Burning Issues

Understanding and Misunderstanding
The Middle East: A 40-Year Chronicle

Burning Issues

Understanding and Misunderstanding
The Middle East: A 40-Year Chronicle

John Mahoney, Jane Adas, and Robert Norberg, Editors

Americans for Middle East Understanding

Americans for Middle East Understanding
475 Riverside Drive, Room 245
New York, New York 10115-0245
www.ameu.org

Cataloging-in-Publication Data

Burning issues : understanding and misunderstanding the
  Middle East : a 40-year chronicle / Jane Adas, John
  Mahoney, and Robert Norberg, editors ; Americans for
  Middle East Understanding.
    p. cm.
  Includes bibliographical references and index.
    LCCN 2006934586
    ISBN 0-9701157-0-9

    1. Arab-Israeli conflict. 2. Israel—History—20th
  century. 3. Palestinian Arabs—History—20th century.
  I. Adas, Jane, 1942- II. Mahoney, John, 1935-
  III. Norberg, Robert, 1935- IV. Americans for Middle East
  Understanding.

    DS126.5.B87 2006   956.9405
                             QBI06-600406

Printed in the United States of America

10 9 8 7 6 5 4 3 2 1

Dedicated to the Memory of

Jack B. Sunderland
AMEU Co-Founder and President,
1967 – 2005

and

Henry G. Fischer
AMEU Co-Founder and Vice-President,
1967 – 2006

Contents

Acknowledgment

AMEU acknowledges with gratitude the gift from Board Member John Goelet that made this anthology possible.

Introduction

Much has happened since March 1967, when a group of men and women, representing various professional backgrounds, came together in New York City to found Americans for Middle East Understanding. AMEU's purpose then, as now, was to create a deeper understanding of the history, culture, and current events in the Middle East. The founders believed that a lack of understanding, particularly in the United States, could cause a serious rift between two important regions of the globe. Time, it seems, has justified their concerns.

As we approached the year 2007, the current directors decided to publish an anthology of *Link* issues from the past 40 years. When feasible, articles have been updated. All past issues of *The Link* and a number of our public affairs papers are available for download at www.ameu.org.

Two of AMEU's founders, Jack Sunderland and Henry Fischer, died during the preparation of this anthology. Jack was a successful entrepreneur, active in humanitarian causes; Henry was curator, and later curator-emeritus of Egyptology at the Metropolitan Museum of Art in New York City. It is in their memory specifically, and in memory of all our past directors, National Council members, and supporters, that we dedicate this forty-year review.

Part I: An Historical Survey

Political Zionism emerged in Europe in the late nineteenth century. Its goal, in the words of Chaim Weizmann, former president of the World Zionist Organization and first president of Israel, was "to make Palestine as Jewish as England is English." To do this, two things had to happen: hundreds of thousands of indigenous Palestinians had to be pushed out, and hundreds of thousands of Jews from other countries had to be brought in. And to do this, Zionists had to secure the moral and financial backing of the reigning superpower, initially Great Britain, then the United States.

Lest We Forget

Jane Adas, Editor

Dr. Jane Adas is an accomplished cellist who teaches music at Rutgers University in New Jersey. In the early '90s she did volunteer work for AMEU—and still does, though now as AMEU's vice president. She is the editor in charge of periodic updates of "Lest We Forget."

The Israeli lobby in Washington has successfully influenced the U.S. Congress to give billions of non-repayable dollars each year to Israel on the premise that Israel's loyalty and strategic importance to the United States make it an ally worthy of such unprecedented consideration.

Is it?

In his Farewell Address, George Washington warned Americans to avoid a passionate attachment to any one nation because it promotes "the illusion of an imaginary common interest in cases where no real common interest exists."

In 1948, U.S. secretary of defense James Forrestal, an opponent of the creation of a Jewish state in Palestine, warned that, even though failure to go along with the Zionists might cost President Truman the states of New York, Pennsylvania, and California, "it was about time that somebody should pay some consideration to whether we might not lose the United States."

Israeli actions over the past 53 years involving U.S. interests in the Middle East seriously challenge the "strategic asset" premise of the Israeli lobby. Some of these actions are compiled in the list that follows:

September 1953: Israel illegally begins to divert the waters of the Jordan River. President Eisenhower, enraged, suspends all economic aid to Israel and prepares to remove the tax-deductible status of the United Jewish Appeal and of other Zionist organizations in the United States.

October 1953: Israel raids the West Bank village of Kibya, killing 53 Palestinian civilians. The Eisenhower administration calls the raid "shocking," and confirms the suspension of aid to Israel.

July 1954: Israeli agents firebomb American and British cultural centers in Egypt, making it look like the work of the Egyptian Muslim Brotherhood in order to sabotage U.S.-Egyptian relations.

October 1956: Israel secretly joins with England and France in a colonial-style attack on Egypt's Suez Canal. Calling the invasion a dangerous threat to international order, President Eisenhower forces Israel to relinquish most of the land it had seized.

1965: 206 pounds of weapons-grade uranium disappear from the Nuclear Materials and Equipment Corporation plant in Pennsylvania. Plant president is Zalmon Shapiro, a former sales agent for the Israel Defense Ministry. C.I.A. director Richard Helms later charges that Israel stole the uranium.

June 1967: Israel bombs, napalms, and torpedoes the USS *Liberty*, killing 34 Americans, wounding 171 others, and nearly sinking the lightly armed intelligence ship. The chairman of the Joint Chiefs of Staff, Admiral Thomas Moorer, charges that the attack "could not possibly have been a case of mistaken identity."

June 1967: Against U.S. wishes, Israel seizes and occupies Syria's Golan Heights.

June 1968: Israeli prime minister Golda Meir rejects U.S. secretary of state William Rogers' Peace Plan that would have required Israel to withdraw from the occupied territories; she calls upon Jews everywhere to denounce the plan.

March 1978: Israel invades Lebanon, illegally using U.S. cluster bombs and other U.S. weapons given to Israel for defensive purposes only.

1979: Israel frustrates U.S.-sponsored Camp David Accords by building new settlements on the West Bank. President Carter complains to American Jewish leaders that, by acting in a "completely irresponsible way," Israel's prime minister Begin continues "to disavow the basic principles of the accords."

1979: Israel sells U.S. airplane tires and other military supplies to Iran, against U.S. policy, at a time when U.S. diplomats are being held hostage in Teheran.

July 1980: Israel annexes East Jerusalem in defiance of U.S. wishes and world opinion.

July 1981: Illegally using U.S. cluster bombs and other equipment, Israel bombs P.L.O. sites in Beirut, with great loss of civilian life.

December 1981: Israel annexes Syria's Golan Heights, in violation of the Geneva Convention and in defiance of U.S. wishes.

June 1982: Israel invades Lebanon a second time, again using U.S. cluster bombs and other U.S. weapons. President Reagan calls for a halt of all shipments of cluster bomb shells to Israel.

September 1982: Abetted by Israeli forces under the control of Defense Minister Ariel Sharon, Lebanese militiamen massacre hundreds of Palestinians in Beirut's Sabra and Shatila refugee camps. President Reagan is "horrified" and summons the Israeli ambassador to demand Israel's immediate withdrawal from Beirut.

September 1982: Israeli prime minister Menachem Begin rejects President Reagan's Peace Plan for the occupied territories.

January–March 1983: Israeli Army "harasses" U.S. Marines in Lebanon. Defense Secretary Caspar Weinberger confirms Marine commandant's report that "Israeli troops are deliberately threatening the lives of American military personnel . . . replete with verbal degradation of the officers, their uniforms and country."

March 1985: Israeli lobby in Washington pressures the U.S. Congress to turn down a $1.6 billion arms sale to Jordan, costing the U.S. thousands of jobs, quite apart from the financial loss to American industry. Jordan gives the contract to Russia. A frustrated King Hussein complains: "The U.S. is not free to move except within the limits of what AIPAC [the Israeli lobby], the Zionists, and the State of Israel determine for it."

October 1985: Israeli lobby blocks $4 billion aircraft sale to Saudi Arabia. The sale, strongly backed by the Reagan administration, costs the U.S. over 350,000 jobs, with steep financial losses to American industry. Saudi Arabia awards contract to England.

November 1985: Jonathan Jay Pollard, an American recruited by Israel, is arrested for passing highly classified intelligence to Israel. U.S. officials call the operation but "one link in an organized and well-financed Israeli espionage ring operating within the United States." State Department contacts reveal that top Israeli defense officials "traded stolen U.S. intelligence documents to Soviet military intelligence agents in return for assurances of greater emigration of Soviet Jews."

December 1985: U.S. Customs in three states raid factories suspected of illegally selling electroplating technology to Israel. Richard Smyth, a NATO consultant and former U.S. exporter, is indicted on charges of illegally exporting to Israel 800 krytron devices for triggering nuclear explosions.

April 1986: U.S. authorities arrest 17 persons, including a retired Israeli general, Avraham Bar-Am, for plotting to sell more than $2 billion of advanced U.S. weaponry to Iran (much of it already in Israel). General Bar-Am, claiming to have had Israeli government approval, threatens to name names at the highest levels. Rudolph W. Giuliani, U.S. attorney for the southern district of New York, calls the plot "mind-boggling in scope."

July 1986: Assistant Secretary of State Richard Murphy informs the Israeli ambassador that a U.S. investigation is under way of eight Israeli representatives in the U.S. accused of plotting the illegal export of technology used in making cluster bombs. Indictments against the eight are later dropped in exchange for an Israeli promise to cooperate in the case.

January 1987: Israeli defense minister Yitzhak Rabin visits South Africa to discuss joint nuclear weapons testing. Israel admits that, in violation of a U.S. Senate anti-apartheid bill, it has arms sales contracts with South Africa worth hundreds of millions of dollars. Rep. John Conyers calls for congressional hearings on Israel–South Africa nuclear testing.

November 1987: The Iran-Contra scandal reveals that it was Israel that had first proposed the trade to Iran of U.S. arms for hostages. The scandal becomes the subject of the *Tower Commission Report*, Senate and House investigations, and the Walsh criminal prosecution inquiries.

April 1988: Testifying before U.S. Subcommittee on Narcotics, Terrorism and International Operations, Jose Blandon, a former intelligence aide to Panama's General Noriega, reveals that Israel used $20 million of U.S. aid to ship arms via Panama to Nicaraguan Contras. The empty planes then smuggled cocaine via Panama into the United States. Pilot tells ABC reporter Richard Threlkeld that Israel was his primary employer. The arms-for-drugs network is said to be led by Mike Harari, Noriega's close aide and bodyguard, who was also a high officer in the Israeli secret services and chief coordinator of Israel's military and commercial business in Panama.

June 1988: Mubarak Awad, a Palestinian-American advocate of nonviolence, is deported by Israel. The White House denounces the action, saying, "We think it is unjustifiable to deny Mr. Awad the right to stay and live in Jerusalem, where he was born."

June 1988: Amnesty International accuses Israel of throwing deadly, U.S.-made gas canisters inside hospitals, mosques, and private homes. The Pennsylvania manufacturer, a major defense corporation, suspends future shipments of tear gas to Israel.

November 1989: According to the Israeli paper *Ma'ariv*, U.S. officials claim Israel Aircraft Industries was involved in attempts to smuggle U.S. missile navigation equipment to South Africa in violation of U.S. law.

December 1989: While the U.S. was imposing economic sanctions on Iran, Israel purchased $36 million of Iranian oil in order to encourage Iran to help free three Israeli hostages in Lebanon.

March 1990: Israel requests more than $1 billion in loans, gifts, and donations from American Jews and U.S. government to pay for resettling Soviet Jews in occupied territories. President Bush responds, "My position is that the foreign policy of the U.S. says we do not believe there should be new settlements in the West Bank or East Jerusalem."

June 1990: Officials in the Bush administration and in Congress say that Israel has emerged as leading supplier of advanced military technology to China, despite U.S.'s expressed opposition to Israeli-Chinese military cooperation.

September 1990: Israeli foreign minister David Levy asks the Bush administration to forgive Israel's $4.5 billion military debt and dramatically increase military aid. Israeli defense minister Moshe Arens expresses concern over expected $20 billion in U.S. arms sales to Saudi Arabia and asks for an additional $1 billion in military aid to Israel. Facing rising congressional opposition, White House backs off from plan to sell Saudi Arabia over $20 billion in military hardware. Bush administration promises to deliver additional F-15 fighters and Patriot missiles to Israel, but defers action on Israel's request for more than $1 billion in new military aid. Arens questions U.S.'s commitment to maintain Israel's military advantage in the Middle East.

October 1990: "Aliya cabinet" chair Ariel Sharon encourages increase in settlement of Soviet Jews in East Jerusalem, despite his government's assurances to the U.S. that it would not do so. Bush sends personal letter to Prime Minister Shamir urging Israel not to pursue East Jerusalem housing. Shamir rejects appeal.

November 1990: In his new autobiography, former president Reagan says Israel was the instigator and prime mover in the Iran-Contra affair and that then-prime minister Shimon Peres "was behind the proposal."

January 1991: White House criticizes Israeli ambassador Zalman Shoval for complaining that U.S. had not moved forward on $400 million in loan guarantees and that Israel "had not received one cent in aid" from allies to compensate for missile damage (in Gulf War)." U.S. says comments are "outrageous and outside the bounds of acceptable behavior."

February 1991: Hours after long-disputed $400 million loan guarantees to Israel are approved, Israeli officials say the amount is grossly insufficient. Next day, Israel formally requests $1 billion in emergency military assistance to cover costs stemming from the Gulf War.

March 1991: Israeli government rejects President Bush's call for solution to Arab-Israeli conflict that includes trading land for peace.

In a report to Congress, U.S. State Department says Soviet Jewish immigrants are settling in the occupied territories at a higher rate than the Israeli government claims. During tour of West Bank settlements, Housing Minister Sharon says construction of 13,000 housing units in occupied territories has been approved for next two years. Plans contradict statement by Prime Minister Shamir, who told President Bush that the Israeli government had not approved such plans.

April 1991: Prime Minister Shamir and several members of his cabinet reject U.S. secretary of state Baker's suggestion that Israel curtail expansion of Jewish settlements in the occupied territories as gesture for peace. U.S. calls new Jewish settlement of Revava "an obstacle" to peace and questions Israel's timing, with Secretary Baker due to arrive in Israel in two days. Hours before Baker arrives, eight Israeli families complete move to new settlement of Talmon Bet. U.S. ambassador to Israel William Brown files an official protest with the Israeli government about establishment and/or expansion of settlements in the West Bank. Housing Minister Sharon says Israel has no intention of meeting U.S. demands to slow or stop settlements. Secretary Baker, in a news conference before leaving Israel, says Israel failed to give responses he needed to put together a peace conference.

May 1991: Israeli ambassador to the U.S. Zalman Shoval says his country will soon request $10 billion in loan guarantees from Washington to aid in settling Soviet Jewish immigrants in Israel. Secretary Baker calls continued building of Israeli settlements "largest obstacle" to convening proposed Middle East peace conference.

May 1991: President Bush unveils proposal for arms control in Middle East. U.S. administration confirms that Israel, which has not signed the Nuclear Non-Proliferation Treaty, has objected to provision on nuclear weapons.

June 1991: Prime Minister Shamir rejects President Bush's call for Israeli acceptance of a greater United Nations role in proposed Arab-Israeli peace talks.

July 1991: Israeli housing minister Sharon inaugurates the new Israeli settlement of Mevo Dotan in the West Bank one day after President Bush describes Israeli settlements as "counterproductive."

September 1991: President Bush asks Congress to delay considering Israeli loan guarantee request for 120 days. Ignoring pleas of U.S. administration, Israel formally submits its request. Prime Minister Shamir says U.S. has a "moral obligation" to provide Israel with loan guarantees, and that Israel would continue to build settlements in the occupied territories.

October 1991: *The Washington Post* reports that President Bush waived U.S.-mandated sanctions against Israel after U.S. intelligence determined that Israel had exported missile components to South Africa.

November 1991: Hours after concluding bilateral talks with Syria, Israel inaugurates Qela', a new settlement in the Golan Heights. Secretary of State Baker calls the action "provocative."

February 1992: Secretary of State Baker says U.S. will not provide loan guarantees to Israel unless it ceases its settlement activity. President Bush threatens to veto any loan guarantees to Israel without a freeze on Israel's settlement activity.

March 1992: U.S. administration confirms it has begun investigating intelligence reports that Israel supplied China with technical data from U.S. Patriot missile system.

April 1992: State Department inspector issues report that the department has failed to heed intelligence reports that an important U.S. ally—widely understood to be Israel—was making unauthorized transfers of U.S. military technology to China, South Africa, and Chile.

May 1992: *The Wall Street Journal* cites Israeli press reports that U.S. officials have placed Israel on list of 20 nations carrying out espionage against U.S. companies.

June 1992: U.S. Defense Department says Israel has rejected a U.S. request to question former General Rami Dotan, who is at center of arms procurement scandal involving U.S. contractors.

July 1992: General Electric Company pleads guilty to fraud and corrupt business practices in connection with its sale of military jet engines to Israel. A GE manager had conspired with Israeli general Rami Dotan to divert $27 million in U.S. military aid with fraudulent vouchers. U.S. Justice and Defense Departments do not believe that Dotan was acting in his own interest, implying that the government of Israel may be implicated in the fraud, which would constitute a default on Israel's aid agreements with the U.S.

June 1993: U.S. House of Representatives passes bill authorizing $80 million per year to Israel for refugee settlement; bill passes despite $10 billion in U.S. loan guarantees to Israel and against evidence from Israeli economists that Israel no longer needs U.S. aid.

October 1993: CIA informs Senate Government Affairs Committee that Israel has been providing China for over a decade with "several billion dollars" worth of advanced military technology. Israeli prime minister Rabin admits Israel has sold arms to China.

November 1993: CIA director James Woolsey makes first public U.S. acknowledgment that "Israel is generally regarded as having some kind of nuclear capability."

December 1993: *Time* magazine reports convicted spy Jonathan Pollard passed a National Security Agency listing of foreign intelligence frequencies to Israel that later was received by Soviets, ruining several billion dollars of work and compromising lives of U.S. informants.

December 1994: *Los Angeles Times* reports Israel has given China information on U.S. military technology to help in joint Israeli-Chinese development of a fighter jet.

January 1995: When Egypt threatens not to sign the Nuclear Non-Proliferation Treaty because Israel will not sign, the U.S. says it will not pressure Israel to sign.

July 1995: U.S. ambassador to Israel Martin Indyk demands Israel abolish import barriers that discriminate against U.S. imports.

November 1995: Israel grants citizenship to American spy Jonathan Pollard.

April 1996: Using U.S.-supplied shells, Israel kills 106 unarmed civilians who had taken refuge in a U.N. peace-keeping compound in Qana, southern Lebanon. U.N. investigators, Amnesty International, and Human Rights Watch condemn the shelling as premeditated. The U.N. Security Council calls on Israel to pay reparations. Resolution is vetoed by the United States.

June 1996: U.S. State Department hands Israeli defense officials classified CIA report alleging Israel has given China U.S. military avionics, including advanced radar-detection system and electronic warfare equipment.

December 1996: Israeli cabinet reinstates large subsidies, including tax breaks and business grants, for West Bank settlers. U.S. says the move is "troubling" and "clearly complicates the peace process." Israeli government rejects President Clinton's criticism of the settlements and vows to strengthen them.

February 1997: FBI announces that David Tenenbaum, a mechanical engineer working for the U.S. Army, has admitted that for the past 10 years he has "inadvertently" passed on classified military information to Israeli officials.

March 1997: U.S. presses Israel to delay building new settlement of Har Homa near Bethlehem. Prime Minister Netanyahu says international opposition "will just strengthen my resolve."

June 1997: U.S. investigators report that two Hasidic Jews from New York, suspected of laundering huge quantities of drug money for a Colombian drug cartel, recently purchased millions of dollars worth of land near the settlements of Mahseya and Zanoah.

September 1997: Jewish settlers in Hebron stone Palestinian laborers working on a U.S.-financed project to renovate the town's main street. David Muirhead, the American overseeing the project, says the Israeli police beat him, threw him into a van, and detained him until the U.S. Consulate intervened. U.S. State Department calls the incident "simply unacceptable."

September 1997: Secretary of State Albright says Israel's decision to expand Efrat settlement "is not at all helpful" to the peace process. Prime Minister Netanyahu says he will continue to expand settlements.

May 1998: Thirteen years after denying he was not its spy, Israel officially recognizes Pollard as its agent in hopes of negotiating his release.

June 1998: Secretary of State Albright phones Prime Minister Netanyahu to condemn his plan to extend Jerusalem's municipal boundaries and to move Jews into East Jerusalem, particularly in the area adjacent to Bethlehem. Ignoring U.S. protests, Israel's cabinet unanimously approves plan to extend Jerusalem's municipal authority.

August 1998: Secretary Albright tells Prime Minister Netanyahu that the freeze in the peace process due to the settlement policy is harming U.S. interests in the Middle East and affecting the U.S.'s ability to forge a coalition against Iraq.

September 1998: Dutch newspaper *NRC Handelsblad* reports that the Israeli airliner that crashed in Amsterdam in 1992 was not carrying "gifts and perfume," as the Israelis claimed, but three of the four chemicals used to make sarin nerve gas. According to the plane's cargo manifest, the chemicals were sent from a U.S. factory in Pennsylvania to the top-secret Israeli Institute for Biological Research.

November 1998: Israeli foreign minister Sharon urges Jewish settlers to "grab" West Bank land so it does not fall under Palestinian control in any final peace settlement.

May 1999: U.S. denounces Israel's decision to annex more land to the Ma'ale Adumim settlement.

June 1999: The Israeli company Orlil is reported to have stolen U.S. night-vision equipment purchased for the Israeli Defense Forces and to have sold it to "Far Eastern" countries.

April 2001: Prime Minister Sharon announces plans to build 708 new housing units in the Jewish settlements of Ma'ale Adumim and Alfe Menashe. U.S. State Department criticizes the move as "provocative."

May 2001: The Mitchell Committee (headed by former U.S. senator George Mitchell) concludes that Jewish settlements are a barrier to peace. Prime Minister Sharon vows to continue expanding the settlements.

May 2001: U.S. is voted off the United Nations Commission on Human Rights for the first time since the committee's establishment in 1947. *The Financial Times of London* suggests that Washington, by vetoing U.N. resolutions alleging Israeli human rights abuses, showed its inability to work impartially in the area of human rights. Secretary of State Colin Powell suggests the vote was because "we left a little blood on the floor" in votes involving the Palestinians.

November 2001: Secretary of State Colin Powell calls on Israel to halt all settlement building, which he says "cripples chances for real peace and security." Benny Elon, a right-wing minister in the Sharon government, says the settlers aren't worried. "America has a special talent for seeing things in the short term," he says, explaining that Powell's intent was to get Arab support for America's anti-terrorism coalition against Afghanistan.

March 2002: U.N. Sec. Gen. Kofi Annan calls for immediate withdrawal of Israeli tanks from Palestinian refugee camps, citing large numbers of Palestinians reported dead or injured. U.S. State Department says the United States has contacted Israel to "urge that utmost restraint be exercised in order to avoid harm to the civilian population."

April 2002: President Bush repeatedly demands an immediate halt to Israel's military invasion of the West Bank. Prime Minister Sharon rebuffs the President's withdrawal demands, saying the United States and other nations should not "put any pressure upon us."

April 4, 2002: President Bush demands that Israel halt its March 29 incursion into the West Bank, withdraw immediately, and cease all settlement building. Three days later, Secretary of State Powell says Bush's "demand" was a "request."

June 10, 2002: Prime Minister Sharon visits White House. When reporters ask about Israel's ongoing incursions into Palestinian towns, President Bush says, "Israel has a right to defend herself."

November 25, 2002: Israel asks the U.S. for $4 billion in military aid to "defray the costs of fighting terrorism," plus $10 billion in loan guarantees to support its struggling economy.

May 29, 2003: Israel announces construction of a new Jewish settlement of 230 housing units in East Jerusalem.

July 29, 2003: Sharon rejects President Bush's appeal to halt construction of a separation wall that Israel is building on occupied Palestinian land.

October 22, 2003: Former Navy lawyer Ward Boston, who had helped lead the military investigation into Israel's 1967 attack on the USS *Liberty*, files a signed affidavit stating that President Johnson and Secretary of Defense Robert McNamara had ordered those heading the naval inquiry to "conclude that the attack was a case of 'mistaken identity,' despite overwhelming evidence to the contrary."

March 21, 2005: Prime Minister Sharon approves construction of 3,500 new housing units in the Israeli settlement of Ma'ale Adumin to link it to East Jerusalem. The U.S. State Department has no comment.

May 2005: *Newsweek* reports that in the late 1990s, lobbyist Jack Abramoff diverted more than $140,000 from charitable contributions by Indian tribes to the Israeli settlement of Beitar Illit for sniper equipment and training of settler militias.

March 2006: Professors John Mearsheimer of the University of Chicago and Stephen Walt, the academic dean at Harvard's School of Government, co-author a major paper in which they conclude: "For the past several decades, and especially since the Six-Day War of 1967, the centerpiece of U.S. Middle Eastern policy has been its relationship with Israel. The combination of unwavering support for Israel and the related effort to spread 'democracy' throughout the region has inflamed Arab and Islamic opinion and jeopardized not only U.S. security but that of much of the rest of the world. This situation has no equal in American political history."

August 25, 2006: The U.S. State Department investigates Israel's widespread use of American cluster bombs against a civilian population in Lebanon. Although such use violates U.S.-Israeli agreements, several current and former U.S. government officials tell *The New York Times* that "they doubted the investigation would lead to sanctions against Israel, but that the decision to proceed with it might be intended to help the Bush administration ease criticism from Arab governments and commentators over its support of Israel's military operations."

September 4, 2006: Israeli Prime Minister Ehud Olmert authorizes construction of 690 housing units in occupied West Bank settlements of Ma'ale Adumin and Betar Illit. American Embassy spokesman says expansion of settlements runs counter to peace plan supported by the United States. *The New York Times* calls the American criticism a "pro forma" response.

Political Zionism: Its Historical Origins and Growth

By John F. Mahoney

John Mahoney has been executive director of AMEU since 1978.

> ***Zionism, the political movement that led to the formation of the State of Israel in 1948 and that has garnered unprecedented financial and political support from the United States, began a little over a hundred years ago in Europe. This is its history, with a special focus on its relations with the United States.***

Roots of Zionism

In 1894, Alfred Dreyfus, a French-Jewish army officer, was sentenced to perpetual deportation and military degradation for selling military secrets to the Germans. Two years later, the chief of French army intelligence, Col. George Picquart, himself an anti-Semite, concluded that another officer, not Dreyfus, was the traitor. The army ignored the evidence. Then, in 1898, the novelist Émile Zola published "J'accuse," an open letter to the newspaper detailing the army's cover-up. After an arduous series of legal challenges that inflamed French public opinion and deeply divided the Republic, Dreyfus was pardoned in 1899, exonerated in 1906, and returned to the army, where he eventually rose to the rank of lieutenant colonel and was named Officer in the Legion of Honor.

During this period, Alfred Dreyfus came to symbolize for many French the supposed disloyalty of French Jews. On the 100th anniversary of Zola's article, France's Catholic daily, *La Croix*, apologized for its anti-Semitic editorials during the Dreyfus affair. The case, however, had a ripple effect that went well beyond the French.

The Dreyfus affair profoundly affected Theodor Herzl, a Paris-based correspondent for an Austrian newspaper. Up until the Dreyfus trial, Herzl, who was born in Budapest in 1860 to a partially assimilated Jewish family, felt, as did most European Jewish intellectuals, that the best course for Jews lay in assimilation, based on the liberal nationalism of the French Revolution, where the individual citizen was central, the state was constituted by its citizens, and all citizens stood equal before the law. The anti-Jewish attacks Herzl observed during the Dreyfus Affair were some of a number of experiences that brought home to him the power of anti-Semitism even in such an enlightened democracy as France.

The alternative to liberal nationalism was racial nationalism. With its roots in German Romanticism, racial nationalism held that each state belongs to a particular ethnic nation, and that this national group occupies a privileged position in the state. Herzl concluded that authentic communities were formed not by legal bonds but by organic, mystical ties that precede and transcend the political. The "problem" for Jews, said Herzl, was that they "had completely lost their feeling of solidarity as a race:" the solution was for them to carve out a state, which they would own, and which would override the interests of its non-Jewish population.

Racial nationalism infused both Nazism and Zionism. As Norman Finkelstein pointed out in his December 1992 *Link* article, the only Jews for whom Hitler reserved any praise in "Mein Kampf" were the Zionists. The Nazis saw Germans and Jews as two different ethnic and racially based nations and, on this basis, first encouraged the Jews to leave Germany to found their own state, then later sought to exterminate them. This ideological convergence of interests was bemoaned by American Jews in "The Congress Bulletin" of the American Jewish Congress in 1936:

> Hitlerism is Satan's nationalism. The determination to rid the
> German national body of the Jewish element, however, led

Hitlerism to discover its 'kinship' with Zionism, the Jewish nationalism of liberation. Therefore Zionism became the only other flag permitted to fly in Nazi-land. It was a painful distinction for Zionism to be singled out for favors and privileges by its Satanic counterpart.

Initially Herzl, who was personally indifferent to religion, had not thought of Palestine as the new state of the Jews. First he considered Argentina; then the Sinai peninsula and al-Arish; then he asked the British for Cyprus; then asked Portugal for a piece of Mozambique; then asked the Belgians for the Congo; then asked the king of Italy for Tripolitania— only to be rebuffed by the king with the simple reminder that Tripolitania "is the home of others!" Finally, the British offered him Uganda. When he proposed this to the Fifth Zionist Congress in 1903, 295 delegates voted in favor, 177 against. The rejectionists wanted Palestine, which, at the time, was part of the Ottoman Empire. Herzl sided with the rejectionists.

The evolution of Zionism from an improbable movement at the start of the 20th century—Hitler scoffed at the idea it would ever succeed—to a member state of the United Nations in 78 percent of Mandated Palestine, with its military occupying the remaining 22 percent, is indeed the product of a remarkable sequence of historical events.

The Strategy

The key to this achievement, as Herzl and later his successor, Chaim Weizmann, realized, was to enlist the support of a world power.

By 1914, the British estimated the population of Palestine at 689,272, of whom no more than 60,000, or 9 percent, were Jews. The goal of the Zionist hardliners, whose views became dominant, was to usurp the land from its rightful owners, while ingathering all Jews worldwide into the new Jewish nation. As Joseph Weitz, the administrator responsible for the colonization of Palestine, put it: "Between ourselves it must be clear that there is no room for both people together in this country. . . . The only solution is a Palestine . . . without Arabs. And there is no other way than to transfer the Arabs from here to the neighboring countries, to transfer all of them; not one village, not one tribe, should be left."[1] To do this would require sufficient military force and a strong international backer to validate the colonization process.

In 1904, the Zionist leader, Chaim Weizmann, moved to England because he felt that Great Britain, of all the great powers, was most likely to provide support for Zionism. Weizmann was a chemist and, when WW I broke out, he offered his expertise in support of the British war effort.

By August 1914, the lineup for World War I was in place: the Central Powers (Germany, Austria-Hungary, the Ottoman Empire, Bulgaria) versus the Allied Powers (Great Britain, France, Russia, Serbia, Belgium). The Zionists calculated that the Allies would win, the Ottoman empire would be dismembered, and Britain would receive the Mandate for Palestine. The Zionists wanted Britain to promise them "a national home" in Palestine. But what could they offer the British in return?

What the British wanted was for the United States to join the war on their side.

So, in 1916, the World Zionist Organization attempted to establish linkages with the British War Cabinet. In return for Zionist promises to pressure Jews in Austria, Germany, France, and the United States to support the Allied war effort, members of the British cabinet began to look favorably on Zionist political aspirations in Palestine. Samuel Landman, the personal secretary to Chaim Weizmann, may have overstated Zionist influence in the U.S. when he wrote:

> The only way . . . to induce the American President to come into the War was to secure the co-operation of Zionist Jews by promising them Palestine, and thus enlist and mobilize the hitherto unsuspectedly powerful forces of Zionist Jews in America and elsewhere in favor of the Allies on a quid pro quo contract basis.[2]

The United States entered the war in 1917, and later that year—before the war ended, and before Britain controlled Palestine—the British cabinet approved a letter signed by Lord Alfred Balfour, the British Foreign Minister (although most of it was written by Zionist negotiators), and addressed to Lord Baron Rothschild, a leading British Zionist leader. The letter stated that "His Majesty's Government view with favor the establishment in Palestine of a national home for the Jewish people," and added "nothing shall be done which may prejudice the civil and religious rights of existing non-Jewish communities in Palestine."

In 1919, Weizmann told a London audience that the Balfour Declaration "is the key which unlocks the doors of Palestine."[3] And as for the "non-Jews" who composed 91 percent of Palestine, Lord Balfour had this to say: "Zionism . . . is . . . of far profounder import than the desires and prejudices of the 700,000 Arabs who now inhabit that ancient land."[4]

Between 1945 and 1947, the British government tried to find a peaceful settlement to the Palestine problem by promising to limit further Jewish immigration, but was stymied both by acts of Jewish terrorism, most notably the bombing of the King David Hotel, and by pressure from the Truman Administration, which threatened to withhold postwar aid from Britain if it did not allow the immediate immigration into Palestine of 100,000 Jews. By this time, due to years of immigration, the Jewish population of Palestine had jumped to 33 percent, although Jewish ownership of land was just a little over 6 percent.

President Truman, at first, had petitioned the U.S. Congress to allow 100,000 stateless Jews into the United States, but American Zionists made it known to Congress that these Jews should settle in their new "homeland." Delegates to the 1944 Democratic Convention even adopted a resolution favoring "the opening of Palestine to unrestricted Jewish immigration and colonization" and the establishment of a "free and democratic Jewish Commonwealth." Republicans, not to be outdone, called for "the opening of Palestine to . . . unrestricted immigration and land ownership, so that in accordance with the full intent and purpose of the Balfour Declaration of 1917 . . . Palestine may be constituted as a free and democratic Commonwealth."[5] No mention was made by either party of the indigenous habitants.

In the 1946 congressional elections Republicans won strong majorities in both houses of Congress. Truman complained that if more Jews had voted Democratic he would have been able to do more for them.[6]

In May 1947, the British, frustrated, gave notice that they planned to surrender their Mandate in one year's time. The onus then shifted to the United Nations to determine who should govern Palestine once the British left. The choices came down to partitioning the land into two nations, the position favored by the Zionists, or keeping it as one with an Arab majority, the position of the Arab countries. The U.N. created a commission of inquiry composed of 11 states, not one of whom was Arab or African, which recommended partition.

By the fall of 1947, in his bid for reelection, Truman was running in the polls anywhere from 5 to 15 percent behind Gov. Thomas E. Dewey of New York. The president knew he needed every vote he could get and that the Jewish-American population, particularly in the delegate-rich states of New York, Pennsylvania, and California, could make the difference. His problem was, on one hand, that virtually every senior official in his Department of State, the War Department, and the Joint Chiefs was against partition, while on the other hand, the White House was being barraged by pro-partition voices. Truman later complained: "I do not think I ever had as much pressure and propaganda aimed at the White House as I had in this instance. The persistence of a few of the extreme Zionist leaders—actuated by political motives and engaging in political threats—disturbed and annoyed me. Some were even suggesting that we pressure sovereign nations into favorable votes in the General Assembly."[7]

Be that as it may, columnist Drew Pearson reported in the *Chicago Daily Tribune* of February 9, 1948, that "President Truman cracked down harder on his State Department than ever before to swing the United Nations' vote for the partition of Palestine. Truman called

Acting Secretary Lovett over to the White House on Wednesday and again on Friday warning him he would demand a full explanation if nations which usually line up with the United States failed to do so on Palestine."

And the fact is that, with or without Truman's knowledge, smaller countries were pressured into changing their votes in favor of partition. Congressman Lawrence Smith, addressing the Congress on December 18, 1947, recounted what happened:

> Let's take a look at the record, Mr. Speaker, and see what happened in the United Nations' Assembly meeting prior to the vote on partition. A two-thirds majority was required to pass the resolution. On two occasions the Assembly was to vote, and twice it was postponed. . . . In the meantime, it is reliably reported that intense pressure was applied to the delegates of three small nations by the United States' member, and also by officials at the highest levels in Washington. The decisive votes for partition were cast by Haiti, Liberia, and the Philippines. These votes were sufficient to make the two-thirds majority. Previously, these countries opposed the move.

Abba Eban, the former Israeli foreign minister, recounted how, on the opening day of the U.N. session on partition, the delegate from the Philippines had declared: "The issue is whether the United Nations should accept responsibility for the enforcement of a policy which is clearly repugnant to the valid nationalist aspirations of the people of Palestine. The Philippines government holds that the United Nations has the right not to accept such responsibility." Then, the Philippine ambassador spoke by telephone to his president, Manuel Roxas, and told him of the pressure he was under. Congressman Sol Bloom, a Zionist and chairman of the U.S. House Foreign Affairs Committee, had intervened on behalf of partition, as had 26 pro-Zionist U.S. senators in a joint telegram; the ambassador advised that it would be foolish to vote against a policy so ardently desired by the U.S. government at a time when seven bills were pending in Congress in which the islands had a tremendous stake.[8]

The senatorial telegram was also sent to 12 other U.N delegations, 4 of whom would change their votes from *no* to *yes*, and 7 from *no* to *abstain*.

Sumner Welles, former undersecretary of state, wrote: "By direct order of the White House every form of pressure, direct and indirect, was brought to bear by American officials upon those countries outside of the Muslim world that were known to be either uncertain or opposed to partition. Representatives or intermediaries were employed by the White House to make sure that the necessary majority would at length be secured."[9] And Undersecretary of State Robert Lovett noted that "never in his life had he been subjected to as much pressure as he had in three days beginning Thursday morning and ending Saturday night."[10]

Alfred Lilienthal, in his monumental work *The Zionist Connection*, reports on "Operation Partition," the effort of Zionists to influence foreign chancelleries. The three American "masterminds," according to Lilienthal, were New York judge Joseph Proskauer, Washington economist Robert Nathan, and White House assistant "for minority affairs" David Niles.[11]

Robert Nathan targeted Liberia by telling its delegate that he would go after his good friend Edward R. Stettinius, Truman's first secretary of state, who at the time had enormous business interests in Liberia. (The Liberian diplomat actually reported this attempted intimidation to the Department of State.) And Harvey Firestone, of Firestone Tire, with his vast rubber concession in Liberia, sent a message to its representative, directing him to pressure the Liberian Government to vote for partition. In the end, Liberia did.

Lilienthal reports that various South American delegates were also told that their vote for partition would greatly increase the chances of a Pan-American road project.

Bernard Baruch was persuaded to talk to the French, who could not afford to lose their postwar Marshall Plan aid. And Adolph Berle, legal advisor to the Haitian government, made a call to Haiti's president.

Bribes, too, were used. Robert Donovan, in his *Conflict and Crisis: The Presidency of Harry S. Truman, 1945-1948,* reported that one

Latin American delegate was given $75,000 to change his vote; the Costa Rican delegate refused a $45,000 bribe, yet still voted for partition on orders from his government.

When the vote was taken on November 29, 1947, U.N. General Assembly Resolution 181 had the two-thirds majority it needed, barely: 33 to 13, with 10 abstentions and 1 absent. The votes of Haiti, Liberia, and the Philippines proved decisive. No Arab nation voted for the partition.

Because the resolution was a General Assembly vote, it had only the force of a recommendation, as opposed to Security Council resolutions which have mandatory force. What would happen when the British Mandate expired in May 1948 still was uncertain.

Truman seems to have been persuaded that, were the Jews and Palestinians unable to come to some agreement, Palestine should be placed under a U.N. Trusteeship. That was anathema to the Zionists, who continued to lobby the U.S. administration for partition.

But Truman was fed up with all the lobbying and barred all Zionist representatives from the White House. That's when Eddie Jacobson entered the equation. Jacobson was the president's closest Army buddy in WW I and former haberdashery partner in Kansas City; Eddie, it was said, could get in to see his friend with just a phone call. The sequence of events, as recorded by Alfred Lilienthal, is as follows:

> When Dr. Chaim Weizmann, head of the World Zionist Organization, came to the U.S. to petition the president, Truman refused to see him. At this point, Frank Goldman, president and secretary of B'nai B'rith, learned of Eddie Jacobson, who was a B'nai B'rith member. Jacobson agreed to send his friend in the White House a telegram asking that he see Weizmann, but when that failed, he phoned Truman on the morning of March 13, 1949, and requested a personal visit.

> "Eddie," said the president, "I'm always glad to see old friends, but there's one thing you got to promise me. I don't want you to say a word about what's going on over there in the Middle East. Do you promise?"

Eddie promised, and the two met in the Oval Office. Truman later wrote of their meeting:

> Great tears were running down his cheeks and I took one look at him and said, "Eddie, you son of a bitch, you promised me you wouldn't say a word about what's going on over there."

> And he said, "Mr. President, I haven't said a word, but every time I think of the homeless Jews, homeless for thousands of years, and I think about Dr. Weizmann, I start crying. I can't help it. He's an old man and he's spent his whole life working for a homeland for the Jews. Now he's sick and he's in New York and he wants to see you, and every time I think about it, I can't help crying."

> I said, "Eddie, you son of a bitch, I ought to have thrown you out of here for breaking your promise; you knew damn good and well I couldn't stand seeing you cry."

> And he kind of smiled at me, still crying, though, and he said, "Thank you, Mr. President." And he left.

On March 18, 1948, Chaim Weizmann entered unnoticed through the East Gate of the White House and met for 45 minutes with Eddie Jacobson's good friend. The president assured Weizmann that he continued to support partition of Palestine.

On May 14, 1948, at 6:00 p.m. Washington time, the British Mandate expired. At 6:01 p.m., David Ben-Gurion declared the existence of the State of Israel. At 6:11 p.m., the United States gave the new state de facto recognition.

On November 2, 1948, Truman, in an upset victory, defeated Dewey. Later, speaking to a group of U.S. diplomats, Truman explained why he did it: "I am sorry, gentlemen, but I have to answer to hundreds of thousands who are anxious for the success of Zionism. I do not have hundreds of thousands of Arabs among my constituents."

The Nature of Zionism

60 Minutes correspondent Mike Wallace often acknowledges that his mentor on the Palestinian-Israeli conflict was Dr. Fayez Sayegh. The two were good friends and, when Fayez died in 1980, Wallace sent his personal condolences.

Fayez Sayegh was a Palestinian Christian—his father a Presbyterian minister—whose family was forced from their home in Palestine in 1948, along with 750,000 other Palestinian exiles. Twenty-seven years later, in the fall of 1975, Dr. Sayegh, now a representative of Kuwait at the United Nations in New York, spoke to the Third Committee of the General Assembly in support of a draft resolution being prepared for a plenary session of the General Assembly. In summary, this is what he said:[12]

> The subject of the resolution, Zionism, refers to a specific political movement begun in August 1897, in Basle, Switzerland, at the inspiration of Theodor Herzl, whose present-day organizational form is the World Zionist Organization. The WZO has held 28 regular Zionist Congresses which have adopted a number of resolutions constituting the official doctrine and program of Zionism. The proposed General Assembly resolution does *not* refer to Judaism or the Jewish religion. The draft's term "racial discrimination," as defined by the United Nations in its General Assembly Resolution 2106 of November 1963, means "any distinction, exclusion, restriction or preference based on race, color, descent, or national or ethnic origin." The question before the world body is whether Zionism, as defined by the Zionist movement, is a form or racism and racial discrimination, as defined by the United Nations.

Quoting from Zionist sources, Sayegh noted that the central doctrine of Zionism was that the Jews of the world, regardless of the quality of their religious commitment to Judaism, constituted one nation, one separate and distinct people. As such they were entitled to create their own state, that is, a state for *all* Jews worldwide and *only* for Jews. To accomplish this, two steps were required: Jews had to be separated from their respective countries and transplanted to the new state, and non-Jews or the indigenous population had to be removed from their land to make room for the transplanted Jews.

Much had occurred between 1948, when the United States recognized the Zionist State, and 1975, when the United Nations examined the tenets of Zionism. Well aware of the Zionists' long-range plans, the Arabs had rejected the partition plan, which gave 55 percent of Palestine, including its most fertile regions, to Jews who owned no more than 6 percent. Even before the May 14, 1948, declaration of statehood, however, Zionist forces had invaded and occupied large parts of the 45 percent that had been allocated to the Palestinians. With the formal declaration of statehood, Arab armies fought only in those areas allocated to the Palestinians in order to redress the injustice. But they were no match for the paramilitary forces of the Zionists, which were formed during and in the wake of World War II.

As the fighting continued into 1949, and more Palestinians were evicted from their homeland, President Truman sent an angry message on May 28, 1949, demanding that Israel withdraw from territories it had captured and that it take back a certain number of refugees. Israel refused to make any of these concessions. Truman warned that if Israel continued in its attitude, "the U.S. government will regretfully be forced to the conclusion that a revision of its attitude toward Israel has become unavoidable." Ten days later, ignoring the warning, Israel formally told Truman that "the war has proved the indispensability to the survival of Israel of certain vital areas not comprised originally in the share of the Jewish state."[13]

When the Armistice Line between Israel and the Arabs was finally drawn in early 1949, Israel had increased its territory from 55 to 78 percent of Mandated Palestine. Some 750,000 Palestinians found themselves refugees, never to be allowed to return to their homes. A remnant population of 160,000 remained and eventually became citizens of the Jewish state.

Nineteen years later, in what it called a pre-emptive war, Israel attacked Egypt, triggering the 1967 war. Within six days Israel occupied the remaining 22 percent of Palestine (the West Bank and Gaza), along with Syria's Golan Heights and Egypt's Sinai Peninsula. Israel unilaterally annexed the Golan in 1981, having first forced 94 percent of its population out of the region. The Sinai was returned to Egypt in 1982 as part of the Camp David Agreement. Israel continues to rule militarily over 3.3 million Palestinians in the West Bank, including East Jerusalem and Gaza, in what is the longest military occupation in modern history.

In his presentation, Fayez Sayegh documented the discrimination against those Palestinians in pre-1967 Israel where, unlike in the United States, a distinction is made between citizenship and nationality. In Israel, Palestinians are identified as having Israeli citizenship and Arab nationality; Jews, on the other hand, are identified as having Israeli citizenship and Jewish nationality. As Israeli citizens, Palestinians, like Jews, can vote and run for the Knesset or Parliament, although, unlike Jews, they cannot form any independent organization to work for their rights. As Arab nationals, however, Palestinians—as all non-Jews—are denied basic rights enjoyed by Jewish nationals.

Here, again, Sayegh stressed that Jewishness in this context does *not* signify a religious attribute, but a biological one, and he cited a March 10, 1970, law enacted by Israel's Knesset which determined that a Jew was one born of a Jewish mother or a convert. Commenting on this definition, Israeli supreme court justice Haim Cohen was quoted in *The Times of London,* on July 25, 1963, as noting how ironic it was "that the same biological or racist approach which was propagated by the Nazis and characterized the infamous Nuremberg laws should, because of an allegedly sacrosanct Jewish tradition, become the basis for the official determination or rejection of Jewishness in the state of Israel."

One such basic right given to Jewish nationals and denied to Arab nationals is the Right of Return. In 1950, Israel enacted the Law of Return by which Jews anywhere in the world, by virtue of their Jewish nationality, that is, by virtue of being born of a Jewish mother or being a convert, have a "right" to immigrate to Israel on the grounds that they are returning to their own state, even if they have never been there before. Conversely, non-Jewish Palestinians, dislodged from their homeland in 1948 and 1967, have no such right because they are not Jewish. To spell this out more clearly, in 1952 Israel enacted the Citizenship/Jewish Nationality Law, granting every Jew in the world, and only Jews, the status of both Israeli citizenship and Jewish nationality as soon as they step foot on Israeli soil. Sayegh points out that, were the situation reversed, were, for example, those born of a Christian mother in the United States entitled by law to rights that were denied Jews, such a law would be decried, rightly, as anti-Semitic and "racist." Why, then, he asked, is not the same practice, when perpetrated by a Jew against a non-Jew, not condemned as racist and a form of racial discrimination?

Another example cited by Sayegh was the Agricultural Settlement Law of 1967 which banned Israeli citizens of non-Jewish nationality, e.g., Palestinian Arabs, from working on Jewish National Fund lands, i.e., on well over 80 percent of the land in Israel. This law prohibits the sale of state-owned land to non-Jews, the leasing of state-owned land to non-Jews, even the employment of non-Jews on state-owned land. Again, were the situation reversed, were Jews in the United States prohibited by law from owning, leasing, or working on state-owned land, this would instantly be condemned as racist.

Sayegh also pointed out that legal discrimination against non-Jewish nationals, that is, Palestinian Arabs, affected the most vital aspects of their daily life. This is because many state benefits, such as educational allowances, housing and welfare grants, and job entitlements, are all tied to military service. All Jewish nationals— even the relatively small number of Jewish nationals who are exempt from military service—are eligible for these benefits; non-Jewish nationals, with minor exceptions, are not. Again, were the situation reversed and Jews were de facto barred from essential state subsidies, this would rightly be condemned as anti-Semitism and overt racial discrimination.

On November 10, 1975, 72 countries condemned Zionism as "a form of racism and racial discrimination." Thirty-five countries voted against the resolution, 32 abstained. The Arab countries were joined in large part by the Soviet Union, then one of the two superpowers, and by member countries of the Organization of African Unity that were reacting to their own colonial histories. Right after the vote was taken, the U.S. ambassador to the U.N., Daniel Patrick Moynihan, rose from his seat, went over to where Israeli ambassador Chaim Herzog was sitting, and embraced him.

As Fayez Sayegh anticipated, those who opposed the resolution lambasted it as an attack on the Jewish religion. Ambassador Herzog dismissed it as anti-Semitic and anti-Judaism. The U.S. press, with possibly the sole exception of journalist I. F. Stone, called it "An Obscenity" and "Anti-Semitic." Stone, writing in *The New York Times* of November 23, 1975, observed: "The painful point about the United Nations resolution equating Zionism and Racism is that it had an element of truth." At the time, no one thought it would ever be repealed, but things would change.

Israel had begun colonizing the lands it occupied in 1967 right from the beginning. President Carter had complained to American Jewish leaders that, by building settlements, Israel was acting in a "completely irresponsible way." The building, however, continued under President Reagan, but by then, Israel had little to fear from the United States. As Reagan's secretary of state George Schultz told the American-Israel Public Affairs Committee (AIPAC), the leading pro-Israel lobby in the U.S., the goal of U.S. strategic cooperation with Israel was to "build institutional arrangements so that eight years from now, if there is a secretary of state who is not positive about Israel, he will not be able to overcome the bureaucratic relationship between Israel and the United States that we have established."[14]

By the summer of 1991, George Bush was riding high in the polls. The Soviet Union had imploded, and U.S.-led forces in the Gulf War had liberated Kuwait. Israel felt that its restraint in that war had given it what one leading Israeli paper called "the moral and practical right to demand a significant material increase from the United States."[15] What Israel wanted from the U.S. was a $10 billion loan guarantee in order to borrow from U.S. commercial institutions at a greatly reduced interest rate. The money was needed, it said, to finance infrastructure, housing, training, and jobs for one million

Jewish immigrants expected to arrive in Israel from the Soviet bloc countries between 1991 and 1995.

On September 12, 1991, leading Jewish organizations in the U.S., at the behest of Israel's Prime Minister Yitzhak Shamir, sent over 1,200 citizens, mostly Jews, through the halls of Congress to lobby for the $10 billion. President Bush, however, said he would veto any foreign aid bill that contained the loan because of Shamir's policy of putting the new immigrants in West Bank and Gaza settlements. Shamir himself made his position crystal clear in the *Jerusalem Post* of January 15, 1990: "We need the space [in the Occupied Territories] to house all the people. Big immigration required Israel to be big as well. . . . we must have the Land of Israel and we have to fight for it, struggle for it."

The lines seemed drawn: a popular president versus a powerful lobby and an adamant Israeli prime minister.

Just after 1 p.m. on that September 12th—a "day that would live in infamy" for many Jews—George Bush went before the TV cameras and gave his famous "one lonely little guy" speech. He said: "We're up against very strong and effective groups that go up to the Hill. I heard today there were something like a thousand lobbyists on the Hill working the other side of the question. We've got one lonely little guy down here. I think the American people will support me."[16]

Morris Amitay, the former head of the American Israel Public Affairs Committee, charged that the president's words "came as close to the line of inciting anti-Semitism as a public figure can go." In the weeks that followed, the president and Republican Party strategists were warned that the remark could cost them much needed reelection campaign cash.

Suddenly, George Bush's vice president, Dan Quayle, emerged as the president's defender. Quayle, a self-declared Zionist who did not consider Jewish settlement an obstacle to peace, was looked upon by Jews as their best friend in the White House. To improve his boss's standing in the Jewish community, Quayle recommended he push for the repeal of the U.N. resolution equating Zionism with racism.

On September 23, 1991, President Bush, in an address to the

United Nations General Assembly, declared: "To equate Zionism with the intolerable sin of racism is to twist history and forget the terrible plight of Jews in World War II and indeed throughout history. Zionism is not a policy; it was the idea that led to the home of the Jewish people."

Over the next three months the U.S., now the world's one remaining superpower, worked to convince U.N. members that revocation of the resolution was in the interest of Middle East peace, as it was a condition insisted upon by Israel for its participation in the Madrid Peace Conference then in progress. On December 16, 1991, the U.N. repealed Resolution 3379 by a vote of 111 to 25, with 13 abstentions.

Within the next year, Shamir would lose his reelection bid to Yitzhak Rabin, George Bush would lose his reelection bid to Arkansas governor Bill Clinton, and Israel would secure its $10 billion in loan guarantees. The Madrid Conference would lead to the 1993 Oslo Accords, and within the next five years, Jewish settlements on occupied Palestinian land would double. By the year 2002, some 72 percent of the West Bank, 89 percent of Arab East Jerusalem, and 25 percent of Gaza would be expropriated for settlements, highways, by-pass roads, military installations, nature preserves, and infrastructure. Over 200 settlements would be built, and over 400,000 Israeli Jews would cross the 1967 boundaries, in the process rendering a viable Palestinian state improbable at best.

Whither Zionism

Rabbi Elmer Berger, the former executive director of The American Council for Judaism, often pointed out that the State of Israel was never the end purpose of Zionism; that purpose was and is to nationalize the lives of all Jews worldwide, ultimately ingathering them into the State of Israel from their "exile," or *Galut*, the Zionist term for Jews who don't live in Israel.[17]

Fayez Sayegh called this the "pumping-in operation" of Zionism, the corollary to its "pumping-out operation." With so many Palestinian exiles, Zionists urgently needed Jews to fill the vacuum, especially agricultural workers, manual laborers, and military recruits to defend the seized lands.

The closest Jews were those living in Arab countries. In 1948, there were 717,000 Jews in Israel. In the years following the Arab defeat in the 1948–49 War, more than half a million Jews from some ten Arab countries began migrating to Israel. Ben-Gurion fully accepted the Zionist doctrine (*'Avoda Ivrit)* that only the "conquest of labor" by Jews and not the mere conquest of land would assure the realization of Zionism and the attainment of a Jewish majority. Eleven years later, on his return from a visit to South Africa, Ben-Gurion reported that he had told the South African prime minister that "the white settlers made a mistake—they should have done what we have done here with *'Avoda Ivrit.* Then they would have been spared their present troubles."[18]

The second largest pool of Jews was Soviet Jewry. In 1972, Richard Perle, an aide to Senator Henry "Scoop" Jackson (D-WA), helped draft the Jackson-Vanik law linking U.S.-Soviet trade relations with Jewish emigration rights. Jews who were allowed to leave the U.S.S.R. traveled to Vienna, where they were given the right to choose where they wanted to live; most opted for the United States. In 1980, e.g., of the 21,471 Soviet emigres, 81 percent came to the United States. The chairman of the Jewish Agency charged the U.S. Jewish community with being anti-Zionist and anti-Israel for not insisting that all the emigres go to Israel. A compromise was reached whereby Soviet Jews with immediate family in the U.S. could go there; all others went to a camp in Naples, Italy, where they would stay until deciding to go to Israel. The problem was that many decided to stay in the camp rather than go to Israel. Still, between 1948 and 1995, over 800,000 Soviet Jews immigrated to Israel.

Today the largest remaining pool of Jews is in the United States. The problem here, though, is that most U.S. Jews don't want to move to Israel. Back in the late '40s and early '50s, Ben-Gurion had pled unsuccessfully with American Jews to come to the new Jewish state. Jewish leaders in America told him, "We are not Zionist in your sense of the word. We can be Zionist as American patriots. We'll give you financial support."[19]

To convince American Jews to immigrate to Israel in significant numbers—and to stem the flow of Jews now leaving the Jewish state—Israel's economy will have to make a major recovery. This means that the constant threat of terrorist attacks will have to end, the "Palestinian problem" will have to be resolved, and relations with Israel's Arab neighbors will have to be improved.

So the question arises: how closely does President Bush's pro-Israel position reflect the policies of Israel's government? On February 18, 2003, Prime Minister Ariel Sharon told a group of visiting U.S. congressmen that America's impending war against Iraq was of vital importance to Israel. He went on to say that Israel was concerned about the security threat posed by Iran, and stressed that it was important to deal with Iran even while American attention was focused on Iraq.

Ariel Sharon has long opposed a Palestinian state on the West Bank and Gaza, saying that the Palestinians already had a state, it's called Jordan. After the '67 War, General Sharon deployed armed Jewish settlers into the West Bank under the pretext of creating a defense perimeter. From 1977 to 1981, Minister of Agriculture Sharon oversaw the settling of 25,000 Jews on the West Bank. And by 1990, Housing Minister Sharon was settling Jews from the old Soviet Union in the occupied territories.

More recently, on March 21, 2001, at an event sponsored by Israel Bonds in New York City, Sharon spoke of his political vision which, he said, consisted of four pillars, the first being immigration. "We need to bring one million more immigrants over the next 10 to 15 years," he said, adding: "The goal is that by the year 2020 the majority of Jews will be living in Israel." Jews had emigrated from Russia, Brazil, South Africa, France, and Ethiopia, he said; now the "time has come to see a strong aliyah from the United States as well." Sharon's other three pillars were: integrating Zionism and Jewish education, building strategic settlements (he called them communities), and competing in today's global marketplace. He concluded: "It is time to be proud Zionists again, and to wave the flag of renewed Zionism. . . . We have accomplished great things in the past 120 years of Zionism."[20]

Update

Prior to his debilitating stroke in January 2006, Prime Minister Ariel Sharon did the math. The large-scale Jewish immigration he was calling for never happened, while the annual birth rate for Palestinians was nearly double that of Israeli Jews. To incorporate the West Bank and Gaza, with all its Palestinians, would quickly spell the end to Jewish majority rule.

So Sharon began to build his Separation Barrier, a complex system of electronic fences and concrete walls, up to 24-feet high in population areas, ultimately stretching 420 miles. Hundreds of acres of West Bank land would be confiscated just for the Barrier's construction, which would also include all of East Jerusalem plus the major Jewish settlement blocs on the West Bank.

Left over for the Palestinians will be approximately 10.8 percent of historic Palestine. This, said Sharon, could be their "state," as long as they understood that they would not have sovereign control of the air above them, the water beneath them, nor the borders around them.

On his assumption of the post of acting prime minister, Ehud Olmert confirmed the mathematical imperative, declaring, in his first policy speech, that Israel will have to give up parts of the West Bank, but not the main settlement blocs and not East Jerusalem. This, he said, was necessary in order to preserve a Jewish majority inside Israel's borders. He explained: "The choice between allowing Jews to live in all parts of the Land of Israel and living in a state with a Jewish majority mandates giving up parts of the Land of Israel. We cannot continue to control parts of the territories where most of the Palestinians live."

Such unilateral withdrawal was heresy to Sharon's Likud party, whose charter calls for "persistence in settling and developing all parts of the Land of Israel, and annexing them." Knowing this, Sharon, shortly before his stroke, left the Likud party and founded the Kadima party. Several other Likud members, including Ehud Olmert, followed. The new party instantly won the support of former prime minister and Labor Party leader Shimon Peres.

Of note, here, is that neither Likud nor the new Kadima party— nor, for that matter, Labor—rejects the claim that all of historic Palestine constitutes the Land of Israel. The difference here is one of strategy, not unlike that employed back in 1948 by Ben-Gurion when he accepted 56 percent of historic Palestine, but never gave up the Zionist claim to all of it.

Many Palestinians, seeing their land continually being taken away from them, vented their frustrations in late January 2006 by giving a near 2 to 1 parliamentary victory to the Islamic party Hamas. While Hamas's charter calls the land of Palestine an Islamic trust, "left to the generations of Muslims until the day of resurrection," Hamas leader Abdel Aziz Rantisi said back in 2002, two years before he was killed in an Israeli missile strike, "The main aim of the intifada is the liberation of the West Bank, Gaza and Jerusalem, and nothing more. We haven't the force to liberate all our land."

So it seems that Zionism hasn't the people to annex all of Palestine, while Palestinians haven't the power to liberate all of it.

The next chapter—some say the last chapter—of political Zionism is about to be written.

U.S. Aid to Israel: The Subject No One Mentions

By Richard Curtiss

AMEU's September–October 1997 Link, "The Subject No One Mentions," was written by Richard Curtiss, executive editor of the Washington Report on Middle East Affairs, *and recipient of the Edward R. Murrow Award for Excellence in Public Diplomacy, the U.S. Information Agency's highest professional recognition. This is a condensed version of the original article with updated figures.*

> *Israel receives favorable treatment and special benefits that may not be available to other countries or that may establish precedents for other U.S. aid recipients. Israel's supporters justify the unusual treatment accorded to Israel because of the special relationship between the United States and Israel and because of Israel's unique economic and political status.—* **Congressional Research Service Issue Brief, 27 May 1997**

Quotations about Israel from some U.S. government publications read almost like pleas from inside the federal bureaucracy for media attention to the obvious abuses in the U.S.-Israel relationship. Dissecting the quotation above, the "favorable treatment and special benefits" Israel receives definitely are not "available to other countries," no matter what services they provide to the United States, from basing rights for U.S. military forces to participation in political, military, and economic alliances and treaties with the United States. And, fortunately for U.S. taxpayers, few of the privileges Israel receives have as yet established "precedents for other U.S. aid recipients."

As for the "special relationship" cited above, it is one in which Israel's very effective lobby in Washington can make Congress do things desired by the Israeli government even when they are contrary to U.S. interests, or can only be carried out at great expense to the U.S. Treasury. Few U.S. presidents or secretaries of state have been willing to put pressure on Israel out of fear of domestic political consequences stirred up by Israel's lobby and the national Jewish organizations that support it.

The special benefits Israel enjoys are not visible in the simple annual totals recorded by the Congressional Research Service. The fact is that a dollar appropriated to Israel costs the U.S. taxpayer more than a dollar appropriated to other countries because of bookkeeping tricks. The most visible of these is the early transfer of U.S. aid to Israel.

Other recipient countries receive their U.S. foreign aid in quarterly installments. However, in 1982 Israel asked that its Economic Support Funds (ESF) be transferred in one lump sum. Since then, Israel has received its ESF during the first 30 days of each fiscal year. This enables Israel to invest the funds in U.S. Treasury notes at prevailing interest rates, drawing its money from interest-bearing accounts as needed. Meanwhile, the U.S. is paying interest on the Treasury notes it has been forced to issue in order to come up early with all of Israel's ESF.

As an example, Israel earned about $86 million in U.S. Treasury note interest in 1991, according to USAID officials. Meanwhile, it costs the United States between $50 million and $60 million annually to borrow funds for the early, lump-sum payment.

The foreign aid appropriation bill signed on November 5, 1990, provided that henceforth Israel also would receive its Foreign Military Sales (FMS) aid in a lump sum during the first month of the fiscal year rather than in quarterly installments, thus duplicating the special benefit accorded for economic aid. With FMS then at $1.8 billion, the economic benefits to Israel and added interest liabilities to the United States in connection with the lump-sum payments approached $150 million annually.

Other special benefits are more difficult to quantify, but they save Israel tens of millions of dollars by making the U.S. bear costs that normally are assumed by the recipients of U.S. aid. Here is a partial listing:

Cash flow financing. Israel is permitted to set aside foreign military sales (FMS) funds for current year payments only. Most other countries must set aside the amount needed to meet the full cost of multi-year purchases. Egypt and Turkey now also benefit from cash flow financing, a privilege not accorded to any other foreign aid recipients. This practice effectively commits the U.S. government to future aid to Israel, because Israel has to make only current-year payments on multi-year contracts.

Cash transfer. The U.S. provides all ESF funds directly to the Israeli government without asking Israel to account in advance for how the funds will be used. Some other aid recipients receive part of their ESF as cash transfers, but not under such flexible, unmonitored conditions.

Unique FMS funding arrangements. Other countries deal with the Department of Defense (DOD) for purchase of U.S. military items. Israel, however, deals directly with U.S. companies for 99 percent of its military purchases in the United States. Other countries have a $100,000 minimum purchase amount per contract. Israel is allowed to purchase military items for less than $100,000. According to a Government Accounting Office (GAO) report in May 1990, Israel processed more than 15,000 orders for less than $50,000 in 1989, with no DOD review of the purchases as would be required in the case of purchases by other countries. Other countries have the U.S. government disburse funds to companies directly, but the Israeli Purchasing Mission in New York pays the companies and is reimbursed by the U.S. Treasury.

FMS offsets. U.S. contractors selling military materials to Israel agree to offset some of the costs to Israel's FMS account by buying components or materials from Israel. This is a common practice in normal commercial contracts, but, in the words of the U.S. General Accounting Office, offsets on FMS sales are "unusual," because FMS is intended to *sell* U.S. goods and services to foreign countries.

Loans with repayment waived. Apologists for Israel never tire of saying that Israel has never defaulted on repayment of a loan from the U.S. government. In fact, however, Israel has not been required to repay its U.S. government loans, some of which are extended on the understanding that repayment will not be made. This was the case when, following the 1973 war, President Richard Nixon asked Congress for emergency aid for Israel, including "loans" for which repayment would be waived.

The Israeli government insisted that this aid be described as loans rather than grants to avoid having a U.S. military mission established in Israel to oversee a grant program. In the words of the CRS Issue Brief: "Technically, the assistance is called loans, but as a practical matter, the military aid is [given as] grants."

This special benefit amounts to having a U.S. military aid program without U.S. military personnel administering it. The same benefit applies to U.S. economic aid. In other countries receiving bilateral U.S. economic aid, there is an AID mission within the U.S. embassy that must approve in advance the manner in which the money is to be spent, and then audit the actual expenditures to detect abuses or deviations from the approved program. There is no such AID mission in Israel. Israel spends its economic aid as it pleases and can prevent the U.S. from learning when, where, and how the money actually is spent.

In Israel's early years, private contributions from Jewish Americans and from U.S. Jewish organizations were a major source of support. They were so important that after Israeli military forces occupied Egyptian Sinai in 1956 and refused to heed President Dwight D. Eisenhower's demands that they withdraw, he threatened to cut off the U.S. tax exemption that donations to Israel enjoyed. Faced with the threat, Israeli prime minister David Ben-Gurion withdrew his forces.

At that time tax-exempt donations by Americans to Israel were about $40 million a year, and annual sales of State of Israel bonds (which are not tax exempt) in the U.S. were between $50 million and $60 million. Fueled by the unique U.S. law that grants U.S. tax exemption to donations from the United States to any Israeli institution that is exempt from Israeli taxes, the total of tax-exempt U.S. donations to Israel now approaches $1 billion annually.

These generous congressional gestures to Israel are subject to massive abuses, because the recipient institutions are outside the reach of U.S. law or oversight. A donor can claim a $1 million donation to an Israeli charity, and deduct this from his U.S. tax liability. But there is no way to prove the donation actually was for the amount claimed, if it went to the organization claimed, or even if it was made at all.

Suppose, for example, that the claimed Israeli recipient organization was prepared to testify that it had received the donation, but in fact there was a prior understanding that the $1 million would instead be donated to pro-Israel political action committees, whose role is to aid members of Congress who support aid to Israel. The potential for abuse is endless, as are the permutations in which such an unpoliceable tax benefit can be exploited to strengthen Israel's domestic lobbying apparatus. Since all of the institutions involved are outside U.S. legal jurisdiction, there is no possibility of proving fraud or punishing the perpetrators, including Americans who may be lending themselves to Machiavellian foreign intrigues, or simply cheating on their U.S. taxes.

In any case, if there were no cheating, the cost to U.S. taxpayers of this exemption for Israeli charities could be up to 38 percent of the estimated $1 billion in claimed donations.

Israel also turns to the U.S. government to guarantee repayment of commercial loans. The first time Israel sought this sweetheart deal was in late 1990, when it sought to borrow $10 billion from U.S. commercial institutions with U.S. backing. Israel said it needed the money to finance infrastructure, housing, training, and jobs for one million Jewish immigrants expected to arrive in Israel from the Soviet Union between 1991 and 1995. If the U.S. would guarantee payment in case of default, Israel could obtain a greatly reduced interest rate from lending institutions.

In April 1991, however, Israel requested emergency compensation for damages it said it sustained during the Gulf War. In the ensuing negotiations, the Israeli government agreed to postpone its request for loan guarantees until September 1991.

By that time, President George Bush had become alarmed by the reluctance of Israeli Prime Minister Yitzhak Shamir to participate in the Madrid Conference, which the U.S. and Russia were convening to open direct peace negotiations between Israel and its Arab neighbors.

As a result, Bush asked Congress to delay consideration of the U.S. loan guarantees until January 1992, because he feared that granting them would jeopardize Secretary of State James Baker's delicate negotiations at Madrid.

When Congress convened that January, Secretary Baker said the administration would support the loan guarantees on condition that Israel freeze all Jewish settlement activities in the Occupied Territories. Subsequent negotiations reached no agreement and, largely as a result of the impasse with the Bush administration, Shamir's Likud Party government fell, and new Israeli elections were called.

In June 1992, a Labor Party government headed by Gen. Yitzhak Rabin was formed. When Rabin visited the U.S. in July, Bush, facing a re-election campaign of his own, announced that the U.S. would provide the guarantees. His concession won him no pro-Israel support and no respite from press criticism, however. It was only after Bush lost the November election that Congress approved the loan guarantees in December 1992, to take effect in fiscal year 1993.

In three-way negotiations involving Congress, the administration, and Israel, it was agreed that the requested $10 billion in loan guarantees would be spread evenly over five fiscal years, that Israel would be allowed to complete Jewish housing projects underway in the Occupied Territories but not start new projects, and that each year's $2 billion in guarantees would be reduced by an amount equal to Israeli government expenditures during the previous fiscal year on settlements in the Occupied Territories.

On September 30, 1993, President Clinton notified Congress that the $2 billion in loan guarantees for FY 1994 would be reduced by $437 million, the amount the U.S. government calculated Israel had spent on Jewish settlements in 1993. These reductions continued over the five years the agreement was in effect, but President Clinton reinstated part of the reductions for "security reasons," resulting in a total reduction for settlement activity of $1.3588 billion and a reinstatement of $585 million—for a net reduction of $773.8 million.

In addition to the loan guarantees for resettling Soviet refugees, the U.S. also provided Israel a total of $600 million in housing loan guarantees spread over eight fiscal years. The largest annual guarantee was $400 million in 1990, with $200 million having been provided between 1972 and 1980.

What Israelis actually have received from the United States is considerably less than what it has cost American taxpayers to provide it. The principal difference arises from the fact that so long as the U.S. runs an annual budget deficit, every dollar the U.S. gives to Israel has to be raised through U.S. government borrowing.

As shown in Table I, Israel has received $98.7 billion in grants, loans, and commodities since the country's establishment through fiscal year 2006. Table II, which takes into account military aid dispensed through the Department of Defense budget plus interest for early disbursement, puts total direct aid to Israel at more than $110 billion. In addition to the economic and military aid, Israel has received some $10 billion in U.S. loan guarantees, and perhaps $25 billion or more in tax-exempt contributions from American Jews.

No other country in the world has received anything approaching these raw numbers. In per capita terms, probably no other country has received more than $100 per citizen over the past 60 years. In the same period, Israelis will have received nearly $17,500 per citizen from the U.S. alone, and more than $20,000 per citizen when German assistance is included. (Germany, the major non-American donor to Israel, has given the Jewish state more than $30 billion in grants and preferred loans.)

The true cost of Israel also includes assistance to Egypt, a payoff from U.S. taxpayers for Egypt's having made peace with Israel in 1979. According to the Congressional Research Service, U.S. aid to Egypt from FY 1979 through FY 2006 totaled more than $47 billion (compared to $4.2 billion for the preceding 26 years), averaging more than $1.7 billion per year.

There are other factors to consider as well. These include lost American export markets because of Arab and Muslim anger over U.S. support of Israel; the upward pressure on world oil prices caused by Middle Eastern instability stemming largely from Israel's refusal to enter into land-for-peace settlements with the Palestinians, Syria, and Lebanon; and the costs of having to station large U.S. air, naval, and ground forces in the Mediterranean, Persian Gulf, Indian Ocean, and Arabian peninsula.

When these real-life pressures on the United States are added to the formal outlays to Israel by the U.S. government, it seems that George Balls's estimate was right on the money. In his book *The Passionate Attachment: America's Involvement with Israel*, Ball, the former undersecretary of state in the Kennedy and Johnson administrations, figured Israel was costing the U.S. treasury $11 billion a year.

Table I: Aid to Israel
(millions of dollars)

Year	Total	Military Grant	Economic Grant	Immigrant Aid*	ASHA**	Other***
1949-96	68,030.9	29,014.9	23,122.4	868.9	121.00	14,903.0
1997	3,132.1	1,800.0	1,200.0	80.0	2.10	50.0
1998	3,080.0	1,800.0	1,200.0	80.0	?	?
1999	3,010.0	1,860.0	1,080.0	70.0	?	?
2000	4,131.9	3,120.0	949.1	60.0	2.75	?
2001	2.876.1	1,975.6	838.2	60.0	2.75	?
2002	2,850.7	2,040.0	720.0	60.0	2.65	28.0
2003	3,745.2	3,086.4	596.1	59.6	3.05	?
2004	2,687.3	2,147.3	477.2	49.7	3.15	9.9
2005 est.	2,612.2	2,202.2	357.0	50.0	2.95	?
2006 est.	2,563.5	2,280.0	240.0	40.0	3.00	0.5
Total	$98,719.5	$51,326.4	$30,780.0	$1,478.2	$143.30	$14,991.7

Source: Congressional Research Service Report to Congress: "U.S. Foreign Aid to Israel," dated January 5, 2006. Also FY2006 Foreign Operations Appropriations Bill, HR 3057

*Migration and Refugee Assistance begun in 1973 to assist in resettlement of migrants to Israel.
**American Schools and Hospitals Abroad program.
***Military and economic loans, Food for Peace grants, loans, etc.

Editor's Note: Figures above do not include funds from Department of Defense for joint research and development projects, interest lost to the U.S. from early lump-sum disbursement of aid rather than in increments over the fiscal year (as is done with other aid recipients), and billions in aid to Egypt resulting from its 1979 peace treaty with Israel.

Table II: Estimated Cumulative Aid to Israel (millions of dollars)

CRS Total thru FY 2006 (Table I)	$98,720
Est. Total for FY 2007	$2,600
Est. Department of Defense	$7,000
Est. Interest from Early Disbursement	$2,000
Total Direct Aid 1949-2007	$110,320

Note: Military aid to Israel from the Department of Defense is mostly for specific projects. In computing interest for early disbursement, very conservative figures were employed based on prevailing interest rates for the time periods under consideration. According to the Congressional Research Service, "Israel is the largest cumulative recipient of foreign assistance since World War II. From 1976-2004, Israel was the largest annual recipient of U.S. foreign assistance, having recently been supplanted by Iraq. Since 1985, the United States has provided nearly $3 billion in grants annually to Israel."

Veto

By Phyllis Bennis

Phyllis Bennis is with the Institute for Policy Studies in Washington, D.C., where she is responsible for U.N. and Middle East programs.

> *While U.S. dollars fuel Israel's colonization of Palestinian land, it is U.S. vetoes that shield Israel from international censure. The U.S. has used its veto 40 times on Israel's behalf, frequently as the only dissenting voice. Violence and abuse against civilians is a prevalent theme of the resolutions, as is failure to comply with resolutions that even the U.S. felt compelled to support. The full account of how the U.S. shields Israel from U.N. censure can be found in Ms. Bennis's* Link *article (January–March 2003) at www.ameu.org. The list of vetoes that appeared in her article has been updated below.*

U.S. Vetoes of U.N. Security Council Resolutions Condemning Israeli Actions

1. **S/10784, 9/10/1972.** Calls on all parties to cease military actions. 13 for, 1 abstains.
2. **S/10974, 7/24/1973.** Deplores Israel's continuing occupation of territories and requests the secretary-general and his special representative to pursue a solution to the Middle East problem. 13 for, 1 abstains.
3. **S/11898, 12/8/1975.** Condemns Israeli air raids on Lebanon and Palestinian refugee camps. 13 for, 1 abstains.

4. **S/11940, 1/25/1976.** Affirms inalienable rights of the Palestinian people to self-determination, an independent state, and return to homes. 9 for, 3 abstain.

5. **S/12022, 3/25/1976.** Deplores Israel's failure to stop actions changing the status of Jerusalem and calls on it to desist from land expropriation and settlements. 14 for.

6. **S/12119, 6/29/1976.** Repeats S/11940. 10 for, 4 abstain.

7. **S/13911, 4/30/1980.** Repeats S/11940. 10 for, 4 abstain.

8. **S/14832, 1/20/1982.** Condemns Israel's failure to comply with SC Res. 497 concerning Israel's annexation of Golan Heights. 9 for, 5 abstain.

9. **Rev. S/14943, 4/2/1982.** Denounces Israel's dismissal of elected Palestinian officials and other human rights violations in occupied territories. 13 for, 1 abstains.

10. **S/14985, 4/20/1982.** Condemns attack at al-Haram al-Sharif in Jerusalem. 14 for.

11. **S/15185, 6/8/1982.** Condemns Israel's non-compliance with SC Res. 508 and 509 and demands all hostilities in Lebanon cease within six hours. 14 for.

12. **S/15255, 6/26/1982.** Demands all parties cease hostilities in Lebanon and withdrawal of Israeli and Palestinian armed forces from Beirut. 14 for.

13. **S/15347, 8/6/1982.** Condemns Israel for not implementing SC Res. 516 and 517 which call for a cease-fire in Lebanon. 11 for, 3 abstain.

14. **S/15895, 8/2/1983.** Calls Israeli settlements in the occupied territories illegal, deplores continued settlement building, and calls upon all states not to give Israel aid to be used for settlements. 13 for, 1 abstains.

15. **S/16732, 9/6/1984.** Calls on Israel to respect rights of civilian population and demands that it lift restrictions in the areas it occupies in southern Lebanon, western Bekaa, and Rashaya District. 11 for, 3 abstain.

16. **S/17000, 3/12/1985.** Condemns Israeli practices against civilian population in southern Lebanon, western Bekaa, and Rashaya District. 11 for, 3 abstain.

17. **S/17459, 9/13/1985.** Deplores Israeli repressive measures against civilian population in the occupied territories and calls for them to stop. 10 for, 4 abstain.

18. **S/17730, 1/17/1986.** Deplores Israeli violence against civilians in southern Lebanon. 11 for, 3 abstain.

19. **S/17769, 1/30/1986.** Deplores provocative acts by Israelis which violate the sanctity of the Haram al-Sharif in Jerusalem. 13 for, 1 abstains.

20. **S/17796, 2/6/1986.** Condemns Israel's interception of a Libyan civilian aircraft. 10 for, 4 abstain.

21. **S/19434, 1/18/1988.** Deplores Israeli attacks against Lebanese territories. 13 for, 1 abstains.

22. **S/19466, 2/1/1988.** Calls on Israel to cease policies violating human rights of Palestinians in the occupied territories. 14 for.

23. **S/19780, 4/14/1988.** Urges Israel to rescind deportation of Palestinian civilians and condemns Israeli violations of human rights in occupied territories. 14 for.

24. **S/19868, 5/10/1988.** Condemns Israel's invasion of southern Lebanon. 14 for.

25. **S/20322, 12/14/1988.** Deplores Israeli military activities against Lebanon. 14 for.

26. **S/20463, 2/17/1989.** Deplores Israeli policies towards Palestinians in occupied territories. 14 for.

27. **S/20677, 6/9/1989.** Deplores Israeli human rights violations in occupied territories. 14 for.

28. **S/20945, 11/7/1989.** As S/20677, adding particularly the siege of Beit Sahur. 14 for.

29. **S/21326, 5/31/1990.** Establishes SC commission to examine situation in the territories. 14 for.

30. **S/1995/394, 5/17/1995.** Confirms that Israel's expropriation of land in East Jerusalem is invalid and calls upon Israel to rescind the expropriation orders. 14 for.

31. **S/1197/199, 3/7/1997.** Calls for Israel to reverse its decision to begin construction of the Jabal Abu Ghneim settlement. 14 for.

32. **S/1997/241, 3/21/1997.** Demands Israel cease construction of the Jabal Abu Ghneim settlement. 13 for.

33. **S/2001/270, 3/27/2001.** Calls for U.N. observer force, protection of Palestinian civilians, and end to closures of occupied territories. 9 for, 4 abstain.

34. **S/2001/1199, 12/14/2001.** Calls for withdrawal of Israeli forces from Palestinian-controlled territories, and condemns acts of terror against civilians. 12 for, 2 abstain.

35. **S/2002/1385, 12/20/2002.** Condemns Israel for death of three U.N. staff and destruction of U.N. warehouse in Gaza. 12 for, 2 abstain.

36. **S/2003/891, 9/16/2003.** Demands that Israel desist from any act of deportation and cease any threat to the safety of the elected president of the Palestinian Authority. 11 for, 3 abstain.

37. **S/2003/980, 10/14/2003.** Decides that construction by Israel of a wall in the occupied territories is illegal and must be halted and reversed. 10 for, 4 abstain.

38. **S/2004/240, 3/25/2004.** Condemns Israel's extrajudicial execution of Sheikh Ahmed Yassin and six other Palestinians outside a mosque in Gaza City and calls for complete cessation of extrajudicial assassinations. 11 for, 3 abstain.

39. **S/2004/783, 10/5/2004.** Demands that Israel halt all military operations in northern Gaza and withdraw its occupying forces from area. 11 for, 3 abstain.

40. **S/2006/508, 7/13/06.** Calls for the unconditional release of an Israeli soldier captured earlier as well as Israel's immediate withdrawal from Gaza and the release of dozens of Palestinian officials detained by Israel. 10 for, 4 abstain.

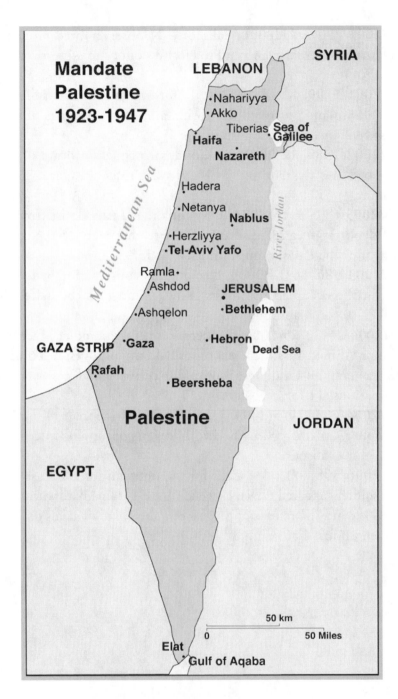

Original British Mandate in Palestine
1923 -1947

In the Beginning, There Was Terror

By Ron Bleier

Ronald Bleier is a writer-researcher based in New York City. He edits the Demographic Environmental and Security Issues Project web site.

Much of the history of terrorism in today's Middle East has been thrust down the Orwellian memory hole due to the highly effective campaign over the past 50 years to suppress information prejudicial to Israel.

Blowing up a bus, a train, a ship, a café, or a hotel; assassinating a diplomat or a peace negotiator; killing hostages, sending letter bombs; massacring defenseless villagers—this is terrorism as we know it. In the modern Middle East, it began with the Zionists who founded the Jewish state.[1]

The Original Sin

Israel's original sin is Zionism, the ideology that a Jewish state should replace the former Palestine. At the root of the problem is Zionism's exclusivist structure, whereby only Jews are treated as first-class citizens. In order to create and consolidate a Jewish state in 1948, Zionists expelled 750,000 Palestinians from their homeland and never allowed them or their descendants to return. In addition, Israeli forces destroyed over 400 Palestinian villages and perpetrated about three dozen massacres. In 1967, the Israelis forced another 350,000 Palestinians to flee the West Bank and Gaza, as well as forcing 147,000

Syrians from the Golan Heights. Since 1967 Israel has placed the entire Palestinian population of the Territories under military occupation.

The effects of the dispossession of the Palestinians and other Arabs are with us to this day, in the shattered lives of the millions of people directly affected, and as a sign of the West's war against the entire Arab nation and Muslims everywhere. Arguably, the original sin of Zionism and its effects on the peoples of the Middle East were central to the motivation behind the events of 9/11, the most important consequence of which is the ongoing "war on terrorism" that is smothering our political landscape.

Assassinating the Peace Negotiator

One of the most notorious acts of Israeli terrorism occurred during the 1948 war when Jewish forces, members of the LEHI underground (also known as the Stern Gang), assassinated Swedish count Folke Bernadotte, a U.N.-appointed mediator. Bernadotte was killed on September 17, 1948, a day after he offered his second mediation plan which, among other things, called for repatriation and compensation for the Palestinian refugees.

The assassination of Bernadotte highlighted one of the biggest policy differences at the time between the United States and Israel—namely, the fate of the Palestinian refugees. By that time, Jewish/Israeli forces had already forced more than half a million Palestinians from their homes. The resultant international outcry focused attention on the implications for Middle East peace as well as on the suffering of the refugees. Moreover, the fate of hundreds of thousands of Jews who resided in the Arab world, mainly in Iraq, Morocco, Yemen, and Egypt, was placed at risk because of Israeli expulsion policy.

The day before the assassination, Israeli foreign minister Moshe Sharett publicly accused Bernadotte of "bias against the state of Israel and in favor of the Arab states." Stephen Green points to evidence that the Israeli government was itself directly involved in the killing. On the night of the assassination, the Czech consulates in Jerusalem and Haifa were busy processing some 30 visas for Stern Gang members "who had been rounded up for their involvement in the planning and execution" of the assassination. "Between September 18 and September 29, most if not all of the 30 left Israel on flights for Prague, Czechoslovakia." The "scale, precision, and speed of the evacuation-escape" made the State Department "suspicious that the Stern Gang was not involved alone." The U.S. wondered whether the "operation might have been planned and prepared in Czechoslovakia, and that a specially trained squad had been flown into Israel from Prague for that purpose."[2] In addition, historian Howard Sachar notes that "Yehoshua Cohen, a friend of Ben-Gurion, is widely believed to be the trigger man."[3]

Eight months later, the Israelis revealed to the U.N. that the majority of the Stern Gang members rounded up in the "purge" had been released within two weeks. Those not released were held until a general amnesty was granted on February 14, 1949.[4] No one was ever put on trial for the killing.

The assassination of Bernadotte made international headlines, and for a time more attention was paid to the issue of the Palestinian refugees. In the end, pressure to repatriate them was never successfully mustered. Arguably, from the point of view of Israeli expulsion policy, the assassination was a success, since none of Bernadotte's successors was able to focus sufficient pressure on the Israelis to make any concessions. Had Bernadotte lived, he might have succeeded where others had failed. At the least, his murder was a warning to any who might have tried to follow his activist example.

Dynamiting a Public Building

One of the most notorious examples of Jewish/Zionist terrorism in the post-war period (1945 - 1948) was the bombing of the King David Hotel on July 22, 1946. The bombing developed out of an atmosphere in which the Zionists were enraged when the British Labor Party's sweeping victory in the summer of 1945 did nothing to liberalize the previous government's policy on Jewish immigration.

British insistence on maintaining their restrictive immigration policy led to the unification of the three major factions of the Jewish fighting forces into a United Resistance. The three forces comprised the Jewish Agency's Haganah, led by David Ben-Gurion: the LEHI; the Stern Gang, led by Nathan Yellin-Mor; and the Irgun, led by Menachem Begin, who in his book *The Revolt* bragged that he was "Terrorist Number One." At the end of October 1945, they formally agreed to cooperate on "a military struggle against British rule."[5]

Their joint attacks, including the Night of the Trains, the Night of the Airfields, the Night of the Bridges, and other operations, were so successful that they led finally to forceful British retaliation. Immediately after the Night of the Bridges, June 17, 1947, British Army searches for terrorists were conducted, arrests were made, and Jews were killed and injured in clashes. A much larger British operation that came to be known as "Black Sabbath" began two weeks later. Thousands of Jews were arrested. British troops ransacked the offices of the Jewish Agency in Jerusalem, seized important documents, arrested members of the Jewish Agency Executive, and carried out searches and arrests in many kibbutzim.

As a direct result of the Black Sabbath operation, the Haganah command decided on July 1 to conduct three operations against the British. The Palmach (the elite Haganah strike force) would carry out a raid on a British Army camp to recover their weapons. The Irgun would blow up the King David Hotel, where the offices of the Mandatory government and the British military command were located. (The LEHI task, blowing up the adjacent David Brothers building, was never carried out.)

Just at this moment came an appeal from Chaim Weizmann, president of the World Zionist Organization, urging that the armed struggle against the British be halted. As a result of his appeal, the supreme political committee decided "to accede to Weizmann's request." However, Moshe Sneh, the Haganah liaison with the Irgun and LEHI, strongly opposed the Weizmann request and did not inform Begin of the committee resolution but merely asked him to postpone the action.[6]

The King David Hotel was brought down by means of 50 kilos of explosives placed beside supporting pillars in the hotel's La Regence restaurant. Timers were placed for 30 minutes. After the bombers made their escape, telephone messages were placed to the hotel telephone operator and to *The Palestine Post.* The French Consulate, adjacent to the hotel, was warned to open its windows to prevent blast damage, which it did.[7] Some 25 minutes later, a terrific explosion destroyed the entire southern wing of the hotel—all seven stories. The official death toll was 91: 28 Britons, 41 Arabs, 17 Jews, and 5 others.

The Sharett Diaries

Moshe Sharett's résumé included being head of the Jewish Agency's political department (1933–1948), Israel's first foreign minister (1948–1956), and its second prime minister (1954–1955). Following his death, his son edited his personal diary, which covered the period from October 1953 to November 1957. The diary was published in 1979 in Hebrew only. It may well have received little attention outside of Israel had it not been for Livia Rokach.

Livia Rokach, daughter of Israel Rokach, minister of the interior in the government of Israeli prime minister Moshe Sharett, later moved to Rome, where she identified herself as "an Italian writer of Palestinian origin." In the early 1980s, she translated excerpts from the Sharett diary and inserted them into a book: *Israel's Sacred Terrorism: A Study Based on Moshe Sharett's Personal Diary and Other Documents.* Despite legal threats from the Israeli foreign ministry, the book was published in the United States by the Association of Arab American University Graduates (AAUG). Israel never took legal action, fearing that, in the words of Knesset member Uri Avneri, "stopping the dissemination of the booklet would be a mistake of the first order, since this would give it much more publicity."[8]

In her book Rokach charges that from the earliest days of the state, Israel cynically and with cold calculation used its military power under the banner of security in order to dominate the region. She explains that Israel's leaders were unhappy with the 1949 armistice borders even though, as a result of the 1948 war, they increased Israeli territory from the U.N. allotment of 56 percent of Mandate Palestine to 78 percent. The Israeli government understood that it needed to transform the fledgling state into a regional power in order to conquer the rest of Palestine as well as some of the territory of its Arab neighbors.

Rokach concludes from Sharett's journal that the Israeli political establishment never seriously believed in an Arab threat to the existence of Israel. She writes that Israel deliberately attempted to drive the Arab states into confrontations and wars in order to dominate the Middle East. Such ambitions could not be achieved on the basis of the earlier Jewish moral superiority doctrine and thus "inevitably presupposed the use of large scale, open violence." According to Rokach, "Terrorism and revenge were now to be glorified as the new moral . . . and even sacred values of Israeli society." Such a transformation of the Israeli population could not be achieved automatically, but required the generation of fear and anxiety on the part of its population and its supporters. They also understood that "the lives of Jewish victims also had to be sacrificed to create provocations justifying subsequent reprisals. . . . A hammering, daily propaganda, controlled by the censors, was directed to feed the Israeli population with images of the monstrosity of the Enemy."[9]

In late 1953, Israeli prime minister Ben-Gurion decided to take a two-year sabbatical during which he would withdraw from government activity. His retirement was "presented as a spiritual exercise," but Rokach contends that it was done for strategic reasons. The "moderate" Sharett was to replace Ben-Gurion in order not to alarm the West about Israel's intentions. "In the short range the Israeli design was aimed at slowing down the negotiations between Arab states pressing to be armed and the West which was reluctant to arm them." The timing of Ben-Gurion's sabbatical indicates that already only four years after the war of 1948–49, the security establishment was contemplating a strategy for regional destabilization. Its modus operandi was to be the political military policy known under the false name of "retaliation." The point of the retaliation policy was to provoke conflict and tension in the area, to destabilize the Arab regimes by demonstrating that they could not protect their citizens from Israeli attacks, and to set the stage for general war.[10]

Massacring Villagers

An instance of Sharett's documentation of Israeli "retaliation" is the notorious Kibya affair. On the night of October 12, 1953, a grenade was thrown into a Jewish settlement east of Tel Aviv, killing a woman and two children. Ben-Gurion and others planned a powerful retaliatory blow against a Jordanian village from which it was determined the attack originated. Sharett argued against the raid; on October 14, 1953, he recorded:

I told [Pinchas] Lavon [a staunch supporter of the retaliation policy, soon to become the minister of defense] that this [attack] will be a grave error, and recalled, citing various precedents, that it was never proved that reprisal actions serve their declared purpose. Lavon smiled . . . and kept to his own idea. . . . Ben-Gurion, he said, didn't share my view.[11]

Two nights later, Ariel Sharon's Unit 101 killed 60 people in the Jordanian border village of Kibya. Sharett heard reports that 30 houses had been demolished in one village.

This reprisal is unprecedented in its dimensions and in the offensive power used. I walked up and down in my room, helpless and utterly depressed by my feeling of impotence. . . I was simply horrified by the description in Radio Ramallah's broadcast of the destruction of the Arab village. Tens of houses have been razed to the soil and tens of people killed. I can imagine the storm that will break out tomorrow in the Arab and Western capitals. (15 October 1953)

I must underline that when I opposed the action I didn't even remotely suspect such a bloodbath. I thought that I was opposing one of those actions which have become a routine in the past. Had I even remotely suspected that such a massacre was to be held, I would have raised real hell. (16 October 1953)

Bombing a Public Bus

In addition to the Israeli retaliation policy against the Arabs, Rokach devotes a chapter to possible Israeli "false flag" or "black propaganda" operations whereby Israel's own Jewish citizens were deliberately sacrificed. In her chapter entitled "Sacred Terrorism," Rokach details an incident from March 1954 in the course of which attackers killed 10 passengers on a bus from Eilat to Beersheva at the Ma'aleh Ha'akrabim crossroads. Four passengers survived. To this day the circumstances of the attack are shrouded in mystery. Who were the attackers? Rokach wrote that the Israeli cover story was "too strange" for outsiders to believe, noting:

> Colonel Hutcheson, the American chairman of the mixed Jordanian-Israeli Armistice Commission, did not take it seriously. Summing up the Commission's inquiry, Colonel Hutcheson in fact officially announced that "from the testimonies of the survivors it is not proved that all the murderers were Arabs."

The details of the operation were so unclear that even American press reports made mention of the Jordanian version "according to which the Ma'aleh Ha'akrabim massacre was committed by the Israelis." Although in public and private, Sharett was reluctant to believe the Jordanian version, Rokach speculates that "deep down in his heart" Sharett must have had his "unconfessed doubts."[12]

Although Sharett managed to block the Israeli military from forceful retaliation for the bus massacre, a pretext was soon found to launch a massive attack on the village of Nahalin, near Bethlehem, killing dozens of civilians and "completely destroying" another Palestinian village in the West Bank. The neighboring Arab countries "were persuaded that the Israeli escalation of self-provoked incidents, terrorism, and renewed retaliation meant that Israel was preparing the ground for war. They therefore took strong measures to prevent any infiltration into Israel." Israeli general Moshe Dayan told a journalist friend in May 1954 that "the situation along the borders is better than it has been for a long time and actually it is quite satisfactory." But quiet borders simply spurred more Israeli incursions, and Rokach explains how the military adopted new tactics using small patrols for sabotage and murder in Arab villages, in which Ariel Sharon's infamous Unit 101 played a decisive role.[13]

Today with Ariel Sharon as prime minister, the same dynamic of Israeli use of terror for political gain repeats itself shamelessly. As Rachel Corrie, the American volunteer recently crushed to death in Gaza by an Israeli bulldozer, said in a letter home to her parents: "Sharon's assassination-during-peace negotiations/land-grab strategy is working very well now to create settlements all over [and is] slowly but surely eliminating any meaningful possibility for Palestinian self-determination."[14]

Bombing British, U.S., and Egyptian Property

One of the most historically significant "false flag" schemes documented by Sharett is the infamous Lavon Affair, which is one of the few such operations that the Israeli government was forced to acknowledge. In July 1954, about 10 Egyptian Jews under the command of Israeli agents planted bombs in British and American properties and Egyptian public buildings in Cairo and Alexandria. The spy ring was caught and broken up on July 27, when one of its members was caught after a bomb exploded in his pocket in Alexandria.

There was a trial, and two of the accused were condemned to death and executed, while the three Israeli commanders escaped and a fourth committed suicide. A scandal subsequently ensued in Israel that turned on exactly who ordered the operation. In 1954–55, Sharett anticipated the findings of the commission which ultimately established that Chief of Staff Moshe Dayan, Director General of the

Ministry of Defense Shimon Peres, and Intelligence Chief Colonel Benjamin Givli were the culprits. Sharett confided to his diary on January 10, 1955:

> [People] ask me if I am convinced that "he [Defense Minister Pinchas Lavon] gave the order?" . . . but let us assume that Givli has acted without instructions. . . . doesn't the moral responsibility lie all the same on Lavon, who has constantly preached for acts of madness and taught the army leadership the diabolic lesson of how to set the Middle East on fire, how to cause friction, cause bloody confrontations, sabotage targets . . . [and perform] acts of despair and suicide?

At the time of the bombings, negotiations were at their height between Cairo and London for the evacuation of the Canal Zone, and between Cairo and Washington for arms supplies and other aid in connection with a possible U.S.-Egyptian alliance. Stephen Green presents an even more cynical picture: top Israeli officials initiated the terrorist operation in order to sabotage Prime Minister Sharett's ongoing and quietly successful negotiations with Egyptian President Gamal Nasser.[15]

Today, a standard, even routine method of sacrificing Israelis on the altar of politics is the Israeli tactic of provoking Palestinian attacks by assassinating high-profile activists. One such example was so clear that a leading Israeli journalist forecasted the Israeli casualties that would result from an Israeli "targeted assassination." On November 23, 2001, the Israelis assassinated Mahmud Abu Hunud, a top Hamas operative. Two days later, Israeli journalist Alex Fishman, in a front-page article, explained that before the assassination of Hunud there had existed a "secret" and unacknowledged gentlemen's agreement between Hamas and the Palestinian Authority that "Hamas was to avoid in the near future" suicide bombings in Israel. As Fishman wrote: "Whoever decided upon the liquidation of Abu Hunud knew in advance" that the agreement with Hamas would be "shattered. . . . The subject was extensively discussed by both Israel's military echelon and its political one."[16] Just as Fishman had predicted, Hamas soon struck back, and less than a week later, on December 1 and 2, suicide bombings in Jerusalem and Haifa killed 25 Israelis. The effect of this cycle of violence was predictably to heighten tensions and to dramatically weaken the constituency in Israel and the U.S. in favor of peace negotiations.

Raiding a Camp in Gaza

Rokach's *Israel's Sacred Terrorism* provides previously unavailable documentation relating to Israel's preparations for the October 1956 surprise attack by Israel, France, and Britain against Egypt. In that operation, the Allies conquered the Suez Canal, Eastern Sinai and the Gaza Strip. The combined invasion occurred at a time when the U.S. sought to stabilize the area. But the Israeli interest was precisely the opposite. It was to exacerbate tensions and make it difficult or impossible for Egypt to gain the weapons it needed to deter Israel from war.

An important incident leading up to the October 1956 war was a massive raid on an Egyptian Army camp in Gaza, "the bloodiest incident between Egypt and Israel since the 1948 war."[17] The raid took place in a period "of relative tranquility following the enforcement of repressive measures decided on by the Egyptian administration of the Strip." On the night of February 28, 1955, the Israelis sent in 50 paratroopers, who wound up killing 39 Egyptians and wounding 30 others. Sharett approved the operation but was "shocked" by the loss of life, as he wrote on March 1, 1955:

> The number [of Egyptian victims] . . . changes not only the dimensions of the operation but its very substance; it turns it into an event liable to cause grave political and military complications and dangers. . . . The army spokesman, on instructions from the Minister of Defense, delivered a false version to the press. . . . Who will believe us?

It is widely acknowledged that the Gaza raid was a decisive turning point in Nasser's relations with Israel. From then on, the Egyptian president took every opportunity to explain to visiting diplomats that the attack "was a moment of truth" when he "finally perceived the dimensions of the Israeli problem." He soon decided to turn to the Soviets for arms in order to defend his country.[18]

In the aftermath of the Gaza raid, Sharett instructed his embassies to go on the offensive despite what he knew of the origins of the attack. He hoped to counter the "general impression that while we cry out over our isolation and the dangers to our security, we initiate aggression and reveal ourselves as being bloodthirsty and aspiring to perpetrate mass massacres."[19]

Sharett was very much concerned about U.S. pressure to reduce tensions in the area. He understood, as seen in his March 12, 1955, entry, that the U.S. interpreted the Gaza raid as "signaling a decision on our part to attack on all fronts. The Americans . . . are afraid that it will lead to a new conflagration in the Middle East, which will blow up all their plans. Therefore they wish to obtain from us a definite commitment that similar actions will not be repeated." However, Ben-Gurion had recently emerged from retirement to rejoin Sharett's government as Defense Minister precisely to prevent Israel from committing to discontinuing such reprisals. Indeed, within days of rejoining the government, Ben-Gurion proposed that Israel proceed to occupy the Gaza Strip, then controlled by Egypt, this time for good, a proposal that Sharett managed to defeat.

But the Israelis would not agree to a U.S. initiative for a security pact because, as Sharett wrote:

> We do not need [Dayan said] a security pact with the U.S.: such a pact will only constitute an obstacle for us. . . . The security pact will only handcuff us and deny us the freedom of action which we need in the coming years. Reprisal actions which we couldn't carry out if we were tied to a security pact are our vital lymph. . . . they make it possible for us to maintain a high level of tension among our population and in the army.[20]

Sharett put the implications of Dayan's view into his own words in a May 26, 1955, entry:

And above all—let us hope for a new war with the Arab countries, so that we may finally get rid of our troubles and acquire our space. (Such a slip of the tongue: Ben-Gurion himself said that it would be worthwhile to pay an Arab a million pounds to start a war.)

In addition to creating tensions, Israel hoped to isolate the Nasser regime and prevent Egypt from obtaining weapons and other aid from the West. The Israeli sanctions program was so successful that "after years of contacts and negotiations," Egypt received nothing more than a "personal present made to General Neguib in the form of a decorative pistol to wear at ceremonies."[21]

In the end, an enraged President Eisenhower, who was not informed of tripartite plans to make war on Egypt, forced the Allies to halt the attack and eventually to give up virtually all the territory they had captured. Eisenhower's actions make clear that he understood that American interests lay in a stable Middle East and an Israel confined to its 1949 borders.[22] Immensely popular as he was, Eisenhower was largely able to shake off the pressures placed by the Jewish lobby on Congress and the White House. His relative independence was virtually the last such example in American history.

Update by the author, Ronald Bleier

Prescription for Terror

New York City—As I reread my 2003 article on Israeli terror for *The Link*, I had to recognize that the bleak outlook expressed there for future prospects for the human and national rights of the Palestinian people and for regional stability has been more than borne out. Ehud Olmert has stepped into the shoes of the legendary Ariel Sharon without missing a beat. In its focus on alienating the Palestinians from their land, Israeli policy has been unwavering. Through the use of every means of state terror at its disposal, including targeted assassinations, air strikes, invasions, torture, land confiscations, closures, economic strangulation, and more, the Israeli government relentlessly pursues its anti- Palestinian agenda.

Even the rollback of the Israeli occupation of Gaza has been tempered by the closure of its borders, resulting in millions of dollars in lost produce and lost pay, putting a stranglehold on Gaza's economy. Hospitals are running out of the most basic supplies, and even such staples as flour and cooking oil are often difficult to obtain. After the Hamas electoral victory, Dov Weinglass, an adviser to Israel's prime minister, blandly announced his prescription for maximizing the pressure on the Palestinians to just short of provoking an effective international outcry. He said that they should be "put on a diet, but not starved to death." So far his prescription seems to be working.

Part II: Individuals of Courage

From his collection of poems on Palestine and Iraq (see entire collection on our web site), AMEU co-founder Henry Fisher wrote:

> O do you know that it is so,
> And if you do, can you be quiet?
> Would you not cry, would you not cry it?
>
> Do you not know that it is so
> Appalling you cannot forgo
> The need to tell them, who deny it?
>
> On this, on any day of woe
> Would you comply with what you know
> To be a lie, and justify it?
>
> O can you know that it is so,
> And yet be quiet.

Over the past 40 years we have profiled numerous Americans who did know, often through personal experiences, the tragedies inflicted upon the Palestinians. They could not be quiet. We profile five of them; others can be found in our internet archive.

Deir Yassin Remembered

By Daniel A. McGowan

In 1996, when he wrote this issue of The Link, *Daniel McGowan was professor of economics at Hobart & William Smith Colleges in upstate New York. Today he is retired and devotes his time to the project he founded, Deir Yassin Remembered.*

> *Early in the morning of Friday, April 9, 1948, commandos of the Irgun, headed by Menachem Begin, and the Stern Gang attacked Deir Yassin, a village with about 750 Palestinian residents. It was several weeks before the end of the British Mandate. The village lay outside of the area that the United Nations recommended be included in a future Jewish state.*

Deir Yassin had a peaceful reputation, had cooperated with the Jewish Agency, and was even said by a Jewish newspaper to have driven out some Arab militants. But it was located on high ground in the corridor between Tel Aviv and Jerusalem, and one plan, kept secret until years afterwards, called for it to be destroyed and the residents evacuated to make way for a small airfield that would supply the beleaguered Jewish residents of Jerusalem.

By noon over 200 people, half of them women and children, had been systematically murdered. Four commandos died at the hands of resisting Palestinians using old Mausers and muskets. Twenty-five male villagers were loaded into trucks, paraded through the Zakhron Yosef quarter in Jerusalem, and then taken to a stone quarry along the road between Givat Shaul and Deir Yassin and shot to death. The remaining residents were driven to Arab East Jerusalem.

That evening the Irgunists and the Sternists escorted a party of foreign correspondents to a house at Givat Shaul, a nearby Jewish settlement founded in 1906. Over tea and cookies they amplified the details of the operation and justified it, saying Deir Yassin had become a concentration point for Arabs, including Syrians and Iraqis, planning to attack the western suburbs of Jerusalem. They said that 25 members of the Haganah militia had reinforced the attack and claimed that an Arabic-speaking Jew had warned the villagers over a loudspeaker from an armored car. This was duly reported in the *The New York Times* on April 10.

The final body count of 254 was reported by *The New York Times* on April 13, a day after they were finally buried. By then the leaders of the Haganah had distanced themselves from having participated in the attack and issued a statement denouncing the dissidents of Irgun and the Stern Gang, just as they had after the attack on the King David Hotel in July 1946.

The Haganah leaders admitted that the massacre "disgraced the cause of Jewish fighters and dishonored Jewish arms and the Jewish flag." They played down the fact that their militia had reinforced the terrorists' attack, even though they did not participate in the barbarism and looting during the subsequent "mopping up" operations.[1]

They also played down the fact that, in Begin's words, "Deir Yassin was captured with the knowledge of the Haganah and with the approval of its commander" as a part of its "plan for establishing an airfield."

Ben-Gurion even sent an apology to King Abdullah of Trans-Jordan. But this horrific act served the future State of Israel well. According to Begin:

> Arabs throughout the country, induced to believe wild tales of "Irgun butchery," were seized with limitless panic and started to flee for their lives. This mass flight soon developed into a maddened, uncontrollable stampede. The political and economic significance of this development can hardly be overestimated.[2]

Of about 144 houses, 10 were dynamited. The cemetery was later bulldozed and, like hundreds of other Palestinian villages to follow, Deir Yassin was wiped off the map. By September, Orthodox Jewish immigrants from Poland, Rumania, and Slovakia were settled there over the objections of Martin Buber, Cecil Roth, and other Jewish leaders, who believed that the site of the massacre should be left uninhabited. The center of the village was renamed Givat Shaul Bet. As Jerusalem expanded, the land of Deir Yassin became part of the city and is now known simply as the area between Givat Shaul and the settlement of Har Nof on the western slopes of the mountain.

The massacre of Palestinians at Deir Yassin is one of the most significant events in 20th-century Palestinian and Israeli history. This is not because of its size or its brutality, but because it stands as the starkest early warning of a calculated depopulation of over 400 Arab villages and cities and the expulsion of over 700,000 Palestinian inhabitants to make room for survivors of the Holocaust and other Jews from the rest of the world.

Why Me?

In 1989 I knew nothing about Deir Yassin, and six years later I had started *Deir Yassin Remembered* to work toward building a memorial to the Palestinian victims massacred there on April 9, 1948. People often ask me why. I am not Jewish and I am not Palestinian. It is a project totally unrelated to my fields of study, namely, monetary theory, personal finance, and forensic economics. The work absorbs a monumental amount of time. It has generated financial, social, and academic costs, and it has strained personal relationships that had been built over several decades.

It started around 1985 when colleges and universities were overwhelmingly demanding that their pension funds no longer invest in South Africa. As a conservative professor of economics at Hobart and William Smith Colleges in Geneva, New York, I disagreed with such prohibitions and political obstructions to the free flow of capital.

I began to ask questions publicly, such as:

If apartheid is evil, why is it bad for South Africa and acceptable for Israel? Why is the expropriation of land for the exclusive use of whites condemned, while the expropriation of land for the exclusive use of Jews condoned? If Krugerrands are to be banned, why not diamonds; does cutting them in Israel remove the Black blood on them?

Such uncomfortable questions for comfortable members of the college community were largely answered by silence. The one exception was the flamboyant Richard Rosenbaum, Vice Chairman of the Board of Trustees of Hobart and William Smith Colleges and later a gubernatorial candidate for the state of New York.

In a letter to the *Chronicle of Higher Education,* Rosenbaum expressed "grave concern . . . that a professor might be teaching students distorted and, in some cases, totally false information." He promised, in writing, to take me "on a mission" to Israel, "in the certain knowledge that anyone with a shred of an open mind would come back a friend of Israel."

But alas, Mr. Rosenbaum could not get Malcolm Hoenlein, the Executive Director, Conference of Presidents of Major American Jewish Organizations, to pay for the trip. In reneging on the offer, Mr. Rosenbaum passed on a parting insult that he said originated with "a wise man" with whom he had shared my correspondence: "Why take him to Israel; he's obviously a bigot, and that experience will make him think he's an informed bigot."

But if Rosenbaum and friends found my questions on the efficacy of divestment and the comparisons with Israel to be offensive, others, like Walter Williams, the John M. Olin Distinguished Professor of Economics at George Mason University, found raising them to be courageous. Invariably they would first ask if I had tenure; when informed that I did, they would encourage me to use it and freely express opinions and beliefs which, although politically incorrect, were well founded or irrefutable.

The South African divestment confrontation caused me to begin to study Israel and to use it in pedagogical examples. When lecturing on international trade, for instance, I would point to the fact that the Israeli diamond industry provided a living for some 20,000 people and accounted for over a fifth of the value of the country's visible foreign trade (1990 figures).

For the United States to ban the sale of Krugerrands was a politically acceptable way to fight apartheid; to ban the sale of diamonds would have caused an uproar.

When studying labor markets, I often stimulated discussion by illustrating disequilibria caused by ethnic or religious discrimination. For example, I would point out that when workers from Gaza go to Israel they work largely with no benefits in a country with a very strong labor union orientation, at least for Jews. So it is no surprise that as Palestinians they are confined to jobs in agriculture, menial construction, and sanitation.

I wanted to study Islam, not extensively, but at least at the introductory level. The religion department at our colleges had five full-time faculty and offered 39 courses, 10 on Judaism and the Holocaust. But there was no course on Islam.

I was astounded! Not a single course was offered on this major religion to which roughly 25 percent of the world's population subscribe. I compared it to an economics department with no courses in macroeconomic theory, or a math department with no calculus.

In response to my queries, the religion department said that Islam was very complicated and that there was no one qualified to teach such a course. One member defended the department's shortcoming, saying the colleges had very few Muslim students, as if that mattered. By that analogy, colleges without Russian students have no reason to teach Russian.

A unique feature of our colleges is that the faculty is encouraged to teach new courses, especially those that cross disciplines, involve women's studies, and lead to travel abroad. I proposed such a course, called "Palestine and the Palestinian People: Political, Social, and Economic Issues," to begin in the winter semester of 1990. The course was to be a senior forum taught by three professors: a political scientist, an anthropologist, and an economist.

The course precisely met the stated curriculum goals and was approved by the committee on academic affairs, despite some Zionist reservations and the administration's insistence that at least one of the professors be Jewish. The latter demand was met by adding a second political scientist who was Jewish, although not a Zionist.

To learn more about Palestinians, I went to my first meeting of the American-Arab Anti-Discrimination Committee (ADC) in the spring of 1989. It was there that I learned of ADC's Eyewitness Israel Program, which took small groups of Americans to visit Palestine and observe first-hand the brutality of the occupation.

I immediately applied for the program and was rejected, probably because I did not fit the stereotypical profile: I was not a doctor, a sociologist, a labor union leader, a minister, or an organizer for human rights. I was a conservative, an economist, and a lifetime member of the National Rifle Association, and those were not considered good credentials. Nevertheless, I continued to call and write to ADC, eager to go to Palestine. When another participant dropped out at the last minute, I was ready with passport and money to pay my own way.

While in Palestine I lived in Jabalia, the largest of the refugee camps in Gaza. I visited hospitals and cottage industries and spoke with doctors, social workers, lawyers, and leaders in the intifada. I photographed Israeli patrols shooting both live and rubber bullets at children who routinely attacked them with stones.

I went to Hebron, Jerusalem, Ramallah, and Jenin. I tried to visit the Jewish settlement of Kiryat Arba, for which permission was denied, and offered the Israeli lawyer Lea Tsemel $2,000 to take me to the Ketziot prison camp in the Negev. (She was unable to take me, but she remembered my visit and unhesitatingly joined *Deir Yassin Remembered* when I asked for her help six years later.) I made many contacts among the Palestinians and some among the Israelis.

Teaching a course on the Palestinians at a liberal arts institution is daunting, especially where 20 percent of the students, key people in the administration, and key people on the board of trustees are Jewish.

In 29 previous years of college teaching, I had never been summoned to the provost's office. In the second week of the term, I was summoned and told that there were grave concerns—a now familiar warning—about the course, and that it might "need to be canceled" unless it was immediately given "more balance," meaning, of course, a pro-Israeli spin. I pointed out that the course was already balanced and that canceling it for such a spurious reason would most certainly damage the colleges' reputation when the argument was aired in the *Chronicle of Higher Education* or the local press.

But it was not just Zionist criticism by some administrators that made teaching or saying anything positive about the Palestinians difficult. It was a sense of constantly being on guard and of having to back up any statement with a Jewish source.

If you wanted to talk about Palestinian refugees, you first had to refute the Zionist propaganda that there were no Arabs living in Palestine when the Jews returned; many students came convinced of the well-worn myth that it was a "land without people for a people without land." You had to get by the propaganda in Golda Meir's claim that there is no such thing as a Palestinian; they are all just Arabs. You had to break the image that the Arabs were Nazis, that Palestinians are inherently anti-Semitic, and that today's settlers are invariably peace-loving, devoutly religious pioneers. You had to correct the impression that the Six Day War was started by the Palestinians; you had to clarify that a "preemptive strike" is when our side initiates war, and a "sneak attack" is when the other side fires first; you had to show that making reference to Israel's attack on the USS *Liberty* is not a gratuitous, anti-Semitic footnote, but an unresolved piece of American history which has been flushed down the memory hole, where unpleasant things are put to be deliberately forgotten.

To lecture about Palestinians, you inevitably were forced to speak about the Holocaust, to which the Palestinians did not contribute, which was a genocide committed by Christians, and which had nothing to do with Muslims. In spite of Zionist tales of Hitler-meets-the-Mufti, the Palestinians no more collaborated with the Third Reich than did the Stern Gang.

Yet if guilt for the Holocaust cannot be laid on the Palestinians, its horror serves as the final apology for injustices committed by Jews against Palestinians. The apology goes something like this: "Yes, what the Zionists have done, and continue to do, to the Palestinians is not

right, but you really can't blame them after all Hitler did to the Jews."
It is the ultimate excuse which covers not only Zionist behavior
immediately after World War II, but every year and every generation
since then.

The course, after all, was about Palestinians, and it was frustrating
to have to get to that subject only after first reviewing the darkest
chapter in Jewish history, a chapter which shows Jews to have been
far greater victims than any victimization the Palestinians can ever
imagine.

The fact is that if every Palestinian in the West Bank and Gaza
were executed tomorrow, the number of victims would not equal
half of the number of Jews executed in World War II, but so what?
Why does a description of the political, social, and economic
characteristics of one people have to be prefaced and twisted to fit the
history of another? Many courses are given on Jews with no mention
of Palestinians; no courses are given on Palestinians without extensive
discussion of Jews and Zionism.

In spite of pressure, more subtle than overt, it is a tribute to Hobart
and William Smith Colleges that such a course on the Palestinians
was allowed to be taught at all. Yes, I was forced to "balance" the
course—the film *Days of Rage* was balanced with *Exodus; The Gun
and the Olive Branch* was read along with *The Israel-Arab Reader;*
and Mubarak Awad was "countered" by Phillipa Strum.

But I was allowed to buy "Palestinian" books for the library,
although there was no special budget as there is for Judaic Studies. I
was even encouraged by the president of the colleges to present a
"balancing" speaker when Benjamin Netanyahu visited the campus;
Professor Edward Said filled the role with his usual eloquence.

I also was encouraged to invite Hanan Ashrawi to "balance" a
presentation by Elie Wiesel. Both were invited to join the Board of
Advisers of *Deir Yassin Remembered;* Professor Ashrawi readily
accepted; Professor Wiesel has declined even to answer.

Teaching a course on Palestinians sparked interest all across the
college community. After an Israeli woman artist and close friend of
the provost held an art exhibit, I secured support for an exhibit by

the Palestinian artist Kamal Boullata. The art department helped with the exhibit; seven pieces of Boullata's work were purchased by people in the local community, and his moving film, *Stranger at Home,* was shown with hardly a dry eye in the audience.

It was trendy at the time for Hobart and William Smith professors to use vanity license plates to stimulate interest in their disciplines. A geology professor's plate read "DEVONIAN"; a science professor's read "BOTANY." The plate on my old Peugeot read "INTIFADA."

People who didn't know *intifada* from *enchilada* began to recognize the word and to understand its meaning, a "shaking off" of occupation and control.

Although some people were nervous about riding in a car with INTIFADA license plates, I drove the car for four years, including trips to New York City, with no incident other than a few finger gestures. Parked in front of the colleges on Main Street, the license plate was said to have turned away some potential students and some potential donors, but there was never pressure to remove it. To the contrary, the plate became a symbol of someone standing up for the human rights of a people others had learned to despise at worst and to ignore at best. It caused me to be invited to present lectures to local community groups and to colleges throughout upstate New York.

Beyond Knowing

I have come to believe that it is not enough "to see the light" regarding Palestinians, their victimization, and their struggle to survive as a nation. Crying for the world to recognize injustice and to do something is no more a realistic solution for Palestinians than it was for Jews under the Nazis or the Bosnians under the Serbs. The path for Palestinians to follow in achieving human rights and a national state has been blazed by others, including Gandhi and Mandela, and by Jews on so many levels who have built the state of Israel. "Righteous Gentiles" can see the light, work tirelessly for the cause, and even sacrifice their own lives for it, but only the victims, in this case Palestinians, can make the change a reality.

When *Deir Yassin Remembered* was founded, its board was structured to include half Jews, half non-Jews, half men, and half women. This was not simply an attempt to be politically correct or to be in keeping with the northeastern liberal arts environment in which its director is employed. Rather, it is based on the belief that both victim and victor need to remember Deir Yassin and take part in its memorial.

Nor was the massacre simply "a male thing." Palestinian women and children were brutally slaughtered, and Jewish women took part in the attack and in the subsequent mopping-up operations. Jacques de Reynier, a French Red Cross employee who arrived after the massacre, described the Irgunists and Sternists as follows:

> All are young men and women, including teenagers, armed to the teeth with pistols, machine guns, grenades, and large cutlasses, most of them covered with blood, in their hands. A young woman, beautiful but with eyes of a murderess, shows me her cutlass, still dripping with blood as she carries it around like a trophy. They are the "mopping up team," which probably goes about its business very conscientiously.[4]

Even Nathan Friedman-Yellin, successor to Stern Gang founder Yair Stern, condemned the "shocking" murder of women, termed the attack a "massacre," and said it was "too cruel." He complained that it was not authorized by the leadership and that it spoiled "our image" in the eyes of the Soviet Union. Others, like his Sternist rival, Yisrael Scheib (Eldad), and Menachem Begin insisted that without Deir Yassin "the State of Israel could never have been established."[5]

Today there are 17 members on the DYR board, three short of our goal. The board represents a remarkable collection of leaders with one common thread—a strong conviction that the memory of Deir Yassin should be preserved.

Given the small number of board members, its diversity is astounding—Muslims, Jews, Christians, and agnostics, some very rich, some very poor. There are politicians turned academics and academics turned politicians. There are those with tenure and security and others whose involvement could cost them their jobs and endanger their families. All stand ready to rebuff criticisms of anti-Semitism or self-hatred. They seek to restore the tradition of critical thinking demonstrated by Walter Benjamin, Hannah Arendt, and Martin Buber, and the moral vision of the Jewish people seeking justice for all. They want to open the doors of the silent side of Elie Wiesel and others who systematically ignore the injustices against the Palestinians.

Most Israelis and most visitors to Israel do not go to Deir Yassin. Tour guides in Jerusalem are mostly Jewish or Christian and they do not know, or do not care to know, its location and the true story of the massacre. Most of our board members also have not been there. Yet Deir Yassin remains largely intact in the form of a mental hospital in the Givat Shaul district of West Jerusalem. The remaining Palestinian buildings are beautiful, quite distinctive in style and color from other buildings in the area. They are surrounded by the Orthodox Jewish settlement of Har Nof and the industrial area of Givat Shaul.

There are no markers, no plaques, and no memorials at Deir Yassin; parking is a problem, and access to the mental hospital grounds is, understandably, restricted. But tourists today can help keep memory alive and reinforce our efforts to memorialize Deir Yassin by asking about and visiting the site.

Most visitors and virtually all politicians visit the most famous Holocaust museum, Yad Vashem. Literally, Yad Vashem means "a monument and a name," figuratively "a monument and a memorial." The name is drawn from Isaiah where God says to those who keep his covenant, "I will give them . . . a monument and a name . . . an everlasting name that shall never be effaced." Conceived in 1942 and codified in the 1953 "Law of Remembrance of Shoah and Heroism— Yad Vashem," this memorial park is Israel's preeminent national shrine.

One of the most important tasks of Yad Vashem has been to record the names of every Jewish victim of the Germans to perpetuate the memory of the martyrs whose graves are unknown and unmarked. In his book *The Texture of Memory,* James Young writes, "The function of memory in this project is precisely what it has always been for the

Jewish nation; in addition to bringing home the 'national lessons' of the Holocaust, memory would work to bind present and past generations, to unify a world outlook, to create a vicariously shared national experience."[6]

Of course, this is exactly the underlying task of *Deir Yassin Remembered* in its quest to build a memorial. For Palestinians, whose culture and history are largely oral, passed down in stories from generation to generation, the memory of Deir Yassin is paramount and cannot be denied.

It is a chilling fact that the Deir Yassin massacre took place within sight of Yad Vashem. The irony is breathtaking.

Did those who conceived of the noble and necessary project of building the most important Holocaust memorial realize that the site they had chosen was tainted by brutalities of the past? While the idea of Yad Vashem was conceived long before the massacre, construction began years after it. Were the ghosts of Deir Yassin ignored or simply bulldozed over? In dedication ceremonies at Yad Vashem, did no one ever look to the north and remember Deir Yassin? Did no one speak of it? Were its martyrs so deeply buried that their cries for justice could never be heard?

Update by the author, Daniel A. McGowan

Geneva, NY—Since the founding of *Deir Yassin Remembered* we have written two books, dozens of articles, and hundreds of blogs telling the truth about Palestinian dispossession and ethnic cleansing in the lands of Israel/Palestine. We have held hundreds of commemorations on the anniversary, April 9th, most with dozens of participants, some with hundreds. We have made a video depicting the massacre and explaining the purpose of *Deir Yassin Remembered*. The 33-minute movie was the first segment of *Palestine Trilogy*, which opened to a sold-out crowd at Toronto's Royal Theatre in January 2006.

Yet still there is no memorial, no recognition, not even a historical plaque at Deir Yassin. Across the valley at Yad Vashem there is a whole new museum, complete with a spectacular view of "Jewish Jerusalem," which ironically includes the fuel tanks under which lie the bodies of Palestinians shot in the quarry of Deir Yassin. Jews continue to demand and receive restitution for crimes against them in WWII; Palestinians get no restitution for crimes against them in 1948, 1967, and today. Ketziot remains an Israeli concentration camp for over 4,000 Palestinians, and the media looks the other way. Elie Wiesel continues to lie about the *Nakba* and refuses to recognize, let alone apologize for, the atrocity committed by his employer at Deir Yassin. The American media dwells on Oprah at Auschwitz, with virtually no coverage of the suffering of 1.4 million Palestinians locked down and starving in Gaza.

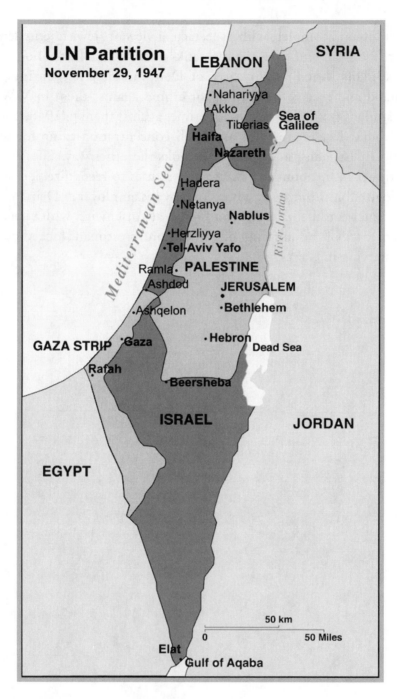

U.N. Partition Plan of the Palestinian Mandate, 1947

Politics *Not* as Usual

By Rod Driver

In 1998, when he wrote this issue of The Link, *Rod Driver was a professor of mathematics at the University of Rhode Island and a former four-term member of the Rhode Island House of Representatives. Today he is retired from teaching, but not from telling his fellow citizens how their money is being used to deny Palestinians their most basic human and civil rights.*

This will have to be "reviewed," said the manager of the advertising office at *The Providence Journal* last August.

I had just submitted a small display ad for publication in Rhode Island's main newspaper describing demolition by the Israelis of Palestinian homes in Bir Naballa.

After seven calls and eleven days of getting the runaround, a message came down that the paper's lawyer had reviewed the ad and found it to be "unacceptable as a matter of policy."

Unable to compel the paper to accept the money and run the ad, I prepared a different one and submitted it a week later. The new ad consisted of a statement from B'Tselem, a highly-respected Israeli human rights organization, calling for an end to the Israeli practice of holding Palestinian prisoners indefinitely without trial. The statement called for either trial or release of hundreds of Palestinians. It had already been published in a major Israeli newspaper with the endorsement of five prominent Israeli authors.

But *The Providence Journal* still had to get it "reviewed" by the lawyer. This time the "no" came in just two days: "The newspaper won't run editorial content in a display ad."

Now I was getting angry.

If this really were the paper's policy, it would come as a surprise to other political activists, labor unions, and businesses which routinely present their points of view in display ads. The lawyer at the paper would not return my calls.

The question now was: Were the ads being rejected by the top management of the paper, or just by some officer in the legal department? So I asked for the publisher and chairman of the board. He was away. And the president was away. So they put the lawyer on the line. I may not have been very polite in telling him that he was not the person I wanted to speak with at this point.

A day later I got through to the executive editor. After a short discussion he agreed that the paper would publish my ad provided I used a typeface different from the one the paper uses, put a border around the ad, and repeated the word ADVERTISEMENT several times across the top of the ad.

My reputation for making a nuisance of myself may have given me an edge over others who might try to run a "politically incorrect" ad. In the 1970s, thanks to the ACLU, I had won a court case against the CIA for opening my mail. During eight years as an elected member of the Rhode Island House of Representatives, I had exposed and challenged disreputable practices of the state legislature. In 1996, I went to court to stop the state Lottery Commission from introducing a new type of gambling without voter approval. The governor later joined my lawsuit, the TV bingo game was blocked before it began, and the Lottery Commission had to pay refunds to thousands of ticket holders.

Anyway, the ad based on B'Tselem's text finally appeared five weeks after the process began. Having in mind a series of ads, I labeled this one "Untold Stories No. 1." This was the beginning of an effort to open people's eyes via paid advertisements. Today it includes television. But let me start closer to the beginning.

Why Bother?

Why would anyone spend his or her money to advertise about the mistreatment of Palestinians?

The Providence Journal and other papers had already published several of my commentaries on the subject. But there was never enough space to report more than a fraction of the abuses. It is difficult for an outsider to get more than one column or letter per month published in a major newspaper. And after submitting a column or letter, the writer waits with no idea when or whether it will appear.

Meanwhile, each day's e-mail included six to eight messages about new cruelties visited upon the Palestinians. These were rarely covered by the news media in Rhode Island, so the public didn't know what was happening. Occasionally the paper inserted one or two column inches mentioning a tragedy. Twice last year it even ran pictures of families whose homes were being bulldozed or confiscated. But these infrequent little stories were buried on inner pages of the paper and were dwarfed by daily stories of the Holocaust and other Jewish suffering.

Most Americans would not permit a dog or a cat to be thrown out of its home, beaten, imprisoned without charges, or tortured. So I have to believe that the horrors being inflicted on human beings in Palestine would not continue if the American people, who pay Israel's bills, learned of them.

But it hadn't occurred to me until last summer to buy newspaper ads to report what the news media wouldn't.

The Ad Series

When my first ad about the Palestinians was finally accepted by *The Providence Journal*, I signed a contract with the paper to spend a total of $10,000 on ads within a year. This resulted in a slightly lower rate per column inch. Advertising rates usually relate to the size of the expected audience. The *Providence Journal* has a circulation of about 180,000.

Ten thousand dollars may sound like a lot, but, to put it in perspective, it is a little more than what I was annually putting into a voluntary retirement plan. And how does it compare with the life savings lost, the dreams shattered, and the anguish inflicted on just one Palestinian whose home is demolished, whose land is confiscated, or whose father, mother, husband, wife, brother, sister, son, or daughter is killed, crippled, or imprisoned?

During a visit to the West Bank in January 1997 my wife and I met Palestinians who had been shot, beaten, or interrogated by the Israelis. One victim was a two-year-old boy beaten by an Israeli soldier. We visited Palestinians whose homes had been demolished or stolen; and we happened to be there and stood helplessly alongside members of one family as an Israeli bulldozer uprooted their olive trees and took more of their land. This strengthened our appreciation of Palestinian suffering.

"Untold Stories No. 1" included my name, address, home phone number, and picture. This was intended to draw attention to the ad and to help dispel the attitude that one dare not be publicly identified with any criticism of Israel. I put the word "CENSORED" at the top of the ad in a further effort to attract readers' attention.

Palestinian "Cooperation"

Daily e-mail messages from Palestine tell of home demolitions, violence against Palestinians by Israeli settlers and soldiers, restriction on travel for Palestinians, and denial of water for their crops. So one need not look far for topics to write about. I thought it would be easy to write "untold stories"—even on a weekly basis.

It wasn't! While trying to confirm the details of a story or to obtain pictures for use in the ads, I encountered unexpected problems:

(1) The Palestinians whom I called were willing to say they would do it "tomorrow." But apparently "tomorrow" is a meaningless word. After watching my mail each day for two or three weeks, I'd phone them again. And again they would promise to send the material "tomorrow." Sometimes it took two months and many phone calls to get a picture or other item. Often they never sent it at all.

(2) It was difficult to determine whether two stories were really different stories. Palestinians may have several different names, and they sometimes use one and sometimes another.

Arabic characters must be transliterated into English letters, and different translators use different systems of transliteration—if they use systems at all. Similar problems can arise with respect to village names.

(3) Palestinians and Americans working with them were often careless about details. Perhaps, with all the tragedies they see, it didn't seem worth determining whether an Israeli who killed a Palestinian had been fined one agora (one-hundredth of a shekel), was just "under investigation," or had been forgotten. Perhaps it seemed unimportant to report that certain homes were demolished on February 16 when the demolition really occurred on February 17. But this can make a person in Rhode Island believe he is hearing about two or more different incidents rather than one, especially when the problem is compounded with name discrepancies.

In attempting to get some video footage that had been shown on Israeli and Palestinian television, I was told repeatedly that Reuters had it, or perhaps AP. After more than a dozen phone calls, I discovered that neither agency had it. It would have been so much easier if someone in Palestine had made the phone calls for me. Instead, I was usually told to simply make more trans-Atlantic calls—with all the complications of a seven-hour time difference. My phone bill has ranged from $100 to $175 per month since I began this project.

Jewish human rights activists in Israel, especially those at B'Tselem, are often more responsive than Palestinians. I also spoke three times, more than an hour altogether, with a spokesman for the Israeli forces in the Occupied Territories to obtain Israeli figures on home demolitions.

After a couple of months I had pictures of home demolitions suitable for use in ads No. 2 and No. 3, plus information I could trust. Without objection, the paper ran these ads, each a quarter page or more, showing pictures of Palestinian families and the furniture they had rescued before their homes in Bir Naballa were demolished. One family, three adults and five children, had only half an hour to remove its possessions.

Responses

I had spent days and weeks checking and cross-checking to make sure everything I said was correct. But each ad drew angry responses from Israeli apologists who made up stories with no regard for the truth. They simply sent them to the newspaper, and their letters or columns seemed to get onto the editorial pages almost immediately.

Itzhak Levanon, the consul general of Israel to New England, wrote, and *The Providence Journal* published, a column complaining about my "misleading advertisements." His column, he said, would "provide readers with a clarification of the rules and regulations surrounding Israel's decision to destroy homes." What followed was an outrageous assortment of fabrications.

He declared: "In Bir Naballa, the houses demolished were those of terrorists who blew themselves up on Ben Yehuda Street and Mahane Yehuda market, leaving more than 40 women, children, and elderly civilians dead."

Nothing could be further from the truth. The paper published my response under the heading MORE LIES BY ISRAEL two weeks later. The proof of Mr. Levanon's deceit requires only a simple calendar. My ads about Bir Naballa actually appeared before the Israelis destroyed four homes in retaliation for the suicide bombings—and these were in Asira Ashamaliya village—far from Bir Naballa. The homes in Bir Naballa, and dozens more, were bulldozed by the Israelis in the spring and summer of 1997—weeks and months before the bombings of July 30 and September 4 that Levanon offered as an excuse. The reason the Israelis themselves gave for destroying homes in Bir Naballa was that they were built "without a license."

What truly amazed me about Mr. Levanon's response, however, was his readiness to defend the destruction of homes occupied by wives, children, mothers, fathers, and siblings of "suspected terrorists." Mr. Levanon claimed "the Palestinian families of these suicide bombers gave them refuge, help, and food in advance of their vile criminal act."

"What civilized society carries out such collective punishment?" I asked in my column. "Imagine the United States destroying the homes of families or acquaintances of Ted Kaczynski or Craig Price (a teenage killer in Rhode Island). Israel doesn't destroy the homes of Israeli killers such as Baruch Goldstein or Yigal Amir. Only Palestinian families suffer such cruelty."

Effectiveness

It is difficult to measure the effectiveness of advocacy advertising. Who knows how many people see an ad and are affected by it but don't bother to respond. I had expected more responses than I got to the first three ads. Many of my most sympathetic friends simply had not seen the ads.

Perhaps placement was the problem. I had always requested placement "upper right." But each of these three ads was printed "lower left." In my paranoia, I wondered if this was entirely by chance.

After I complained about placement, the paper gave me an excellent position, page three, for ad No. 4. This ad recounted the killing of a Palestinian by an Israeli "undercover squad," or "death squad." (It had taken months to get someone in Palestine to visit the victim's family and get me a picture of the victim, Muhammad al-Hilu.) Once again Zionists directed protests at me and the newspaper.

Since the newspaper was under attack for running the ad, I decided to visit the vice president for advertising at the paper. When he saw the extensive documentation behind the ads, he was well satisfied that I could back up everything.

Ad No. 5 featured a picture of a two-year-old Palestinian boy standing crying in the ruins of his newly demolished home. This had been the cover photo of the December 1997 *Washington Report on Middle East Affairs*. I paid the newspaper an extra 25 percent to place this ad on the op-ed page for greater visibility.

The paper soon published a column by the president of the Jewish Federation of Rhode Island attacking the ad. In addition to more fabrications, the writer objected that the picture of a child crying amid the rubble "plays on our most basic emotions."

And he noted, rather accurately, that, "We rely on gatekeepers—newspapers and magazines, broadcasters and analysts, friends and academics—to help select our information for us." My ad, obviously, had not been stopped by his "gatekeepers."

Ad No. 6 was the strongest of all—describing some of the methods used by *Shabak* and other Israeli interrogation agencies to extract "confessions" from Palestinians. In hopes of preempting any possible rejection by the paper, I decided not to submit this ad through the advertising representative for my account. Instead, I went directly to the vice president for advertising and showed him documentation from Human Rights Watch, Amnesty International, and the U.S. State Department.

He accepted the ad and ran it as submitted—again on the op-ed page. It is reasonable to suppose that this ad would not have been accepted if it had been the first one submitted.

When the ad appeared, a woman called to tell me I was anti-Semitic. She told me that if Palestinians had been arrested they must be guilty (of something) and deserved to be punished (tortured, I presume).

A second call came from a fundamentalist Christian who told me that the Jews had been expelled from their land by the Romans in 78 AD, and Palestinians had no right to be there. So I suggested that we shouldn't be here because this land belonged to the Native Americans. "No," he explained, "God gave land to the Jews. God didn't give any land to the Indians." And suffering inflicted on the Palestinians is punishment from God, he added.

A week after "Untold Stories No. 6" appeared, Mark Patinkin, a regular writer for *The Providence Journal*, wrote a column headed "A Lesson for Professor Rod Driver." Although I had included a statement in the ad—using bold type—that the Palestinian Authority "has a horrific record of torturing Palestinians," Patinkin said I had overlooked that fact, and he made this "oversight" a refrain throughout his column. His thesis, apparently, is that it is okay for the Israelis to torture Palestinians because the Palestinians torture Palestinians. My response, printed four weeks later, included this passage:

I am painfully aware of the Palestinian abuse of Palestinians. And I can't explain it any more than I can explain why an abused child grows up to be a child abuser, or why Jews whose parents were brutalized by Nazis now brutalize Palestinians.

Putting the ads on the op-ed page was worth the extra cost. Starting over again, I would pay the 25 percent premium to place them all there, where they are most likely to reach the right audience.

During 20 months of writing columns and ads—nine months for the ads themselves—I have had supportive calls or letters from about 60 people. I also keep meeting people who have seen one or more of the ads and thank me for them, although they had not bothered to call or write.

Why Not Television?

A few months ago, I first saw the "infomercial" titled "On Wings of Eagles," then running on a local TV station at 6 a.m. on Sundays. Professionally produced, this 30-minute program asks the viewer to contribute $300, $600, or more. Each $300 will "rescue" one Russian Jew and bring him or her "home to Israel," it says.

It occurred to me that those of us who care about the abuse and suffering of the Palestinians could learn from the Zionists. Why couldn't we produce TV commercials to begin to tell Americans how the Israelis use the billions of dollars we give them to destroy Palestinian homes, take Palestinian land, and otherwise oppress the people who have lived on the land for generations?

Isn't TV the medium to reach people who simply don't see letters and newspaper ads?

Some video that I thought would be especially good for use in a TV spot was filmed in 1995 by Reuters Television, Jerusalem. It shows Israeli police and soldiers forcibly removing a Palestinian family from its home in East Jerusalem, shooting and arresting neighbors who come to help the family, and then bulldozing the home.

It took a few weeks to find someone to help me get permission to use it—but not as long as it might have taken if I hadn't learned from past experiences. Based on my earlier troubles getting information and pictures, I had decided that if you want something from Palestine, you call. Then you call again tomorrow and again the next day until something happens. When I got to the right party, Reuters kindly gave me permission to use the footage.

While wrestling with the problem of editing five minutes of dynamic video down to a 30-second spot, I also started inquiring about buying airtime on local TV stations.

One station asked to see the spot. Since it didn't yet exist, I faxed a preliminary version of the script to the station. That was enough! A few days later, I got a familiar message:

"The station won't accept the spot."

"Why not?"

"We're not required to give a reason."

This was reminiscent of *The Providence Journal*'s initial response to me in August 1997. That problem had been resolved when I made a nuisance of myself with top management at the paper.

Running for Congress

In the case of television, there is a different solution: Under federal law, a bona fide political candidate can buy advertising time on television, and a station cannot reject the ads—unless it rejects advertising from all candidates in the race in question.

So early in May I filed papers with the Federal Elections Commission to become a candidate for the Republican nomination for Congress in Rhode Island's second district.

I finally got the TV spot edited down to 30 seconds. It would have started airing on May 20 on a local station, but the station decided that my permission letter from Reuters did not have quite the right wording. Reuters promptly faxed me a revised letter, and the spot began running on May 26 on one broadcast station and several cable channels.

On television, as in newspapers, the cost of advertising depends on the size and nature of the audience you are reaching. The programs I selected are not the ones with the biggest audiences in Rhode Island and hence not the most expensive.

Conventional wisdom about advertising says that a viewer must see a spot several times before it "registers." (Think how many times you have seen ads for Tums, Toyota, Total, Slim Fast, or Pepsi Cola.) By staying with the lower-priced airtimes, I hoped to achieve adequate repetition, with a select group of viewers, for a few thousand dollars.

Editing the commercial cost about $1,000, plus many hours of my time. I paid another $9,000 for the initial buy of broadcast time. For that amount of money in this "market," one could get about five spots of local airtime during *60 Minutes,* or about 11 spots during *48 Hours.* Instead I opted to have more spots on less popular local programs. I plan to put in more money to run the ad on another station. (The $1,000 federal limit on contributions to a campaign does not apply to a candidate's contributions to his own campaign.)

The ad is dramatic. It shows family members resisting and screaming as Israeli police forcibly remove them from their home. Soldiers shoot and arrest neighbors who come to help the family; then the home is bulldozed.

The television station that first broadcast it decided to precede the spot with a disclaimer. White letters on a black background and an announcer's voice warn the viewer:

THE FOLLOWING POLITICAL ADVERTISEMENT CONTAINS SCENES WHICH MAY BE DISTURBING TO CHILDREN. VIEWER DISCRETION IS ADVISED.

This added four-second announcement, which I did not have to pay for, probably attracts attention to the ad. The spot is obviously having an impact. Apparently this is an ad that makes an impression the first time one sees it—let alone the ninth or tenth time. Several people have told me they were shocked to learn what the Israelis are doing.

The broadcast station and the cable channels that ran the ad soon began to feel the heat. They wanted to talk with me about it. They had not kept track of the number of hostile calls, but they were obviously alarmed.

The broadcast station decided to explain its position on the 6 o'clock news. So on June 5 it spent more than three minutes showing excerpts from the spot and explaining to its audience that, under federal law, it had no choice but to run the commercial—that it could lose its license for refusing.

The station then read a statement from the Anti-Defamation League saying that "the ADL supports (Driver's) right to free speech, but we urge audiences to take a critical eye to his propaganda." (Free speech was alive and well only because Zionists had not succeeded in knocking the ad off the air with their protest calls to the television stations, Reuters, and the Republican Party.)

GOP Assails TV Spot

On June 9, *The Westerly Sun,* which serves southern Rhode Island and eastern Connecticut, carried a press release from Joan Quick, chairwoman of the Rhode Island Republican Party, declaring that my TV ad "offends millions of Jewish Americans in its pro-terrorist portrayal of ongoing conflict in the Middle East between Palestinian terrorists and the State of Israel."

I called Ms. Quick and asked if she had been getting complaints about my ad. Yes, indeed she had! I asked where she got the notion that the people seen in the ad were "terrorists." She said the wording for the press release came from the national GOP. I then faxed a rebuttal to AP and newspapers throughout the state. The *Westerly Sun* used part of it, but I have not heard that it was used anywhere else.

On June 11, *The Providence Journal* ran a front-page story about the TV ad. The headline stated: "Candidate Aims to Disturb with Violent Anti-Israel Ad." Beneath that was a subheading: "Richmond's Driver Makes No Apologies for Exploiting an Exemption to Rules on Advertising Content."

In the same issue, columnist M. Charles Bakst, who frequently writes in praise of Israel, took aim under the heading "RI Doesn't Need Driver's Campaign for U.S. Congress" and alleged that the ad "has high-voltage rhetoric about home demolitions and bitterly disputed data on what has been going on over there, or perhaps has gone on in exactly that fashion only in Driver's mind."

Bakst quotes Itzhak Levanon, Israel's consul general in Boston, as saying that the TV spot "revolts me" and makes "false allegations." (Levanon is the man who earlier used absolute falsehoods in responding to my ads about home demolitions.) Bakst consulted and quoted others to buttress his attack. The one person he did not contact was the person he was writing about.

On June 12, *Waterbury [CT] Republican-American* carried an AP story under the headline "Man Runs Only to Get Ad on the Air." The same story ran in *The Westerly Sun* (and goodness knows where else). The article says, "The commercial depicts what [Driver] claims are Israeli police dragging Palestinians from their homes."

Although none of the stories has been complimentary, they have called attention to the effort. In the immediate aftermath, I got nine calls of support, including five from "new" people.

The Providence Journal articles resulted in a five-minute interview on one radio program, a 50-minute participation in another station's call-in talk show, and a one-hour interview on a local cable program.

On the evening of June 11, and in a rerun the following Sunday, the local PBS station's weekly program *The Lively Experiment* gave me a good going-over—in my absence, of course. One of the panelists, Thomas L. DiLuglio, a former lieutenant governor of Rhode Island, said, "It doesn't add up that he would want this kind of ad aired in Rhode Island. This is an international matter! Who is he aiming at? What is the purpose of it, unless these numbers add up to bigot?" He went on to suggest that airing this ad (about an international matter) in a congressional campaign is "bizarre and erratic behavior." I am seeking an opportunity to appear on the program to respond.

I hope to put together another TV spot based on the al-Atrash family's persistent but nonviolent response to the Israeli "security" forces that demolished their home near Hebron in 1988. They rebuilt, and their new construction was again turned to rubble on March 3, 1998.

Still the family refused to give up. On March 22, their Palestinian neighbors and peace activists from Israel and the U.S. labored alongside Mr. and Mrs. al-Atrash and their 10 children as they continued to rebuild. This time Israeli forces, who came to the site to confiscate a small cement mixer, responded violently. Seventeen-year-old Manal al-Atrash was beaten so severely she was hospitalized for a week. Her parents, Yusef and Zuhuur, and an older brother Hosham, were brutally arrested, and a 14-year-old, Wilah', was left in charge of her seven younger brothers and sisters.

Although the authorities left the site without destroying the home, they returned on June 11. The family had been working until 3:00 that morning to finish the cement floor. By 10:30 a.m., the Israeli forces had demolished the home for yet a third time. It is the March 22 footage of the violence of the arrests and beatings that I hope to acquire for my new TV spot. Maybe viewers will begin to understand just who the "terrorists" are.

The Race

The race for Congress will be difficult. It is hard for any Republican to unseat an incumbent Democrat in Rhode Island. Second, the incumbent, Bob Weygand, plans to spend one million dollars on his re-election campaign. And third, in boldly questioning the use of our tax dollars to oppress Palestinians, I am going where—to my knowledge—no other candidate for Congress has gone before.

The campaign does offer a chance to raise public discussion of a tragedy which, for 50 years, people have been afraid to mention. And it will raise the question: Should the American taxpayers be required to continue giving Israel more than $3 billion per year?

I plan to put on a major campaign and will talk about many issues besides Palestine. One cannot win an election by talking only about the plight of the Palestinians.

If I win the Republican primary on September 15, there will be opportunities for debates with Rep. Weygand in the general election campaign. Since taking an Israeli-guided tour, Weygand has been willing to jump as the Israeli lobby— AIPAC—requires it. He signed a recent letter telling President Clinton not to pressure Israel to return any land or rights to the Palestinians unless Israel wants to.

Update by the author, Rod Driver

Supporting Palestinian Rights—As a Candidate

West Kingston, RI—In 1998 I lost the Republican primary for Rhode Island's second-district congressional seat. The Republicans didn't care about winning the seat. They just wanted to make sure there would not be a Republican candidate who supported Palestinian rights. After the primary, the Republican Party ignored the race, and the Democrat got 72 percent of the vote.

So in 2000 I ran as an independent for the same seat. We worked hard and spent about $270,000, mostly from my retirement accounts. But we finished a distant second to Democrat James Langevin. This was the only district in the nation where a major-party candidate, the Republican in this case, finished third. (Some districts had no Republican candidate.)

In 2002 I was foolish enough to think I could win the Republican primary. So I repeated the race I lost in 1998— and lost again for the same reason.

Next I founded a non-profit organization, Justice First Foundation, Inc., to "provide information about injustices and to appeal for help in correcting them." The IRS granted us tax-exempt 501(c)3 status.

Months before Mr. Bush attacked Iraq, Justice First produced a 30-second TV spot with the following script:

> **Video** (from my trip to Iraq in January 2001) showing traffic and people on the street, in a Presbyterian church in Baghdad, in a field with sheep, in a hospital, in a school— all accompanied by singing from that Presbyterian church choir plus the following voiceover:
> **Narrator**: "These are some of the people who will suffer or die if we bomb Iraq. The Congressional Budget Office estimates that war with Iraq would cost American taxpayers more than $100 billion. Please contact the President and your

members of Congress. Your call *will* make a difference."
On-screen at the end: President Bush 1-202-456-1111;
Congress 1-800-839-5276

Our two biggest TV stations, the Rhode Island affiliates of NBC and CBS, refused to sell us airtime for the ad. (They can do this without even giving a reason, unless the advertiser is a candidate for federal office.) The spot did run on some Cox cable TV stations and on the local ABC affiliate. You can see it at www.roddriver.com/index_foreign.html.

Another 30-second spot produced by Justice First was on the demolition and rebuilding of Palestinian homes. The audio script (accompanied by appropriate images) was:

Narrator: "Imagine a bulldozer coming to destroy your home. Soldiers fired tear gas into Salim's home to force his children out. Then they beat Salim and demolished the house."
Rabbi Arik Ascherman (from Rabbis for Human Rights): "Thousands of people have been made homeless this way."
Jeff Halper (from the Israeli Committee Against House Demolitions): "The bottom line is to create conditions so difficult that the Palestinians will leave the country."
Narrator: "But some Israelis are saying 'no' to their government's policies."
Halper: "Sometimes dozens or hundreds of Israelis join Palestinians to rebuild the house. We refuse to be enemies."
On-screen: To support this work, call call 412-820-3204 or go to www.RebuildingHomes.org.

This too was rejected by the Rhode Island affiliates of NBC and CBS.

In 2006 I am running for Congress again as an independent. Among other things, I have placed ads in *The Providence Journal* (Rhode Island's biggest paper) about Mr. Bush's lies to justify war against Iraq. The first was on the implication that Iraq attacked us on 9/11. The second was about the "uranium-from-Africa" scam. In each case the paper made me prove what I was saying. For example, I showed them where to find (in their own paper of September 18, 2003) Bush's confession that there was no evidence linking Iraq to 9/11.

The incumbent representative Langevin has a habit of voting for bills without reading them. He voted for the "Patriot Act" without reading it. He votes for funds to continue the undeclared war in Iraq whenever President Bush asks for more money. He even voted against requiring President Bush to get authorization from Congress if he decides to attack another country. He voted to denounce the International Court of Justice for its ruling against the wall Israel is building around Palestinian communities. He has been taken to Israel by pro-Israel lobbyists at least twice, and he has returned blaming the Palestinians for the fighting and praising Ariel Sharon as a man of peace.

Being a congressional candidate, under FCC rules, I would be able to get TV ads broadcast without censorship if we had the money. Anyone who cares to help can send contributions to Friends of Rod Driver, PO Box 156, West Kingston, RI 02892, or call 401-539-7985.

Inside H-2

By Jane Adas

Jane Adas joined the AMEU Board in 1998 and was elected a vice president in 2004. She "discovered" Palestine when she learned that her college roommate was Palestinian. Throughout the years, Jane has not forgotten her college friend nor the land she came from.

> **Jane Adas is a member of the Christian Peacemaker Teams, a pacifist group whose role is to place themselves nonviolently between conflicting parties in areas of open hostility. In 1995, the mayor of Hebron invited CPT to come to his divided city. In this September-October 2001 issue of The Link, Jane tells of her fourth six-week assignment in the City of the Patriarchs.**

The airport security inspector had me open my bag as I entered Ben-Gurion Airport.

"Who did you see during your visit?" I was asked.

"I don't have to tell you," I replied.

"You took pictures?"

"Yes." The inspector wanted to see them. I obliged.

"Who are these people?" the inspector asked, pointing to Palestinians.

"I don't have to tell you," I said.

The inspector handed them back to me and motioned me on.

As I closed my bag, I was glad I had left the pamphlet "Know Your Rights: Everything You Wanted to Know about Ben-Gurion Airport . . . But Didn't Know Who to Ask" on top of my clothes, in plain view, just inside my bag.

What the inspector did not ask for was my diary.
That follows here . . .

Wednesday, May 9, 2001: Took a shared taxi to Hebron, passing several tanks stationed along the road. Bethlehem roads completely closed. Two massive roadblocks of Jersey barriers piled high with dirt and rubble on main road into Hebron; cars only able to get through one at a time. Arrived in Hebron. Walked from Baab al-Zawwiye in H-1 down into H-2. Shuhada Street seemed deserted.

An Israeli soldier in front of Beit Hadassah settlement stopped and questioned me. Palestinians are no longer allowed to walk in front of the settlement, but must climb up and around broken stone steps. Since I am not Palestinian, I can walk along the street. When I suggested that it isn't fair that he and I, both visitors to the area, are free to walk on the public street when non-settler residents cannot, he answered, "We soldiers are here because of chaos. These are my orders. What can I do?"

As soon as I arrived at the CPT apartment, just off Shuhada Street in the chicken market, CPTer Anita Fast called for people to come immediately to Gross Square, which is actually a circle with a monument erected for a yeshiva student killed by Palestinians years ago. Anita was showing a small group of Canadian church dignitaries around the area when three settler women, one with a baby in her arms and another pregnant, tried to prevent Palestinian men from repairing shops that settlers had bombed a month earlier. The women were throwing stones, spitting, and pushing. Soldiers used to stand around watching such scenes. This time they danced around the three women in order to prevent them from making contact with the Palestinians. In the midst of this, a settler man approached Anita and the church leaders, yelling, "Nazis! Haven't Christians killed enough Jews?" He saved his spittle for a Palestinian photographer who approached. We later learned that two settler boys had been beaten to death in a cave near Tekoa. When a settler is killed anywhere at all, Hebron settlers rampage and destroy Palestinian property.

Several of us went to Beit Ummar, a village between Hebron and Bethlehem. Israel is planning a bypass road in the area, but has not revealed its exact location. This has caused anxieties, because any Palestinian homes along its projected path are doomed.

Ghazi, who works as an electrician at the municipality, is our translator. Two months ago, Ghazi's brother, Yusef, was shot at the Beit Ummar checkpoint. When I offered my condolences, Ghazi said not to worry: "If Yusef weren't my brother, he would have been somebody else's brother."

Thursday, May 10: CPTer Rick Carter, Zleekha Muhtaseb, another translator, and I visited Im Mohammed Jaber. She and her husband live just below Harsina settlement, east of Hebron in Area C. Recently, her 12-year-old nephew was sitting in his father's fruit stall in Ramallah while clashes were going on in the street. A rubber bullet hit him in the eye. Doctors were unable to save his eye.

Im Mohammed said settlers drive at night on the new road they have made above her house on confiscated Jaber property. The settlers park their car with the lights on, and do nothing. A couple of weeks ago, the sewage pipe from Kiryat Arba settlement flooded much of the valley, destroying young crops and attracting snakes and rats. The farmers in the area turned the outlet pipe away from the cultivated areas, but nobody from the settlement has repaired the pipe.

Two of Im Mohammed's sons and their families couldn't stand living near Harsina, so they moved to Jabal Jobar, to an apartment right below a Palestinian elementary school. Last fall, the Israeli military took over the school, raised the Israeli flag, and put tanks in the schoolyard from which they shell the Abu Sneineh neighborhood. The noise must be deafening. Im Mohammed's sons, their wives and children cannot use their front door, ever, for security reasons.

Her husband, Abu Mohammed, has a butcher shop in H-2, near the Ibrahimi Mosque. When the curfew was imposed in October, he couldn't travel between his home and shop. The family and neighbors ate what he couldn't sell. Since then, he has not been able to replenish his supplies. The Hebron Rehabilitation Committee has urged store owners to open their shops even if they have no customers, in order to be a presence so that settlers don't move into the shops. Abu Mohammed invited me to his shop for coffee. The shop was absolutely bare; but he was open for business.

From there we went to Abdel Jawad Jaber's for lunch with several neighboring farmers. Last month, the retail fruit and vegetable market adjacent to the Avraham Avinu settlement was trashed by settlers and closed off with barbed wire by the Israeli military. Since then, the vendors have moved to Bab al-Zawiye in H-1 . But this makes the area extremely crowded and more difficult to get to with produce. The Hebron Rehabilitation Committee is urging fruit and vegetable vendors to move back to H-2, because the settlers are pushing deeper into the market. The farmers understand this but are reluctant. They ask who will protect them from rampaging settlers and from losing business during curfews?

I went next to see Rudeina, the wife of Abdel Jawad's son 'Ata. They are expecting their fourth child in July. Rudeina has had several miscarriages, hardly surprising given all that has happened. 'Ata lost his job in an Israeli hotel during the first intifada. Encouraged by the Oslo process, he began building a home for his family on his own property in 1993. Three years later, Israel built bypass Road 60 through the Jaber family's fields, destroying thousands of dollars of crops and separating 'Ata's home from his father's and brother's. On August 19, 1998, the Israeli army demolished 'Ata's home. With help from the Israeli Campaign Against Home Demolitions, 'Ata rebuilt a small, two-room structure next to the demolished house. The army demolished that on September 11, 1998. 'Ata is now rebuilding a third time, with oral permission, but much higher up the mountain.

But not high enough. Last December 8th, dozens of settlers took over 'Ata's home, then in the final stages of construction. Because it was a Friday, with Shabat beginning at sundown, the army refused to remove the settlers until Sunday morning. The settlers bashed in walls, left Hebrew graffiti everywhere, and set a fire in the lower level, burning a lot of clothing and mattresses. When they vacated, Israeli soldiers moved in, declaring 'Ata's house a closed military zone. The soldiers left a lot of garbage around. And the civil administration confiscated all the surrounding land up to one yard from the house, bulldozing Rudeina's garden in the process.

'Ata and Rudeina were only able to move back in three weeks ago. Rudeina walked me around the house, pointing out the damage. She and 'Ata are still cleaning up the settlers' and soldiers' mischief, and slowly, slowly finishing the building. 'Ata said what hurt him most was [the destruction of] the stone he had specially made that was engraved with "By the grace of God, this is the house of love and peace. Anno 2000." He carried the stone up the hill and set it himself. Settlers smashed it and left the broken pieces at the front door.

Friday, May 11: Three a.m., settler men and boys noisily marched in Shuhada Street, singing and playing clarinets. Someone suggested it might be a celebration for the boys' first haircut. At 3 a.m.?!

Later that morning, three of us went to a demonstration against settler expansion in Deir Istya, near Nablus. Following the demonstration, Benjamin, a French reporter who was with us, interviewed the Israeli captain. Captain: "The villagers are outlaws." Benjamin: "What about the settlers?" Captain: "Don't talk politics!"

Saturday, May 12: CPTer Greg Rawlins and I went to Aroub refugee camp for a children's *hafla* (party) in honor of Aroub's martyrs from the second intifada. We met Ibrahim, a 20-year-old student in hotel management at Bethlehem University; he told us how Israeli soldiers enter the camp at night, knocking on doors, shooting for the hell of it, searching homes, and upsetting everything.

Sunday, May 13: Around 5 p.m., Kawther Salam, a journalist for Al-Hayat al-Jadida, staggered into our apartment, obviously upset. Soldiers near Gross Square had pushed her down, knocking her camera out of her hands. Two of us walked her back to her apartment. As we neared Gross Square, settler men and boys threw rocks at TIPH observers and us. The boys swarmed around us, jeering in Arabic, *"Kalbe, iskuut"* (Dog, shut up). Then soldiers arrived and did their choreographed intervention so that we could pass without further incident.

In the evening the electricity went out. This happens about once a week. From the roof we could see Beit Hadassah and Avrahim Avinu settlements; they were ablaze with lights.

Monday, May 14: I spent the next three days in Beit Ummar.

Tuesday, May 15: Went to visit a preschool, Ahlam al-Tifuul ("Dream Kids School"). Walking down Road 60 to meet Fariba, a volunteer with Doctors Without Borders, I noticed tanks positioned on both sides of the road near Al Aroub camp. The Israeli Army was apparently nervous about Nakba Day, or Day of Catastrophe, the day each year when Palestinians mourn Israel's expulsion in 1947–48 of over 750,000 Palestinians from their homes.

Fariba's major concern is the psychological effects of occupation. She is annoyed with the media because it covers only clashes and funerals. She feels the real story is what is happening daily to ordinary Palestinians. For example, what is life like for Palestinian families when soldiers have declared the roofs of their homes closed military zones and occupied them? Fariba is an Iranian Kurd who left her homeland for Australia in 1988. She says, "Believe me, I know what are terrorists. There are no Palestinian terrorists in Hebron. If there were, Israeli soldiers would not strut in the streets."

Laila, a volunteer, showed us around Dream Kids School. Because of Nakba Day, only half of the 100 children, aged five and under, were present. Laila says the children have so many emotional problems. They can't sleep, can't concentrate, fall silent, their hair falls out. Four of the children have relatives, three uncles and one father, who have been killed in the current intifada. Recently, an older boy threw a stone at a soldier, then ran into the school to hide. Soldiers chased after him, broke the window in the door with their guns, and entered, searching all the rooms. When they found the boy, they dragged him outside and beat him. All the children were crying.

Wednesday, May 16: Ghazi told us all was quiet in Beit Ummar yesterday because most of the older boys went to Hebron. Ten were injured in clashes there. Ghazi took CPTer Anne Montgomery and me on a five-hour tour of Beit Ummar neighborhoods where families have received home demolition orders.

There is a Jimmy Carter Street in Beit Ummar because the former president once visited here. Ghazi wants to write to Carter to invite him back and to ask him for help in stopping home demolitions, in rebuilding demolished homes, perhaps as a Habitat for Humanity project, and in getting access to water for the Al Mintarah neighborhood for 300 people currently without water. All they need is two kilometers of iron pipes and connections to hook into the main water pipe that serves Kiryat Arba, Beit Ummar, and Al Aroub

Technical College. The residents are willing to do all the work. The problem is that Al Mintarah is in Area C, so no foreign government will help, even if Israel were willing. It would cost about $16,000, the amount we U.S. taxpayers give Israel every three minutes.

Thursday, May 17: Four Machsom Watch Israeli women came to see checkpoints in Hebron. *Machsom* is the Hebrew word for checkpoint. The women were concerned about Israeli soldiers' treatment of Palestinians at checkpoints. They began in January with a handful of women; now 30 women, in groups of three or four, regularly monitor four checkpoints in the Jerusalem area. They talk to soldiers, letting them know that they know that ID checks should not exceed 20 minutes. If they spot soldiers abusing Palestinians, they intervene assertively, but not in a confrontational manner. They hand out fliers in Arabic advising Palestinians on who to call if they have a medical emergency or if soldiers have damaged their property. They photograph incidents and have just completed their first written report, which they will send to human rights groups in Israel, the Department of Defense, and the Chief of Staff. The women have found that the way soldiers behave is arbitrary and inconsistent, and that checkpoints have nothing to do with security, but rather are intended to inflict humiliation on Palestinians and to alleviate boredom among young soldiers.

We took them to checkpoints at Beit Hadassah, Gross Square, and Kiryat Arba. They were shocked to see settlers walking around with rifles, and shocked, too, by the Hebrew graffiti: "Arabs Out," "Kill All Arabs," "Arab Blood Is Fair Game." They said they felt more tension here than any place else they'd been.

Friday, May 18: Rick and I went for an overnight with 'Ata and Rudeina in their almost finished house. We were getting ready to eat when we noticed about 20 Israeli settlers who had come down the Harsina road and set up a roadblock with their cars. When Palestinian cars failed to turn around in time, the settlers stoned them. At 5:15 p.m. we telephoned Israeli police. They showed up 25 minutes later. Meanwhile, Israeli military jeeps passed through the settler roadblock as though it were normal, and settlers set brush fires on either side of the road. When the police arrived, they didn't do much at first. Then, when more police arrived, they set up roadblocks on either side of the settler roadblock about 100 yards away. With no Palestinian traffic passing by to harass, the settlers dispersed.

The rest of the evening was spent in pleasant conversation under the single lightbulb that 'Ata has rigged up from a neighbor's outlet.

Saturday, May 19: Three a.m., we were awakened by a phone call from the CPT office in Chicago asking if we are all right. That's how we learned that Israel had bombed Nablus, Ramallah, Tulkarem, and Gaza using American-made F-16s. Following breakfast we returned to Hebron where we found all the shops closed for mourning. The streets were utterly empty. Around 7:30 p.m. we heard three big booms. Then around 11:30 p.m. we heard an hour of heavy gunfire.

Sunday, May 20: Walking in Hebron in the early afternoon, I saw people with their necks craned up towards the sky. They were watching four F-16s flying in strange patterns directly overhead. The jets dropped flares that were at first red, then turned white. Walked on a bit and saw young Palestinians with stones. A bit farther then heard bangs. Retreated into a friend's clothing store. The clash didn't last long.

Eleven-thirty p.m., more shooting, lasting for over an hour. Some shots sounded really close.

Monday, May 21: Curfew imposed on Palestinians in H-2, but not on Israeli settlers, journalists, and the observers from TIPH and CPT. F-16s roaring overhead all morning.

Eleven a.m., I was walking up Shuhada street alone to meet Osaid, a translator, when heavy shelling began. It sounded close, but since I was near Beit Hadassah settlement, I figured it was the safest place possible. My knees apparently didn't accept this logic. They refused to behave normally. I was at the halfway point, so decided to proceed shakily up the empty street.

Made it to Osaid's home in H-1, but he was delayed in returning from the hospital where he works because the curfew necessitated his going out of his way on back roads. We realized it would be impossible to avoid H-2 in going to the families we wanted to visit. Osaid is not exempt from the curfew, and the risk for him of being caught in H-2 is simply too great. To cheer him up I told him that an official of the International Committee of the Red Cross had just declared settlements to be war crimes. Osaid shrugged. "Just words," he said. "The U.S. will block any action."

Later, Kawther came by to tell us an awful result of last night's shooting. At least two Israeli bullets were fired into Alia Hospital in the Hart al-Sheikh neighborhood, one in the intensive care unit on the third floor that didn't hit anybody, and one into a room on the second floor that injured a 22-year-old woman in her bed. Majdaleen Alrai, from Al Aroub refugee camp, had been in the hospital for a week for treatment of diabetes. The bullet hit her in the abdomen. She had a three-hour operation to repair the damage to her liver, kidney, colon, and intestines.

CPTer Bob Holmes and I went with Kawther to meet Majdaleen's mother and fiancee. The mother, Im Maher, had been sleeping next to Majdaleen when she was shot. She said Majdaleen screamed, struggled to the corridor, and collapsed. After doctors arrived to care for Majdaleen, Im Maher tried to telephone her family, but the phone was closed. She was finally able to reach Mohammed, Majdaleen's 25-year-old fiancee. He told Majdaleen's family what had happened and brought some of them to the hospital. That is when Im Maher learned that about an hour after Majdaleen was shot, Israeli tank fire had completely damaged the family's home in Al Aroub camp, which is why the telephone was not working.

When we arrived, Im Maher was sitting on the floor outside the intensive care unit. She still was unable to stand. But she did have questions: "Why does the Arab world keep silent while Israel destroys our homes over our children's heads? Why does the world enforce U.N, resolutions against Iraq and not against Israel? Where can somebody feel secure if not in a hospital bed?"

Back in the CPT apartment that night, we heard several loud booms. When Anne looked out of our bedroom window, a soldier yelled at her and ran to the door, as if to enter. Then we heard more booms. It was an Israeli military robot blowing up suspicious objects, in this case our CPT garbage in black plastic bags. We resolved that in the future we would put our garbage out in the morning instead of the night before.

Tuesday, May 22: Curfew continues. Two observers from TIPH visited us. They said the occupation forces have imposed curfew on Palestinians in H-2 because other Palestinians in H-1 threw stones. The observers said Israel punishes Palestinians in H-2 in order to turn them against Palestinians in H-1.

Several of us attended a dialogue group, tentatively calling itself "Circle of Sanity," that meets weekly at Tantur, a beautiful property belonging to the Vatican on the Jerusalem side of the Bethlehem checkpoint. Present were seven Israelis, seven internationals, and four Palestinians. None of the latter have permits to enter Jerusalem. They attend such meetings at considerable personal risk.

Several of the Israelis said that the problem was only between "those of us who are suffering—Israelis and Palestinians," the implication being that the internationals were superfluous. One Israeli woman said, "I have to remind the internationals that Jews have died too." My impression was that, in spite of their good intentions, these Israelis have little comprehension of what daily life is like for Palestinians if they imagine that the two groups are equally discomfited by the occupation and the present intifada.

When we walked the Palestinians out the back way through Tantur to avoid the checkpoint, they told us that they have had no work in eight months. Unemployment is at 70 percent in Bethlehem.

Wednesday, May 23: Abdel Hadi Hantash stopped by to update us on land issues. This remarkable man knows every acre in the Hebron District. If the army bulldozes trees or confiscates land, or settlers burn crops or add even a single caravan, Abdel Hadi knows about it. He has worked full-time since 1978 as a surveyor for the Hebron Municipality. On his own time, as a volunteer, he is one-half of the Hebron branch of the Land Defense Committee. This is an organization, founded in 1995, with 16 members in offices in every West Bank district, whose purpose is to monitor, document, and challenge land confiscation in the Israeli courts. Abdel Hadi has testified in such court cases more than a hundred times. But he is fighting an uphill battle. Israel has confiscated 62 percent of the land in Hebron District, almost half of that since the Oslo process began.

Thursday, May 24: Harriet Taylor arrived to join the team. Her taxi was stopped at one checkpoint across which she had to drag her luggage. She then got a ride in a pickup truck that was stopped at another checkpoint. After climbing over that, her next ride was in a big tire truck. It was stopped at the edge of Hebron. Two more taxis brought her the rest of the way to walking distance of the CPT apartment. The trip from Jerusalem took two and a half hours and five vehicles. Welcome to Palestine.

Friday, May 25: Translator Zleekha and CPTers stopped for tea before heading out to the Beqa'a. Across the street we noticed a Palestinian man standing in the sun for an ID check while soldiers were lounging about. He was still there when we left 40 minutes later. TIPH observers were photographing the scene and writing a report.

The Palestinian's name is Jawdat. A teenaged soldier had taken his ID and rudely demanded to search him. Jawdat refused and asked to see an officer. The standoff had lasted nearly an hour when an officer arrived. Jawdat explained what had happened. The officer asked if he could search him. Jawdat said yes, since the officer asked politely. The officer retrieved Jawdat's ID and sent him off—without searching him.

Gene Stoltzfus, the Chicago-based director of CPT, arrived to spend 10 days with the team.

Saturday, May 26: The whole team was invited to dinner with a Palestinian family in Jerusalem. Our host, Sami, has an antiquities shop in West Jerusalem. He said Palestinians with Jerusalem IDs don't suffer as much as those in the Occupied Territories, but they still experience discrimination. He has to pay the full *arnona* (merchants' tax), but his Jewish neighbors get all kinds of discounts, e.g., for serving in the army, which Sami, as a Palestinian, can't do. He has been taken to court several times for putting dollar rather than shekel prices on his sales tags. His neighboring Jewish-owned stores do the same thing, but have never been prosecuted for it.

Sunday, May 27: Harriet Lewis, an American-born Israeli and long-time peace activist, spent two days with the team. She, Zleekha, Gene, and I went to the Beqa'a to visit Anwar Sultan, head of the Society for Housing Project. We went our usual way, which is to take a taxi to Road 60, get off near the home we intend to visit, then duck under barbed wire, walk across fields, vineyards, and over stone walls. Harriet was nonplussed. "This is ridiculous. There has to be an easier way." But that is the point of bypass roads. They are designed to accommodate settlers and inconvenience Palestinians.

Anwar explained that the Society for Housing Project owns 18 acres on the tops of two hills: Jabal Jaber and Jabal Sultan, both too rocky to cultivate. Sixty municipal employees, mostly teachers, pooled their money to buy the land in order to build affordable housing for themselves. But, in 1997, before they could begin construction, the Israeli Civil Administration declared both sites state land. When the Society showed proof of ownership, the Civil Administation Captain said, "In that case, the land is confiscated." In May 1998, settlers bulldozed a road around Jabal Jaber. Israeli soldiers and military police were present to prevent Palestinians and CPTers from interfering with the settlers. The following year, settlers began bulldozing a road around Jabal Sultan. This time the Society, with Israeli lawyer Shlomo Lecker, took the issue to court. On 25 May 1999, the High Court issued a decision that nobody, neither Palestinians nor Israeli settlers, should build on the two sites, nor make any use whatsoever of the land, until a final answer is reached.

Then, two months ago, a lone, armed settler from Givat Harsina, named Natty, parked a large Mercedes van on the site. Anwar called the police and the Civil Administration. They both acknowledged that Natty's presence is illegal, but have done nothing to remove him. Meanwhile, Natty has expanded. He has built a stone house, brought in goats that he turns loose in Palestinian vineyards, guard dogs, a water tank, and put up barbed wire. He is usually joined by other young settler men. With attorney Lecker, the Society is taking the issue to the High Court.

Anwar brought out a pile of legal documents. Among them was one in Hebrew: "Kiryat Arba 2000." Harriet read it in amazement.

The master plan indeed projects a tourist site with a hotel on Society lands and specifies that all Palestinian homes in the area are to be demolished within five years. It is signed by Yossi Segal, Head of Neglected or Absentee Property.

From Anwar's house we walked over to Natty's camp. The dogs were chained, thank goodness. Two settler men in the van got on the mobile phone and, within minutes, Natty himself drove up. He is a Yemeni Jew who spoke in Hebrew to Harriet and in Arabic to Zleekha. To Harriet he said that Palestinians may invite her for tea, but they laugh behind her back. To Zleekha he said that Palestinians respect people like him more than peace activists like Harriet because he speaks their language and, like them, knows how to live on the land. Zleekha was courteous and refrained from telling Natty what Palestinians say behind his back.

Tuesday, May 29: Stepped out of the apartment at 10:00 a.m. to find a fracas. Settler women were throwing rocks past the barrier on our street at Palestinian men, and soldiers were rushing to the scene. A TIPH observer told me that a settler had been shot dead near Nablus. He was a high-ranking official of settler security and a brother of prominent Hebron settlers. This looked like a major to-do, so I got Gene to come with me. We found a large crowd of settlers at Gross Square. They pelted us with eggplants and beat us with cornstalks. When they ran out of produce, they switched to rocks. Methodically they smashed the building blocks that Palestinians had piled up to rebuild their bombed-out stores. Then they tried to get into the market itself, but soldiers prevented them. This was the first time I ever saw soldiers and police physically lay hands on settlers to restrain them. Relative calm was restored when soldiers pushed Palestinians back up the streets and ordered them to go into their homes.

Meanwhile, other settlers had breached the barrier on the street leading to our apartment. The CPTers who had remained there, unable to get out the door, watched from the roof as settlers hurled rocks and bottles at Palestinians gathered deeper into the market.

One Palestinian boy, nine or ten years old, threw a bottle that landed far short of the settlers. Instantly police rushed in, grabbed the boy, hauled him out past the mob of irate settlers, and took him to the police station, where he was detained a few hours, then released.

Later that afternoon we got a call from 'Ata that settlers had again set up a roadblock. Gene and I set out. En route, 'Ata called again. "Come quickly. Settlers are attacking my father's house." Our taxi was forced to stop at a distance from the Jaber home because settlers were stoning any cars that got near. As Gene and I approached on foot, we found Abdel Jawad, 'Ata's father, sitting by the side of the road with blood on his leg where settlers had struck him with a stone. Two Israeli soldiers were bandaging his wound. 'Ata's mother, brother, and sister-in-law had also been wounded. Huge rocks were lying everywhere, and the whole family was traumatized.

As we were trying to take in what had happened, we noticed three settler men, one of them with a gun slung over his shoulder, walking up the dirt road to Abdel Jawad's house. The thought went through my head, "I must stop them." I walked down to meet them, trying to make myself as big as possible, and heard myself asking them, "Can I help you?" The big one brushed me away with a "Go to hell" in unaccented English.

They went around and behind Abdel Jawad's house, obviously looking for something. I followed them, but couldn't see what they picked up. As they were leaving they had a few angry words with Israeli soldiers who had by then shown up, then joined the other settlers swarming on Road 60 below. They were pulling up the irrigation tubing that 'Ata's brother, Jowdi, had laid that morning.

Gene and I decided to sit on a rock under a tree towards the end of the dirt road. At one point I walked up to the house, but glancing back saw about 20 settler men, women, and children turning up the road. I raced back and found Gene surrounded. A settler man demanded Gene's film. Gene's response that it was a digital camera and had no film seemed to bewilder the settler. He then demanded mine. I said, "I don't have to give it to you," then, looking at a policeman who had joined us, "Do I?" The policeman gave the sweetest smile and shook his head.

The men and boys left, but two women stayed to talk with us. Well, one talked, the other spat. The talker asked why we were there on her land. We responded that we were guests of Palestinian friends. She said, "I pity you. Palestinians are dogs. They murder Jews." The spitter spat, and they too left.

'Ata, from across the road, had called a Red Crescent ambulance. It tried three or four times to come the shortest way, up Road 60, but every time settlers stoned it. So it finally came up a back road, arriving around 8:30 p.m. The wounded family members had to walk across several fields to reach it. Gene stayed with the rest of the family and I rode in the ambulance back to Hebron. All four Jabers were slumped over and moaning. The ambulance was detained at a checkpoint for about 10 minutes, then allowed to proceed to Alia Hospital.

Walking back to the CPT apartment, I was stopped by a soldier in front of Beit Hadassah settlement. My nerves were shot. "What now!" I growled at him. He seemed startled and immediately became apologetic: "It's been a bad day, but don't take it out on us."

Wednesday, May 30: Anne and I went back to Abdel Jawad's in the morning. He, his wife, son, and daughter-in-law were treated at Alia Hospital and returned home by taxi late last night. We surveyed yesterday's damage: broken windows, damaged water tank and satellite dish on the roof, about half the $400 worth of irrigation tubing pulled up and destroyed, plants near the house crushed under huge stones. The family is shaken, yet offered us mint tea, fruit, and coffee. We saw no sign of roving settlers, so returned to Hebron.

Late that afternoon we got a call from Jowdi, 'Ata's older brother: "They're back!" Three of us rushed out, but by the time we got there it was all over. Five teenage settler boys had heaved rocks over the fence behind Abdel Jawad's home—a fence that guards new settlement construction on land confiscated from Abdel Jawad in 1998.

That night Gene and I were musing about how settlers repeatedly break the law in the presence of police and get away with it. We decided to write a Letter of Inquiry to the Kiryat Arba police, asking them to clarify the legal status of Israeli settlers. We planned to include photographs of settlers in the act of damaging property in case the police needed help identifying lawbreakers. While we were planning this, Arik Ascherman of Rabbis for Human Rights telephoned. He had been thinking about settlers rampaging with impunity and wondered what could be done about it. Gene said it was a sign that the spirit was moving among us.

Thursday, May 31: A CPT delegation arrived and we all went to Abdel Jawad's. While there, the settlers did their roadblock thing again. We called the police who said they knew about it and would stop it. They did so by turning away Palestinian cars on either side of the settler roadblock. Eventually the settlers left.

Gene spoke with Palestinian attorney Jonathan Kuttab about our Letter of Inquiry. He thought it a good idea and suggested we send copies and photographs to the Ministers of Justice and Internal Security, the State Comptroller, and the National Police in Jerusalem.

Friday, June 1: Long-time CPT friend Hisham Sharabati was married today. Gene went to the men's gathering at noon, where everybody ate a lot. We three CPT women went to the women's function in the evening, where there was no food, but lots of dancing. The room was packed with women. The only male present was the bridegroom. As is the custom, he presented his bride with gold jewelry.

Saturday, June 2: I joined the CPT delegation to go to Dura to hear Khaled Amayreh, a political analyst who writes for *Middle East International*. He said no Israeli government will dismantle settlements, and no Palestinian state is possible with them present. Israel's solution is to narrow Palestinian horizons to the point of claustrophobia until life becomes so unbearable that they leave. Amayreh advocated one country with equal rights for all. If Jews can live anywhere in Palestine/Israel, Palestinians should have that same right.

Sunday, June 3: Eight of us went to Jerusalem in a shared taxi. There were many new checkpoints, roadblocks, and tanks alongside the road. We were stopped for 30 minutes at a checkpoint outside of 'Efrat settlement. Two of the three Palestinians in our van were not allowed to continue. They had to wait for a taxi returning to Hebron.

In Jerusalem we met with the Machsom Watch women. They will address and mail copies of our Letter of Inquiry and photos to the various ministries.

Monday, June 4: CPTer JoAnne Lingle and I went to meet a member of the Jaber family, Naim, at the Kiryat Arba police station where together we would deliver our Letter of Inquiry and photographs. It turned out to be quite an education into how the Israeli police handle complaints from Palestinians.

Not knowing better, JoAnne and I walked in through the settlement's front gate. We had to get by two checkpoints, where soldiers never asked us a thing. The whole police compound seemed deserted. We wandered around at will until we found a cook who showed us where to find the Palestinian gate. This is at the back of the station, behind huge concrete blocks. Palestinians reach the gate by a dead-end dirt road. There is a guard post at the gate, but it was unmanned the whole time we were there.

Standing on the outside of the gate was a Palestinian man and a little boy, obviously his son. The man held his head at a funny angle and was clearly in pain. He had been beaten by a settler the night before and had brought a medical report to register a complaint. He had been waiting for an hour with nobody in sight. I went into the compound and, hearing footsteps, found a policeman and took him to the injured man. The policeman was very polite, assured me he would find the soldier with the key, and left. An hour later, when nobody showed up, the man and boy left.

By then Naim and another man had come. The new man is a Hebronite, but has a wife and children in Jerusalem. When he applied for family reunification, he was ordered to come to the police station about an irregularity in his application. He had spent the whole previous day waiting outside the gate. Again I went to find someone to help. This time it was a man in a *kippa* (skullcap) who is from Jerusalem and teaches Torah at Kiryat Arba. He walked me to the front gate and in Hebrew explained the situation to the soldier on guard duty, who in turn said somebody would come immediately. Walking back, the Torah teacher asked me why I was there. I explained that my friend had been harassed by settlers. He said, "What's a settler?"

An hour passed and nobody came. I tried again. This time I found another policeman who asked if I were a lawyer. When I said no, he replied, "Then I don't talk to you." Another hour and another try. This time I was sent from one person to another, phone calls were made, and finally, after three hours, a policeman came to the gate. He told the family reunification man to go away and wouldn't tell him what his application needed. When we explained that Naim had come to complain about the damage settlers had done, the policeman replied "Is that all?" He unlocked the door, let Naim in, and put JoAnne and me out, with a "Good day, ladies." He refused to accept our letter and photos.

While we were waiting outside, two more men showed up. I tried to explain in my limited Arabic why we were there and understood from them that they had been told to come to pick up a letter. One of them went away and came back with juice for us all. After a couple of hours, JoAnne and I decided to walk around to the settlement entrance. Again we got in easily. The same soldiers at the two checkpoints didn't ask how we got out or why we were going in again. We asked for Naim and, after being sent from one person to the next, learned that he had been taken to the Beqa'a to photograph the damage. So we walked back to Hebron.

We told Arik Ascherman what had happened. He made several phone calls, then called back to say that somebody would receive the letters the next morning. He also said that Israeli attorney Leah Tsemel expressed an interest in prosecuting the case. A woman from the U.S. Consulate suggested that we contact B'tselem since they had recently published an information sheet on "Tacit Consent: Israeli Law Enforcement on Settlers in the Occupied Territories." Our project had taken on a cooperative dimension, involving several Israeli human rights groups.

Tuesday, June 5: Anita and I returned to the Kiryat Arba police station. We asked for the name Arik had given us and were taken to his office. He took us to Amitai, the "Good day, ladies" man. He did seem somewhat interested in the photographs, then his superior, Yossi, came in and the mood changed. Amitai put the letter and photos in a drawer and slammed it shut. Yossi asked if CPT was neutral. Anita said, "No, we stand with the oppressed." Yossi responded that "unlike CPT, the police are neutral and protect both sides. Good day." Having been dismissed, we trudged back to Hebron.

Wednesday, June 6: We had heard that yesterday soldiers detained a woman for a considerable period outside the main entrance to the

Old City. Zleekha arranged for us to talk with the woman. But when a CPT delegate and I walked through the market to meet Zleehka, we found soldiers blocking the exit. Beyond the soldiers were the settlers, including the Go to Hell guy and spitting woman. When I moved up to take photographs, settler women threw some liquid and bottles at us. I was soaked.

Taking an alternate route through the Old City, we met Zleehka and walked back towards the main entrance near the Ibrahimi Mosque, where we were stopped by two soldiers. Suddenly one of the soldiers ran into the courtyard with his gun raised. Apparently someone had thrown a stone from the roof, although I hadn't heard anything. The soldier grabbed a boy, who couldn't possibly have been the stone thrower, and dragged him into a corner. Within a minute, three soldier-filled jeeps, TIPH observers, and reporters arrived. The boy's mother and grandmother rushed out to plead with the soldiers. A female soldier pushed Zleekha backwards down some steps. After 15 minutes the boy, his mother, and grandmother went into an apartment, followed by two soldiers. The two original soldiers then prevented anybody from passing through the area and threatened to arrest the three of us if we didn't leave immediately.

Eventually we did make it to see the woman who had been detained yesterday. As she explained it to us, she had been in front of her home with her two sons, ages 3 and 4 ½. Several settler boys around 12-years-old began kicking and pushing her sons. When the mother rushed up with a stone, a soldier said to her, "Don't do it," but she threw it anyway. By then the settler boys had run away, well beyond her throwing arm. When the soldiers detained her, she asked, "They hit my children. Why are you stopping only me?" They let her go after an hour.

On the way home we saw two volunteers from Doctors Without Borders. They are frustrated because a Red Crescent ambulance filled with antibiotics they desperately need was not allowed into Hebron. They will try to bring the antibiotics from Ramallah in a Doctors Without Borders car.

Thursday, June 7: Three of us went with a translator to visit Abu Samir's family. They live just up the hill from the four heavily sandbagged settler caravans that comprise the Tel Rumeida settlement. The entire front and sides of Abu Samir's house are enclosed by a metal cage, donated by the Palestinian Authority to protect the family from settler attacks.

The purpose of our visit was to hear what happened two nights ago. More than 30 adult settlers attacked Abu Samir's and two other Palestinian homes. Some stones made it through Abu Samir's metal caging and broke windows. Dozens of soldiers were present but did nothing. The settlers dispersed only when Israeli police arrived.

Abu Samir said his grandchildren are always late for school. They wait until the settler children leave in order to avoid getting beaten up. But they still have to walk home from school, past two checkpoints and a tank. Last week one of Abu Samir's grandsons was attacked by settler children before he could make it inside his cage. For the children to play outside their home is out of the question.

Friday, June 8: The entire team, along with a Palestinian friend smuggled in with us, went to Jerusalem for the Women (and Men) in Black vigil. More than a thousand Israelis, along with Palestinians and internationals, gathered to protest the occupation. A large area was reserved for counter-demonstrators, but only a half dozen showed up. The organizers gave everyone black balloons. When they were all released at once, the sky over Jerusalem became polka-dotted. It was a happy event, but perhaps most impressed was our Palestinian friend. She said it made her realize that not all Israelis think and behave like Hebron settlers.

While still in Jerusalem, we got a call from Palestinian journalist Kawther Salam saying she had been attacked. I telephoned her as soon as we got back to Hebron. She was just being released from the hospital. I met her at her office, where she told me what had happened. She had spent the morning filming soldiers entering and searching Palestinian homes. Two soldiers pushed her into a tunnel and blocked the entrance. So she went out the back way, up onto the roofs, and continued filming.

That afternoon she went out to visit her family. As she approached Gross Square, the two soldiers who had pushed her ran up to her. They had a large toy water pistol and sprayed her in the face with a noxious smelling liquid. Kawther collapsed, unconscious, in the street. When she came to, her hand was in spasm and an ambulance was en route. One of the soldiers crowded around her said the fluid in the gun was "love wine." The water gun was on the ground near Kawther, but when she reached for it, an Israeli officer stomped on it.

At the hospital, medical personnel treated Kawther, but were unable to determine what had been sprayed on her. That evening, she vomited and was feverish, but the symptoms faded by the following morning. Kawther contacted her lawyer, Israeli attorney Leah Tsemel, who advised her to take the clothes she had been wearing to an Israeli hospital to analyze the fluid. They intend to pursue the case. To date, no disciplinary action has been taken against the two soldiers.

Saturday, June 9: Around 10:00 a.m. we were surprised to see two soldiers on the roof of the Turkish bath just opposite our porch. We lined up like spectators to watch them gingerly walking over the rounded domes encrusted with glass that make up the roof of the bath. When they realized they had an audience, one of them said, "Just doing our job." That evening we learned that they had broken in the front door to enter the baths.

Sunday, June 10: Kawther telephoned. Soldiers were in her building searching the apartments. Two of us went over. The outer door was locked, but Kawther's neighbors let us in. Soldiers had just left the apartment. Every drawer and door was open, and all the furniture cushions were on the floor. The soldiers had photographed the people and the rooms and made sketches of the floor plan. The neighbors offered Kawther and us coffee. While drinking it we heard a commotion. Five soldiers were trapped behind the locked outer door. They seemed befuddled. When another neighbor unlocked the door for them to leave, they strutted off, in control again.

Kawther returned with us to the CPT apartment. As we approached Gross Square, a soldier ran to us and said Kawther was not allowed to pass. Kawther asked, "Why? It's a public street." The soldier responded, "If you pass in front of the settlers, they will make trouble." She replied, "Then send them away." Kawther refused to give in. The soldier relayed a call to his commander, and she was allowed to pass by the settlers.

A South African documentary film crew was at the apartment interviewing another CPTer. When they met Kawther, they wanted to film her story as well. Kawther chose the location—Gross Square, where the soldier had sprayed her with the "water" pistol. She stood there, stylishly dressed with matching parasol, describing the incident, while settlers and soldiers, including her two attackers, watched apoplectic and bug-eyed.

After Kawther finished the filming, we walked up Shuhada Street. As we neared Beit Hadassah, a middle-aged, stocky settler I had never seen before was getting into his car. He had what looked like a pistol tucked in his belt. Kawther flinched and grabbed my hand. We kept walking, but were visibly apprehensive. The man called us back. "What's the matter?" he said. "I have no quarrel with you. Come over here." He offered us candy, high-fived Kawther, and shook my hand.

We continued on our way to visit a family Kawther wanted to interview. They live on the steep street that leads to Tel Rumeida settlement. Last Monday, the oldest daughter, 12-year-old Ala', was standing on the steps in front of her home with her 10-month-old sister Ayah in her arms. Three teen-aged settler girls grabbed Ayah and ran up the hill to Tel Rumeida. Ala' ran after them, screaming "My sister! My sister!" Some neighbors joined her in pursuit. Soldiers guarding the settlement stopped the three girls, who then dropped the baby to the ground and fled into the settlement. The baby rolled down the hill, unconscious. When Ala' returned home with Ayah, their mother screamed and ran with Ayah all the way to Alia Hospital. When we saw the baby, five days after the incident, Ayah seemed to be all right, except for a nasty bruise on the back of her head. No attempt had been made to ascertain the identity of the three settler girls.

Monday, June 11: Two of us went to visit Jamal and Sadiyya and their three children in Beit Ummar. Now completely closed off with huge checkpoints, Beit Ummar is an economic disaster. The residents get around the lack of money by helping each other out. Jamal is building his house himself little by little. All the materials have been donated by friends. In return, Jamal, a barber, cuts their hair for free. Nobody says no to a request for help. Although not all needs can be met. Sadiyya can't get out of the village to take their infant daughter for her vaccinations.

Tuesday, June 12: Zleekha and I visited families in the Beqa'a. In one family the grandmother told us that several months ago settlers stole their water pipes and uprooted all their cauliflower plants. She and her son went to Kiryat Arba police station to make a complaint. They waited at the gate for three days. On the third day the police came and went with them to evaluate the damage. Seeing the rotting cauliflower plants in the field, the police asked, "How do you know settlers and not Palestinians did this?" The grandmother explained that settlers regularly came into their fields and asked them, "Why do you grow things here? This is our land." The police said there was insufficient evidence to register a complaint. The field remains fallow because the family does not have the money to replant or replace the water pipes.

Wednesday, June 13: Two of us visited George Rishmawi in Beit Sahour, in the Bethlehem area, who showed us some of the homes that had been bombed in Beit Jala and Beit Sahour. It took three taxis to return to Hebron. The first was stopped just outside Bethlehem, where soldiers had just closed the road. We climbed over the roadblocks to a second taxi. When this driver saw an unexpected checkpoint, he drove off the road, through a field, then an olive grove. He was finally stopped at a third checkpoint. Again, we had to climb over the mounds of dirt and broken cement and take a third taxi to Hebron. What normally would be a 20-minute ride took over an hour and cost three times as much.

Thursday, June 14: I went with Kawther to visit a woman in the Old City whose roof is an Israeli army post. Her husband died of a heart attack in December during an argument with soldiers. On this morning, two bored young soldiers were amusing themselves by yelling obscenities and throwing stones at her. When Kawther tried to talk with them, they propositioned her, saying, "We're cute soldiers, come up on the roof right now." We left.

Later the woman called Kawther. The two soldiers had hit her in the eye with a stone. Kawther called Doctors Without Borders, who rushed to help. By the time Kawther got there, the soldiers were harassing the doctors and making crude comments to the women among them.

The two soldiers then began throwing stones and pieces of metal on all the families below them. The people in the homes were screaming for help. Kawther ran into the street and brought back five other soldiers. But instead of disciplining the two soldiers, they arrested a 12-year-old Palestinian boy. He was taken away by border police and released later that day.

That afternoon two of us went with Zleekha to Tel Rumeida. Settlers there had begun an archeological excavation in the hope of finding evidence of Abraham or David. When it turned out to be a Byzantine site, they began building an apartment complex over the site. Two neighboring Palestinian families and an Israeli archeologist took them to court and won a stop-work order.

So we were surprised to see five Chinese "guest" laborers now working on the site. A TIPH observer told us that the stop-work order had been lifted. To find out more, we visited Abu Hani, who lives next to the site. He told us the Civil Administration had ordered work to resume, but that they had no right to do so because they are a defendant in the lawsuit that brought about the stop-work order. Legal proceedings were initiated by an Israeli archeologist and joined by two neighboring Palestinian families, including Abu Hani. The archeologist had noticed settlers carrying off antiquities found at the site.

Abu Hani told us that settlers offered to buy him any house he wanted if he would leave the area. In 1997, an American, Dr. Irving Moskowitz, offered him millions of dollars and a car for his house and land. Abu Hani refused. "No. I built this house. I love this area. I won't leave until I die." He said Palestinians are denied permits to build or make additions anywhere in the Tel Rumeida neighborhood because it is a historical area; yet settlers build right on top of an archeological site.

That evening around 6:00 we got a call that Abu Hani urgently needed the digital photographs we had taken of the workers at the archeological site. We hurriedly printed them and rushed the copies to Abu Hani's daughter, Hana, who faxed them to the High Court just before the 7:00 p.m. deadline.

Friday, June 15: I went with Zleekha to the Beqa'a to say my goodbyes. We found new problems. Yesterday settlers and soldiers widened the road behind the military camp by appropriating seven yards of land belonging to Palestinians. Widening the road cuts off access to it for Palestinian vehicles. The only road now available to them is unpaved, stony, and barely passable.

While we were visiting one family, we received a call that settlers were again attacking Abdel Jawad's house. We phoned the Kiryat Arba police and were pleased that they responded immediately and stopped the attack.

Saturday, June 16: Zleekha and I went to see Abu Hani's daughter Hana to find out about the stop-work order. Hana was jubilant. The Israeli High Court ruled that the stop-work order is in effect and is unappealable until a final decision is taken. Yesterday, Civil Administration authorities arrived and made the Chinese workers stop.

It was good to leave Hebron this time with a small victory, even though it may not last long.

Update by the author, Jane Adas

Highland Park, NJ—Indeed, the stop-work order was only a hiccup in Israel's colonial settlement project. A three-story Jews-only apartment building now stands over the Byzantine archeological site in Tel Rumeida. Abu Hani died last year, but his and Abu Samir's families remain in their "caged" homes. Beaten down by constant Israeli settler and soldier harassment, most of the other Palestinians who lived in the area have left to become internal refugees.

In 1997 US-AID reconstructed Shuhada Street, the main road connecting H-1 to the Old City, with the aim of improving the lives of both Jewish colonists and Palestinian residents. Today it is closed to all Palestinian vehicular and pedestrian traffic along its entire length and is now another Jews-only road.

The Hebron Accords of 1997 stipulated that the Hisbeh (wholesale market) near the Avraham Avinu settlement was to be returned to its Palestinian owners and allowed to reopen. But the whole area, formerly the commercial heart of the Old City, has now been taken over by Israeli settlers. Adjacent to the Hisbeh on a road leading into the Old City was the bustling retail fruit and vegetable market. On a visit in 2004, I was stunned to find it completely empty, the barricaded entrance manned by Israeli soldiers: "Forbidden to approach! Forbidden to photograph!"

Abu Mohammed's butcher shop is one of more than 60 Palestinian-owned stores in H-2 that were closed by military order in 2005. The Israeli military had by that time installed iron barriers on all but two entrances to the Old City. The more than 30,000 Palestinian residents of H-1 may enter and exit the Old City via one of the two "open" gates—one at a time through a revolving metal door.

After receiving death threats and intensifying harassment from Israeli soldiers and settlers, the journalist Kawther Salam was granted asylum in Vienna. Persons unknown shot and killed Natty, the settler-squatter who had bragged that Palestinians respect people like him.

This is not a happy update, yet good people continue to do good work. Machsom Watch has grown to be a formidable force. Zleekha Muhtaseb has established the Hebron Center for Social Development to help women and children cope with living among Israeli colonists and the soldiers who guard them. Abdel Hadi Hantash of the Land Defense Committee has had some success in Israeli courts in forcing Israel to reposition its separation barrier, resulting in less confiscation of land. And CPT is still there.

Rachel

By Cindy Corrie

Cindy Corrie is the mother of Rachel Corrie, the 23-year-old American who was crushed to death by an Israeli bulldozer on March 16, 2003. In this December 2003 issue of The Link, *Cindy reflects on her daughter's sacrifice.*

My daughter, Rachel Corrie, was one of those brave activists, now numbering in the thousands, who have made the journey from the safety of their own countries and homes to the Occupied Palestinian Territories. They go to see for themselves, to join in solidarity with the Palestinian people, and to work for a more peaceful world.

Rachel connected with the International Solidarity Movement (ISM), a group of Palestinian-led international activists who use nonviolent methods and strategies to confront the Israeli occupation. According to Huwaida Arraf (one of the co-founders), ISM was formed "to provide the Palestinian people with a resource, international protection, and a voice with which to resist, nonviolently, an overwhelming military occupation force."

In March and April of this year [2003], three ISM activists suffered tragedies at the hands of the Israeli military. On March 16, Rachel, 23-years-old and in the spring of her life, died when she was crushed by an Israeli bulldozer while trying to prevent the demolition of a Palestinian home in Rafah near the Egyptian border. On April 5, another U.S. citizen, Brian Avery, 24-years-old, from Albuquerque, New Mexico, was shot in the face by a burst of machine-gun fire from an Israeli armored personnel carrier in Jenin. On April 11, Tom

Hurndall, 21-years-old, from the U.K., was shot in the head as he tried to help two young Palestinian girls to safety.

Rachel, Brian, Tom. All three, members of ISM. All three, tragic victims of the U.S.-Israeli-Palestinian conflict. They join the ranks of those who have died or been severely injured in the occupation. Like so many others who have suffered or been lost in both Palestine and Israel, Rachel, Brian, and Tom were unarmed and nonviolent. And as with so many other killings of unarmed civilians in the Occupied Palestinian Territories, the Israeli military has assumed no responsibility.

In the months since Rachel's killing, our family has had numerous opportunities to talk with ISM volunteers from the U.S. and from other countries. We have been struck by their thoughtfulness, their intelligence, their dedication, and, of course, their courage. They are young and old and in between—college students and retirees. They come from the United States, from the United Kingdom, Canada, Sweden, Denmark, Japan, South Africa, Australia—from many countries in the world. They are students, teachers, accountants, lawyers, poets, mothers, fathers, grandmothers. They are Christians, Jews, Muslims, and undoubtedly come from other faiths as well. They have gone to Palestine because, in 2001, the U.S. vetoed a United Nations resolution calling for international human rights monitors in the Occupied Territories. In remarks at a U.N. conference last year, Huwaida Arraf stated that there are only two stipulations for joining ISM: one must believe in the right to freedom of the Palestinian people based on the relevant United Nations resolutions and international law; and one must agree to use only nonviolent, direct-action methods of resistance. She added, "The strength of ISM activists is not in arms. Their strength is in the truth and justice of the Palestinian cause, and in believing that the Palestinian people deserve equal rights."

To validate her own life, Rachel had a need to resist the injustices she saw impacting the lives of others. This is what drew her to ISM and to the Occupied Territories. She went in January to Rafah because she believed the world had forsaken this place. She became our eyes and ears as she told us about the tanks and bulldozers passing by, about the homes with tank-shell holes in their walls, and about the rapidly multiplying Israeli watch towers with snipers lurking along the horizon.

She told us about Ali, the eight-year-old Palestinian boy shot and killed two days before she arrived, and about large groups of Palestinian men rounded up and held for hours at a time. She wrote of sleeping at night beside water wells to protect them from being damaged by Israelis; she recalled standing with other activists to protect Palestinian municipal water workers who were being fired upon while trying to repair the wells. She drank sweet tea with Palestinian grandmothers, held wiggling babies, and danced with children in the street. She wrote, "Know that I have a lot of very nice Palestinians looking after me. I have a small flu bug, and got some very nice lemony drinks to cure me. Also, the woman who keeps the key for the well where we sleep keeps asking me about you. She doesn't speak a word of English, but she asks about my mom pretty frequently—wants to make sure I'm calling you."

On March 16, according to six eyewitness accounts, Rachel was crushed by an Israeli D9R-type bulldozer while trying to prevent the demolition of the home of a Palestinian pharmacist, his wife, and three young children near the Egyptian border.

One of the eyewitnesses described the bulldozers that day, "plowing up the land in front of the buildings" and "making occasional runs at houses." From a distance, the activists stood and sometimes sat in the bulldozers' path, indicating their intention not to move. The bulldozer would approach very close to the activists but would always stop in time to avoid injuring them. At one point the bulldozers retreated from the area, and the activists felt they had been successful.

But then the bulldozers returned, and shortly thereafter one of them began to approach a home where Rachel had slept numerous times and had played with the children. She wrote about this family:

The two front rooms of their house are unusable because gunshots have been fired through the walls, so the whole family—three kids and two parents—sleep in the parents' bedroom. I sleep on the floor next to the youngest daughter, Iman, and we all share blankets. . . . Friday is the holiday, and when I woke up they were watching "Gummy Bears" dubbed in Arabic. So I ate breakfast with them and sat there for a while and just enjoyed being in this big puddle of blankets with this family watching what for me seemed like Saturday morning cartoons.

Eyewitnesses tell us that the bulldozer began a straight run at this house. Rachel, wearing her fluorescent orange jacket with reflective striping, knelt down well in front of the bulldozer and began waving her arms and shouting, just as activists had done many times earlier that day. But this time, the bulldozer, with its two operators on board, continued moving straight for Rachel and did not stop.

Months ago, the U.S. Department of State notified our family that the Israeli Military Police had completed their investigation, that no charges would be brought, that the case was closed, and that Israel declined to release a report to the U.S. government. With some pressure from the U.S. government, Israel has now permitted a few U.S. officials and my husband and me to read the report and to take notes.

Recently, the Israeli Military Advocate General, "pursuant to the letter dated July 3, 2003, from Secretary Colin Powell to the Minister of Foreign Affairs, regarding the death of U.S. citizen Ms. Rachel Corrie," has reconsidered his position and has released to us and to members of the U.S. government the final section of the report which summarizes its findings. The Advocate General concludes that the bulldozer operators did not see Rachel and suggests (after apparent follow-up with the professor who conducted the autopsy) that her death was caused by an injury or by falling on building debris and not by direct contact with the bulldozer. The report itself, however, has still not been released to the U.S. government. The Israeli military has concluded that the bulldozer operators did not see Rachel.

On April 5, during the second day of a curfew in Jenin, Brian Avery, the 24-year-old ISM activist from Albuquerque, and a companion had left their ISM headquarters to investigate gunfire they heard coming from a distance. When they entered the street, two armored personnel carriers advanced toward them at low speed. There were no Palestinians in the street. Brian was wearing his fluorescent orange vest with a reflective cross. He and the other activist raised their arms in the air. At a distance of about 55 yards, the first armored personnel carrier issued a burst of machine-gun fire.

Brian's left cheek was almost completely shot off. He spent over two months having surgery and other treatment in Israel. He is now at home with his parents in North Carolina and continues to be treated for the severe injuries to his face.

We have met Brian. He is able to speak now. He has become creative with a blender since he still can eat only a liquid diet. With the best smile that he can manage, he tells us his goal is to be able to bite into an apple. His mother tells us that he will never smell again and that doctors think they may not be able to correct his blurred vision.

Brian speaks quietly, thoughtfully, and tells us that when he is stronger, he wants to travel in the United States to tell people about what is happening in Palestine. He says he wants to return there one day to continue the work that was halted so abruptly in that street in Jenin.

But first there will be more surgeries, and Brian has no medical insurance. The University of North Carolina at Chapel Hill Hospitals are funding Brian's medical procedures for the present time.

In a command report, the Israeli military says it was not in the area when Brian Avery was injured. There has been no further investigation.

On April 11, ISM activists had joined Palestinians in an action to set up a tent in an area of Rafah that Israeli tanks had used to shoot into the houses and streets of Yibna refugee camp and to prevent access to a local mosque. One of the activists was a 21-year-old aspiring photojournalist from London, Tom Hurndall. When live rounds were fired from a tank in the area and from a security tower, the activists called off the action and were in the process of leaving when they noticed children who had been playing on a roadblock in the area.

Some of the youngsters ran off, but a few remained. Tom Hurndall lifted a five-year-old boy to safety but then saw two small girls who were in danger. When he reached out his hands to them, he was shot in the back of the head.

Tom, like Rachel and Brian, was wearing a fluorescent orange jacket that marked him as an unarmed civilian. Tom's mother writes that when she first saw Tom in an Israeli hospital, there was a young Israeli girl beside him who kept repeating, "I am so sorry for my country."

Tom is now home in the U.K. where he continues to lie in a deep coma and is not expected to recover.

The Israeli government continues to deny shooting Tom with intent. After months of delay, Israel has recently begun a Military Police investigation into Tom's killing.

We must keep Rachel, Brian, and Tom's stories alive. The world must demand credible explanations for what happened to each of them. Truth. The world, and especially people here in the United States, must hear about these tragedies and in doing so come to understand the magnitude of the violence and oppression that the Palestinian people have lived with for so long.

Rachel, Brian, and Tom were unarmed, nonviolent peace activists trying to prevent the demolition of Palestinian homes, orchards, gardens, wells—trying to support the Palestinian people who nonviolently resist daily by going about their lives as best they can in the face of an unimaginably oppressive occupation.

Rachel stood that March day before the Israeli bulldozer because of the failure of her own country and of the international community to stand for the innocents in Palestine. Rachel stood there that day protesting Israeli military actions that her own country is on record opposing yet fails to stop—actions that the U.S., in fact, contributes to through its funding of the Israeli military.

Rachel believed through the depth of her being that her nonviolent activism would make Palestinians, but also Israelis, Americans, and the world, more secure. She worked with Jewish-Americans and with Israelis who also work to end the occupation. She consulted with Israeli peace activists as she tried to better understand the destruction of the Palestinian water supply. She received guidance from a reservist in the Israeli military, a father of two teenage sons, who taught her Hebrew phrases to shout through her megaphone when she encountered bulldozer and tank operators.

As she lay dying, Rachel was held by one of her ISM friends who is Jewish and has cousins in Israel whom she fears for whenever she hears of a suicide bombing. Rachel wrote to me, "The scariest thing for non-Jewish Americans in talking about Palestinian self-determination is the fear of being or sounding anti-Semitic. Reading Chomsky's book and talking to my non-Zionist Jewish friends has helped me think about this. I just think we all have the right to be critical of government policies . . . any government policies . . . particularly government policies which we are funding."

After the Killing

Since these incidents, the International Solidarity Movement and other human rights groups in the Occupied Territories have come under attack.

On May 9, nearly 20 military vehicles surrounded the ISM media office, seized computers and video equipment, pillaged files and photos, broke equipment, and damaged office space. Activists were arrested and deported. Access to Gaza was severely restricted. Israel established new rules for foreigners entering Gaza requiring that they sign a statement in which they absolve Israel of all responsibility in the case of their injury or death.

On August 25, an ISM volunteer named Kate was with another international and three Palestinians delivering food to the Old City in Nablus when she was stopped by a jeep, taken into custody, and forced to sit at a makeshift base with two tanks, many jeeps, and armed vehicles. She writes:

> I cannot describe the horror. The soldiers were all around me and then there were clashes; rocks and glass were being thrown—sound bombs, tear gas, tank firing, machine guns,

automatic weapons. The whole nine yards were being shot and the soldiers were all next to me. They were shooting at the Palestinians. They shot someone in the head. Every time a child would look out the window, they would point their guns and scream at them and cock their triggers. For five hours, I was there next to the firing guns and tanks. I tried distracting them by talking to them, which worked quite a bit, so that they wouldn't notice Palestinians breaking curfew. I prayed, I prayed, and I prayed that God would warm their hearts so that they would stop this madness. I was so scared. They were all around me shooting. I knew that I was supposed to experience this, because now I have seen the war from the soldier's point of view. Now, I know what they do, say, somewhat feel, and how they act. . . . there is nothing I can tell you to express the pain I feel and what it was like being in the middle of the soldiers shooting and bombing my friends. I wish I could make you see, but then again, I wouldn't wish today on anyone. I am glad the soldiers released me.

More recently, on August 27, two internationals with ISM were deported after being held in an Israeli jail for 10 days after chaining themselves to the inside of a family home in the Balata refugee camp to try to prevent the Israeli Army from demolishing it, the home of Abu Salim, his wife and four children.

Huwaida Arraf wrote on August 26 of ISM:

We're frustrated with the politics of governments and the complacency that is allowing this to continue. There can be no *hudna* or "road map" without restraints put on the Israeli military and government. We are going to keep telling you what's happening on the ground in Palestine and urge you to take action. We are going to continue to organize to resist the Israeli occupation nonviolently, and urge you not to ignore us.

Our Search for Answers

In September my husband, Craig, and I went to Israel and Palestine. We wanted to walk where our daughter walked, to see what she saw, and to try to discover why she was killed.

We have called for an independent U.S. investigation. Rep. Brian Baird of Washington State and 50 cosponsors have offered a resolution in the House of Representatives, HCR 111, calling for the U.S. government to conduct a "full, fair, and expeditious investigation into the death of Rachel Corrie," and for the Israeli government and the U.S. government to work together to make sure that something like this doesn't happen again. Cosponsors include the following:

Neil Abercrombie (HI), Tammy Baldwin (WI), Earl Blumenauer (OR), Dave Camp (MI), Lois Capps (CA), John Conyers, Jr. (MI), Danny K. Davis (IL), Peter A. DeFazio (OR), Norman D. Dicks (WA), John D. Dingell (MI), Lloyd Doggett (TX), Jennifer Dunn (WA), Rahm Emanuel (IL), Anna G. Eshoo (CA), Bob Etheridge (NC), Sam Farr (CA), Raul M. Grijalva (AZ), Rush D. Holt (NJ), Michael M. Honda (CA), Jay Inslee (WA), Darrell E. Issa (CA), Jesse L. Jackson, Jr. (IL), Sheila Jackson-Lee (TX), Eddie Bernice Johnson (TX), Patrick J. Kennedy (RI), Carolyn C. Kilpatrick (MI), Ron Kind (WI), Dennis J. Kucinich (OH), Ray LaHood (IL), Rick Larsen (WA), Barbara Lee (CA), John Lewis (GA), Zoe Lofgren (CA), Edward J. Markey (MA), Jim McDermott (WA), James P. McGovern (MA), George Miller (CA), James P. Moran (VA), Sue Myrick (NC), Eleanor Holmes Norton (DC), James L. Oberstar (MN), John W. Olver (MA), Nick J. Rahall (WV), Martin Olav Sabo (MN), Adam Smith (WA), Fortney Pete Stark (CA), Mark Udall (CO), Melvin Watt (NC), Lynn C. Woolsey (CA), and David Wu (OR).

We have had some support from some newspapers. *The Houston Chronicle*, for example, has called for an independent investigation. Mecklenburg County in North Carolina and Berkeley, California, have passed resolutions calling for support of HCR 111. Over 70 national and local organizations have called on the U.S. government to conduct an independent investigation into Rachel's killing. These include the following:

Academics for Justice, American-Arab Anti-Discrimination Committee, American Friends Service Committee, Amnesty International, Arab American Institute, Episcopal Peace Fellowship, Fellowship of Reconciliation, Global Exchange, Grassroots International, The Green Party, Lutheran Peace Fellowship, Middle East Children's Alliance, Mothers for Peace—International, Muslim Public Affairs Council, Presbyterian Peace Fellowship, Tikkun Community, Unitarian-Universalist Peace Fellowship, Veterans for Peace, U.S. Campaign to End the Israeli Occupation, AFL-CIO-Washington State, Not in My Name—Chicago, NOW—Washington State, Jews Against the Occupation—New York, N.Y., Gush Shalom, and the Israeli Peace Bloc.

In Israel, the investigation into Rachel's killing remains closed, the bulldozer drivers fully exonerated. On March 19, Richard Boucher of the U.S. Department of State said in reference to Rachel: "When we have the death of an American citizen, we want to see it fully investigated. That is one of our key responsibilities overseas, to look after the welfare of American citizens and to find out what happened in situations like these."

Our family could not agree more, and that is why we continue to call for release of the complete copy of the Military Police Final Report with supporting evidence and for an independent U.S. investigation into Rachel's death. Based on our reading of the report, on a memorandum prepared by members of the American Embassy who have read it, and on six eyewitness statements from ISM members which conflict with the report findings, we believe there are unanswered questions and inconsistencies which demand further investigation.

The Israeli report concludes that the bulldozer operator could not see Rachel. Rachel was standing in front of a bulldozer and, according to ISM's practice, kept her eyes on the cab of the bulldozer, so that someone who wanted to look out could see her. We should remember that there was not only an operator in the bulldozer, but also a commander of the bulldozer. That day there were two bulldozers, two people in each bulldozer, plus an armored personnel carrier. That's a lot of eyes.

My husband, Craig, was a buck sergeant in Vietnam, in 1970, with the combat engineers and the first air cavalry division of the U.S. Army. He was in part in charge of bulldozers, and he says it was his responsibility and the responsibility of all who drove those bulldozers to know what was in front of that blade.

Craig notes that the Israeli inquiry quotes Rachel's autopsy report accurately, but adds that the doctor who did the autopsy suggested that her death was probably caused by tripping on the debris or perhaps by being covered by the debris. Craig wants to ask that doctor how many times he has seen somebody with many broken ribs, broken vertebrae of the spine, broken shoulder blades, and ruptures of a lung —all from tripping!

We arrived in Tel Aviv on September 12. From the 15th to the 20th, we were in the Gaza Strip, primarily in Rafah. There we met with many of Rachel's friends: those she had worked with in ISM, the families in whose homes she had stayed to try to offer some international protection, the children she had worked with in the youth parliament, and the community members she had met as she tried to build connections between Rafah and her hometown of Olympia, Washington.

In Rafah, we witnessed some of the violence of the occupation: the nightly machine-gun fire from tanks, and the fear of walking to a home after dark because the family that invited us to dinner lived on a street exposed to gunfire from Israeli watchtowers. We also witnessed the simple and profound dignity of our host walking slowly down the center of that same street to escort us from his home back to the relative safety of our car.

We went to the water wells where Rachel and other activists stood watch so municipal water workers could repair them. We saw there in the faces of the workers concern for our safety and for the safety of the children who followed us. At one of the wells, we saw, too, the shrapnel and bullet holes from the Israeli firing of the night before.

We returned a second time to a home along the border where we had lunched with a family on a previous day. On this latter visit, we found the wall of the room where we had eaten now pushed in and debris piled against the side of the house. We heard how the previous night the IDF soldiers had sent dogs into the house, followed by soldiers that remained for five hours harassing the family.

We saw the ditch they had dug in the front yard, destroying a garden, but proving that, indeed, there were no gun-running tunnels.

We visited the site of Rachel's death. The home she was protecting still stands. Because of its location along the border strip in an area where bulldozers are frequently working, the Israeli military wanted 20 minutes' notice before our arrival, wanted to have a description of the vehicle we would come in, the license plate identification, and the number of people in the car. We complied. Prior to driving to the border area, we called our assigned contact in the IDF and provided all of this information. The Israeli military knew who was coming to Dr. Samir's home. But shortly after our arrival, as we were preparing to join the family for lunch, Palestinians in our group anxiously alerted us to activity outside. An armored personnel carrier had taken a position across the street, approximately 30 yards from the door. When Craig looked through a crack in the garden (the same crack from which Dr. Samir had on March 16 witnessed Rachel's killing), he saw a bulldozer heading straight for the house.

I felt as though we had been trapped. Craig immediately called back to our IDF contact to report what was happening and how we felt about it. About five minutes later he received a call back from the captain wanting to know, "Where are they now?" By this time, the bulldozer had changed course and was, instead of approaching the house, moving sideways to it. This seemed a shockingly aggressive and provocative action by the Israeli military, considering that they absolutely knew who we were and why we had come.

After the machines had moved away and I felt safer, I was, in a way, grateful that it had happened, because it gave me a chance to see the bulldozers and APC's and how they operate.

We also saw the high, steel border wall being constructed from west to east, separating the land, neighborhoods, and families of Rafah in Palestine from Rafah in Egypt.

We witnessed the voracious appetite of the Israeli bulldozers, consuming ever one more block of one community's homes in the name of another community's security.

We visited with groups that are continuing projects in Rachel's name: a kindergarten with its smiling children chanting a song of welcome at the top of their lungs, and a youth cultural center with its plans for a library and computer center still in search of funding. We planted olive trees and drank sweet tea with friends.

And we learned that in her adopted city of Rafah, as in Olympia, Rachel was always expected just around the corner, with her bright smile, her friendly concern, and usually with a small band of children.

Then we left Gaza and experienced the lonely walk through Erez checkpoint, where we were nearly the only people passing through, and our new friends—Rachel's friends—were left trapped in Gaza, waving goodbye to us. It was emotional. My husband said to me, "It's like all the movies we've watched where someone is finally walking out of prison and they leave their friends behind."

We spent time in Jerusalem and the West Bank as well. In Jerusalem we went to a memorial at the site of a bus bombing and learned of Shiri Nagari, Rachel's age, who was killed last year. We listened to her uncle describe Shiri with the same love and pride that our family uses when speaking of Rachel. We learned that the pain does not stop at the Green Line.

In the West Bank we witnessed the strategy of separation taking physical form in the web of fences, walls, identification cards, and checkpoints that separate not only Palestinians from Israelis, but Palestinians from Palestinians, farmers from their fields, children from their classrooms, workers from their jobs, the sick from their healthcare, the elderly from their grandchildren, municipalities from their water supplies, and ultimately, a people from their land.

As I stood in the checkpoint coming from Ramallah into Jerusalem, we had to wait about 45 minutes—a short wait, relatively speaking. We were packed into this little area with families and children. I think it was there that I really felt the humiliation that Palestinians feel. At one point a gentleman looked at me and spoke quietly in English: "This is the occupation." It affected me deeply to think about that daily humiliation of trying to get from work to home, from home to school, from home to medical treatment.

We saw acres of crumpled aluminum, the jagged and torn remains of the once thriving marketplace of Nazlat Isa, a stark reminder of the occupation's devastating effect on the economy of both peoples.

In East Jerusalem, we witnessed the horror on a woman's face and listened to her screaming at Israeli soldiers as her cousin's home was being demolished nearby. We watched as two determined members of Rabbis for Human Rights challenged the soldiers blocking the street that led to the demolition site.

And on the eve of the Jewish new year, we celebrated Rosh Hashanah with Israeli friends in their synagogue and home. We shared their bread, beets, and pomegranates, their stories of the last year, and their hopes for the new one. We shared their music: the songs of so many centuries of suffering and courage, but also, through it all, of joy.

Before leaving to return home, Craig and I gave a statement to the press, the last lines of which recalled something my daughter wrote to me about the occupation:

> This has to stop. I think it is a good idea for us all to drop everything and devote our lives to making this stop. I don't think it's an extremist thing to do anymore. I still really want to dance around to Pat Benatar and have boyfriends and make comics for my coworkers. But I also want this to stop.

Update by the editors

New York City—Cindy and Craig Corrie, Rachel's parents, continue to organize against all odds, and to resist against all odds.

In April 2006, the Rachel Corrie Foundation sponsored a conference in the Corries' home state of Washington, the purpose of which was to find ways of bringing about a just end to the Palestinian-Israeli conflict. Proposals included promoting more eyewitness visits to the Occupied Territories and supporting the campaign to divest from companies, especially Caterpillar, that are involved in the construction of Israel's illegal settlements and its illegal wall, both of which are being built on confiscated Palestinian land.

The Corries received international attention in March 2006, when the "progressive" New York Theatre Workshop cancelled its planned production of *My Name Is Rachel Corrie* because it feared offending unnamed Jewish groups. The one-person play, based on Rachel's own journal and e-mails, had a successful run in London, and its cancellation in New York triggered worldwide debate. Writing in the *Nation* (April 3, 2006), Philip Weiss reflected:

> In this way, Corrie's words appear to have had more impact than her death. The House bill calling for a U.S. investigation of her killing died in committee, with only seventy-eight votes and little media attention. But the naked admission by a left-leaning cultural outlet that it would subordinate its own artistic judgment to pro-Israel views had served as a smoking gun for those who have tried to press the discussion in this country of Palestinian human rights.

Good news came in June, 2006, when James Hammerstein Productions said it would bring the critically acclaimed play to the Minetta Lane Theater in New York's Greenwich Village. The play was scheduled for 48 performances, opening on October 5 and closing November 19.

More on the Corries' efforts is available on Rachel's web site (www.rachelcorriefoundation.org).

A Polish Boy in Palestine

By David Neunuebel

David Neunuebel is co-founder and principal in Neunuebel Minor, a financial consulting and wealth management practice located in Santa Barbara, CA. He is also founder of Americans for a Just Peace in the Middle East. *In this December 2005 issue of* The Link *he tells how he fell into the "black hole" called Palestine-Israel.*

Very often I'm asked, "What's a nice Polish white boy like you doing in a conflict like this?"—meaning the Israeli-Palestinian conflict.

Let me explain. In 1997 I fell into this black hole called Palestine-Israel and now I can't get out. It all started when I was in seventh grade.

My mother was Polish, grew up poor and was often treated badly, being called "Pollock" and any number of other pejoratives most of her life. This kind of treatment was very formative in the development of her moral compass. She was always caring for others and treating them, especially those of color, with grace and dignity.

For most of my life my day-to-day contact was with white people, but when I went to Brentwood High School in St. Louis in 1961 I began to have daily contact with blacks. One day I brought my best friend Steve home for lunch. The next day at school and in my neighborhood, I was called "nigger lover," because Steve was black. When I told my mother, she said to invite Steve's whole family to lunch next time.

Every summer my family traveled to Florida to visit my grandparents. Along the way we'd see "White Only" drinking fountains and "White Only" restrooms, and "Colored Only" drinking fountains and "Colored Only" restrooms. I'd never seen this before, but I'd always drink out of the "Colored Only" drinking fountains and use the "Colored Only" restrooms.

When I got drafted into the U.S. Army in 1966 I made friends with a lot of black guys. One time, while in Texas, my friends and I went to a restaurant where my friends were refused service because they were black. I was stunned and angry. I wanted to do something, but my friends said we should just walk away.

Another time, on a Texas beach during spring break, I watched dozens of white kids beat up four black kids, throwing full beer bottles down on their faces at point blank range, and setting their brand new car on fire.

All these experiences formed much of the basis of my perceptions of what I was to see years later in Palestine-Israel. The time was the late 1990s. A friend of mine, Dr. Richard Cahill, then Director of the Middle East Studies Program (MESP) for the Council of Christian Colleges based in Cairo, Egypt, asked me to assist him in taking his students to Palestine-Israel.

A few days after arriving in Cairo, I boarded a bus with Rick and 22 students and traveled through the Sinai Peninsula. When we came to the end of the Sinai and were about to enter Israel through the Rafah crossing at Gaza, Israeli soldiers instructed our driver to pull over and park. We got off the bus with our luggage. Suddenly our bus driver drove off, back into the Sinai, leaving us there alone. It was a little alarming, since most of us thought this was the bus that would take us all the way.

Rick directed us into the checkpoint building and told us to say only the minimum of what was asked and not to let the Israelis stamp a visa in our passports; later in the semester the students were going to Syria and Lebanon, which would not allow entry if they knew we had been in Israel. When we got through passport control, we gathered outside on the other side of the checkpoint. We were now busless in Gaza.

Rick made a call on his mobile phone and spoke with our new driver, who had been detained at other checkpoints and was running late. Rick decided to use the time to give the students an exam. He handed out maps of the Middle East without any names of countries, cities, or landmarks. The goal was to name as many countries, capitals, rivers, mountain ranges, and other landmarks as possible before the bus arrived. It was a good exercise and something these kids knew a lot better than I did. It dawned on me that, like me, most Americans know very little about the Middle East.

The bus arrived and we began the long trip to Jerusalem. When we arrived at the Old City at Stephen's Gate we gathered our luggage and walked about 100 yards down the old stone street to the Austrian Hospice, since our bus was not allowed into the Old City. After we checked in we met in a conference room where Rick gave us an overview of the next few weeks. It was an eclectic itinerary that had us going many places and meeting several people and organizations.

A year later I made this same trip with Rick and his students and have returned every year since, once as a delegate with the Christian Peacemaker Teams (CPT), and several times on my own.

Let me share some of the epiphanies on those trips that changed my life.

My Mentors

Allegra Pacheco. The first of several times I met Allegra Pacheco was with Rick and the students. She is a Jewish Israeli attorney who grew up in an Orthodox Jewish family in Brooklyn, New York. As she began to describe her work of defending Palestinians in Israeli courts and the situation on the ground in Israel and the Occupied Territories, I asked her, "How did a nice Jewish girl like you end up defending Palestinians?" She gave us a short tour of her growing-up years in Brooklyn and how Leah Tsemel, a Jewish woman who became a lawyer and human rights activist, was her hero.

Allegra explained to us that there are two sets of laws, one for Jews and one for Palestinians. When a student asked, "Isn't Israel a democracy?" Allegra explained that Israel's Basic Law states that Israel is a "Jewish and democratic state," but that this does not mean equal rights for all its citizens. It amounts to "democracy for some, dispossession for others," she said.

She pointed out that Israel does not have a constitution to determine who is (or is not) a citizen, nor has it ever legally established its geographic borders. She said, "In any other place in the world, a country established for the benefit of only one ethnicity would be distasteful, but here, it's the norm." Israeli policy is guided by Zionist ideology, which deems that Israel will be a Jewish state. "When a government wants to establish a state based on only one ethnicity," she noted, "it never works for long."

In the Occupied Territories there is an entirely different set of laws from those within the Green Line. (The Green Line is the 1949 armistice line separating Israel from the West Bank.) Israel recently withdrew its fewer than 6,000 settlers from Gaza, where they had been living among 1.4 million Palestinians. In the West Bank— excluding East Jerusalem, which Israel illegally annexed in 1980, and where 200,000 settlers live—the Jewish state continues to add to the 250,000 settlers who live among 2.5 million Palestinians. Here the Civil Administration administers military law to Palestinians, while Jewish settlers are governed by Israeli law.

Allegra explained that in her opinion all the settlers and settlements are illegal according to international law, particularly the Geneva Conventions. When a student asked how Israel gets away with it, she said that Israelis and American supporters of Israel have worked hard to ensure that the United States supports and protects Israel under all circumstances, even when Israel violates international laws and commits human rights violations.

Allegra went on to explain one method Israel uses to steal land from Palestinians for Jewish-only neighborhoods and settlements: demolish Palestinian homes under the pretext that they lack building permits. The problem with this, she said, is that when most of the Palestinians built their homes there were no permits to be gotten, since the Israeli government didn't even exist. But now, a Jew can move to Israel from New York or Los Angeles, instantly become an

Israeli citizen with all rights and benefits, build a house near a Palestinian home that has been there for hundreds of years, and have the Palestinian home demolished to make room for this new Jewish-only house.

Allegra said that Jewish Israelis still have this idea of "preserving their privilege," and that Americans need to understand where their tax dollars are going in support of Israel. She added that if Americans didn't put up with racism in the United States, they shouldn't put up with it in Israel. She said it took South Africa a hundred years to bring down apartheid and it may take that long in Israel, too.

Bob Lang. Because I think it is important to understand the viewpoint of the settlers who occupy Palestinian land, I include Bob Lang. I met him with Rick and the students on my first visit to Palestine-Israel. He is an American Jew who lives in the all-Jewish settlement of Efrat just outside Jerusalem.

Bob spoke perfect "American" English and began telling us why he moved from America. As a Jew he wanted to "return" to the "land God gave the Jews" and to fulfill the Zionist dream of creating a Jewish state in the land of Israel. He told us how Jews had been persecuted throughout history and how Zionism, an ideology that Jews should gather together to create their own state for their own protection, got its beginning in 1897 with Theodore Hertzl at the first Zionist conference in Basel, Switzerland. After the Holocaust this ideology took on a new urgency, and the Zionist leadership determined that Palestine, which embodied the ancient Holy Land for Jews promised to Abraham by God, would be the place for the Jewish state.

He showed us maps to illustrate where Israel was within the Middle East. He said that little Israel is surrounded by larger, hostile, Arab states. Therefore Israel must defend itself. After the 1967 war this included expanding Jewish settlements throughout Judea and Samaria, a.k.a the West Bank, which is where Efrat is located.

As he kept referring to Israel's small, defenseless size, I asked him, "Doesn't Israel have nuclear, biological, and chemical weapons and the largest, best-equipped military in the Middle East?" Bob concurred and re-emphasized the necessity of all this because Israel is surrounded by such large, hostile Arab states. I said that when I was in grade school we had maps with all the states in the United States in their proper geographic size, but we also had different maps sizing the states on, say, cotton production or orange production. These maps would show Mississippi larger than Alaska because it produced significantly more cotton, that Alaska would be the size of Delaware. So I asked Lang, "If we sized Israel based on its nuclear weapons and military capability it wouldn't be small at all. In fact, it would be the largest state in the area by a huge margin and dwarf these Arab states, not in land mass but in what really counted, wouldn't it? Or if we sized Israel by its economy and per capita income, again, it would be the largest state in the area." Bob responded that the reality was that Israel is a very small state surrounded by hostile Arab neighbors who want to destroy it, so Israel must do all it can to defend itself.

Jessica Montell. Jessica Montell is the Director of B'Tselem, the Israeli Information Center for Human Rights in the Occupied Territory, on the web at www.btselem.org. Her work is to monitor, document, and report human rights abuses and violations of international law in the Occupied Territories. She told us how difficult it is for Palestinians to get around, not only from the West Bank to, say, Tel Aviv, but, as the Israelis set up more and more blockades and checkpoints, even within the West Bank. Palestinians can't even go from Ramallah to Birzeit, which is a mere 10 miles away, without having to go through several checkpoints, which might take several hours. Sometimes they can't get through at all. As a result, Palestinians can't get to their jobs, go to school, or get to a hospital. She reported that there are several cases of women being unable to get to a hospital to have a baby, and that an alarming number of women are forced to give birth at checkpoints; sometimes the baby dies, in a few cases even the mother has died.

She told us of one young girl, written up in one of B'Tselem's reports, who had to get dialysis treatment at a hospital that was only a few miles from her home. But because of the checkpoints and blockades she had to make a three-hour trip on potholed back roads.

Then she had to do the whole thing over again to return home. This was her life in trying to get proper medical treatment. Jessica added that Palestinian ambulance drivers are often shot at by the Israeli Army, and sometimes killed, even after they've been given approval by the army for safe travel.

Jessica said she and every other Israeli never experience this kind of living and go about their daily lives virtually unaffected by any of this.

Then Jessica told us about water, and how Israel has strategically placed several important settlements in the West Bank on the water aquifers in order to control them, leaving Palestinians little access to water. (These are the "established neighborhoods" President Bush has assured Ariel Sharon that Israel will be able to keep in any peace settlement.)

But B'Tselem is also critical of Palestinian violence. Jessica said she can't understand how someone could blow himself up and that these acts were clearly terrorist acts and in violation of international law. She pointed out that Israel has a legal right to defend itself and its citizens, but added that many of the methods Israel uses—collective punishment, extrajudicial assassinations, and bombing entire neighborhoods—are clearly violations of international humanitarian provisions.

Christian Peacemaker Teams. To get to Hebron from Jerusalem I had to take several taxis, each taking me only up to the next blockade or, if a checkpoint, as far as the color of its license plate would allow. At each blockade I'd get out and go over a mound of dirt and boulders with other Palestinians to get into another taxi on the other side. Then that taxi would take me as far as it could go. On and on this would go until I finally got to Hebron. During all this up and down, in and out, I'd noted a highway a couple hundred yards away with cars and trucks driving at highway speeds with no trouble. That road, it was explained, was what is called a bypass road and is for Jews only. So traveling the Palestinian way amounted to taking three hours and five taxis to make a 20-minute trip.

Upon the signing of the Hebron Agreement in January 1997, Hebron was divided into two parts: H-1, an area of some 11 square miles (80 percent of the city) with 115,000 Palestinians, was handed over to complete Palestinian control. H-2, in which 35,000 Palestinians and 500 settlers live, remained under Israeli security control. H-1, however, can still be and often is controlled by the Israelis if they want to shut it down, so Palestinians have only "a mirage of control."

Settlers in Hebron mostly live in the settlement of Kiryat Arba, and most are followers of the radical Rabbi Meir Kahane, the founder of the Kach Party, a racist group that both the Israelis and the U.S. consider a Jewish terrorist group.

One follower of Kahane, Brooklyn-born physician Baruch Goldstein, on February 25, 1994, during the Muslim holy month of Ramadan, decided to actuate the Zionist dream of annihilating the Arab existence in Palestine by entering the Ibrahimi Mosque, the Tomb of the Patriarchs in Hebron, and, turning his automatic weapon on the Muslim worshipers, killing 29 and wounding over 100, before other Palestinians killed him. The Jewish settlers placed an inscription on his gravesite that reads:

> *Here lies the saint, Dr. Baruch Kappel Goldstein, blessed be the memory of the righteous and holy man, may the Lord avenge his blood, who devoted his soul to the Jews, Jewish religion and Jewish land. His hands are innocent and his heart is pure. He was killed as a martyr of God on the 14th of Adar, Purim, in the year 5754 (1994).*

I had met the Christian Peacemaker Teams (CPT) on two occasions with Rick and the student groups and eventually joined a CPT delegation. CPT is a group from the Mennonite/Quaker tradition of nonviolence whose motto is "Getting in the Way" of violence and injustice.

When I was a CPT delegate our team bought groceries in H-1 before we went to the CPT apartment in H-2. To go from H-1 to H-2 we had to go through a fenced-off Israeli checkpoint. Walking from H-1 to H-2 was weird because the noise and hustle and bustle of Palestinians shopping, shouting, and honking in H-1 dropped like a rock to near dead silence in H-2. There were no people on the streets of H-2 except for Jewish settlers and Israeli soldiers. All the Palestinians were under curfew and could not leave their homes for any reason. The curfew had been going on for several weeks, with only brief trips allowed out of the house to get food and provisions.

It was Shabbat, Saturday, the Jewish day of worship, when we entered H-2. Dozens of observant Jews on the streets, but no Palestinians. As we carried our bags of goods and supplies through the crowd of settlers, a teenage Jewish boy tried to slap my camera from my hand. When he was unsuccessful he kicked me as I passed. I quickly turned to protect myself, but he backed away and we were allowed to pass. I was told later that the kid was representative of most of the Jewish young people who live in Hebron, many of whom carry American-made M-16 rifles.

Once in the CPT apartment, there was a frantic phone call from a Palestinian farmer saying that Jewish settlers were destroying his crops and tearing out his irrigation pipes. One of the full-time CPT members asked if anyone wanted to go along to help protect the farmer in the nearby valley. I grabbed a second camera and we were off. That night I filmed a group of settler kids setting fire to tires and the farmer's land and rampaging through his farm, tearing out the irrigation pipes.

When the Israeli Army arrived they did nothing. In fact, the settler kids made fun of them and ran them ragged. The CPT member said that if these kids had been Palestinians, most of them would have been shot or beaten or both.

The entire time in Hebron with CPT was pretty much like this. Emergency calls from Palestinians for assistance, CPT responding. You might think CPT doesn't accomplish much, but simply being present, intervening in situations, and speaking with settlers, Israeli soldiers, and Palestinians in a gentle voice often calms things down. But of course, sometimes not. Several times CPT members have been beaten so severely by settlers that they required hospitalization. Still, the Palestinians of Hebron are grateful they are there.

Jeff Halper. Dr. Jeff Halper lives in a modest house in West Jerusalem. He is an American Jew from Minnesota and has been Professor of Anthropology at Ben-Gurion University in the Negev for 20 years. He is currently the coordinator for the Israeli Committee Against House Demolition, on the web at *www.icahd.org.* ICAHD is an organization made up of Israelis and Palestinians who try to prevent the Israeli government from confiscating Palestinian land and demolishing homes.

In a meeting with Jeff, someone asked why so many Palestinian homes have been demolished. Jeff pointed out that Palestinian homes are destroyed to make room for Jewish-only settlements in the Occupied Territories or to control the Arab population within Israel. In East Jerusalem, for example, the Israeli government's confiscation policy is designed to annex all the area around Jerusalem in order to render it impossible for a future Palestinian state to have any claim to Jerusalem.

Jeff said the pretext of "security" is always used to justify the expropriation of land and the demolition of homes. When a settlement is established in the Occupied Territory, a bypass road must also be built in order to provide a travel route for the settlers to go to and from Israel. This means that a corridor of hundreds of yards on each side of the bypass road must be established for "security purposes," which means that even more Palestinian land is expropriated and homes demolished to make room for this wide swath of highway. Needless to say, these roads are for Jews only.

Jeff explained that a legal justification for the demolition is that Palestinians have no permits to build. He said, "It is the official policy of the Civil Administration not to give permits to Palestinians."

Jeff mentioned that over 100,000 houses have been built for Jews in the Occupied Territories, while none have been built for Palestinians. And, when it comes to water, Israeli settlers get as much water as they want, and often have green lawns and even swimming pools, while Palestinians get one-tenth as much water as settlers and pay twice as much for it. He said it is not uncommon to be in a Palestinian village starving for water and look over the fence into a settlement and see kids playing in swimming pools.

I asked Jeff how other Israelis feel about all this, and he said most Israelis just want what he called "industrial peace," peace that will keep the Palestinians "quiet" and "over there" so they, the Israelis, can go about their day-to-day business. The basic operational model that Israel has for the Palestinians is that of a prison, and Palestinians need to shut up, know their place, remain in their cells, and not forget who the guards are. If they forget their place or get "uppity," they will be put down harshly.

Ilan Pappe. Dr. Ilan Pappe is Senior Lecturer of Political Science at Haifa University and the head of the Emil Touma Institute for Palestinian Studies in Israel. Born in 1954 to a German Jewish family in Haifa, at the age of eighteen he began military service in the Israeli Army, which introduced him to other groups and to the host of social problems facing Israeli society.

In the 1970s, at Hebrew University as an undergraduate in the department of Middle Eastern history, he was exposed to the plight of the Palestinians in Israel. It was then that he found his love for history and formed his belief that the present cannot be understood and the future changed without first trying to decipher its historical dimensions.

It was clear to him that this could not be done freely inside Israel, especially if its own history was to be the subject matter. So he went to Oxford in 1984 as a PhD student. His thesis was on the 1948 war in Palestine. He wrote about the Zionist intentions to ethnically cleanse Palestine of the indigenous population.

His extensive research brought him face to face with declassified Jewish archives of the period. He discovered things that he'd never heard or known before, things that contradicted the official Zionist narrative he'd been taught as a child.

As Pappe discussed his work with me in his office at Haifa University, he pointed out several Zionist myths. The first myth he spoke of was what he called the myth of David and Goliath. This is the myth that the Jews (Zionists) were a small, weak, defenseless, poorly numbered and poorly armed group defending themselves against the massive, overpowering, well armed, Arab hordes. Winning the war made Israelis Invincible Supermen. "Even Hollywood portrays the Israelis as heroic and the Arabs as dirty cowards, an example of which is the movie *Exodus*," he said.

He pulled out maps of that period which showed large, thick arrows from the Arab side and small, thin arrows from the Israeli side which were meant to suggest the size and strength of the competing armies, thus feeding the propaganda that the Jews were small and defenseless.

The truth is that the Jews had the upper hand from the beginning, financially, militarily and politically. The Jewish leadership knew exactly the balance of power and that they had the advantage. This was partly due to agreements they made with Jordan, the strongest Arab military at the time, not to attack in specified areas. This substantially reduced any Arab threat, although the Jordan army did fight when the Zionists reneged on their promise not to invade areas around Jerusalem.

Pappe states, "For us, as Israelis, this was very important, because it was not just a question of whether we were superhuman or not, because there was a very normal explanation as to why we won the war, which had nothing to do with our being David and the Arabs being Goliath. The real myth was that Israel was supposedly on the eve of a second holocaust or extermination. It was not. Jewish leaders produced an atmosphere of fear to raise the commitment from others. But they knew that such a threat did not exist."

Selling this myth to America was also very important as we can observe today in the overwhelming bias the U.S. government shows toward Israel and against Arabs and Palestinians. It also shows up in the level of political intimidation, if not political extortion, of anyone in Congress who might speak out in favor of Palestinian human rights.

The second myth he spoke of was that the Arab leadership told the Palestinians to leave their homes because the war was coming. "This is the official Israeli narrative taught in schools," Pappe said, and is considered the primary reason Palestinians left their homes and became permanent refugees. "This is not true," he said, "they were forced from their homes, driven away by the invading Jewish army." In the special archives in London, British documents of every radio transmission from 1936 through the 1948 war reveal no proof of any such messages transmitted by the Arabs. Pappe says, "It was Israeli propaganda, a myth to cleanse the Jewish conscience of any responsibility for the Palestinian refugee problem."

Pappe stated that, on March 10, 1948, the Jewish leadership decided that the new Jewish State would take over 80 percent of Palestine even though a minority of Jews lived where over 900,000 Palestinians also lived. This decision was made before the 1948 war. He said there was a specific decision to "ethnically cleanse Palestine of Palestinians." The vast majority of Arabs were expelled by force. People who had lived there for thousands of year were expelled. Five hundred villages were destroyed along with 11 towns making 700,000 people refugees. Houses were looted and destroyed, careers were stopped.

The Zionists who were responsible for this, according to Pappe, were David Ben-Gurion, Moshe Dayan, and "Mr. Transfer" himself, a name even the Jewish leadership used to describe Yosef Weitz. Weitz was responsible for the transfer of Palestinians and the settlement of their land with Jews. Before the war Weitz looked at all the fertile land and determined which part he wanted for the Jewish Agency, and created transfer committees in each region to deal with how to execute the transfer. The Zionists used intimidation and scare tactics, trucks to transfer people, and even massacres.

Pappe pointed out that there was more than one massacre committed by the Zionists. The massacre at Deir Yassin is the only one the Israeli government has ever admitted to, but "to suggest that there was only one massacre is ridiculous," he said, "There were dozens of massacres."

The third myth he spoke of is one that suggests that the Israelis extended their hand in peace and the Arabs refused. The truth, according to Pappe's research, is the exact opposite. The Arab side offered to reach a compromise with Israel based on U.N. guidelines and international law to divide the land into two states, to allow Palestinian refugees to return to their homes, and to internationalize Jerusalem. Even United States President Truman supported this Arab position and found it to be quite reasonable. In fact, the United States government exerted some pressure on Israel to accept the deal. But

Israel refused. From his research Pappe concludes: "The Arabs offered to negotiate a peace and the Israelis rejected it."

Telling Others What I Saw and Learned

On each of those trips with the students, one of the things they always asked was, "Does anybody know this is going on?" Each time I returned from Palestine-Israel I felt a strong obligation to tell about these new realities I'd discovered. I found myself as incensed about the injustices Israel perpetrates on the Palestinians as I was by the injustices white people perpetrated on blacks in America.

I began to write letters-to-the-editor about the water inequities, collective punishment of Palestinians, the expropriation of land and demolition of homes to make room for Jewish-only settlements and bypass roads, and extrajudicial assassinations. While some of my letters were published in my local newspaper, many were not.

After a while I began to buy ad space to tell what I felt needed to be told. (You can see several of the ads we've created on our web site: www.ajpme.org under "Flyers"). As I began to buy my message into the public arena with these ads, I started receiving positive inquiries from people in my community. I was, indeed, getting a message across and, for the most part, being well received. People wanted to know who we were, could they help, could they join. The problem was, there was nothing to join. I was it. Just a guy who went, heard, saw and needed to tell about it. As Martin Luther King, Jr. once said, "A time comes when silence is betrayal." I was doing a small thing and people were responding. But advertising is an expensive sport. I needed to find a better way.

Beyond the Mirage

One of the most important things that happened in America during the Civil Rights movement was when Americans saw, on black and white TV, the brutal treatment of blacks by whites. Blacks were beaten with clubs by white cops, devastated by water hoses, and attacked by dogs. There was something wrong with America and most

Americans didn't like what they saw. Many would say, "This isn't us, this isn't who we are as Americans, this isn't who we want to be," and the Civil Rights movement came into full swing. So I bought a digital video camera. I filmed each trip to Palestine-Israel and every interview in order to make a documentary to show the American people a view of Israel that is generally unavailable to them.

I finished my first documentary, *Beyond The Mirage: The Face of the Occupation,* in June 2002, just in time to attend the American-Arab Anti-Discrimination Committee convention in Washington, DC. I purchased a booth to display my ads and flyers, photos and other materials, and showed the documentary on a 36-inch TV by our booth. As the documentary ran over and over, people came by to watch it and ask about it. I'd taken two hundred copies of the documentary and returned home with none. It was very validating and encouraging.

It was at this conference that I first met John Mahoney, Director of AMEU. He asked if he could get some copies to sell through AMEU, which he has done ever since. He's been an enormous encouragement to me and my work.

Americans for a Just Peace in the Middle East

As I continued to receive positive feedback from more and more people in my community, I became curious as to just how many people felt as I did. I thought maybe I could organize and make something out of our shared ideas and values. So I decided to contact all the people who'd responded and see if they'd show up at a meeting at our community library. I expected ten people. More than 50 showed up.

As I presented who I was and what I was trying to do it became evident that a more formal organization ought to be created. My feeling was we should become an official 501(c)3 nonprofit. This way we would be a legitimate California corporation and donations would be tax-deductible. The next step was what to call ourselves. We spent a lot of time throwing around different ideas until we settled on Americans for a Just Peace in the Middle East (AJPME).

The next day I contacted some attorney friends in Washington, D.C. and over the next several months they worked on incorporating us in California and preparing the application to the IRS for nonprofit status. In November 2002 we were granted 501(c)3 nonprofit status and have been operational as such ever since.

Imagine...

On a return trip to Palestine-Israel in 2003, I was waiting for a taxi in the lobby of my hotel with my translator. We were going to Ramallah to see Yassir Arafat and then on to Birzeit University to interview students about the rigors of getting an education. In the lobby, I overheard an older couple who were also waiting for their taxi. Their conversation revealed that they were in agreement with many of my concerns regarding the Palestinian-Israeli conflict, so I went over to talk with them. The man, in his eighties, was an Auschwitz survivor and, as we chatted, it became clear he was very critical of Israeli policies against the Palestinians. I asked him if I could interview him. He agreed but said it would have to be another time since their taxi had just arrived.

The next day, I approached him in the hotel garden café and asked again about an interview on camera. He said he would be happy to be interviewed. I ran to my room, got my camera equipment, found a quiet place in the hotel, put a microphone on him and interviewed him for an hour.

His name is Hajo Meyer. He is a Jew who lives in The Netherlands and is part of a Jewish group that works to show the world that Israeli policies toward the Palestinians are unjust and need to change. The interview resulted in my second documentary, "Imagine...," which focuses on the state of Palestinian education under Israeli occupation. Meyer introduces the video by noting that one of the things he learned in Auschwitz was that you can kill people without gas chambers by denying young people access to education. He explains: "One of the most important things for any conscious living being is to develop his or her own potential. If you deny young people access to education, you rob their future. If you have no future you have no life. If you have not developed yourself to the full, you are at least handicapped, and although you may still walk around, you are dead."

The documentary notes that during the first intifada, Israel made it effectively illegal for Palestinians to pursue their education. Students were arrested for attending underground classes in people's homes and community centers, and even for carrying their books in public. Today over 250,000 Palestinian students under Israeli occupation cannot go to school because of the wall Israel has illegally put up in the northern part of the West Bank. Elsewhere, Palestinians are confronted with checkpoints and roadblocks all over the West Bank that make it extremely difficult to attend classes on a daily basis.

The vigorous Mr. Meyer concludes the documentary with these words: "When the Nazis gassed the Jews the world was silent. Now, the world is silent while the Jews or the Israelis harass, humiliate, and steal away land from the Palestinians. And the world is silent. And I want to awake the world."

"Imagine…," which runs for 15 minutes, and is particularly good for campus groups and seminars, is also available through AMEU.

Final Thoughts

On Facing Opposition. As I began to move beyond letters-to-the-editor to paid advertisements to get my message across, I occasionally got hate mail and hate phone calls. I was becoming known to the community, in good ways and in threatening ways.

As things moved toward organizing AJPME, the attacks on the World Trade Center occurred. That night a call was left on our voice mail stating, "You have blood on your hands. You better watch out for the FBI. We're going to get you."

The attacks on the World Trade Center were unsettling enough, but to get a call like this was of deep concern. I immediately called the police and gave them the access code to our voice mail service. They listened to the message, called me back and said, "You better call the FBI." I immediately called the local FBI. The next morning, about 4:00 a.m., I got another call from the same caller who said pretty much the same thing and asked if I'd had any contact from the FBI. I told him, "Yes, in fact I've called the FBI and had them listen to your voice mail." He hung up and I never heard from him again.

A few days later a local FBI agent called me. We talked about the call which he also listened to. He asked about AJPME and said he wanted to meet with me. He came to Santa Barbara where we spent a few hours talking about the incidents. He took lots of notes. I gave him our AJPME brochures and literature. He was very nice and understanding. He also seemed interested in the work of AJPME. As we finished the meeting he said he would contact me later about coming to their office to discuss all this with an FBI Middle East expert. He gave me his card and told me to call him any time.

Several months later he called and asked me to come to Ventura to meet with the Middle East expert. About a week later I went down for this meeting. I met first with my agent and his associates in a small conference room. A few moments later another man entered the room, introduced himself, said he was an agent specializing in the Middle East and gave me his card. I gave him the whole story about how I got involved in the Middle East, specifically Palestine-Israel, and how I started AJPME. I gave him our materials and brochures and gave each person in the room a DVD of our documentary, *Beyond the Mirage: The Face of the Occupation*. They were all very interested. We finished the interview in a couple hours; I left and have never heard from them since.

On Security and Freedom. It seems to me that the rhetoric of this whole thing, that Israel needs security and the Palestinians need to be free, is backwards. I think it's the other way around. The Palestinians need security and Israel needs freedom, freedom from Zionism. As Jeff Halper puts it, to attempt to create a state for Jews only, especially with such a large indigenous Palestinian population present, is, "in the modern sense, ethnic cleansing." You cannot do it and still call yourself a democracy.

I realize that it is often not the "accepted wisdom" of many Americans whom I meet. I encourage them to look at the videos and to read many excellent books on the subject. But, most of all, I urge them to go, as I did, and see the situation with their own eyes. As Rachel Corrie wrote in one of her last e-mails home to her parents before an Israeli soldier killed her with a Caterpillar bulldozer, "No amount of reading, attendance at conferences, documentary viewing and word of mouth could have prepared me for the reality of the situation here. You just can't imagine it unless you see it."

This conflict must stop. The whole world is at risk. But it will not stop unless there is a just peace. If the Israelis, in their quest for security, feel it is necessary to build a wall around themselves, fine. But they should build it on the Green Line and not throughout the West Bank, further destroying Palestinian lives and reducing them to living in Bantustans, rendering a two-state solution impossible. In a world that has recently seen the fall of the Berlin Wall and the Iron Curtain, to build a wall in the name of security is antithetical to modern reason and is unjust in the way it is preceding.

Former Israeli Prime Minister Shimon Perez once stated, "You can't expect 100 percent security unless you give the other people 100 percent freedom. Israel's future security depends more on a just peace for Palestinians than on borders marked by barbed wire and fortifications." There is a better way.

Miroslav Volf, Professor of Theology at Yale Divinity school and a Croatian who survived his own country's conflicts with the Serbs, in his book *Exclusion & Embrace: A Theological Exploration of Identity, Otherness & Reconciliation,* states, "When we are looking at each other through the sights of our guns we see only the rightness of our own cause. We think more about how to increase our own power than to enlarge our thinking; we strive to eliminate others from our world, not to grant them space within ourselves." We all must enlarge our thinking to bring a just peace in the Middle East.

To me justice looks like this. It is based on the fact that all people are created in the image of God and that God loves all the little children of the world, no matter what color their skin or how old they are. It is also based on the fact that all people are created equal and endowed by their creator with certain inalienable rights which means liberty and justice for all, not just some.

So, if white people can eat at that restaurant, then black people can too. If white people can live in that neighborhood, then black people can too. If white people can go to that school, then black people can too. If Jewish people can eat at that restaurant, then Palestinians can too. If Jewish people can drive on that road, then Palestinians can too. If Jewish people can live in that neighborhood, than Palestinians can too. And if Jewish people have the right of return, then Palestinians do too.

Part III: The Media

Besides their uncommon determination, what the individuals we just profiled have in common is the difficulty they encountered in trying to tell about their experience in newspapers, on radio, or on television. In this section we hear from various media professionals who themselves encountered this media bias.

Palestine after the 1949 War

Censored

By Colin D. Edwards

Colin Edwards was a Middle East correspondent, documentary maker, and lecturer for over 40 years. In the 1980s and early '90s, he was a commentator on station KALW-FM in San Francisco. A friend of Moshe Menuhin, father of violinist Yehudi Menuhin, Edwards served as Moshe's literary agent for his autobiographical work, The Decadence of Judaism in Our Time, *in which Moshe protested against the identification of Judaism with Zionism. If you can't find the book in your library, Edwards tells you why.*

While the Iron Curtain has disappeared, what I would call the Zion Curtain lives on, heavily damping and distorting news concerning the Middle East as it appears in the world's news media, very particularly the print and broadcasting media in the western world. Since my work has been mostly in the field of news reporting and documentary production, I will concentrate in this article on what I have experienced of Zionist censorship in these fields.

This goes back to January, 1949, when a Jewish friend in the United Nations Secretariat warned me that I had been put on the death list by people in Israel who had belonged to the Irgun terrorist organization. They had found out that I would be passing through Egypt on my way to an appointment as a Military Observer in Southeast Asia after a year and a half of free-lance journalism at U.N. headquarters.

In view of the fact that I had nothing published to that point on the Middle East, it seemed ridiculous that I would be thought important enough to be assassinated. However, my friend reminded me that at some party of U.N. people in New York (before Israel was established in May 1948) I had expressed the opinion that it would be dangerous for everyone in the Middle East, including the Jews there, and for world peace, if a Jewish state were set up in Palestine on Zionist principles of Jewish superiority, discrimination against non-Jews in every walk of life and expulsion of the indigenous Muslim and Christian Arabs, and especially if it pursued the expansion of its borders to include all the territory to the East as far as the Euphrates and North to Turkey proper, as had been put forward by the Zionist leadership prior to and during the Peace Conference at Versailles, following the end of the first World War.

It seemed much more sensible and fair, in my view, for Palestine to go through the process that was happening in some other British-ruled territories, like India and Burma; that is, of being granted independence, with equality of political, cultural, religious and personal rights guaranteed in a constitution to all its inhabitants. I felt it would be madness for the U.N. to let a European settler minority with no valid ancestral claim to the land of Palestine establish a state there encompassing more than half of its territory, including the bulk of its fertile areas.

Almost all Central and East European Jews are descendants of the ancient Khazars,[1] a mixed Turko-Ugrian[2] people who had once ruled a large and powerful empire in Ashkenaz (what is now Southern Russia, the Ukraine and the Crimea). Very few, if any, had ever been seen in Palestine before the start of, first, spiritual and, then, political Zionist emigration from Czarist Russia to Palestine in the 19th and 20th centuries.

The Zionist claim of a religious connection to Palestine was equally weak, since the vast majority of Central and East European Jews, including most of the Zionist leadership, were atheists or agnostics by the 20th Century. In fact, it is not at all certain that the order by the Khazar Khan a dozen centuries before had resulted in all his subjects seriously adopting Judaism as their religion.

Saying all this apparently got me into the bad books of the Zionists.

Censorship at the Commonwealth Radio Systems

Nothing untoward happened on my passage through the Middle East in 1949. I returned there in 1969, doing straight reportage and recording dozens of interviews in Egypt, Jordan, Syria and Lebanon for Commonwealth radio systems. CBC-Radio Canada and the New Zealand Broadcasting System used an hour-long conversation I recorded in Beirut in 1969 with Laila Khaled, the Palestinian former schoolteacher who had hijacked a TWA plane in the Middle East in an effort to get the U.S. government to pressure the Israelis into releasing some members of her political faction, the Popular Front for the Liberation of Palestine, who—they believed—were being tortured in an Israeli prison. When I submitted it to BBC they turned it down, but according to friends of mine at the CBC office in London, segments of it were used a year later (without informing me) when Miss Khaled hijacked an Israeli airliner.[3]

My interview with Laila Khaled was the first of a series of my programs on the Middle East that NZBS had accepted. But before the second could be put on the air, the NZBS executive who had handled my contributions to their programming for many years told me that, because of political pressures exerted through members of the New Zealand Parliament, NZBS was having to cancel the rest of the series—with deep regret.

In the next few months I completed more programs, including major documentaries, out of the recordings I had made in the Middle East and sent them up to the CBC in Toronto. I had been supplying the CBC with reports from other regions of the world, without any trouble, for most of the previous ten years. Suddenly, I found that a brick wall had gone up as far as receptivity at CBC for my work went. The explanations were politely evasive: "We have covered this subject already," when I knew they had not, at least not in any depth. The "Zion Curtain" had dropped. Zionist influence is strong and pervasive in Toronto.

During a 1970 visit to the CBC's Toronto headquarters, where I had been the Program Organizer of a network documentary series in the early 1960s, I was invited by the executive in charge of another CBC radio network program to produce a one-hour documentary on the history of the Palestinian resistance. He happens to be Jewish, a Jew who—like vast numbers of other Jews—has seen through the Zionist pretension to be the sole representatives of the Jewish people and their traditions and the true heirs of the millions of victims of the Nazi Holocaust.

In that program I put extracts from interviews I had recorded with leading figures in most of the major factions of the P.L.O. Before it was broadcast all across Canada and into U.S. areas along the border, the same CBC executive put out press releases everywhere to emphasize its importance.

However, CBC staff members told me that other program departments of CBC, ones that could take more frequent contributions from outside producers like myself, had received word from a different Jewish executive that my work should not be used.

Gratifying as it was to have the documentary on the Palestine Resistance broadcast, it was clear that my concentration on the Middle East had jeopardized my capacity to make a decent living in radio, unless I was willing to compromise on my duty to bring out all the relevant facts of a situation.

That compromise was one I could not accept.

Censorship at the Pacifica Radio

If I could not get through the "Zion Curtain" in the Commonwealth radio systems on which I had been broadcasting for so many years, perhaps there was a chance in the United States with Pacifica Radio, a non-commercial radio system for which I had done many documentaries and a commentary series on Asian affairs for four years. By then it had stations in Los Angeles, New York and Texas, as well as the "mother station" in Berkeley, California. However, Pacifica was to prove that it itself was not immune.

As I finished the work on each program, I made a copy and gave it to the Public Affairs Director at the Pacifica station in Berkeley, KPFA-FM, Elsa Knight Thompson. She had always welcomed programs I had done around the world and in the U.S. and had put them on in the first available open space in the station's schedule, usually the nightly Open Hour. This was created to accommodate new developments in the political scene. Frequent announcements were made during the day that my latest documentary would be aired that evening, and a repeat broadcast would be scheduled so that it could be included in the next KPFA folio.

However, that scenario ceased after the airing of the first of the programs made from the material I had recorded in the Middle East in 1969. Mrs. Thompson received the tapes of the subsequent programs as graciously as ever—but they were not put in the first available slot, nor by the time I had completed the next ones, nor until six months after the day I gave her the first.

In May 1970, Mrs. Thompson was promoted to Program Director, and Don Porsche, who had been News Director, succeeded her as Public Affairs Director. He discovered that for the third anniversary week of the June 1967 war she had scheduled eight programs produced in Israel or by Zionist organizations in the United States. In a cupboard he found the tapes of my recent Middle East documentaries that she had chosen not to air, so he decided to put five of these on in the same week as the eight Zionist programs, to provide some sort of balance.

Mrs. Thompson had gone on vacation but, when the first of my latest documentaries had been broadcast, bringing on a storm of protests from local Zionists, she rushed back. Porsche lost his job and the last two or three of my programs were canceled. The time allotted for the last one was reallocated to a round table discussion where I was confronted by a panel of three highly antagonistic Zionists.

Several of the top staff people at the other Pacifica stations were protégés of Mrs. Thompson and soon my programs were banned on all of them. However, non-Pacifica public radio stations around the country that had purchased the right to use a certain number of Pacifica programs each year wanted to continue to receive the programs I was producing. The staff of the Pacifica Foundation, which owned the operating licenses for Pacifica stations, handled the distribution of programs to these non-Pacifica stations. It continued to meet requests for the backlog of my documentaries that it still had, despite strenuous efforts by Mrs. Thompson, without the knowledge of the station manager, to stop it doing so. Shortly after a new manager, Larry Lee, was installed at KPFA, a KPFA staff member told me that Lee had called her and her colleagues to a meeting and told them that he was a Zionist and would not stand for any programs of mine being put back on the air.

The station's engineer told me that, during the week in June 1970, when the first couple of my programs on the Middle East were broadcast, the station's doors were shot out twice.

In that same period I received four or five death threats on the phone and one day when I went up the steps from my house to the street above, where my car was parked on the left, I thought they had become serious. Settling into the driver's seat I noticed in my rear view mirror a car parked on the other side of the road, facing in my direction, in the shade of some eucalyptus trees, about a hundred yards behind me. As I was about to put the key in the ignition I remembered something I needed to take with me that I had left in the house. I jumped out and was just a few steps down towards my front deck when I heard a car drive by and the sound of shattering glass. I went up to the car and found a bullet hole through the front passenger window. The car down the road had disappeared. An Oakland police officer investigated and said that it was probably just a random drive-by shooting.

A week or so later, on a Friday, I found on my answering machine an abusive message that I was to be killed the following Monday. I told the police. They said that I should inform the telephone company and reiterated this when I told them that this seemed like a criminal matter. "The telephone company has a special office to deal with these things," they said.

I called up the telephone company, where a customer service representative did not seem to know of any such office. She said someone at the company would call me. On Sunday evening (which seemed peculiar) I got a call from a man who identified himself as from the telephone company. He questioned me about the message and asked whether I had received any similar calls before. I said "Death threats, yes, but none of them mentioned a specific date until this time."

"Have you ever actually been attacked?"

"Shot at once. At least I believe I was the target. You can get the police report."

"Well, if you get any more threats, let us know." And that was that. Fortunately, the threat was not carried out.

When I mentioned this incident to a Jewish friend who was a student at the Berkeley campus, he told me that an attempt had been made, not long before, to recruit him into the Jewish Defense League, which had carried out many terrorist actions in the United States, resulting in deaths and injuries.[4] He did not want any part of it. What was even more interesting was that the JDL recruiter who had approached him was a long time member of the university faculty, a man I had sat beside at a luncheon in the faculty club for a visiting Israeli military officer, who was on campus to give a talk to U.C.'s R.O.T.C. unit.

I saw Elsa Knight Thompson when I next called in at KPFA to recover the tapes of my programs. In trying to explain the difficult position that my work had put the station in with some of its wealthiest supporters, she said they were threatening not only to withhold their annual contributions and cut the station out of their wills but also to organize a boycott of the station by all its subscribers.

She also told me that she had been beaten up on the street outside the station, "Who would want to beat you up, Elsa?" I asked.

"Oh, from what they were shouting at me I gathered they were some young Zionists who did not understand that I was a Zionist," she replied.

"Why didn't you tell all this—on the air—to your listeners? Lou Hill established KPFA to be a station that could resist all outside pressures. I am sure your listeners would have rallied around the station."

"We could not afford to lose our big contributors," she replied.

"We would put at risk the very existence of the station, which would mean also all the other programs that we do that commercial stations dare not do, for fear of offending the sponsors."

"You are falling into the same trap, Elsa. Lou Hill wouldn't like it." And on that note, we parted.

Cassette Censorship

In the 1970s, a group of people connected with a church in Los Angeles that had been trying to get discussion going on the problems of the Middle East invited me to speak at a rally there with a P.L.O. representative and Rabbi Elmer Berger, president of American Jewish Alternatives to Zionism. The L.A.P.D. provided us with police protection but a pipe bomb exploded outside the home of a lady involved in the organizing of our appearances.[5]

While continuing to supply programs—on subjects other than Middle East politics—to Commonwealth broadcasting systems, I began spending more time lecturing at colleges up and down the West Coast. Since early in 1969 I had been on the speakers' panel of the College Association for Public Events and Services (C.A.P.E.S.), an organization set up by smaller colleges in California, Oregon, Washington and Arizona to arrange lecture tours of these colleges by people with some expertise in a wide variety of fields.

This gave me the opportunity to continue getting out to the public what I had learned about the politics of the Middle East, as well as on Southeast Asia, my other specialty at that time. Some of the colleges where I spoke on the Middle East were told by local Zionists that if I were invited back they would cut off their financial contributions to them. They also wanted me taken off the C.A.P.E.S. speakers' list.

To its great credit, the C.A.P.E.S. staff and board resisted these attempts at censorship and kept me on its panel of lecturers year after year but, since C.A.P.E.S. left it to the colleges to choose which speakers would appear on their respective campuses, the "Zion Curtain" pressures began to tell on my bookings, and my last record of a talk under C.A.P.E.S. sponsorship came at the end of 1974.

By that time I had embarked on another means of getting my work out to the public. The University of California Extension Media Center in Berkeley asked me in November 1966 if I would allow them to distribute tape and cassette copies of my documentaries and interviews to universities, colleges and organizations. They started with 12. By 1971 the list had grown to 43, many of which did not deal with the Middle East.

In September that year, with the approval of the U.C. Extension Media Center, I signed an agreement with an audio-cassette program distributor in North Hollywood, C.C.S. (the Center for Cassette Studies), for them to distribute a hundred of my other programs, and C.C.S. selected an additional 38 during the following eight months. These it began selling to schools, colleges and libraries around the U.S.

Among the one hundred and thirty eight programs on which the distribution rights had been bought by C.C.S., 23 dealt with the politics of the Middle East. When I granted C.C.S. the rights on the programs, I was assured that there would be no censorship of them. However, as the new C.C.S. catalogues of its audio-cassette offerings appeared in the following months and years, I noticed that none of my Middle East programs was among them. Inquiring about this I learned that the C.C.S. staff member who had selected my programs originally had left the company and his place had been taken by a former Israeli army officer.

About this time, U.C.E.M.C. (the University of California Extension Media Center) asked me if I could give them more programs, including a strong collection on the Middle East. Fortunately, I had been spending a good deal of time in the Middle East, Asia and Europe, recording interviews for further documentaries and lecturing, so I set to work preparing another forty or so programs.

As U.C.E.M.C. distributed these around the country and the world (many orders for those on the Middle East coming from U.S. military institutions) pressure, exerted by California Zionists, began to build on U.C.E.M.C. to drop them. When its director and staff held firm, the Zionists turned to the university's Board of Regents, one of whom was a prominent Zionist. U.C.E.M.C. was obliged to submit to special meetings of the board its justification for distributing my Middle East programs. Faculty members who were experts on the Middle East were asked to evaluate my programs for accuracy—and they declared favorably on them. However, U.C.E.M.C. was subjected more than once to this time consuming process of justifying its retention of my programs in its catalogue. In what seemed to me a move to placate the complaining Regent, U.C.E.M.C. added to its audio tapes catalogue a large collection of Zionist-prepared or Zionist-approved programs. Eventually, in 1978, U.C.E.M.C. shut down its entire audio-cassette distribution program and concentrated its efforts on selling documentary films.

The Menuhin Censorship

Early in the Seventies I had recorded 16 hours of conversation with Moshe Menuhin, Yehudi Menuhin's father, about his life, beginning in Czarist Russia, where he experienced the pogroms, and proceeding on to his school years in Palestine in the early years of this century, to his years in America and then Europe and around the world, and to his retirement in Los Gatos, California. After I had pared the recordings down into 11 one-hour programs, these were distributed by U.C.E.M.C. Also, they were broadcast on KPFA in Berkeley, in a rare let-up of the ban on me.

Moshe Menuhin and I had become good friends and early in 1979 he asked me to work with him on his autobiography. When we had finished, near the end of that year, Moshe startled me by asking me to act as his literary agent, a profession in which I had no experience. I repeatedly declined his request but he was insistent. He was one of the many anti-Zionist Jews whose views are almost totally ignored by the mass media and he feared that, if he died and left the manuscript in the hands of a regular literary agent, that agent might yield to a publisher's wishes to remove or dilute Moshe's strong political statements in it. He felt he could trust me not to allow that.

After approaching several American publishers and recognizing a reluctance to publish a manuscript containing lengthy explanations of how Moshe came, as a Jew from a strongly religious family,[6] to reject Zionism as a political philosophy, I suggested that I show it to some publishers in Britain, where I thought the "Zion Curtain" was not quite so all-enveloping. If *The Menuhin Saga*, as we had titled it, achieved the hoped-for success in Britain, then it would be harder for U.S. publishers to turn it down out of hand.

So, off I went to London to talk with publishers there. Many expressed the same reservations about its anti-Zionist viewpoint but eventually I found five of Britain's leading publishers who were ready to make offers. Within days of these being communicated to me, the editorial directors at three of these publishing houses telephoned me with the news that, despite the favorable recommendations of their editorial boards to their board of directors, the decisions to offer to publish *The Menuhin Saga* had been reversed.

This left me with two publishers willing to bring out *The Menuhin Saga*, Quartet and Sidgwick & Jackson. We chose Sidgwick & Jackson. While cutting the manuscript down to make a 280-page book I was told by the publisher that we could not leave in it a reference by Moshe to the Zionist collaboration with the Nazis before and during World War II [on page 229], unless I could provide documentation. I gave them more than five hundred lines of references, mostly Jewish sources, like Jewish newspapers of the 1930's, as well as official documents in archives in Europe and Israel. Only ten lines of my documentation appear in the final published form of *The Menuhin Saga*.

The British edition of *The Menuhin Saga* was published in the Fall of 1982 but only two small ads were placed in the media for it, one in a London neighborhood paper and one in the London Zionist newspaper, *The Jewish Chronicle*, which ran a nasty article on Moshe without really addressing the issues that he was raising in the book. The book was not displayed at the Frankfurt Book Fair that October, nor even in Sidgwick & Jackson's display window, below its offices, in London, at least not on the days I checked there.

The Literary Editor of *The London Times* placed *The Menuhin Saga* on a list of the most interesting books published in Britain that week, but the *Times* did not publish a review. Neither did any of the other national papers. There were reviews in provincial papers and in *The Irish Press*, Dublin, and almost all were laudatory.

Despite the lack of advertising but probably due to the good reviews in the smaller papers, sales of *The Menuhin Saga* seem to have gone well. Unfortunately, instead of 8,000 copies being produced in the first printing, as I had been told would be done when I was discussing the contract with Sidgwick & Jackson, only 2,000 were printed. This I discovered much later.

In my approaches to publishers on the European mainland, to interest them in producing translations of *The Menuhin Saga*, I needed to let them have copies of the British edition, but I found that Sidgwick & Jackson could not round up enough copies to sell to me for this purpose. I had to look in bookstores on the Continent that I knew carried English-language books. Many of the fifty I ended up buying I found in bookshops in Zurich, Luzern, Lausanne and Geneva.

In Paris I suspected that the branch there of W.H. Smith would not be selling it, and this proved to be true. The only chance was Brentano's, on the Avenue de l'Opera. I telephoned in advance, to make sure. "Oh, yes," a male voice said, "We have it."

"I'll need a dozen," I said.

"Ah, I am afraid we are having to ration our customers to two each. There is such a demand for it."

"O.K. I'll come over and get two."

When I got to Brentano's, I could not immediately find the gentleman there to whom I had spoken, so I looked around to see where *The Menuhin Saga* was displayed. It was nowhere in sight. When the salesman who had talked to me on the phone appeared, I asked if all the copies had been sold. "No," he said. "We keep them in a cupboard."

In the same year that the British edition appeared, a French translation of *The Menuhin Saga* was published by Editions Payot, in Paris, under the title *La Saga Des Menuhin*. With very few exceptions, the French edition got good reviews in French newspapers. It has sold out and a new publisher, to do a reprint, is being sought, as also for the sold-out British edition.

In 1985 Schweizer Verlagshaus in Zurich brought out, in hardcover, under the title *Die Menuhins*, a German translation of *The Menuhin Saga* by Lexa Katrin Grafin von Nostitz, a relative of a gentleman I had interviewed about his role in getting Jews and dissidents out of Nazi Germany. More than a hundred German publishers had turned down the book, mostly with the explanation that it was difficult for them, as Germans, to handle a book that was critical of Israel. They feared that might be considered pro-Nazi, despite the fact that the author was a Jew. They would not be swayed by my pointing out that the people they were afraid of offending had collaborated with the Nazis in the 1930s during the war.[7] I faced the same problem with German publishers when I tried to get them interested in books by some other friends: Lenni Brenner, Alan Hart, Alfred M. Lilienthal and Donald Neff, whose well-documented works upset Zionist sensibilities.

However, in 1987 one of the leading German pocketbook publishers, Deutscher Taschenbuch Verlag, in cooperation with Barenreiter Verlag, produced a paperback edition of Grafin von Nostitz's translation of *The Menuhin Saga*.

Dutch and Scandinavian publishers proved particularly resistant to the idea of issuing translations of Moshe's book, sometimes saying that they would not want to offend Israel and the Jews, making no distinction between them. In the case of a publisher in Finland and one in Denmark, they were on the point of signing a contract when they decided that they had better first ask a prominent Jew they knew about his reactions to the book. In each case, the Jew they chose to consult disagreed strongly with Moshe's viewpoint, and the publishers withdrew their offers for the Finnish and Danish translation rights.

In 1989, Forlaget Hovedland in Arhus published a Danish translation of *The Menuhin Saga* under the title *Min Familie: Menuhin-Sagaen*.

I must have talked personally with around two hundred U.S. publishers about their issuing an American edition of the Saga, and I provided copies of the British edition to twenty or thirty, few of whom returned them. Some told me frankly that they did not dare touch it, because of Moshe's strong antipathy towards Zionism. Others said that it did not suit their list. So far, only one publisher here has expressed a willingness to bring out a U.S. edition and that offer came with the condition that we take out of the book a warm letter of praise and appreciation Moshe had received from Yasser Arafat.[8] Believing that Moshe would not have been willing to have that deleted, we declined the offer.

So, Americans who wanted to read *The Menuhin Saga* have had to order copies from England, and the publisher's stock there was completely exhausted years ago. Two American libraries that ordered it while copies still were available are the San Francisco Public Library and the Berkeley Public Library. I received a postcard from the San Francisco Library telling me that it had arrived. There is much about San Francisco and the history of its symphony orchestra in Moshe's account of his life, because he spent eight years as the founder and superintendent of the Hebrew schools there, attended the San Francisco Symphony's performances regularly with his wife and small son Yehudi (who gave his first concerts in the city) and, in 1934, had a hand in bringing Pierre Monteaux in to rebuild that orchestra after a period in which its standards had declined.

I telephoned the San Francisco Library and inquired as to which section they had chosen to place *The Menuhin Saga* in. I was interested in knowing if it had gone into the music department or was among the books on history. I felt the latter would be a more appropriate choice. They told me it was in a special section devoted to books on San Francisco history.

On my next visit to that city I called by at the library to introduce myself. I showed the postcard to the lady at the special collection desk and she disappeared into an office. Soon, another lady appeared and in a very agitated voice declared that they did not have the book, that they had never ordered it. I asked, "But the postcard! And when I telephoned, I was told it had arrived and was in this section."

"No. There must have been a mistake."

"Will you be ordering it? There is a lot about San Francisco in it."

"No. We won't." She was visibly nervous and walked away.

When the Berkeley Public Library informed me that they had

purchased a copy of the British edition of *The Menuhin Saga*. I stopped by and found it in the card catalogue in the music department, but it was nowhere to be seen on the shelves. "It must be out on loan," a librarian said.

There were quite a number of people I know in Berkeley who were checking frequently to see if it was on the shelf or if they could reserve it but, in the ensuing eight years, neither they nor I have been able to find it. Recently, a librarian friend there said that it must have been stolen.

Censorship at KALW-FM San Francisco

In March 1990 a producer at KALW-FM, a public radio station owned by the San Francisco Unified School District, invited me to do a weekly commentary, of an "Op-Ed" nature, on world affairs. After decades of just straight reporting, producing documentaries and recording interviews in many countries, I thought it was time that I shared with the public some conclusions I had arrived at, as well as some historical background on situations abroad that were important, especially information that had been sadly lacking in the mass media, as I had observed it. I would bring out facts that correspondents would tell you if you sat down personally with them but had not been able to say on the air or get into print.[9]

These commentaries went on the air on March 28, 1990. I was allowed ten minutes and they were broadcast at 9:35 a.m. each Wednesday. Among the governments I dealt with very critically in the next two years and three months were, in addition to Israel: Lebanon, Cambodia, Thailand, South Africa, Malaysia, Indonesia, Taiwan, Singapore, Saudi Arabia, Vietnam, Korea, Turkey, Yugoslavia, Germany, Burma, Kuwait, England, Iraq, the United States, and my own land of origin, Wales.

Beginning with the August 22, 1990 commentary, my weekly air time was cut to between five and six minutes.

My reports and comments on Israeli government actions brought frequent complaints from local Zionist organizations and individuals. Station Manager Daniel Del Solar told me of these every time I encountered him at the station. In a letter responding to a pro-Israeli listener who had complained of some things he claimed I had said (but had not) in my "vile" commentaries, Del Solar identified a senior member of his staff as "a strong supporter of Edwards." I considered this a betrayal by him of a subordinate. Also, what if that listener was a member of the murderous Jewish Defense League or had friends in it? They might have gone after that named staff member. I am the only one who should be responsible for my remarks and I accept the risks associated with them. No one else should be victimized on account of me.

One day, when I encountered Del Solar at the station, he said: "Aren't you anti-Semitic?" On another occasion, when I suggested he invite William M. Mandel, author of *Soviet But Not Russian*,[10] about non-Russian republics and minorities in the old Soviet Union, and six other books on the U.S.S.R., to do some commentaries on the breakup of that empire, Del Solar replied: "No. I don't think so. He was a member of the communist party, as you were."

The fact is that Mandel quit the communist party in 1956, over the Soviet invasion of Hungary and the Russians' brutal suppression of the Hungarian revolution, and he has a considerable reputation as a scholar. As for myself, I never was a member of the communist party. In fact, ever since I became politically aware in my secondary school days I have regarded the totalitarian communist system of single party rule, denial of freedom of speech, secret police methods and labor camps for political dissidents as repugnant.

I saw Del Solar's sly insinuations as attempts to provoke me into "walking out" of the station in high dudgeon and giving up my program slot but I remembered what some senior members of his staff had told me once: "Just ignore him. We do." After all, my real relationship there was with my listeners, dozens of whom had written letters praising my programs and many more who had telephoned the station expressing their strong support for them. I did not want to let them down just because of the idiotic remarks of Del Solar.

Del Solar's animosity took on a more insulting tone at one stage. Shortly after I started doing my commentaries for KALW, the station staff had told me that the tape I was using to record them in the small studio I have in my home was not up to their standard and that I must use some of their tape. Since I was not being paid for my commentaries, nor for my expenses in delivering them to the station in San Francisco from my home across the Bay, they felt that the station should provide the tape, anyway.

When recording my commentaries, I often did some last minute editing, which means that there were splices in them. The station staff made it very clear that they did not reuse tape with splices in it. I was glad to hold on to the tapes because I had discovered that KALW did not maintain the old radio custom of making and keeping "air-checks" (i.e. recordings) of its broadcasts. Knowing that I might be challenged on what I was saying in my commentaries, I wanted a record—on tape—of them all.

One day I received a phone call from Del Solar accusing me of taking station property because I had used station tape and retained the recordings of my commentaries. I was outraged at this but he continued to put that construction on the arrangement I had with his staff. So, from then on I purchased tape out of my own pocket to do my commentaries.

On June 30, 1985, I had read in that day's *San Francisco Examiner*, the Hearst flagship newspaper, a report on an interview with a member of the San Francisco Board of Supervisors (City Council), Quentin Kopp, titled "Kopp's Israel Diary." In it, Kopp described the month he had just completed as a "Volunteer for Israel," unpacking military supplies at a warehouse on an Israeli jet fighter base in the Negev. The article said: "It's difficult to see how the Israeli Defense Forces got their money's worth out of San Francisco Supervisor Quentin Kopp... In the volunteer program, interested persons pay $500 for plane fare. In exchange, Israel gives them boots, fatigue uniforms, three meals a day and a warm place to sleep. They also get buck-private's jobs on Israeli military bases for thirty days."

Illustrating the interview was a photo of Kopp and two friends, all in Israeli uniform, at the air base near the town of Arad. Describing what Kopp had told him of one incident there, the reporter wrote:

"Kopp and his friends made the mistake of wearing their uniforms on a visit to the Red Sea resort of Taba Beach, and they got rousted by Israeli soldiers in civvies. That's because both Israel and Egypt claim Taba Beach and, in the Camp David Accords, Israel promised not to station uniformed troops there."

In the July 3, 1985 issue of *The San Francisco Chronicle*, that city's principal morning paper, there were two articles referring to Supervisor Kopp and the program that took him and other foreigners, Jews and non-Jews, to Israel to don Israeli military uniforms. One of the articles was titled "A Stint in the Israeli Reserves: Rewards of Roughing it in Reserves." It noted that "since 1982 and the start of the Lebanon war, more than 3,000 Jews, most of them American but including English and South African, have paid their way to Israel to ease the shortage in the Israel Defense Force."

"Easing the shortage in a military force" well describes the function of a military reserve.

The other article, illustrated by two more snapshots of Kopp in Israeli uniform, consisted of excerpts from Kopp's diary for the 30 days he spent in the Israeli military in 1985. They included the following verbatim statements: "May 22 : ... In the afternoon I help Limor (another volunteer) move a bomb to the flight repair shop... May 22: about 9:30 a.m. there's a flamboyant ceremony to celebrate the promotion of Ori, Miri and a third soldier (Dorit) to corporal... June 16: ... We turn in our uniforms."

The day after those articles appeared in *The San Francisco Chronicle*, I happened to hear Kopp describing his service on the Israeli air bases on a radio talk show, the Ron Owens program, on the ABC radio outlet in San Francisco, KGO. Kopp recommended a stint in the "Volunteers for Israel" program to Owens and his listeners, explaining that anybody between 18 and 65, or 62, years of age, including women, were welcome to join. He repeatedly gave an address and a telephone number through which interested persons could get information and application forms. "If you are stuck and can't get through [on the phone] or something," he said, "call my office and I'll be happy to give you the information... I've already had somebody write me from Walnut Creek who isn't Jewish, an ex-Marine Corps pilot. As a matter of fact, he flew Skyhawks, he said, and he wants to get into the program. And so I sent him the address and the telephone number."

At least a couple of callers on the program described how they had been going over to Israel as "volunteers for Israel" year after year, one to serve as a tank driver.

I recalled all this when I was preparing my September 11, 1991 KALW commentary, in which I was remarking on Zionist influence in American politics and said that I had heard of public officials in the U.S. serving in "the Israeli armed forces reserves," and gave Quentin Kopp, by now a California State Senator, as a local example.

That term "reserves" had been used twice by *The San Francisco Chronicle* in its description of the "Volunteers for Israel" program and I think the words "armed forces reserves" accurately describes the nature of the "Volunteers for Israel" program, even though "armed forces volunteer reserves" would have been more precise. They all constitute forms of "military reserves."

From a friend who reads the *Northern California Jewish Bulletin* regularly I heard that its November 22, 1991, issue had an item reading: "California State Senator Quentin Kopp (Independent, San Francisco) retracted his threat to file a libel suit against S.F. radio station KALW this week after the station promised to air an apology for broadcasting a statement that Kopp had been in the Israeli military. Colin Edwards, an occasional [*sic*] guest commentator on the station, told a radio audience, September 11, that Kopp had served in Israeli Defense Force [*sic*] and advocated other Americans join the Israeli reserves. Actually, Kopp had lent his services to Volunteers for Israel, an American organization that places Americans—who pay their own way—in non-paid IDF support positions for several weeks at a time."

I had not received from KALW's manager, Daniel Del Solar, any indication that it had been threatened with a lawsuit by Senator Kopp because of anything I had said on the air, or that it intended to apologize to him. This was an extreme discourtesy to me but when I brought this up with Del Solar he was absolutely unapologetic.

I supplied him with copies of the 1985 issues of the *San Francisco Chronicle* and *Examine*r containing the articles quoting Kopp on his service at the Israeli air force base and the photographs of him in Israeli uniform, as well as verbatim transcriptions of the relevant Kopp remarks on the Ron Owens talk show. Yet, Del Solar said he planned to go ahead with his broadcast apology to Kopp.

On November 27, 1991, Del Solar went on the air on KALW and apologized to Kopp for my allegedly "erroneous statements" in my September 11 commentary.

Early in 1992, Del Solar told me he was giving the Israeli Consulate General a chance to respond to remarks made about his government's actions by myself and another KALW commentator, Sasha Futran (who was also taken off the air soon after me). It was to be a lengthy interview conducted by Del Solar. In his introduction to the interview, Del Solar declared: "In the June, 1967 War, Israel was not considered the aggressor. It was under attack by Egypt, Syria and Jordan and, when it fought back, it occupied the land." (Del Solar apparently didn't know that even Israeli generals and politicians have discarded this myth.)

On June 22, 1992, a KALW staff member telephoned me to say that I was being taken off the air on the orders of Daniel Del Solar. I called Del Solar and he said it was because he needed my six-minute commentary spot for programming of a more educational nature. I remarked: "Oh, come on, your decision was political." "Everything is political," he responded.

My last commentary was broadcast on July 1, 1992. At its end I told the listeners: "This is the last of my regular commentaries on KALW. It was not my decision to stop. This station has received many objections to my remarks from the Israeli Consulate General and Zionist organizations and individuals."

When listeners telephoned Del Solar to object to my commentaries being taken off the air, Del Solar told them that my statement was a lie. That he was not responding to any outside pressure.

An investigative reporter for *The San Francisco Weekly*, the only Bay Area paper to say anything about my termination, wrote in its July 19, 1992 issue:

Outspoken radio commentator Colin Edwards has been fired
from KALW-FM after a months-long campaign by the Jewish
Anti-Defamation League and the threat of a lawsuit by state
Senator Quentin Kopp... The Kopp incident spurred the Anti-
Defamation League (ADL) into action. Assistant Director
Nancy Diner said last week "We started transcribing
[Edwards'] shows to check for accuracy. We wrote many
protest letters to the station." Diner said that, although it was
not the ADL's intention to force Edwards off the air, one
member of the group recently compiled a list of Edwards'
alleged inaccuracies and took them to station manager Daniel
Del Solar in a personal effort to get Edwards fired.

Del Solar denied that the campaign against Edwards figured
in his decision to end Edwards' four-year-old program. "He
was getting boring," Del Solar said. But producer Alan Farley
confirmed that outside pressure provoked the firing.
"Edwards' commentaries have drawn a lot of flack from the
Israeli consulate and elsewhere in the Jewish community," he
said. "Our station manager finally got tired of dealing with it."

Loyal listeners, upset at the decision, jammed the station
switchboard with irate calls for half an hour after Edwards
announced that the July 1 program was his last, Farley said.

Del Solar responded to the article in a letter to the editor of *The
San Francisco Weekly*, stating: "Mr. Edwards' journalistic integrity was
completely compromised in my mind by the lie he stated on the air
during his six-minute KALW commentary. Edwards said, or inferred
strongly enough for listeners to consider as fact, that I had been forced
by the Israeli Consulate and other 'Zionist forces' to remove Edwards
from the air."[11]

Nancy Diner of the ADL wrote to *The San Francisco Weekly*
disclaiming "credit for something with which we had little to do. For
our part, we simply asked KALW's management for an equal
opportunity to be heard. No attempt at censorship. No attempt to

get Edwards fired. Kudos to KALW for recognizing its editorial responsibility."[12]

Her letter brought a rejoinder from a member of KALW's advisory board, Herbert G. Susmann, who wrote, in a letter to the editor of *The San Francisco Weekly*: "I was present at a KALW board meeting on April 30 when the then-manager [Daniel Del Solar] read a letter from B'nai B'rith asking for the removal of Mr. Edwards. ...In fact, in a July 31 memo to a member of the school administration, the station manager stated that "important organizations in the Jewish community communicated their desire to have Mr. Edwards removed from KALW.'"

The final paragraph of a July 15, 1992 *San Francisco Weekly* article on my being taken off the air by Del Solar reads: "The San Francisco school district runs the station, and school board member Tom Ammiano called for an investigation into Edwards' firing. 'I am concerned about censorship,' he said. 'It's not up to Del Solar to decide these things. The board sets policy. We don't want to look as though we cave in to pressure, although we always do.'"

Knowing of the Board of Education's pressing financial problems I delayed getting in touch with it until March 22, when I wrote to its president, Mr. Ammiano, demanding a public apology for Del Solar's public attacks on my journalistic standards and personal integrity. The Schools Superintendent wrote to me a few days later, saying that I would receive a response within ten days but, despite a further enquiry (by phone) and another promise of an early response, to this date of writing (May 25, 1993) I have heard nothing further from the Board regarding my demand for an apology, nor has there been any news of an investigation into Del Solar's actions.

Epiphany at Beit Jalla

By Donald Neff

Donald Neff served as Time *magazine's Jerusalem bureau chief from 1975 to 1978. In this December 1995 issue of* The Link, *he writes of the media bias he brought with him and the experiences that changed him. Books by Neff include three major works on the Arab-Israeli wars of 1956, 1967, and 1973, and his 1995 book* Fallen Pillars, *a survey of U.S.-Israeli relations.*

It was two decades ago when I first arrived in Israel. Like many Westerners, and I suppose like most Americans at the time, I was something of an unwitting Zionist in my sympathies. If I did not embrace Israel's history of expansionism, I did not necessarily reject it either. I believed that the Jews deserved a secure state of their own, as the Nazi Holocaust had proved, and it followed that Israelis had a right to look out for their own safety.

This included Israel's continuing occupation of three-quarters of a million Palestinians in Jerusalem and the other territories captured by Israel in 1967. Even after eight years, the occupation was being described by Zionists as the "most benign in history," and the American media had little hesitancy in repeating that claim. As a strong believer in human rights, I wasn't comfortable with such a facile slogan. I didn't believe any occupation could be less than evil, a blasphemy against freedom and democracy, and ultimately corrupting of the occupiers. But, if an exception existed, I assumed a case could be made for Israel's special needs.

Palestinian rights had never been of high concern to the media or most Americans, especially in the Congress and the White House.

Moreover, the Palestinians themselves had shown little talent for making their own case. Their prevailing image abroad was as hijackers of airliners and terrorists at Munich and elsewhere. I was unaware of any credible record of Israeli abuses, and the Palestinians seemed incapable of producing one. In the circumstances, the occupation was a troubling but distant subject for me.

This was the rough outline of my mindset when *Time* magazine sent me to Israel in January 1975. Although I had been a reporter for more than 20 years and seen my share of the world, I had never worked in the Middle East. My attitude toward the region reflected pretty much the pro-Israel biases of the media and of Americans in general, unleavened by history or sophistication about Zionism.

Like any seasoned foreign correspondent, I took my first task to be looking out for my own health and comfort. That is how I found myself shortly after my arrival driving the hilly streets of Beit Jala, next to Bethlehem and just a few miles from Jerusalem. It was my first visit to an Arab town; however, I was not there out of curiosity about the Palestinians, but because it was reputed to have one of the best tailors around. He made me two marvelously warm tweed jackets, leaving me with sunny thoughts of Beit Jala, an image that was to change dramatically three years later.

As my tour extended into years, I could not ignore a disturbing blindness in some of even the most gentle Israelis. They did not seem to see the Palestinians all around them. Nor did they seem to see the degradation and injustice imposed on them by Israeli rule. In general, this was just as well; when most Israelis did notice Palestinians, their reaction to them was one of loathing or fear that quickly could escalate into violence. I had not seen such an instinctive hatred of another people since living among southerners many years earlier.

"Filthy Arab" was the routine and most printable description uttered by Israelis. Mindless and violent attacks against Palestinians were not rare, particularly in flashpoints like the West Bank city of Hebron. Palestinians were forcefully kept out of Jewish areas after nightfall, facing arrest and worse if they were caught on the street, and there was no question of any of them being welcomed in restaurants, hotels, or other public facilities. Their access to jobs was almost nonexistent, except at the lowest levels as farmhands, construction workers, and trash collectors. Their cars were issued license plates of a different color than Israelis, and their identity cards clearly marked them as not being Israelis. These were ironic reminders of the yellow stars Nazis forced Jews to wear so they could be differentiated from other Germans.

I had trouble giving credence to such blind prejudice, because it seemed to me almost unthinkable that a people who had suffered so much could be so unfeeling toward another people. No doubt that was why it took me so long to recognize the reality around me. It was many months before the daily witness of my eyes and ears began to work its way into my consciousness.

In the end, and with all the goodwill in the world toward Israelis, there was no escaping the brutal reality that Palestinians were treated like a lesser form of humanity, to put it mildly. Although their housing was insufficient and overcrowded, Palestinians were strictly denied housing in Jewish areas. At the same time, some of the most desirable homes in Jerusalem and elsewhere had originally belonged to Palestinians but were now occupied by Israelis.

The enormity of the displacement of the Palestinians hit me one night while I was having dinner with an Israeli couple I was especially fond of. Theirs was a saga that would have been from a story book almost anywhere else. She was a German Jew incarcerated in a Nazi concentration camp, and he was an Israeli from Austria serving with the British forces who liberated the camp. He returned for her after the war and they took up married life in Israel.

They were among the most charming and sophisticated couples I had ever met. And she was one of the best cooks, so an offer of dinner at their house, conveniently located near the center of Jerusalem, was always welcome. At one point, over an after-dinner brandy before flames of olive wood in the fireplace, she remarked that, of course, the house had originally been Palestinian.

She said it without the slightest shred of compassion, this woman who herself had suffered so much. True, after what she and her family had been through, the loss of a home was not the worst fate. Yet there was not the least hint of sympathy or guilt, or even irony, about the fact that immigrants from Europe were now living in the home of Palestinians, a people who had had nothing at all to do with the Nazi Holocaust.

I was still mesmerized enough by the heroic version of Israel's history not to challenge my hosts. But the seed had been planted. I began to wonder: What right, really, did European Jews have to Palestinian homes—or, for that matter, to Palestine itself? Was this conflict about two people with an equal right fighting for the same land, as the Zionist slogan had it, or a premeditated scheme by foreign immigrants to displace the legitimate local majority population?

It was thus by fits and starts, between long periods of numbness, that I slowly became aware of the Palestinian dimension of the conflict. As time passed and the new U.S.-Israeli relationship settled into a state of intimacy, I made it my business to get around the Occupied Territories more, meeting Palestinians and glimpsing life through their eyes. My interest doubled with the arrival in the White House of President Jimmy Carter, who became the first—and only—president to call Jewish settlements illegal and speak out on Palestinian rights.

This greater exposure to the Palestinians did not lead me to any sudden revelations. A large part of the reason is that it was so difficult to grasp what was really going on in the Occupied Territories. This was because it was almost impossible to determine who was telling the truth between two bitter enemies. While some Palestinians angrily complained about the cruelty of the occupation, Israeli officials insisted with great sincerity and persuasiveness that the occupation was as humane as it could be.

They denied confiscating Palestinian land, although new settlements were going up all the time in the occupied areas. They claimed the Palestinians were far better off economically than they would have been under Jordanian rule, although the sorry state of Palestinian villages displayed desperate poverty. They insisted that the military government of the occupation respected Palestinians' rights, although increasing numbers of arrests in the middle of the night without charge or trial told a different story. So too did the blowing up of Palestinian houses and the forceful exiling of Palestinians, who were deposited by their captors in the Jordanian desert or the mountains of Lebanon.

They even insisted that security forces acted only to keep the peace, although it seemed to me that the fatal incidents were increasing. Hardly a week seemed to go by without another killing, six in one memorable day that became known as Land Day. But nobody seemed to be counting or to care.

Such contradictions put a reporter in a particularly awkward situation. Lacking documentation or credible witnesses, a reporter is hard put to challenge the official word of a government. The difficulty was greatly compounded by the lack of documentation or reliable information about the occupation itself, which was still less than a decade old. In fact, looking back, it is hard to believe how little had been published up to the mid-1970s on the Israeli-Palestinian aspect of the conflict going back to the turn of the century. As far as I knew, there was almost no objective research on the Palestinians available to the general public. *The Journal of Palestine Studies* had only begun publishing several years earlier, and I was not yet aware of the level of its scholarship or the reliability of its research, nor was it popular reading in Israel.

What was printed in English for the most part reflected the Zionist view. The prevailing picture in America of the Israelis was that of heroic pioneers right out of the movie *Exodus,* which depicted an Israeli struggle against fanatical Arabs and an inhospitable desert that through their hard labors they made bloom. Menachem Begin and his clique of terrorists were largely ignored or explained away as a lunatic fringe group. Israel was, the Zionists proclaimed, a "light unto the nations." The Palestinians were lumped with the general mass of Middle East Arabs and denied status as a separate people—in Golda Meir's memorable words, they "did not exist."

Without hard documentation and credible witnesses, these stereotypes were almost impossible to shatter. This was so even though my eyes confirmed for me every day they were cartoons of reality. Yet

I could not completely shed the stereotypes, not in my own thinking, much less in stories fit to print.

Ultimately my breakthrough to reality was aided enormously by an unexpected source, the United Nations. Since the 1967 occupation, the General Assembly had become unusually active in challenging Israel's practices and affirming the rights of the Palestinians. Resolutions passed by the General Assembly over the years affirmed the Palestinians' status as a separate people with "inalienable rights," including the right of self-determination and the right to struggle for their freedom.

I have to admit that these resolutions had mainly escaped my notice. In part this was because of my involvement in other assignments, but largely I believe because Israel had been so successful in its efforts to discredit the United Nations among Americans.

Zionists hated the U.N., charging it was prejudiced. In fact, it was the only major institution that actually knew what was going on in the Occupied Territories and dared to speak out. Israel's reaction was not to change its occupation practices but instead to undermine the credibility of the United Nations itself. In this, of course, it was helped by the many other foes of the world body, but Israel's contribution should not be underestimated. By the mid-1970s, the United Nations had essentially ceased to be taken very seriously by the American media.

Interestingly, although Israel lost no chance to denigrate the United Nations, Israel itself did take it seriously. As a result, whatever the United Nations did received prominent and critical attention in Israel. My exposure to what was going on in the United Nations opened up a documentary record on which I could rely.

Israeli scorn of the U.N. turned into rage towards the end of 1975 when the General Assembly passed a resolution saying that Zionism was a "manifestation of racism and racial discrimination." The United States and Israel strongly condemned the single-line statement in the resolution and declared they would never acknowledge it. (In fact, the United States, prodded by Israel, managed to get it rescinded in 1991.)

The resolution was no surprise to me, since numerous Israelis had left no doubt in me that Christians, Muslims, and other non-Jews were not welcome in the Jewish state. But passage of the resolution provoked me to ponder the broader implications of the exclusive nature of a Jewish state—as opposed to a democracy open to all. It had a powerful influence on my evolving attitude toward Israel.

There were other events that aided my education. One was a rare divergence by the State Department from Israeli policy around the time of the U.N. racism resolution. The State Department publicly declared that the "heart of the conflict" in many ways was the Palestinian dimension, adding: "The legitimate interests of the Palestinian Arabs must be taken into account in the negotiating of an Arab-Israeli peace."

Another milestone came in mid-1977 with the publication by *The London Sunday Times* of a major exposé about torture of Palestinian prisoners by Israeli security officials. The newspaper reported that torture was "systematic" and "appears to be sanctioned at some level as deliberate policy." Israel indignantly denied the charges. Nonetheless the *Times* stuck by its report, which had the result of touching off other investigations. (Over the years other reports produced such overwhelming evidence that Israel eventually had to admit their truth. Instead of changing the practice, however, it then passed a law making some torture legal, probably the only country in the world to have a law sanctioning torture.)

But until 1978, nothing influenced me more to reconsider my original bias than the leak to the Hebrew press of a top-secret government report outlining how Israel could rid itself of some of its Palestinian citizens and make the lives of those remaining more miserable than they already were. It had been co-authored in 1976 by Israel Koenig, Northern District (Galilee) Commissioner of the Ministry of Interior, and became known as the Koenig Report.

The report was so diabolical it was hard to believe it was authentic. It warned—correctly, as it turned out—against growing Palestinian nationalism and suggested a number of cynical ways Palestinians of Israeli citizenship could be kept subordinate or even gotten rid of.

These included examining "the possibility of diluting existing Arab population concentrations;" "giving preferential treatment [in the economic sector, including jobs] to Jewish groups or individuals rather than to Arabs;" encouraging Arab students to study difficult scientific subjects because "these studies leave less time for dabbling in nationalism and the dropout rate is higher;" and encouraging Arab students to study abroad "while making the return and employment more difficult—this policy is apt to encourage their emigration."

Despite massive protests by Palestinians demanding the authors' firing, the government maintained the report was merely the personal opinion of two middle-rank officials and not official policy. Koenig remained in his post, and a short time later his co-author, Zvi Aldoraty, was recommended by Prime Minister Yitzhak Rabin as his candidate for appointment as director of the Labor Party's Arab Department.

For me the Koenig Report was a watershed. My stories increasingly began focusing on the occupation and the sly and brutal ways Israel undermined the Palestinian community. Some of my stories were based on information and leads I received from a valiant Palestinian woman, Ramonda Tawil. A wealthy, sophisticated Christian from Ramallah, she became something of a one-woman Palestinian press center in the late 1970s. (One of her daughters, Suha, married Yasser Arafat many years later.)

The stories Mrs. Tawil had to tell were usually unimpeachable, since many of them centered on her own maltreatment by Israeli military authorities. She was imprisoned and abused several times, placed under house arrest, and otherwise brutally and repeatedly harassed because of her outspokenness. Since it was clear what was happening to her—there could be no doubt she was under house arrest—Israel had to admit it was acting against her, thereby providing reporters a rare solid basis for stories about Israel's occupation practices.

My final revelation, my epiphany, so to speak, came in March 1978. It began with a telephone call from a freelance reporter, a courageous American who had become interested in the plight of the Palestinians and was close to Ramonda Tawil. She had heard reports that Israeli troops had just conducted a cruel campaign throughout the West Bank against Palestinian youth. Many Palestinians had suffered broken bones, others had been beaten, and some had had their heads shaved. Some of the victims were in Beit Jala Hospital.

When I repeated the report to my staff, all of them Israelis, they reacted with horror and indignation. The whole group, a secretary, a teletype operator, two stringers, a photographer, and two other correspondents, cast doubt on the story. They all declared that it was unthinkable because "that is what was done to us in the Holocaust."

About this time one of my best friends, Freddie Weisgal, stopped by. He was the nephew of one of Zionism's important theoreticians, Meyer Weisgal, and had been a human rights crusader in the United States before moving to Israel after the 1967 war. His vision of developing a dialogue between Israelis and Palestinians early dissolved in disillusionment. Like most American immigrants, who were not large in number, his ideas about living together with the Palestinians were not taken seriously by the Zionist establishment composed of Eastern European Jews. As a result, he whiled away his time playing chess and the piano, trying to eke out a living selling Hebraic art and artifacts to American tourists. He was the funniest, liveliest, and dearest man I had ever known.

He said something like, "Aw, come on, Don, you know Jews wouldn't do anything like that." He was agitated and indignant, which wasn't all that unusual for him. But there was an underlying tension too. By this time the bureau was in great agitation. Everyone seemed to echo Freddie's indignation. My god, one or another of them muttered or shouted at one time or another, that is what Nazis did to Jews. It was impossible to think of Jews doing that to anyone.

"All right," I said to Freddie, "let's go to Beit Jala and check it out."

We drove in the chill gathering of darkness. We went into the small hospital, and a young Palestinian doctor who spoke English soon appeared. Yes indeed, he said matter-of-factly, he had recently treated a number of students for broken bones. There were 10 cases of broken arms and legs, and many of the patients were still there, too seriously injured to leave. He took us to several rooms filled with boys in their mid-teens, an arm or leg, sometimes both, immobile under shining white plaster casts.

The doctor had a professional, no-nonsense air about him, so as he interpreted I felt I was receiving exactly the story as the victims related it.

They all said that for reasons unknown to them, Israeli troops had surrounded their two-story middle school while classes were underway. In several classrooms on the second floor, the students were ordered to close all the windows. Then the troops exploded tear-gas bombs and slammed shut the door, trapping the students with the noxious fumes. They panicked. In their rush to escape, they fled from the rooms so fast that some of them went flying over the balcony to the asphalt and stony ground below.

About the third time we heard the same story, I noticed Freddie's face. It was gray and stricken. He was shaking his head and wringing his gnarled hands. "Oh, man," he said, "this is too much. I'm getting out of here." And he left, taking a bus back to Jerusalem. Afterwards, he never talked about Beit Jala.

My Israeli photographer, who had followed in his own car, was not looking much better. But he dutifully continued taking pictures of the injured boys.

I talked to them all, and there could be no doubt about what had happened to them. Still, I wanted to see where the attack had occurred. The school was just up the hill. It was dark by now, but I had no trouble finding spent tear-gas canisters with Hebrew lettering littering the playground.

The doctor had told me that similar incidents had been reported at other Palestinian towns, including Beit Sahur and Bethlehem. However, my weekly deadline was looming, and I did not want to go chasing all around the West Bank simply to duplicate what already was clear.

This meant I would not discover the full extent of the Israeli actions. But at this point I was more determined to nail down the aspect of the story that had so upset my staff and astounded me—the cutting of hair. I had to admit to myself that I found it almost too bizarre to believe that Israelis would actually inflict on another people this most humiliating symbol of the Holocaust. On the other hand, my experience told me that Israeli hatred of Palestinians might make anything possible.

I returned to the bureau to find most of the staffers still there, expectant and anxious. To their horror, I displayed one of the used tear-gas canisters. I told them there was no doubt about what had happened.

One of the reporters with excellent military sources and of whom I was extremely fond drew me aside and in confident tones assured me the story was not true. He had checked with his best sources, and they swore to him that it had not happened. I held up the canister. He rolled his eyes and left.

The next morning at Ramonda Tawil's house I met several of the young men who had had their hair shorn. They had not been shaved, but clumps of hair were missing from their heads as though roughly cut by a knife.

They said they had been picked up by Israeli troops for no obvious reason and were ordered to do exercises and pick up litter and weeds, some of them through most of the night. They had heard, they added, that similar scenes had taken place all over the West Bank.

As with the victims in Beit Jala, their stories were entirely believable. I was determined to do a story, but I was nagged by a certain uneasiness. I was not aware of any stories about the incidents in the local media, yet two days had passed. Surely other reporters must have heard of Beit Jala or one of the other incidents that had apparently swept all over the West Bank.

I decided to seek further confirmation from an objective third party. I called one of the few Western diplomats I knew who in the past had proved willing to discuss Israeli occupation practices, albeit on an anonymous basis. We had lunch that same day. To my disappointment, he said he was not able to confirm any details.

But then he said the embassy had heard that Israeli troops had recently gone wild, adding: "There is a widespread feeling that we haven't seen this kind of repression here for years, if ever."

His vagueness and refusal to let me use his name left me not as satisfied as I would have liked to be with the level of evidence I could present my editors. Nonattributed quotes are never as strong as those with names attached. Still, his confirmation that foreign diplomats were aware that Israeli troops had gone wild clinched it for me. Even if my editors would not know the source, I did, and I trusted him.

I returned to a sullen and nervous bureau, where hanging in the air was the question of whether I was going to do a story. I announced I was.

When I walked out of my office several hours later and handed my story to the telegraph operator, there was a deep silence. I was back in my office for some minutes before the silence was broken with shouts and curses, even sobs. Members of my staff upbraided me, furiously charging the story was false and unfair, a libel against the State of Israel. I stood my ground. In response, the telegraph operator firmly announced she would not send such a story. The others seemed in agreement.

I suddenly had a sympathetic understanding of Captain Bligh. As the complaints continued, I reminded the staff that I had used a Telex many times in Vietnam and that, if it came to it, I could do so now. Short of destroying the machine or shooting me, there was nothing they could do. Reluctantly, the story was sent. I left the bureau, relieved to be by myself.

Time gave the story prominent play, and it evoked outrage by Israeli authorities and American Zionists. I had anticipated that. My growing concentration on the occupation had already resulted in resentment from some of my colleagues at *Time* in New York and anger from prominent Zionists, who did not hesitate to lodge their complaints with Time Inc. executives, especially those on the business side.

After Beit Jala, the complaints became shrill. The upper levels of *Time*'s editors were bombarded by complaints from Zionists, and a group of them demanded to meet personally with Time Inc.'s editor-in-chief to complain about my coverage. That was a mistake, since Hedley Donovan was not one to bow under such pressure. In fact, *Time* under his editorship was far in front of the rest of the media in printing stories revealing some of the dark sides of Israel's occupation, and it continued to do so.

The atmosphere in Israel was even harsher. *The Jerusalem Post* printed a cartoon of *Time* under the headline: "Time, Slime." I was attacked to my face as an anti-Semite and shunned by some.

One day as I was entering a restaurant with an Israeli official, he spotted Leon Uris and said he wanted to introduce me. Uris was a long-time propagandist for Israel—the author of *Exodus* among other novels—and owned a home in the Tel Aviv area. As we approached his table, still unseen by him, we could clearly hear Uris mention my name in a highly unflattering way. My diplomatic friend smoothly changed course, and we sat down at another table.

Around the same time strange things began happening to me. One day my mechanic reported that the front tires of my car were so over-inflated that they could blow out at any time. How did it happen, he wanted to know, that the tires had twice the pressure they should have? I didn't have the slightest idea, but I couldn't help musing that it would be an effective way to harm someone.

Another time my third-story apartment was broken into, the only time that had ever happened to me anywhere in the world. It almost certainly was the work of ordinary thieves. But still it spooked me. The old terrorist Menachem Begin was now prime minister, and anything was possible. And no other apartment in the large building had been broken into.

But mainly my worry centered on the disturbing fact that the story had not been picked up by *The New York Times*, which was the morning newspaper read by *Time* editors. They relied on it as the newspaper of record, a reliance not always justified when it came to Israel, certainly not during this period when its editor was A. M. Rosenthal. He was a fanatical Zionist, as his later career as a columnist has revealed.

I was in that unenviable position that reporters dread most. While there is nothing like the joy of getting an exclusive, some exclusives become too exclusive. The implication of a scoop that nobody else prints is that other reporters have looked into the story and found it too flawed to be worthy of publication. The continuing silence by the *Times* cast mounting doubts about my story. My situation became more uneasy as the days and weeks went by.

And then a miraculous thing happened. Ezer Weizman, the father of Israel's airforce and an upright man, personally took the matter into his own hands. As defense minister, he appointed a commission to investigate the matter. It found the Beit Jala story true. When he was presented with the findings, Weizman did something that had never been done before: he publicly fired the military governor of the West Bank, Brigadier General David Hagoel, for abusing Palestinians.

It had taken more than a month, but needless to say, the ending was enormously satisfying, a forthright action that to this day gives me hope that Israel may still have a chance to become the nation it professes to be.

Shortly after Weizman set the record straight I left Israel. I was, quite frankly, worried about my personal well-being under a Begin government, drained by Beit Jala, and heartbroken and discouraged by the display of prejudice and unprofessional conduct of my colleagues, whom I had admired. Not only would they not have used the story if it had been up to them, but after Weizman's confirmation some of them confided to me that from the beginning they had known in their hearts that the story was true.

This amazing confession struck me as the worst example of bad journalism and ugly prejudice I could imagine. The experience left me highly skeptical about the wisdom of employing reporters in areas where they are partisans.

After three and a half years, my last act in Jerusalem was to throw a going-away party for myself and a welcoming party for my successor. It was just as well that I cast it as a welcome party for him; I'm not sure many Israeli guests would have attended otherwise. This was confirmed to me when Teddy Kollek, the mayor of Jerusalem with a reputation in America as a champion of Palestinian rights, arrived. He did not smile. "I am not here to see you," he declared, then turned his back and sought out my successor.

On that graceful note, my tour in Israel ended—but not by any means my interest.

People and the Land:
Coming to a PBS Station Near You?
By Tom Hayes

Tom Hayes, a documentary filmmaker, teaches at Ohio University's College of Fine Arts. In 1989, he and his film crew went to the West Bank and Gaza to make a documentary on Israel's occupation of Palestinian land. From his November–December 1997 issue of The Link, *we excerpt those sections dealing with the censorship he encountered both in Israel and on his return home.*

In the late 1970s I made a film about displaced Indochinese people who were eventually resettled in the United States. The documentary followed a single family, the Nouts, starting with their life in [a refugee] camp and staying with them through their first year in the United States. The resulting film, *Refugee Road,* was broadcast nationally on PBS. It was picked up again by WNET, the New York City PBS affiliate, for a series on immigrants that was broadcast during the rededication of the Statue of Liberty. Never once, in all the screenings of *Refugee Road* I attended, was the term "balance" ever mentioned.

Refugee camps are purposely impermanent constructions—places to drain off humanity into the sky. There is no safe place to hide but sewage-filled trenches when high explosives come screaming in. More than half the population of any refugee camp on the planet is children. You connect the dots—refugee camps, artillery, and children—the results are utterly and ruthlessly predictable. That trip left an impression like a tattoo on my neocortex.

I remember quite clearly the morning I stepped into that black hole marked Palestine. It's funny how the pivotal moments of our lives are so innocuous, with so little preparatory fanfare. I'm having a cup of coffee before class, two newspapers before me—*The New York Times* and *The Columbus Dispatch*. I read a story in the *Times* that goes something like this, "Israel launches air strike against guerrilla stronghold in southern Lebanon, 6 dead."

I didn't think much of it. There wasn't much of it—an inch of copy. I'd seen hundreds of nearly identical inch-long stories without blinking. I reach for the *Dispatch:* "Israel launches air strike against Rashidiyya, a Palestinian guerrilla stronghold in southern Lebanon." And I look up. Just across the dining room table I've tacked up a map of all the refugee camps. And I'm looking right at the word Rashidiyya with a little symbol that says it's a refugee camp. My mind travels at the speed of light back to the Cambodian border, and I'm confused. Israel—the Israel I was so smugly sure of—would never bomb a refugee camp. I know from bombing refugee camps. The shining city on the hill simply wouldn't do that. And I seemed to sense the camouflage that the term "guerrilla stronghold" provided to the act of bombing men, women, and children in a refugee camp. I became very curious about who these Palestinians were and how they happened to be in refugee camps and why the English language was evading these journalists.

So I read everything I could get my hands on, from Menachem Begin to Fawaz Turki. I sought out Palestinians and talked to them about what I'd read and about their lives. If you know anyone who's doing that—informing themselves on this issue, and talking to actual Palestinians—warn them: ROAD CLOSED, PROCEED AT YOUR OWN RISK. Knowledge may very well be power; I have bet my life on that premise. But ignorance may provide a better night's sleep.

It took two years to generate enough "clean" funding (spell that n-o-n-A-r-a-b) to go into production on *Native Sons*. Most of the grants were from the Ohio Arts Council and the National Endowment for the Arts. Hoorah for peer panel review. UNRWA was providing some logistical support, and I had borrowed heavily against my home to make up the balance of the budget.

With nine months of colloquial Arabic study under my belt, I took off for Lebanon, to be followed in two weeks by the soundman and the rest of the equipment. It seems crazy in retrospect. I didn't have any real contacts, had never visited the country before. Six people had died in shelling at the Beirut airport the day before I flew into it.

Life under Military Occupation

Within the Occupied Territories there is a broad sense among Palestinians that the most powerful weapon in their hands is the truth. The camera was not only welcome, but people would take considerable personal risk to make sure we got out with our film.

Jenin, 1989: Riad, John and I are having coffee on the front porch when we hear that characteristic crackle of M-16 fire. It sounds like someone slapping two-by-fours together, not at all the throaty sound of a Kalashnakov. It wasn't long before a neighbor woman came up the front walk shaking with sobs. She told us that a neighborhood boy, Imad Arqawi, had been killed by Israeli troops. Several other people were badly wounded.

A Palestinian journalist drove up and asked whether we wanted to go over to the clinic or up to Imad's house. We opted for Imad's house in Jenin Camp. By this time burning tires are pushing black fingers into the sky all over Jenin.

There was no question we were at the right house as we unloaded our equipment. All the neighbor ladies had come to be with Imad's mother. The collective grief that poured from that courtyard was a sound from hell.

In Islam, as in Judaism, it is customary to bury the dead the same day they die, and martyrs are buried in the clothing they were wearing when they were killed. The Israeli Army, in its role of harasser of things non-Jewish, regularly confiscates the bodies of martyrs for a few days and performs unauthorized autopsies to prevent the observance of this religious custom.

We followed Imad's family to the cemetery, a bowl-shaped field to the east of the camp. It looked like all of Jenin was involved—crowds numbering in the hundreds, chanting for freedom and liberation, pouring down the roads and paths leading to the cemetery.

Imad lay beneath a Palestinian flag in the center of the field, his friends and family kneeling beside him, saying goodbye. The townspeople gathered, surrounding them like a great protecting wall. Neighbor ladies escorted his mother to the shade of an olive tree. One of the women cried out to Umm Imad, "All the boys in Palestine are your sons now." It was then that I started to cry.

The waste of that young life. Never to marry, never to share grandchildren with his parents, never to have lived free for even an instant of his life. His mother held an olive branch in her hand. An olive branch!

The distance between a news item like "One Palestinian Killed" and the human meaning of the murder is such a terrible, unbridgeable distance.

There was a feeling I couldn't shake at that funeral that made me recall tales I had heard of slave funerals in the old South. Imad was free at last, safe beyond the oppressors' long reach.

We had gone down through the crowd to where Imad's body lay. As non-Arabs, we were instantly identified with the occupation. Some people directed their rage at us, but others came forward to lead us to where Imad rested.

I'm not unaware of the ghoulish reputation the media have: "If it bleeds, it leads." But frankly I was so sick of listening to denials of the violence against Palestinians—the so-called "benign occupation"—that I felt compelled to film what we were seeing. Imad had a bullet hole just at the base of his throat, and another about four inches away near his left armpit.

As I bent close to that young body, there was a smell. Not the smell of death; he had only been dead an hour or so. It was a strange, sweet smell, like a baby's smell. I kept smelling that smell for a long time afterwards, like it was fastened to me. Even months later it would just appear in my nose.

We shot all the film we had brought with us. Boys we'd never met, friends of Imad, urged us to get the hell out of there, because the army was going to be attracted to such a large gathering. They held a quick logistical discussion.

One group took off to scout the road. There was no telling which direction or directions the army would come from. The boys were absolutely intent that we not lose our film to the Israelis. We followed in a second car a half mile behind.

The cemetery was actually no more than a quarter mile from where we were staying, but we took a long, circuitous route back to the house. When we got there, the boys asked us for the film and took off through backyards. The footage wound up buried in a garden for two weeks before we could get back to retrieve it.

Then we heard automatic weapons fire from the direction of the cemetery. Usually you hear a burst or two, then it's over. This shooting didn't stop. The army had come to seize Imad's body. I loaded audiotape into the deck and started recording. As I was trying to describe the sounds coming from the distance, I couldn't shake the image of Imad's mother, sitting under that tree, all those other Palestinian mothers gathered around her. Even in death, Imad was pursued. Even in her grief, his mother endured another assault.

What kind of people shoot into crowds at a funeral? What manner of human being? Murdering Imad wasn't satisfying enough? They had to terrorize his family and friends during the funeral?

The unarmed crowd succeeded in holding off the soldiers long enough for Imad to be buried. Another boy, 13, died as a result of chest wounds incurred in the attack. More than a dozen Palestinians were seriously wounded.

Tell me those fairy tales of "Israeli democracy." I'll be looking at you like you just escaped from a mental hospital. Tell me about that shining city on the hill.

Tell me I don't have a balanced viewpoint.

Then balance for me the Khmer Rouge tale with the refugees' tale. I didn't give the Khmer Rouge any face time at all in *Refugee Road.* Not one second. Yet in the 50 plus screenings of *Refugee Road* I attended, no one ever whispered the word "balance."

Balance me apartheid, or the Cheyenne, or the Japanese-Americans' experience during World War II; the slave's tale with the slave owner's. Truth exists beyond balance. It is "justice" that is associated with balance, as in "the scales of." The sound of those high-powered assault rifles being used against a funeral crowd and recorded on my tape is a truth that nothing is going to balance.

How Is Such Distorted Mythology Perpetuated?

That is the salient question.

People and the Land addresses two forms of information control vis-à-vis the human rights situation in Palestine. In fact there are really four distinct pinch points on information before it hits the breakfast table: Funding, filming, getting the footage out of Israel, and dissemination.

The amount of money required for a broadcast-quality media production is staggering. It can take years to mount a project, and funding may be needed from any number of sources to fill in the fiscal recipe. Probably 80 percent of an independent filmmaker's time is spent hacking out proposals. When you finally go into production it's like being released from a cage.

On *People and the Land,* co-producer Riad Bahhur and I were fortunate to get the nod from the Independent Television Service (ITVS). Congress mandated the creation of ITVS through the Corporation for Public Broadcasting to serve underserved minorities and increase programming diversity on PBS.

The total annual budget for ITVS is equivalent to six hours of aid to Israel, or three 30-second Super Bowl commercials. ITVS provides full funding for productions precisely to accommodate PBS funding "concerns."

That makes the process sound so simple: one grant, full funding, out the door. It's anything but simple. It took two years to raise enough money to go into production on *Native Sons.* Five years on *People and the Land.*

Generally you only get one opportunity per year on a specific grant, an annual panel meeting. You can go through whole years turning out nothing but bad paper, the grant-writing days and weeks like pieces of your life sucked into the word processor, then spit into oblivion. A little frustrating. ITVS receives in excess of 2,000 proposals a year. If 20 get funded it's a good year.

Our relationship with ITVS began stormy in 1991, and continues so to this day.

It was July 1991 when ITVS called. They had just completed their first grant panel meeting, and the entire film community was holding its collective breath, each of us praying that the project that was consuming us was going to be recommended for funding. I had trouble controlling bodily fluids when I was told that our project had been selected.

The next sentence that came scratching out of the phone dropped a sinker in my stomach: "We have some questions."

When you have spent a few years doing information work on Palestine, the sound of a qualifying remark from a grant administrator is an icicle to the heart.

"Some questions" from ITVS staff, mostly in the person of John Schott, then executive director, turned into 18 months of battling to keep the grant. Multipage lists of questions streamed in from their offices in Minneapolis. The paper interrogation boiled down to "where did you get every penny that went into shooting the sample work submitted for this grant?" ITVS burrowed through the project records, mining for a justification to kill the funding.

The lasting mental image I have from that 18 months is of my feet pacing my office night after night, trying to figure out how ITVS could pull such a stunt, scoping the next move in that slow chess game.

There was plenty of time for soul-searching. For me, work on Palestine was a test of the relevance of independent filmmaking. If you couldn't get funding and dissemination for work about super-power culpability in cultural genocide, then what exactly was the point of independent filmmaking? Entertainment? Media titillation?

I'm not interested in entertainment, nor am I interested in the programming philosophy embedded in most PBS shows: "If it's dead, shoot it." PBS runs lots of interesting documentaries, nearly all of them about dead people, dead artists, and dead issues. Their one current-affairs documentary series, *Frontline*, is squeezed through the corporate filter of WGBH in Boston, a single executive producer exercising final cut on the entire series. Not a recipe for diversity in the marketplace of ideas.

According to the ITVS grant panel, what I had brought to the table fit its congressional mandate of providing diversity and serving an underserved audience.

It is worth noting that PBS, the Corporation for Public Broadcasting, and ITVS were looking at reauthorization hearings on Capitol Hill within the year. What John Schott described as "administrative diligence" appeared to me like a monster cop-out, an attempt to protect ITVS funding by not having to defend a Palestine project before Congress.

At one point I was told that the project had been disqualified because a Palestinian-American community organization had provided plane tickets and lodgings in Palestine for production trips funded by the Ohio Arts Council. Schott defined that as support from an organization with a direct interest in the topic. "I'd really like to see this project funded, but those are the rules. We can't do anything about it."

Ironically, at the very same time, the Ohio Arts Council was saying that it was going to reduce the final payment on one of our grants because we had not generated adequate matching funds. Their justification was that the travel assistance we had received had no monetary value—the same travel assistance ITVS was defining as having a monetary value that disqualified the project.

Schott's "administrative diligence" on the project was the source of ongoing discussion and division on the ITVS board. At one point, Jackie Shearer, a member of the founding ITVS board, threatened to resign over the affair. She had herself come under the Zionist swatter when she produced a human interest story for a Boston station about Palestinians in America. Jackie knew precisely what was going on.

In December 1992 she became president of the ITVS board. Four months later the preproduction payment for *People and the Land* arrived from ITVS. Jackie Shearer died of a chronic illness some months later. Without her dedication to the principles of diversity and artistic freedom, *People and the Land* would not exist.

With funding in hand, we were ready to film in Occupied Palestine. You learn quickly that cameras are not wanted. It's completely understandable. If you were committing war crimes, would you want camera crews following you around? Israeli antagonism to foreign camera crews is justified on the premise that the entire world is anti-Semitic and therefore only Israelis should be making images for export of the Jewish state in action.

The media obstacle course begins long before entering Israel. The geography of this maze says a lot about the "why" of prevailing Middle Eastern mythology. It starts with domestic issues: equipment, and a document called a carnet.

Once a project is funded, you rent the production equipment. Of course renting anything from a car to a camera is going to require insurance. However, "all-risk" insurance is not available for media equipment to be used under Israeli jurisdiction. I don't know why exactly, but it may have to do with Israeli guys with machine guns taking and breaking crews' camera gear. Not even Lloyd's of London would write insurance against confiscation on equipment going into Israel.

The impact of this insurance problem is a financial bullet big enough to stop a project. Since no one is going to rent you equipment, you have to buy it. This is an expense on the order of buying a house. In light of the kind of resources this equipment consumes, I am very fortunate that my wife and family have been supportive of this work. The lack of insurance means that if the equipment is seized or damaged, you're looking at financial devastation.

Getting the film, the crew, and the equipment into Israel is another can of worms. The carnet is sort of a passport for the equipment. It makes possible the duty-free import/export of the gear. In addition to the carnet, Israel requires a deposit on entry equal to the full value of the equipment you're bringing in. We're talking in excess of $40,000. At that time there were only three countries in the world that demanded a 100 percent deposit on media equipment: South Korea, South Africa, and Israel.

I had a history of unsullied carnet use, so I was able to secure a surety bond for considerably less than $40,000. Still, it's not hard to see how these two issues, carnet and insurance, can limit attempts by independents to document the situation in the Occupied Territories.

Then you have to get through Ben-Gurion Airport. A word to the wise: treat your entrance onto the plane for Tel Aviv as entry into an Israeli military base. Don't discuss your purpose with your crew or anyone else. Just watch the movie and keep your mouth shut.

For a trip in 1989 we had secured letters from the governor of Ohio and Senator John Glenn stating that we were producing a film for PBS and to please extend all normal journalistic courtesies and clearances to the crew. At some point in the flight Dorothy Thigpen, Riad Bahhur, and I checked over the contents of the "letters envelope." Each of us had a full set of originals. When we got into Tel Aviv, the three of us were immediately escorted to the "Welcome to Israel" wing (otherwise known as the Arab Room), where we were taken to separate interrogation rooms. The first thing out of my interrogator's mouth was "let's see the letters."

The management of Interrogations-Are-Us concentrated on Dorothy, the assistant cameraperson. "Who are their contacts?" "Who's helping?" "What did they tell you about where they'll be filming?" She enjoyed their company longer than either Riad or I, although Riad may have been the reason for their interest: an Arab surname, even on a U.S. passport, plus a camera is an irresistible red flag, so we quit traveling together to Israel after that. Entry without Riad was somewhat easier. And we briefed the crew on subsequent trips: no shop talk.

An interesting thing happened after our trip to the Arab Room. Dorothy called her parents to tell them we had arrived unscathed. The moment she said, "The airport was really weird," her call was cut off.

It sends you a simple message—we're listening. In some ways that is what I found most oppressive about working in the Territories. You'd come back into Jerusalem after a few days in the trenches witnessing God knows what new horror, and you'd be dying to talk with your family, hungry for the touch of their support. But you couldn't go near the phone. You don't want the army to know what you have on film, or where you've been, or what you saw. Over time the sense of living under siege became palpable, a ringing loneliness.

By 1993 Israel had put a new twist on keeping down improper image creation. I'm standing in the immigration queue at Ben-Gurion. I hand my documents to the young women in her nice blue uniform and she glances at them. "You are a journalist?" "Yes, a journalist."

"You cannot enter, you don't have a visa. You should have contacted us ahead of time."

"Usual politics of intimidation," thought I. "I don't need a visa; I'm an American citizen. I can enter when I want." She throws me a poisonous glance, stamps the passport, and motions me through. After all, I'm white. I didn't find out until a couple of days later what she was talking about.

We had embarked on the ritual of the Journalist's Credentials. This entails traveling into West Jerusalem to the National Baloney Factory, otherwise known as the Government Press Office at Beit Agroan. This had to be weirdest for Riad—requesting a document from New Yorkers to be able to film in his homeland without getting beat up.

The crew is sitting around filling out applications for press credentials, part of which acknowledges our understanding that as journalists we can't make a phone call or send a fax that discusses the situation on the ground without first getting content cleared through the military censor.

I do most of the camera work, but this time I just wrote "director" as my job description. Barry Congrove, assistant cameraperson on that trip, completed his form and handed it to the clerk. The guy looked at the form and narrowed his eyes at the five of us. "Which of you will be handling camera equipment?" Barry put up his hand. "There's a new law. Foreign camera operators can only have credentials for two weeks." He proceeded to explain that the videographers union persuaded the government to protect Israeli jobs by limiting the amount of time a given project could use non-Israeli camera operators.

On its face this seems pretty reasonable, and it would be reasonable if the army service requirements were different in Israel. Virtually every male between 18 and 50 performs active duty with the Israeli military once a year. Which means that any Israeli cameraman you hire may have—just the week before—been kicking the shit out of the people you're filming.

American networks abide by the law. We would frequently see convoys of Israeli crews in their armored Volvos rolling in from Jerusalem after clashes.

The implications of this policy that "only our people are allowed to interpret our image to the world" are profound. The image conduit to the U.S. is, by law, narrowed to the perspective of Israeli reservists. This is not to say that every Israeli cameraperson is a slack-jawed lackey to the army. On the other hand, if you are raised in a segregationist society, your worldview is going to be shaped by that. The obscene is normal and you may treat it as such in your work.

Mr. Credentials said one other very interesting thing. "You don't need credentials in the Territories, only if you want to film inside Israel." This is a classic bit of Orwellian speak. He may as well have said, "We don't object to you putting your tongue in that light socket." Press credentials are the only protection against the army that you've got in the Territories. And a puny bit of protection it is.

With the camera running, I asked the Keeper of the Credentials, the army spokesman, and the general who runs the "Civil Administration" exactly what the credentials enabled us to do in the Territories. Their answers were the same: "Oh, anything you want." I show their responses in the film as an example of the abyss between official Israeli government pronouncements and the situation on the ground.

The credential itself clips inside your passport. It's worthless plastic in terms of allowing you to do your work, but it can save your skin.

On our first trip into the Territories in 1988, Riad, John, and I decided to enter as tourists. We had letters from the governor of Ohio and a congressman basically saying we were artists working with Ohio Arts Council funds and not to beat us up. We decided to steer clear of the Government Press Office and try to work without credentials. The army was routinely seizing footage and equipment from journalists. We thought we might be able to move more easily if we weren't associated with the press.

One afternoon we shot an interview in Ramallah with a human rights caseworker from Al-Haq (Law in the Service of Man). The shoot dragged on until after dark. Once finished, we brought the car around and surreptitiously began loading the equipment. We had learned early in the game that if the army saw a crew entering or leaving a home they would make a point of visiting the family later, either to smash up the place or to detain the person suspected of talking to the press.

We were making the last turn out of Ramallah for Jerusalem when two army jeeps pulled in front of us and forced us to stop. "What are you doing here?" the leader of the pack yelled into my face. "Trying to get back to Jerusalem." "Where have you been?" "Uh, Nazareth." When we traveled we'd work out our story ahead of time; always use tourist towns for points of departure and destination. "Give us your passports!"

We hand over our passports. Riad is sitting in the back seat trying to make himself invisible. We've stuffed all of the production equipment into the trunk, so we're looking pretty touristy.

The unit commander flips through the three passports. When he gets to Riad's, he steps to his window. "What was your whore mother doing in Argentina?" Riad's passport indicates that he holds American citizenship but was born in Argentina. Riad answers, "My family moved to Argentina before going to the States." "Speak Arabic!" screams the unit commander. "My Arabic isn't very good." The commander, now very agitated, is yelling in Arabic, *"Haki Arabi ibn sharmoota"* ["Speak Arabic, you son of a whore."]

He yells a clipped order in Hebrew. Two soldiers step to either side of the car and point their M-16s at John and me. Two more throw open Riad's door and drag him by his clothing onto the deserted street. The few cars that do approach the intersection are waved through. We are alone in the dark and at their mercy. My knees have started shaking for real.

"Is there a problem? What's the problem?" I go for my door latch and the soldier covering me sights down his rifle as if to say "one more inch and you won't need that head." They are dragging Riad around in the street like a dead animal, the commander screaming at him. Finally they stand him up, shove a rifle in his stomach, and say something in Arabic. Riad turns and says, quietly, "He's ordering me into the jeep. He says they're going to teach me manners."

I had read enough reports of young Palestinian men found in olive groves with their heads staved in to know I would probably never see Riad again if he got into that jeep. I looked the soldier who was covering me in the eye, prayed, and stepped out of the car. Hanging onto the door—my knees didn't seem to be cooperating—I yell as loudly as I can yell, "THIS MAN IS AN AMERICAN CITIZEN. I WANT TO SEE YOUR COMMANDING OFFICER. THIS MAN IS AN AMERICAN CITIZEN. WHAT'S THE PROBLEM?" I'm terrified and very glad to have the door to support me.

Riad pulls out his letter from the governor of Ohio and hands it to the commander. He looks at it, tears it up, and throws it in the street.

While I'm hanging off the car yelling, the other soldier tells John to pop the trunk. He does. They see the camera and tell the commander. Now it's my turn. I'm shoved over to the jeep. "You are journalist?" "Well, uh, media artist, yes." He shoves his face into mine. He's out of control, his spit hitting me in the face. "Your pictures are making a lot of trouble for us!"

You learn quickly in the Territories that carefully measured audacity can be salvation. Never show these punks fear; it just makes them feel more powerful. "This man is an American citizen. I want to see your commanding officer," I yell back. What's to lose at this point? I figured we were all in for it.

He gives me this weird look, like "the subhuman must have some juice or he wouldn't talk to me like that." "I WANT YOU OUT OF HERE NOW!" "Yes, sir, we're gone." John reaches over and plucks the passports from the commander's hand and heads back to the car. The other soldiers look to their boss for orders. He says nothing. Riad and I jump in the car and take off, holding our breath, waiting for the crack of the rifles. Nothing.

We decided that Israeli journalist credentials might not be a bad idea in the future. And we made a hard rule. No traveling in the Territories after dark. Be gone before dark, or stay where you are. The wolf packs come out at night.

Many a long night after that I lay in the darkness of my room polishing that sword named fear. What tomorrow? Will we all get out of here alive?

A year later when we went to get journalist credentials, Mr. Credentials was disturbed by the number of letters from U.S. senators and congressmen that we dropped on his desk. "I've never had anyone bring in a letter from a senator before. Why do you have one?"

I explained that Riad and I had a very unpleasant interaction with Israeli troops on a previous trip and that I had no intention of repeating that experience, and neither had Senator Glenn.

We got our credentials, but had to listen to Mr. Credentials' excuses for why Israeli troops can't control themselves at the sight of an Arab surname. "You don't know what happened to those soldiers before you got there!" That kind of denial is like nails on a blackboard. "I was there. Tell me, do you think there's any excuse for an agent of the government to call someone's mother a whore?"

So you've got some funding, equipment, and credentials—and you're in the Territories. This is where it gets tough.

The army will do anything to prevent you from capturing their tactics on film. And the Palestinian community has little reason to either trust you or put any value in what you are trying to accomplish. Fortunately some Palestinians are committed to outreach work and are willing to help journalists. Still, developing contacts can take years. Riad, as a member of the community, was able to do a great deal in this regard, but we faced a siege mentality in many Palestinian communities: trust people you grew up with, and keep an eye on some of them.

Risk and benefit. Those were two issues we saw weighed before us daily. As Jad Isak, a member of the Palestinian negotiating team and a veteran of Israeli prisons, said, "The sword of administrative detention hangs over the neck of every Palestinian."

You can go to jail for breathing if you're Palestinian in the Territories. Helping out journalists was a pretty good way to guarantee a trip to Ansar III. I think many of the people who did help us make contacts, or who appeared in the film, were convinced enough about the power of video to risk paying the price. The price got very high.

Of the people who helped us on our 1989 trip, 18 received administrative detention and four were shot. Zacharia Talamas almost paid with his life for helping us, and his tale says much about the army's attitude toward journalists. The logic is transparent. If someone can help film Palestinian resistance, they must be part of the resistance and must therefore be taken out of circulation.

The early years of the intifada were the toughest in terms of direct assaults on camera crews. Confiscation of film and equipment, beatings, and shootings were all on the menu. Palestinian journalists were most heavily targeted. Their newspaper offices were welded shut, and a great many were given administrative detention running into years without charge, trial, or family visits.

One of the first people we interviewed in 1988 was Kamel, a Palestinian journalist. He had just been released after a year of administrative detention at Ansar III, the concentration camp in the Negev desert. His wife was six months pregnant with their first child when troops broke into their house and dragged him off into the night. His son was six months old before he met his father.

As foreign journalists, we didn't have to worry too much about being jailed unless we tried to film military prison camps, which would be interpreted as an act of spying. Making the army really angry can result in the Israeli government's declaring you persona non grata—you're out for good. If the army arrests you, that's it. Avoiding arrest and trying to do your work is a knife edge you walk daily.

The primary problem was a sort of geographic censorship. If the army spotted our crew, a soldier would pull out a closure order, wave it in our face, and order us to leave the town. If a journalist was caught in a "closed area," the minimum retribution was arrest and a pink slip out of the country. Some American journalists weren't so lucky. Neal Cassidy, who photographed for the New York City newspaper *Front Line,* was shot in Nablus. Photographer Bill Biggart, who did work for *The Village Voice* and *The Christian Science Monitor,* was caught alone by Israeli troops and thoroughly stomped.

In the course of our filming, we experienced an exciting range of army hospitality. We were shot at and targeted for gassing. Or a soldier would attempt to slam the camera through the back of my head. It's a simple technique: shove the lens hard enough, and the eyepiece will try to spoon the cameraman's eyeball out.

At first the troops can intimidate you into leaving simply by stating, "This is a closed military area, you have to leave." After a while we got wise to the fact that soldiers would lay this line on us whether we were in a closed area or not. We started demanding to see the closure order. This was partly for our own entertainment, and partly a step in the dance of intimidation and defiance.

Denial is a way of life for the Israeli Army: "The press is free to film the army." "The army's role is not to punish people." "There are no death squads." I didn't want anyone on my crew shot in the back by "mistake." We frequently changed the vehicles we were renting—not so much for anonymity, but for license plate color. The basic color code is yellow=Israeli, blue=West Bank Palestinian, white=Gaza Palestinian. Israeli settlers have yellow plates regardless of where they live. This simplifies harassment of Palestinians and minimizes inconvenience to settlers.

Deciding which plate to display on a given expedition is not that simple. If you use yellow, you aren't going to get much trouble from the army. Approach the checkpoint with confidence, you'll slide through. But when you get to where you're going, people will be suspicious that you're settlers come to rain havoc, and you may lose a windshield or worse.

The army is going to home in on the people you film because there's a car with the wrong color plates near the house. We got in the habit of putting yellow-plate vehicles in barns or garages, or dumping them on the outskirts of town after we'd unloaded.

If you show a blue plate, the army will treat you like a Palestinian: long waits, vehicle searches, explanations of why a card-carrying human being is sitting in a car with blue plates. But if you can get to where you're going, you can move about quietly. There's nothing on the vehicle to leave the journalist scent.

Yellow plates are very handy if you want to drive inside Israel at night. It is illegal for Palestinians from the Occupied Territories to spend the night in Israel, so forget the blue or white plates. Swinging through Israel to get back to Jerusalem was something we did several times. If we worked late in Nablus or Jenin, we'd punch across the Green Line in our yellow-plate special and avoid the checkpoints.

If we were playing tourist, we'd take a yellow-plate Israeli rental car into the Territories and keep a checkered *kaffiyya* on the dashboard when moving through Palestinian towns. If we approached a checkpoint, we'd stuff the *kaffiyya* under the seat 'til we'd cleared the troops.

Some strategies for dealing with the army were more perverse. I picked up several corrosively bright shirts at the Salvation Army and wore them constantly. These shirts are guaranteed to make you underestimate the wearer on sight (as in "only a moron would wear that"). I also carried a yo-yo. If soldiers got into that mean kind of kick-yer-ass testiness, I'd pull out the yo-yo and start doing "'round the worlds." I'm older than most of the soldiers. The image: eye-searing shirt, yo-yo, $40,000 camera—full-on ozone cowboy American—worked on several occasions to get the boyz in green to react like I was possibly infectious.

Those are the mechanics of gathering footage in Occupied Palestine, but some discussion of project method, a look at the documentary philosophy behind *People and the Land,* is in order.

We tried to maintain a kind of controlled chaos system during the nearly seven months of filming we did in the Territories: Don't try to make plans; the army's sure to screw them up anyway, and you also risk filming according to the plan instead of catching the situation around you.

I am comfortable inside that kind of chaos, Riad less so, but we kept things very loose. We'd go out the door with the camera loaded, the recorder threaded, and enough charged batteries, underwear, and film for several days of shooting. We shot any manifestation of the occupation we could get away with.

There were things we couldn't film. Unforgettable things. We were trying to get back to Gaza City from Rafah one day. It was close to the first anniversary of the Palestinian Declaration of Independence. The Occupied Territories were seething, and the army was not liking it. Khan Yunis was blocked off—there had been an armed operation against the army—so we took back roads, mostly sand paths, to get around it.

We came into a village well back from the main road, on the eastern side of the Gaza Strip, that was crawling with army. As we turned onto the road that would take us back toward Gaza City we came upon a large ditch completely surrounded by soldiers and jeeps. The males in the village, 70 or so, had been herded down into the bottom. Old men squatted beside their grandsons amidst the trash. You could hear murmured assurance to the little ones. The older faces gazed up at the ring of soldiers and guns on the rim of the ditch, as though memorizing the faces.

A tableau of oppression. But no way in hell we could shoot it.

The Censor: There and Here

As the weeks of filming went on, we all found the ugliness of the situation chewing on us like some black fungus. It's the isolation. You can't really talk to your family back home about what you're seeing, about the realities of the situation. One wrong word on the phone is going to let the perpetual listeners know what we're filming, or where, provide clues about our helpers' locations, or set us up for trouble with the military censor.

Registering as a journalist with Israel requires a signed commitment to clear every fax, every foreign call that involves discussion of the situation, every tape, and every reel of film through the military censor's office at Beit Agroan. Failure to do so is punishable by imprisonment or deportation. While you're filming, you constantly live with the implicit threat that if you mess with the army, the censor isn't going to let you take your footage out of the country.

You can't clear your material bit by bit. No more than 48 hours prior to leaving the country, you have to physically drag the crates up to the censor's office, where armed soldiers decide whether it stays or leaves. All your work, all the risks and sacrifices contained in those crates, comes down to that moment. They can do anything they want, from seizing the entire heap, to screening the material frame by frame. They have guns.

Every story you see on television has been through this process, although the networks rarely acknowledge it. The chronic failure to inform viewers and listeners that material has been cleared through the Israeli Military Censor amounts to a form of systematic distortion. It gives the impression that what is posing as information is coming to you "free and clear."

During the Detroit PBS station's follow-up to the broadcast of *People and the Land,* the moderator slammed the "quality of journalism" in the documentary. I had to laugh. The network he works for hasn't acknowledged censor clearance since the Gulf War. My response was that *People and the Land* held itself to a higher journalistic standard than PBS or any of the networks by disclosing the strictures through which the American people receive the information.

The censor on duty asks for all the cases to be emptied. I drag about 50 cubic feet of film cans and Hi8 tapes onto the floor of the office. "Who is helping you do all this filming? What are their names? What towns are they from? What did you film?" I'm being offered a not terribly subtle bribe: give us some people and we'll let you and your footage go.

"Everybody helps, I don't know their names, we filmed whatever the army allowed us to film." "Holy sites" was also an effective response to the censor's questions. After all, every place in Palestine is a holy place to someone. It's a hard answer to tease any information from and it doesn't antagonize.

At any point the officer can demand to see the footage. In our case this would have meant processing and printing in an Israeli lab. Fortunately the duty officers I encountered weren't in the mood for confrontation. After the questions, they'd hand me a form thick with carbon paper, a legal document on which I was to explain the content of the footage and sign a declaration that nothing in the footage was a threat to state security.

There are events that preoccupy any nation, even occupying nations. World Cup soccer games, for example. I arrive at the censor's office with nine crates of footage, smack in the middle of the Israel vs. Poland match. They've pulled the monitors off their playback decks and are glued to the screens. I'm the last thing in the universe they want to mess with.

The censor hurriedly reads the signed form. The armed soldiers are oblivious to anything but the game. You hold your breath as the censor's seal descends onto the pages. Then all the footage goes back into the cases and he applies a seal to each case. Without the seal, the footage will not leave the country.

We always went to the airport three hours early so there would be plenty of time for our search and interrogation. And every single time Israeli security officers would say that the material was not allowed to leave the country. Censor's seals aside, they let you know that your exit was in their hands. "Who helped you, what are their names, where are they from? You couldn't have filmed all of this on your own." She is in her early twenties, a true believer, her English clipped and precise. "We need to know who helped you, for your own safety." My response is that the military censor has already cleared the footage. I lean into the adage *when threatened be aggressive:* "The right of journalists to maintain confidentiality of sources is internationally recognized."

"Wait right here." She marches off and returns with someone higher in the food chain. He's in his late forties and carries a distinct Philly accent. "Whatah de names o'de people det hepd chu fim?" I know the type; generally you run into them in settlements. I decide to go for the weak spot, racism. "I don't know, everyone's named Mohammed or Ali around here and lives in Beit something." He looks at me hard. After a moment the image—clueless, Hawaiian-shirted American—prevails. He relaxes.

We're still pulled aside with our 27 crates for that special search. Every single thing in every single case comes out. The collapsing miniature darkroom goes up so security can touch the unprocessed negative. Two hours and several thousand dollars in excess baggage fees later our passports are handed back to us and we are instructed to go to the departure lounge and wait for the boarding call before entering passport control.

We grab some breakfast and hope that there are no hitches. You aren't really home free until you leave Israeli airspace. We finally hear the TWA boarding call and hustle up to Passport Control. I hand my passport to the officer, who glances at it, then hands it back. "You haven't received an exit visa. You are not allowed to pass." There wasn't anything to argue about, so I took off in a not too calm search for the security officer who had handled my passport. It wasn't long before I saw her, standing behind a door, watching me through a small window.

"Excuse me, do you remember me? You cleared me but must have forgotten to put the exit visa in my passport." Staring sullenly at me she clips out the words, "I did not forget." I stand there, mute, holding out my open passport like one of my vital organs. She finally takes it from my hand, pulls a little yellow sticker from her pocket, and puts it on the page. "Goodbye, Mister Hayes."

The anvil sitting on my stomach didn't begin to lift until the landing gear left the tarmac and we arced out over the Mediterranean.

Getting footage "in the can" and easing it and a living crew back to the States is all very nice, but there shouldn't be any sense of accomplishment in it. You're no closer to getting it into the nation's living rooms than when you started. The Information Blockade is cocked and waiting like a bear trap.

The first time I got my leg hung in that thing was in the early '80s. I was editing *Native Sons* but had zero finishing funds. Grant writing was getting me nowhere until the George Gund Foundation out of Cleveland awarded us a grant adequate to complete the work, the first time they had funded an independent film project. There was much naive rejoicing.

About a week later there was a tiny squib of a story in the entertainment section of the *Columbus Dispatch:* "The Community Film Association has received a $25,000 grant from the George Gund Foundation for Tom Hayes's project, *Native Sons,* that examines the lives of three Palestinian refugee families in Lebanon." That's all it said, but it changed my world.

My funders and potential funders, and the Community Film Association that administered my grants, received letters from the Columbus Jewish Federation painting me as a PLO stooge, making perverse allegations about the Gund Foundation, and "insisting" on editorial control of the film.

At the same time freelance enthusiasts—Jewish Defense League types—began harassing my family. Phone calls into all hours, obscene threats against my then pregnant wife, threats on her life and mine. I put wire mesh on all the windows except the living room, a simple way to avoid a firebombing. It didn't help; someone came into the yard and busted that window out. At one point our phone line was cut as I prepared to take a business trip. I stayed home.

We talked to the police several times, even providing them a tape of one set of calls. But whenever we got to the question "why would you be having this problem" and I explained what I was working on, they'd sort of wander away, asking quietly over their shoulders if I owned a firearm. This was in Columbus, Ohio, not Jenin or Hebron. Nevertheless, we had begun to feel like we lived in occupied territory.

The whole thing was so dumb. Like I'd forget about the film if enough people hassled me. I had already put my butt on the line precisely because I suspected there were structures preventing a broad base of information on issues Palestinian. These info-terrorists did nothing but affirm the reasons I started this work in the first place. We got scared, sure, and we got busy.

One of the grants the Community Film Association (CFA) was administering came from the Ohio Arts Council. This was a matter of public record. The Columbus Jewish Federation secured that information, and a copy of the Gund Foundation proposal, which was not public record. Under the signature of Eric Rozenman, Director of Community Relations, a second barrage of correspondence went to my funders, trashing the film and me and urging CFA to disassociate itself from the project.

A CFA board member told me that he and other board members had received intimidating phone calls from people at Federation: "You are responsible for Tom Hayes engaging in propaganda with public funds. There's going to be an injunction against this film, and your whole board is going to be sued for their personal assets."

The board was basically a bunch of folks who liked to watch movies and thought it exciting to occasionally help an independent filmmaker. This *Native Sons* thing was giving them a lot of unexpected grief. They called me in to announce that one of their number would screen the rough cut. They sent Dennis Aig, who was at the time active with (I'm sure you can guess) the Columbus Jewish Federation.

Dennis ended his private screening standing on a chair in my cutting room yelling, "You can't say that! You can't say that." His visit was followed a week later by a letter from CFA informing me that the board had found that I was engaging in propaganda and would therefore forfeit a $20,000 reimbursement grant from the Ohio Arts Council.

I had borrowed once again on the house (counting on reimbursement from the grant for repayment) and spent the loan on lab charges. I contacted OAC, howling for help. Chris Nygren, who coordinated the media arts program, informed CFA that it had the right to forfeit the grant. BUT if it followed this course, with its implicit effect on an artist, then CFA could not expect to see another OAC grant. It was some ice-cold line like, "If you forfeit, then you must not want our funding" that did the trick.

Two days later I received a letter from CFA stating that it would complete its commitments on existing grant contracts. The financial heat was off, but the freelancers kept at my family with threats and harassment.

The Ohio State University School of Fine Arts had booked the premiere for a series called Personal Independents and would be using a local theater for screenings. I got a call from the curator, Nancy Robinson, telling me that *Native Sons* was going to have to be shown elsewhere; the theater owner was refusing to show it.

I suggested that she might respond to this censorship by telling the owner she planned to pull the whole series out of his theater. She contacted the owner, and their conversation apparently served as an inducement to him to straighten up and act like a supporter of artistic freedom. Personal interest conquered politics.

A week before the premiere of the film, Alex Odeh, a regional director in California for the American-Arab Anti-Discrimination Committee, was blown in half by a bomb wired to his office door. He had apparently commented on local television that the PLO was the sole legitimate representative of the Palestinian people.

Suddenly the threats felt less like threats and more like impending doom. Bomb squad in place, we premiered the film. At a press conference that night I spoke out against the Columbus Jewish Federation's attempts to limit artistic freedom.

If American Zionists had left the project and my family alone, I doubt that I would have continued work on the topic. They made it personal and they made it part of the politics of my community. I'm old enough to remember that the same tactics of intimidation were used to keep black Americans from registering to vote in the South. There's no way I could walk away and allow intimidation to succeed. I was weaned on *Cry, The Beloved Country.*

I got curious about the American Israel Public Affairs Committee (AIPAC). As I dug around, the rest of the equation of oppression began to lay itself out before me: the U.S. tax dollars that prop up the Zionist enterprise.

Some years later, when we entered into the agreement with ITVS, we stipulated in the contract that no public information about *People and the Land* would be released without our express permission. Important advice to anyone working on a project about this topic: keep quiet until you're done. Talking to the papers is like taping a "kick me" sign on your behind.

One interesting aspect of the contract with ITVS is that their projects are available at no charge to the PBS system for a period of three years. And only to PBS. As producers, Riad and I have no rights to license broadcast or cablecast of the program anywhere in America until the year 2000. This would not have become a problem if the PBS system had picked up the program, or if ITVS had handled itself more carefully.

ITVS submitted *People and the Land* to PBS for national release in February 1997. Gayle Loeber, Director of Broadcast Marketing for ITVS, called some time afterward to inform me that PBS had "declined the program." "Declined? What do you mean declined? What's their reason for declining?" Gayle cut me off, "They are not required to provide a reason."

She went on to describe the next steps in the distribution plan: submit for PBS's *Point of View* series and, if that failed, up-link. ITVS would prepare press materials and arrange a satellite feed to all 283 PBS affiliate stations. This is called a soft feed. A hard feed is PBS core programming, prime-time series, and specials. Stations, at the discretion of the individual program directors, can air any of the dozens of "soft feeds" they receive each week.

The relationship with ITVS, never warm on account of the 18 months they had me swinging in the wind, deteriorated further over the first press release. I had worked by phone and fax with ITVS in preparing it. Their first draft omitted mention of the foreign aid issues that the program starts and ends with—the essence of the program. I wrote a brief paragraph to remedy this defect, they said "fine," and (I thought) we put the project to bed.

When I got my press copy in the mail, the following text had been deleted: *"People and the Land* carries this humanist perspective into a look at U.S. involvement in the Israeli occupation comparing Israel aid figures with cuts in human service programs for American citizens—$5.5 billion in aid to Israel, $5.7 billion in cuts to human service programs."

I called ITVS. "What's up with censoring my press release?" I was told by a staff member that Jim Yee, Schott's replacement as executive director, had called for the copy cut.

In May ITVS called to say that some of the stations requested additional information about the program and would I write a statement about why they should air it. What I was not told was that ITVS had requested Mark Rosenblum, founder of Americans for Peace Now, to review the film. ITVS didn't ask anyone else to review the film. No Palestinian view was solicited, no American historian, just Mark Rosenblum.

ITVS sent this review to every programming director in the PBS system. An introduction signed by Gayle Loeber states, "Mark is uniquely qualified to comment on this program. . . . "

The review, using asterisks to emphasize some words, proceeds to firebomb the film with Zionist mythology: "approximately 20% accurate," "97% of Palestinians are *ruled* by *Palestinian* authorities," and—in a true flight of imagination—"Actually Jews [in Palestine] represented . . . the demographic *majority* since 1870." The document bears a striking resemblance to the ooze that rolls out of the Government Baloney Factory in Jerusalem. A sort of Joan Peters pocket novella.

[Editor's Note: *The Link* contacted Mr. Rosenblum on November 12 to confirm his connection with Americans for Peace Now. He emphatically denied having written a "review" or having put any comments in writing for ITVS, although he said he had expressed certain opinions orally to someone at ITVS whose name he did not recall. He was aware that ITVS had cited him as the authority for the "review" on *People and the Land* that it distributed in May to all PBS stations. Told that he was quoted as saying the documentary was "20 percent accurate," Mr. Rosenblum said he had not stated any percentage of accuracy. He specifically denied saying that 97 percent of Palestinians are ruled by Palestinian authorities (explaining that he might have said that such would be the case if the Oslo Accords were fulfilled). He also repudiated the statements regarding the plurality and majority status of Jews in Palestine in 1820 and 1870. (He said that he might have remarked that Jews had attained majority status in Jerusalem by the turn of the century.) On November 13, *The Link* reached Suzanne Stenson, formerly of the ITVS staff, who said she had transcribed Mr. Rosenblum's comments on a laptop computer during an hour-long phone conversation. Ms. Stenson told *The Link* that prior to its dissemination to PBS stations, the text of the communiqué quoting Mr. Rosenblum was e-mailed to him for review at his personal and business e-mail addresses. No response to these e-mails was received, she said.]

When the Anti-Defamation League sent out its press release expressing outrage that CPB had funded *People and the Land,* ITVS sent a very thoughtful letter to Abraham Foxman at ADL, and sent copies of ADL's condemnation of the program to every station in the system.

Now check me on this: is sending out an utterly negative review of a program a '90s promotion technique that I'm not sharp enough to appreciate? Orwellian promotion: war is peace, promotion is sabotage.

I asked Jim Yee and Suzanne Stenson of ITVS why ITVS had become a mailboy for the ADL. Public agitation by the ADL would have raised the profile of the program and widened the debate, raising censorship and free speech issues. When ITVS delivered the message,

ADL's hands were clean, and the desired results were achieved without public discourse.

These ITVS/ADL/Rosenblum tactics have scored hits. At least one station that we can document, WTIU in Bloomington, Indiana, removed *People and the Land* from its schedule following the communiqués from ITVS. Other stations, in Cleveland and Philadelphia for example, rejected member requests to air the free program by referring to the ITVS material.

These aggressive ITVS "promotion" techniques are ominous when you consider that they have a broadcast lock on the program for three years. However, there have been some victories for information and the "marketplace of ideas." Twenty-three stations have broadcast so far. Many of those screenings were the result of grassroots organizing.

Arab Americans of Central Ohio (AACO) conducted a campaign that resulted in the program's being aired in a prime-time slot on the PBS affiliate in Columbus. AACO's approach constitutes a worthy model for the like-minded:

Step 1) Organization calls the director of programming at the local PBS affiliate to ask when *People and the Land* is going to be broadcast and how the group could help promote the program. (Rather than approaching the issue from an adversarial perspective, assume the station will do the right thing.)

Step 2) Members of the organization sign on, en masse if possible, as supporting members of the station.

Step 3) Organization's board members meet with the director of programming, the general manager, or both if necessary, expressing their concern that their community is under-represented and under-served by the station's programming. (Emphasize that diversity is the issue, not who can field the most "friends of the station.")

Step 4) If successful in getting the program aired, organization members call to thank station management for its commitment to quality and diversity in programming. (Then encourage more of the organization's members to become station members.)

The decision to air or not to air *People and the Land* in any of the 283 communities served by PBS rests in the hands of two people, three at the most: the Program Director, the Station Manager, and the General Manager. It's not a "System"—it's two or three people with phone numbers and offices. ITVS provides the tape free of charge, so the "broke station blues" is not a valid excuse.

Program directors who express ignorance about where to obtain the program can be reminded that ITVS can be reached at 415-356-8383 or by e-mail at itvs@itvs.org. Lois Vossen, manager of marketing and promotion, is the contact person for stations.

The production crew, our colleagues, and friends in Palestine have gone to some lengths to create this information resource. Are there enterprising and energetic people out there who will challenge the blockade at the 260 PBS affiliate stations still sitting on the program?

For those about to rock, we salute you.

Update by the author, Tom Hayes

Columbus, OH—In December of 2004 I returned to the occupied West Bank to film an update to *People and The Land*. I have not seen the human realities any worse in the 24 years that I have been intermittently visiting Palestinian communities, both in historical Palestine and in the refugee camps "outside." There was much less gunfire, but the occupation is now a mass prison system solidified in stone and concrete.

I could not have made *People* under the current conditions. The government press office refused to issue me a press card, something that has never happened to me before in any country. Every checkpoint turned into a drama. "Show me your press card." "I don't have one." "Then you can't be here with the camera!" Or at a checkpoint near Nablus: "You cannot film soldiers or you will be arrested. Film just the pretty hills."

On one trip I hired a driver to skirt the checkpoints to get the crew into Jenin. He did some serious damage to the Mercedes, rolling it through fields and ramming it across dry wadis, but he got us there. When we tried to return to Jerusalem, the army refused to let us pass. I asked if they intended to keep me in Jenin for the rest of my life, and they told me to get out the same way I got in. It took half a day.

What I was able to see and film reminds me of that series on the Animal Planet cable network where animal control officers go around arresting pet owners for neglecting their animals—starving them, denying them needed medical treatment, crowding them together in small pens. That's Palestine today. You couldn't treat an animal in the United States the way Israel is treating the Palestinian population—not without going to jail. I brought back a recording of soldiers in a guard tower calling a 13-year-old Palestinian girl "one that walks on two legs" before they killed her.

I hope to have the new documentary in release by the end of this year. The working title is "Monkey Island."

The Coverage and Non-Coverage of Israel-Palestine

By Alison Weir

Alison Weir, a journalist and lecturer, is executive director of If Americans Knew, *a California-based organization that disseminates news from the Israeli-Palestinian conflict that rarely makes it into the U.S. media. In her July–August 2005 issue of* The Link, *she documents the media's bias.*

> **In the fall of 2004, we visited the Palestinian Territories. Such a simple statement, and such a complicated reality. Let me try again. . . .**

In the fall of 2004, we visited a large, open-air prison. A prison whose guards keep people out, when they choose to, as well as *in,* humiliating and violating those they dislike; a prison into which the jailers periodically shoot and send regiments of destruction; a prison full of mini-prisons and convoluted rules that change with the wind. A complicated, teeming prison in which there are wedding festivals and dancing; where babies laugh and the tea is flavored with mint and sage; and where desperation silently waits.

In fall 2004, my daughter and I traveled to Palestine—to the West Bank. And the Israeli guards let us in. But then we went to Nablus, a historic and ancient city in the northern sector of the West Bank. We stood in the crowded line full of women, men, and children waiting to pass through the double turnstile gate into this interior, mini-prison, until it was our turn, and as we walked, one at a time, through that lonely, eerie 20 feet, the soldiers' guns trained on us, the soldiers waved us back. "You are not allowed in," they pronounced, and ignored our protests and our American passports.

But later we found a back way in, over the hills, and then we saw a little of what they didn't want us to see, and heard about the rest. We visited Balata refugee camp, one of the dense communities around the West Bank and Gaza created by the 1948 *Nakba,* the "Catastrophe," when hundreds of thousands of Palestinians were forced off their land with the creation of Israel. These refugee communities are often on the outskirts of town and bear the major brunt of Israeli invasions. Their residents are among the poorest and most desperate in Palestine, and they contain pockets of resistance to Israeli military occupation.

We talked to a man in his late twenties who had recently adopted nonviolent methods of resistance. He told us that he used to have a group of close friends—about eight other guys who he'd grown up with. They would always hang out together, joke around. When Israeli forces launched a major invasion into Balata and Nablus—100 tanks descended on the area in April 2002—many joined the Palestinian resistance. One by one all these friends have been killed, and now "Sami," as we'll call him, was the only one still alive.

We learned that Israeli forces in armored vehicles periodically invaded Balata, occupying homes and shooting residents without provocation. While sometimes there were small numbers of Palestinian men with guns trying to resist these invasions, often there was no armed resistance at all. In many cases there were only kids throwing stones at these invading vehicles. The Israeli soldiers would then shoot these kids. The main street down which these Israeli armored vehicles would drive was bullet riddled and teeming with children. We also interviewed two old ladies whose home had occasionally been taken over by Israeli soldiers, who would then shoot from the windows at the people below. We saw a cemetery where children played—it was one of the few open spaces in this dense community—and people described how Israeli soldiers would taunt the children. Several kids had recently been killed there.

We were told of an incident that had occurred approximately two weeks before. There had been another of these regular Israeli "incursions" down the main street. The vehicles had stayed there for 20 minutes, asserting their control, and there had been no resistance against them. At one point an Israeli soldier poked his gun out the porthole of his vehicle, aimed at a boy nearby, and pulled the trigger. The boy, who looked to be about 13, was shot in the lower abdomen with a metal bullet coated by rubber. A Reuters photographer had photographed this incident, and an Associated Press cameraman had filmed it. We were told that the video of the incident had been sent to the Associated Press bureau in Jerusalem, but that it had been erased.

We were shocked. On what possible basis could this footage not be considered newsworthy? We decided to look into this incident further. In Balata there was a handful of international peace activists, members of the International Solidarity Movement, who were there to act as witnesses, and who attempted to intercede nonviolently in instances of aggression in order to reduce the violence in the conflict. Several of these people, including an American woman and a British woman, had witnessed this event and described it to us in detail. They had recorded the number of the Israeli armored vehicle, and had written down the names of the two photographers who had filmed the incident. We talked to both photographers, who confirmed the facts. We found the hospital where the boy was still being treated, interviewed the boy himself, his father, his older brothers, and the doctor who had treated him. All the facts confirmed what we had been told. The boy was named Ahmed, and it turned out that he was actually 14, though he looked considerably younger. He had been shot with a rubber-coated steel bullet, which had penetrated his bladder. He had undergone surgery and was still recovering.

The boy told us he was afraid of Israeli soldiers. He showed us a scar on his leg, where he had been shot previously. While we were in the hospital, we came across several other kids who had been shot. One had a fractured femur. He said he hadn't even been throwing stones, but that next time he would. Another boy had been shot in the chest. The doctors had barely saved him. Another boy, a visitor, showed us a scar at the corner of his mouth and missing teeth from when he had been shot. We had a camera along and filmed all of this.

After a few days we returned to Jerusalem.

Again, this sounds so deceptively simple. We made our way through armed Israeli checkpoints, rode in crowded vehicles that were stopped by Israeli police, wondered when or if we would be harassed. When we arrived in Jerusalem, we went straight to the AP bureau. We discovered that it was in a large building in the Israeli section of Jerusalem that appeared to house most, maybe all, of the major U.S. news bureaus. We went up to the eighth floor, still carrying our packs, and entered the AP office.

We walked up to the bureau chief, Steve Gutkin, and asked him about this incident and why the tape was erased instead of broadcast. He became flustered and said he wasn't allowed to say anything, that AP requires its corporate communications office to respond to all requests for information. Later, when we returned to the U.S., we phoned AP Corporate Communications and asked Jack Stokes, director of media relations, about this incident. I told Stokes what I had learned, and asked him whether AP had indeed erased this video, and, if so, why. He said he would look into this and get back to me with the information. When I phoned him a few days later, he said that he had looked into it, and that it was "an internal AP matter" that he could tell me nothing about.

In other words, AP had video footage of an Israeli soldier specifically and intentionally shooting a young Palestinian boy who was not attacking them, and they erased it. I don't know how often they do this.

But back to the West Bank and Steve Gutkin. My daughter and I run a small organization that focuses on the Israeli-Palestinian issue and studies how it is covered in the American media. We were there to present our research into this topic at a conference in Ramallah, as well as to gather more information. Extremely disturbed at what we were discovering about AP news coverage, we decided to investigate further. Months earlier I had heard that AP had a bureau in Ramallah in the West Bank, but when I had phoned AP in Washington, D.C., and New York about this, no one seemed to have heard of it. AP receptionists kept trying to look it up, and then would give me the number for the Jerusalem bureau, saying that was the only one listed.

We traveled to Ramallah, phoned a Palestinian agency, and asked if there was indeed an AP bureau in the city. They said there was, and gave us the phone number. We called this and were readily given directions. When we arrived, we found a fully staffed, professional bureau. While the Jerusalem bureau had appeared to be largely, perhaps exclusively, staffed by Israelis and Jewish Americans, this office appeared to contain journalists of Palestinian ethnicity.

We spoke to the bureau chief at length, and to his associate, an on-camera female reporter. They described how their news process worked. They and other correspondents throughout the Palestinian territories would cover events that took place in the area, then send their reporting to writers in the Jerusalem bureau, who would write the actual article. For example, while we were there, they received a phone call from a correspondent in Nablus. This time a 12-year-old boy had been killed. The boy, Bashar Zabara, had been throwing stones toward Israeli forces approximately 300 meters away. He had been shot in the throat with live ammunition. The bureau chief immediately phoned the Jerusalem bureau with all the details. Journalists in the Jerusalem bureau would then write up the story and send it out to the many worldwide papers that subscribe to AP's services.

The fact that everything reported by the West Bank bureau was vetted by the Jerusalem bureau flagged our attention. AP Jerusalem was the bureau that had recently erased footage of a similar incident. We asked the Ramallah bureau journalists if they could send out wire stories themselves. They said no, that all reports went through the Jerusalem bureau.

I remembered the Ramallah bureau chief's name from having occasionally seen articles with his byline in the past. Confused, we asked him if he ever wrote news stories himself. He said no, that he always called the information into Jerusalem, and that they then wrote the stories there.

We were surprised—and concerned—to learn that the bylines and datelines of stories were being misrepresented in this way. Given the ethnic nature of the Israeli-Palestinian conflict, and the fact that the ethnicities live and suffer in two different (if neighboring) locations, both the location and ethnicity of journalists writing about the conflict are particularly relevant. While it is certainly appropriate to give full credit to journalists who gather information for a story, we felt that it was highly misleading that stories with a Palestinian byline and West Bank dateline were being written by Israeli and Jewish correspondents living in Israel—that one ethnic group in the conflict actually wrote news stories purported to be by reporters from the other ethnic group in the dispute.

If such a situation is for some reason necessary, it would seem important to disclose this fact with more accurate attribution, perhaps in the form of a byline reading "Reporting by . . . , Written by . . ."

Instead, we have articles containing, at least occasionally, a spin that I suspect the authors cited in the byline would be displeased to see, much less to receive credit for writing.

Later, back in the U.S., I looked up AP coverage of the 12-year-old who was shot in the throat while we were in the Ramallah bureau—the report the bureau chief phoned in to Jerusalem while we watched.

I found no story. Apparently, the Jerusalem bureau had not sent out a story on the incident. I did find an AP photo on the internet, but could not find a single American publication that had printed it—perhaps because there was no connecting story.

Also, I saw that AP Jerusalem had sent out no reports about any of the children with shattered bodies that we had visited in the Nablus hospital, despite the on-the-scene presence of paid AP journalists.

Why Israel/Palestine Matters to Us

I had first begun looking into news coverage of Israel-Palestine four years before this visit to the Palestinian territories. I was the editor of a small newspaper in California. I had never studied this conflict before, and knew almost nothing about it. When the current uprising began in the fall of 2000, however, I became curious about it and decided to follow the news more carefully. As I did this, I noticed that news reports seemed to be largely written from an Israeli point of view. Israeli sources were quoted first and far more frequently than Palestinian ones, for example. I began going on the internet to find more information, and was astounded at what I discovered. For months I followed events closely, increasingly drawn in by the immense disparity between the information I was reading from the foreign press and international web sites, and the narrow sliver I was receiving from American media.

Finally, I decided to travel to Gaza and the West Bank as a freelance journalist in February and March of 2001. I traveled independently and alone, and was shocked at the devastation I found and at the depth of human tragedy. I returned with a sense of obligation to tell other Americans the facts I was discovering, and about our connection to them. I founded an organization called If Americans Knew to provide this information to the public, as well as to undertake a systematic study of U.S. media coverage of Israel/Palestine.

The Israeli-Palestinian conflict has been one of the most significant sources of global instability for over 50 years. It is the core conflict in the Middle East and is intimately connected to the "war on terror;" to the situations in Iraq, Iran, and Syria; and to America's disastrously deteriorating relationship with the world's 1.2 billion Muslims. In the "Holy Land" itself, it is the cause of continuing tragedy and daily misery, and according to a number of historians, in 1973 it came close to plunging the region—and perhaps the world—into a nuclear exchange. Many analysts feel such a possibility continues.

While the majority of the American public is unaware of this fact, American taxpayers are primary funders of Israeli actions. More American tax money goes to Israel than to any other nation on earth—over $10 million per day.

In addition to this, approximately $2.1 billion of American tax money goes to Egypt every year (per capita, about one-fourteenth the amount Israel receives). This funding was appropriated as part of an arrangement whereby the Egyptian government would largely refrain from opposing Israeli actions, so this money, too, could be considered in the total amount paid out annually on behalf of Israel.

While the amount of money dispersed to Palestinian organizations is significantly smaller than the above two categories, amounting to approximately $0.23 million per day in 2004, this, too, should be included, bringing the yearly total to over $7.6 billion.

In sum, then, over half of all American tax money sent abroad is connected to Israel/Palestine. In fact, a report commissioned by the U.S. Army War College estimates that the total financial cost to Americans of support for Israel over the years has been about $1.6 trillion.

In addition to this massive financial connection, American citizens are also significant players in this conflict through our government's critical role in representing Israeli interests in the international arena. In the United Nations, for example, the U.S. has exercised its veto 39 times on behalf of Israel.

For all of these reasons, it is essential that Americans be fully and accurately informed on Israel/Palestine, without bias in either direction.

Statistical Studies

To determine how well the American media are fulfilling their critical function, our organization has undertaken the laborious but essential task of conducting statistical studies of media coverage of this issue. Our methodology is to examine clear, significant categories that are as impervious as possible to subjective bias. It is our view that the media's job is to report as accurately as possible the facts on a topic. Indications about the extent to which the press is accomplishing this can be objectively measured.

Specifically, we look at the extent to which certain media outlets— e.g., *The New York Times* or *ABC World News Tonight*—cover the deaths of Israelis and Palestinians in the conflict. This approach allows meaningful statistical analysis that would be impossible in a qualitative study and provides a yardstick that allows us to determine whether media demonstrate even-handed respect for human life, regardless of ethnic or religious background.

We decided to count the number of reports of deaths for each side during a given period, and then compare these to the number of people actually killed. It is our view that deaths among both populations are equally tragic.

Fortunately, reliable data for both populations is available from the widely respected Israeli human rights organization B'Tselem (go to www.btselem.org for a full analysis of their findings).

In our studies we include only those Israeli deaths directly caused by the actions of Palestinians, and vice versa. In addition to analyzing coverage of all deaths, we specifically examine reporting on children's deaths. These tragedies represent an especially human side of the uprising, and one that lies outside of most people's views of acceptable violence in armed conflict. The killing of children is especially repugnant to most people, and these deaths elicit extreme disfavor for those responsible for them. Therefore, we felt that studying how the media covered children's deaths would be particularly significant.

In spring 2005, we completed studies of *The New York Times,* the "newspaper of record," and three of the major network evening news shows, *ABC World News Tonight, CBS Evening News,* and *NBC Nightly News.* Not only are these news media the major sources of information for millions of Americans around the country, they are also the windows through which editors and producers of smaller newspapers and broadcast news stations throughout the nation view the conflict and gauge the accuracy of their own coverage. Their significance in forming Americans' views on Israel-Palestine cannot be overemphasized.

For each of these media outlets we examined coverage of deaths over two separate year-long periods. First, we analyzed coverage for the first year of the current uprising, September 29, 2000, through September 28, 2001. This period was selected for study in order to evaluate viewers' and readers' first impressions, which are crucial as they continue to try to make sense of the conflict. Coverage of this year set the context within which all subsequent reporting on the conflict is viewed, forming viewers' and readers' opinions as to who was initiating the violence and who was retaliating.

Second, we studied the coverage for 2004 to discover whether the patterns we found for the first year had continued, diminished, or increased several years into the intifada.

We looked into two types of reporting on deaths. The first and major focus of our study was on timely/specific reports and mentions of deaths; e.g., "four Palestinians/Israelis were killed yesterday." It is this ongoing reporting of deaths that provides people with their impression of a conflict. We also counted follow-up stories, so, in theory, numbers of death reports could surpass actual number of deaths, giving percentages that exceed 100 percent. We were surprised to find that this frequently occurred—but only for one population.

Secondarily, we examined cumulative reports, e.g., "The violence has left 200 Palestinians dead" or "200 Israelis have been killed in suicide bombings." While we believe that such summaries of deaths can provide useful information, especially when numbers for both populations are given in the same report (which, sadly, rarely occurred), it was our view that such mentions are not the equivalent of 200 individual reports on each of these deaths, and needed to be enumerated in their own, separate category.

For *The New York Times* we studied prominent reporting on deaths—i.e., deaths reported in headlines/lead paragraphs—and then conducted a month-long sub-study on deaths reported in the entire article. (Interestingly, we found that the patterns discovered in our study of prominent reporting essentially held true.)

For the television networks we studied transcripts of the full newscasts in addition to introductions by anchors.

Our findings are disturbingly decisive as they reveal a pervasive pattern of distortion. For every time period, for every news source, for every category except one, one population's deaths were covered at significantly higher rates than the other—in one case 13 times higher. The favored population was Israeli. We found that the only category in which Palestinian deaths were reported at similar rates to Israeli deaths was cumulative reports—"200 Palestinians/Israelis have been killed"—and this only during the first months of the first year. After that, even cumulative reports disproportionately covered Israeli deaths over Palestinian deaths.

In addition, we were startled to find that not only was daily reporting profoundly skewed, but that in 2004 not a single network even once reported the kind of full, two-sided cumulative report one would expect to be a regular feature of news coverage: the number of people killed among both populations since the intifada had begun.

Let us look at what was going on, and then at how this was reported.

In the first year of the current uprising, September 29, 2000, to September 28, 2001, 165 Israelis and 549 Palestinians were killed. In 2004—a period that the media reported as a period of decreased violence—107 Israelis were killed and 821 Palestinians. In other words, the media were using a highly Israeli-centric index for measuring calm/violence. As I will show later, this is common.

This pattern was found to be even greater for children killed in Israel and the Palestinian Territories. In the first year, 28 Israeli children and 131 Palestinian children were killed. In 2004, 8 Israeli children and 176 Palestinian children were killed. In other words, during our second study period, over 22 times more Palestinian children than Israeli children were killed.

Many people have reverse impressions of these death rates and of their trends. Perhaps even more significant, many Americans believe the chronology of deaths in this conflict to be the opposite of its reality. A survey two years after the intifada had begun found that 90 percent of respondents either had no idea which children were killed first in the conflict or thought them to be Israeli children, despite the fact that at least 82 Palestinian children were killed before a single Israeli child—and that this killing of Palestinian children had gone on for three and a half months before a single loss of life occurred among Israeli children. The single largest cause of these Palestinian deaths was gunfire to the head.

Our studies show why so many Americans have such diametrically incorrect impressions.

In the first year of coverage, *The New York Times* headlines and first paragraphs reported on Israeli deaths at a rate almost three times greater than Palestinian deaths. This 2.8-to-1 ratio was the closest to parity that we found in all of our studies. Perhaps that is why some pro-Israeli groups allege that the *Times* is "pro-Palestinian."

ABC, CBS, and NBC covered Israeli deaths at rates 3.1, 3.8, and 4.0 times greater, respectively, than they covered Palestinian deaths.

What does this mean for people who relied on these sources for their understanding of the conflict? One of the most noteworthy aspects of this type of coverage is that it creates an illusion that roughly the same number of Israelis and Palestinians have died in the conflict: all of the media outlets reported similar numbers of deaths on both sides. ABC reported on 305 Israeli deaths and 327 Palestinian deaths. The *Times* reported on 197 Israeli deaths and 233 Palestinian deaths in headlines and first paragraphs. CBS and NBC both reported on *more* Israeli than Palestinian deaths. Hence, they were all giving the impression of balanced coverage of a balanced violence during a time when 3.3 times more Palestinians were being killed.

For children, the disparity in coverage was even larger for all four outlets.

The New York Times reported prominently on Israeli children's deaths at a rate almost seven times greater than Palestinian children's deaths.

Significantly, we found that while the number of prominent *New York Times* reports on Israeli children's deaths exceeded 100 percent when including follow-up stories, prominent reports on Palestinian children's deaths represented a small fraction of the number actually killed.

As a result, the *Times*'s coverage gave the impression that more Israeli than Palestinian children were killed during a time when 4.7 more Palestinian children were actually killed.

Most of the networks were even worse: ABC reported Israeli children's deaths at a rate 13.8 times greater than deaths of Palestinian children, CBS at a rate 6.4 times greater, and NBC at a rate 12.4 times greater.

Again, we saw a pattern among the networks in which there were numerous follow-up stories on Israeli deaths, while only a small fraction of Palestinian deaths were being similarly covered.

In 2004, these distortions were amplified.

The New York Times reported prominently on overall Israeli deaths at a rate 3.7 times greater than Palestinian deaths, and on Israeli children's deaths at a rate 7.5 times greater than Palestinian children's deaths. ABC, CBS, and NBC reported Israeli children's deaths at rates 9.0, 12.8, and 9.9 times greater, respectively, than Palestinian children's deaths.

A chronological graph of actual and reported deaths can be found on our web site, www.ifamericansknew.org. In all four news outlets (*The New York Times*, ABC, CBS, NBC) for both years of study, Palestinian deaths were reported along a curve that closely resembled the Israeli death rate, when in reality the actual curve for Palestinian deaths is far higher and slopes upward far sooner. This provides a striking illustration of the difference between the reality, in which deaths are heavily concentrated on one side, and the impression created in the major American media of a balanced conflict.

In our one-month sub-study of deaths reported in full *New York Times* articles (as opposed to the headlines and lead paragraphs), we found that the disparity in reporting grew even greater. The number of Palestinian deaths that were reported increased when the entire articles were studied—10 Palestinian deaths were reported for the first and only time in the last two paragraphs of articles—but we found that reports of Israeli deaths increased also, and at an even greater rate, due to the repetition of reports on Israeli deaths that had occurred in previous days.

Regarding the *Times*'s coverage of cumulative totals, information that would have at least somewhat ameliorated the above mis-impressions, we found that the paper had never reported numbers for both populations side by side within the first paragraphs or headlines of articles. (Cumulatives were defined as reports summarizing deaths over a period of time greater than one week.)

Once in 2004, the paper reported a partial (e.g., for a shorter period of time than the entire intifada) cumulative figure of Palestinian deaths. Such a cumulative, however, without corresponding statistics for the Israeli population, does little to enlighten readers on the comparative deaths among all people in the region.

In our month-long sub-study of full articles, we found that the *Times* did provide side-by-side cumulative counts of fatalities for both populations twice: once in paragraph 14 and once in paragraph 20 of an article.

The networks, also, rarely provided full two-sided cumulative reports, and partial two-sided cumulatives were only rarely given.

Instead, we found that it was far more common for the networks to report one-sided cumulatives. These, whether full or partial, make it more difficult for the viewer to make a comparison and draw conclusions on the relative levels of violence. In fact, such one-sided cumulatives may at times do more to obscure understanding of the conflict than to enhance it. For example, ABC's March 22 report was typical: "Hamas has killed hundreds of Israelis over the years." We're not told over how many years, or how many hundreds. We're also not told how many Palestinians have been killed during this period—probably at least three times more.

The networks' full one-sided cumulative reports display an interesting pattern. All three networks reported full cumulatives of Palestinian deaths without corresponding numbers for Israelis in the first few months of the uprising, but they quickly discontinued this practice. As the conflict continued, we found that cumulative reports of Israeli fatalities often provided information on extensive periods of time—frequently back to the beginning of the uprising or even before—while cumulative reports of Palestinian deaths tended to cover far shorter periods of time—often only weeks. Thus, similar numbers of deaths were frequently reported in these cumulatives, despite the fact that throughout the conflict Palestinians have been killed in substantially larger numbers than Israelis.

"Balance"

This phenomenon of achieving a deceptive appearance of reportorial "balance," achieved through actual and enormous imbalance, was documented first by analyst Seth Ackerman of the media monitoring organization Fairness and Accuracy in Reporting (FAIR).

Ackerman conducted a study of National Public Radio's coverage of Israeli and Palestinian deaths during the first six months of 2001, and entitled his report "The Illusion of Balance." Ackerman found that NPR, which was being accused by Israel partisans of being "pro-Palestinian," had in reality reported Israeli deaths at a rate almost two and a half times greater than Palestinian ones, and Israeli children's deaths at rates almost four and a half times greater than deaths of Palestinian children. (For his study, Ackerman considered each reported death only once. If follow-up reports had been included, it is possible that the disparity would have been even larger.)

Moreover, Ackerman's study included an additional and extremely interesting category: a comparison of reports on deaths of armed combatants among both populations. He found that while an Israeli civilian victim was more likely to have his or her death reported on NPR, Palestinians were far more likely to have their deaths reported if they were security personnel. Such distortion, of course, gives the impression that the Israelis being killed are civilians, and that the Palestinians being killed are armed fighters. The reality is that large numbers of civilians are being killed on both sides, and that far more Palestinian than Israeli civilians have been killed.

Such distortion on a national scale often grows even greater on a local level, as news stories are cut to fit smaller editorial holes, and editors choose which to place on front pages.

For example, a six-month study of *The San Francisco Chronicle*'s coverage of children's deaths during the first six months of the intifada found that they had reported Israeli children's deaths at a rate 30 times greater than Palestinian children's deaths.

A similar study by Stanford professor John McManus of media monitoring organization Grade the News found that *The San Jose Mercury News* front-page headlines had reported on Israeli deaths at a rate 11 times greater than Palestinian deaths. McManus found that during this period, AP headlines had featured Israeli deaths at twice the rate they reported Palestinian deaths.

We have not yet conducted a formal study of *The Los Angeles Times*'s coverage. In several cases it has run important stories that were omitted from *The New York Times*, and overall its coverage appears less distorted. Yet, one evening in February 2005, a breaking news report on their web site stated that a suicide bombing had "shattered a months-long period of relative calm."

I phoned the foreign desk immediately—there was still time to correct this story before it was published in the following day's print version—and pointed out that this alleged "months-long period of relative calm" had in reality been a time of particularly high Palestinian casualties. The preceding months had included the killing of 170 Palestinian men, women, and children, and the wounding of 379 more.

I was told that the story said the calm was "relative," and therefore would not be modified. Not only did the next day's paper contain this highly false statement, *The Los Angeles Times* refused to print a single op-ed or letter to the editor correcting it, despite receiving many. By the way, the story carried a double byline. I looked into the reporters and found that one was a neophyte to the Middle East, while the other was an Israeli whose son was about to join the Israeli military.

Reactions from the Media

How have these news organizations responded to such studies?

In our reports we write: "Given that the media have a desire and a responsibility to cover this topic accurately, we provide these reports in the hope that our analyses can assist them in achieving this goal." In our conclusions, we use almost the identical words that we used in one of our very first studies: "We assume that *The San Francisco Chronicle* is as disturbed as we have been to find these shortfalls in its quest to provide excellent news reporting to its readers. Now that it has been alerted to these distortions in its Israel-Palestine coverage, we encourage the *Chronicle* to undertake whatever changes necessary to provide accurate news coverage of this vital issue."

Sadly, it appears that the *Chronicle* was indeed as disturbed as we were—but not at the distortion we had documented. Rather, indications have been that the paper was only disturbed that the profound flaws in their coverage were being exposed; there seems to be little interest in remedying the situation. Numerous phone calls to editor Phil Bronstein to present our findings in person remained unreturned. When we had the opportunity to ask Bronstein about it at a community forum, he publicly promised he would meet with us to discuss our findings. However, he has continued to refuse to do so.

It is interesting to note that Bronstein got his start at *The San Francisco Jewish Bulletin*, where one of his early journalistic exposés was on American corporations participating in the international boycott of Israel (Congress, following Israel's directions, had made such financial pressure on Israel illegal).

Despite the *Chronicle*'s lack of interest in our findings, several local organizations and many individuals have found them important and have distributed thousands of summaries of our report throughout the San Francisco Bay Area. We have presented our findings to a variety of Bay Area Rotary clubs, at libraries, schools, and college campuses, and have discussed them on a number of radio programs. In addition, thousands of people have read our report online.

Other editors around the country have been more open to meeting with us. The reception has been mixed. Some editors of smaller papers were extremely surprised at the number of Palestinians actually being killed, and clearly had no idea that their coverage was so distorted. Their frequent conclusion—that the wire services that they subscribe to for international news stories bore much of the blame for this distortion—no doubt holds some validity.

The New York Times, unable to use the same excuse, instead has tried to ignore our evidence. An April 24, 2005, column by Public Editor Daniel Okrent on the *Times* coverage of Israel/Palestine, published a week after we had presented our findings to him in detail during a lengthy face-to-face meeting, omitted all mention of our two-year study of the *Times*'s coverage, the forty-plus pages of documentation we provided, and our significant findings. He did mention our organization, however, in a statement misrepresenting our views.

Interestingly, during the meeting in which we presented our findings, Okrent had asked us what we felt was the cause for the *Times* distortion, and how we would fix it.

We gave two answers: First, we said that figuring out where their system had broken down was up to them. They are the only ones who know the internal workings of the *Times* newsroom and thus are the best equipped to discover what is wrong.

At the same time, I told Okrent that I wondered how diverse their team of editors and reporters working on this issue is. Since Israel's purpose and avowed identity is as "the Jewish state," I commented that it seemed to me there should be approximately equal numbers of Jewish journalists and Palestinian/Arab/Muslim journalists, as well as journalists without ethnic connections to either side—perhaps African-American, Asian-American, or other noninvolved ethnicities.

He responded that there were insufficient numbers of Arab-American or Muslim-American journalists to balance out the many Jewish reporters in this country, and ignored the suggestion that people of other, neutral ethnicities be involved in covering this issue.

In his subsequent April 24, 2005, column, Okrent claimed that we had suggested that if insufficient Arab/Muslim reporters could be found to balance Jewish reporters, then Jewish reporters should "be taken off the beat." Okrent said that he found this "highly offensive." I was shocked to see this misrepresentation of our meeting. If Americans Knew is opposed to discrimination in all its forms; proposing exclusion of any person based on ethnic or religious background is the antithesis of our philosophy. Moreover, there are many journalists of Jewish descent (several mentioned in this article) writing honestly and accurately on this subject (as on others) who bring valuable expertise and ability to their reporting. The last thing I would want would be to exclude such people. Rather than suggesting that any group be *ex*cluded, we had actually suggested that the *Times* *in*clude *more* ethnicities.

Outraged at his misrepresentation, I phoned and wrote several times asking that a correction be published. Finally, at the bottom of his next column, Okrent stated that I felt he had misrepresented our meeting, and added, "interested readers can find her critique at www.ifamericansknew.com."

Interestingly, analysis of the space allotted to the "two sides" in this follow-up column shows more lack of balance. While Okrent juxtaposes If Americans Knew with a pro-Israel organization, and exudes the manner of one taking neither "side," he gives the highly pro-Israel organization 206 words, most of them high up in the column, and If Americans Knew only 44, at the end, and again without informing readers of our detailed study.

As I responded in a letter to the editor, not published, this is a differential of approximately five to one (not even including the additional factor of placement), and an excellent index of the *Times* "balance" on this subject.

In a conversation with *Times* Deputy Foreign Editor Ethan Bronner, I was surprised to find Bronner similarly stating that it was impossible for the *Times* to find Arab- or Muslim-American journalists to report on Palestine: he said that "there aren't hundreds of Arab- or Muslim-American journalists in America." I have no idea how many Arab-American or Muslim-American journalists there are (or how many Jewish-American journalists). All the *Times* needs to balance its Jewish reporters in Israel and the Palestinian Territories, however, is two. I don't know how many editors serve on the *Times*'s foreign desk, but I suspect that attaining some approximation of balance at this level would also entail low single digits. We're not talking armies of journalists here.

(A longer report on my communications with the *Times* is available on our web site.)

What Is Causing the Distortion?

One of the most common responses to our studies is a question: what is causing this distortion? This is an extremely important question, since solutions require that the cause of a problem be correctly diagnosed. Answering it accurately and with precision will require further study, and, given sufficient resources, perhaps this is something we will undertake in the future. We encourage others to investigate it as well. Following are some possible factors to be studied:

1. Do statistical or contextual patterns explain why Israeli deaths are covered more frequently?

For example, do Israeli deaths occur in spurts, while Palestinians die more frequently but in smaller numbers, making the instances less newsworthy?

Analyses of the data on deaths suggest that there are no such patterns. There were cases where small numbers of deaths on the Israeli side resulted in headlines, and large numbers on the Palestinian side did not. Similarly, as we've stated above, civilians are being killed among both populations, children on both sides.

Still, more detailed work on this question would be valuable. Analyses along the lines of Seth Ackerman's work in examining which deaths among both populations are being reported would be useful in clarifying coverage patterns.

2. *Is there a vicious cycle of reporting at work?*

If the type of distortion our studies revealed is not new, then journalists may have developed a particular mindset on this issue based on years of flawed reporting, which then influences how they themselves cover it.

Many journalists follow the news avidly, with media reports providing their contextual understanding of Israel-Palestine. Editors who have neither studied the issue nor visited the region feel they are experts on it, and may find it hard to believe that coverage which is in line with the news they view on television and read in *The New York Times* is distorted. Conversely, accurate facts and reports that don't fit this paradigm may be rejected.

3. *How significant is the fact that American correspondents in the region tend to live exclusively in Israel?*

In some cases (perhaps many or most cases), their partners and spouses are Israeli, as, at times, are their children. One of ABC's major correspondents in the region, Martin Fletcher, is an example.

As noted above, bureaus are in Israel, and are largely staffed by Israelis. It is probably not surprising that these journalists are filing articles from an Israeli-centric perspective. It is important to note, however, that this intimate knowledge of the region they're covering may bring valuable depth to their reporting.

On the other hand, the lack of journalists with this kind of first-hand life experience reporting from the Palestinian Territories may account for the massive imbalance we have found in news coverage. While reports from Palestinian journalists could help to counter this lack, the fact that these reports are being screened and edited by journalists living in Israel can be expected to diminish the balance such reporting could otherwise have provided.

4. *Along these lines, to what extent is personal bias involved in creating the distortion we've found?*

Journalists, like other people, possess prejudices and preferences, loyalties and allegiances. Early conditioning, family pressure, and received narratives are difficult to put aside. Such biases may color, intentionally or unconsciously, one's writing or editing.

An article entitled "Jewish journalists grapple with 'doing the write thing,'" in the November 23, 2001, *Jewish Bulletin of Northern California* looked into this question, interviewing journalism students about how they would cover Israel. Its findings were inconclusive. Some students felt they would cover Israel impartially, some didn't. The *Bulletin* described one of the latter, Uzi Safanov: "'I'm a Jew before being a journalist, before someone pays me to write,' he said. 'If I find a negative thing about Israel, I will not print it and I will sink into why did it happen and what can I do to change it.' Safanov said that even if he eventually wrote about negative incidents that happen in Israel, he would try to find the way 'to shift the blame.'"

Another also spoke of the need to protect Israel: "'On campus there is already so much anti-Israeli sentiment that we have to be careful about any additional criticism against Israel,' said Marita Gringaus, who used to write for Arizona State University's newspaper. 'This is our responsibility as Jews, which obviously contradicts our responsibilities as journalists.'"

Still another felt that her background would inescapably affect her reporting: "Meyers feels a loyalty to Jewish values. 'It doesn't matter if you are a journalist or in another profession. . . . Our Jewish values influence every aspect of our lives. Nobody can be totally objective because we all come with our own perspective, our own biases, and that is going to come through in the writing.'"

On the other hand, there are numerous excellent Israeli and Jewish journalists reporting on this issue accurately. Some Israeli reporters regularly file investigative stories on Israeli abuses in the Occupied Territories. Similarly, some of the student interviewees in the *Jewish Bulletin* article stressed the importance of reporting honestly and without prejudice. For example, "'Journalists have to realize the importance of unbiased reporting, the fairness of portraying both sides. They are not supposed to be agencies.'"

5. How large a part do outside pressure and proactive news dissemination play in shaping news coverage?

Partisan groups are known for organizing phone-calling and letter-writing campaigns; boycotts have been organized against NPR and the *LA Times*, alleging that their coverage was "anti-Israel." An off-the-record comment made by the editorial page editor of a large metropolitan daily is noteworthy: "We write our editorials for our Jewish readers." Has there been a view that Israel is a "Jewish" subject, and that articles should be tailored to a particular, expected readership that these editors think holds a monolithic view on this subject? While pro-Palestinian groups are also beginning to organize media campaigns, these are still far smaller—an editor quoted in *American Journalism Review* estimated them at one-tenth the activity level of pro-Israel efforts.

Similarly, how significant is lobbying by the Israeli government and pro-Israel organizations?

Israel takes great efforts to influence the American media. The Israeli government employs such high-powered public relations firms as Howard J. Rubenstein Associates and Morris, Carrick & Guma to promote its version of events, and there are numerous think tanks such as the Middle East Media Research Institute (MEMRI), the Middle East Forum, and the Washington Institute for Near East Policy actively disseminating information beneficial to Israel. Again, Palestinian officials and partisans are making similar efforts, but their activities are currently far smaller, and their financing a fraction of that being mobilized on behalf of Israel; plus, they entered the game late.

6. *To what degree do financial considerations of the "corporate media" influence news coverage?*

Advertising and consumer pressures of the type noted above, interlocking business arrangements, and the quest for profits all need to be examined. The dynamics of these and the degree to which they're operative on Israeli-Palestinian coverage are unclear, particularly since coverage of Israel-Palestine so often reveals patterns of reporting that seem to lie outside the expected ratings-driven paradigm.

For example, reporting on the killing of Rachel Corrie, a beautiful young American whose actions are seen by many around the world as extraordinarily heroic, would likely have increased viewership and sold newspapers. Yet reports on this incident were minimal, and follow-up stories virtually nonexistent. Similarly, footage of Israeli soldiers shooting at the cross on the Church of the Nativity and taking pot shots at a statue of the Virgin Mary would, no doubt, have generated considerable audience interest. These stories still went unreported.

7. *Finally, to what extent do the views of owners/management set the agenda for coverage?*

Mortimer Zuckerman, at various times the owner of *U.S. News & World Report, The Atlantic,* and *The New York Daily News,* is passionately pro-Israel and is known, in general, for imposing his views on news content. A plethora of other owners/publishers/executives express similarly strong views, sit on pro-Israel boards, exhibit patterns of giving to Israeli organizations, etc. How significant is this factor? Do such individuals set general or specific policies for their news staffs, and if so, how are they manifested?

Without further study it is impossible to know which of the above factors, possible additional factors, or combinations are creating the situation we find today. What is less complex are the results.

Shaping Coverage

Several *San Francisco Chronicle* reporters and writers who had occasionally written about Israel/Palestine have been let go, transferred, or demoted.

The experience of veteran *Chronicle* journalist Henry Norr is a case in point. Norr was fired in 2003 after he took part in an anti-war demonstration. Norr, who reported on technology, not the war, had participated in the demonstration on his own time. He contested his firing and ended up winning a substantial out-of-court settlement from the *Chronicle*. Norr had also been active on the Israeli-Palestinian conflict. He suspects that his activities regarding Palestine, rather than his participation in the demonstration, were the underlying cause of his firing.

In July 2002, Norr wrote about an Intel factory constructed illegally on Palestinian land from which Israel had ejected the Palestinian owners. In a radio interview with Amy Goodman of *Democracy Now!* after his firing, Norr described the *Chronicle*'s reaction to the story, which had received a great deal of criticism from the Israeli lobby: "I was told this was an inappropriate topic and I wasn't supposed to write such things anymore."

Norr went on to discuss a vacation-time trip during which he and his wife participated in nonviolent protest activities in the West Bank. When he returned to work, he described his trip to colleagues:

> I put together a little lunchtime presentation and slideshow, a little discussion of what I had seen and observed and heard. And apparently management didn't like that very much. Apparently there was somebody who attended that presentation . . . [who] reported to management that I made anti-Semitic remarks and so on, which is really a big joke. I mean, I'm Jewish by background, and I don't think I'm the least bit anti-Semitic. However, I'm deeply opposed to the policy of the Israeli government.

Less than a year later Henry Norr was out. Such veiled but firm management policies don't appear unique.

John Wheat Gibson, a former journalist who worked as a reporter and journalism instructor for a number of years before finally leaving for a different career, found a similar pro-Israel climate at Cox Newspapers, one of the nation's top newspaper chains, with 17 daily newspapers, including *The Atlanta Constitution,* and 30 non-daily papers around the country: "As a journalist in the 1970s," Gibson recalls, "I found that a rigid bias against objective reporting and in favor of Israel was a prerequisite for employment with a daily newspaper in the Cox chain. I never understood why, since I saw no evidence the major advertisers in the media market were Zionists."

My own personal experiences with newspaper chains have been illuminating.

A few years ago a reporter from the Gannett newspapers planned to do an article about me and If Americans Knew, which had just begun operating. Gannett is one of the largest news outlets in the nation, with 102 daily newspapers in the United States, including *USA Today*, the nation's largest-selling daily newspaper, for a combined daily paid circulation of 7.6 million readers. Gannett also owns a variety of non-daily publications and *USA WEEKEND*, a weekly newspaper magazine, with circulation of 22.7 million, delivered in more than 600 Gannett and non-Gannett newspapers. As if this weren't enough, Gannett also owns and operates 21 television stations, covering almost 20 percent of the country.

Needless to say, a Gannett article about our fledgling organization was quite exciting. He interviewed me at considerable length about my experiences in the West Bank and Gaza, sent out a photographer to take pictures of me at home, and directed her to Fed Ex them immediately.

Then we waited. After a few months, I e-mailed him to ask if I'd missed the piece. He e-mailed back, no I hadn't missed it. The article had been shelved: "The top guy here feels like the story is 'missing' something." The article, apparently, is still on the shelf.

At the other end of the newspaper chain spectrum is a small company in Rhinebeck, New York. A reporter from this chain also wrote an article about us. To his surprise, his boss axed it. Despite his protests, the piece was never published.

Killing such stories carries significance beyond simply suppressing the specific information they contain. Perhaps of even greater importance, it sends a very clear message to journalists about what one may report, and what one may not, if one is to get ahead in American journalism.

This article has only scratched the surface of the distortion, omission, and suppression I have come across as I have looked into press coverage of Israel and the Palestinian territories over the past four and a half years. Some of the other recent stories that haven't made it into the American media consciousness include the following:

- A story about the 1967 Israeli attack on an American ship, the USS *Liberty*, has been in the works at *Nightline* for over a year; surviving crew members have been interviewed, the Naval officer who blew the whistle on the cover-up on this attack was filmed a year ago. It, too, is still on the shelf.

- A report describing the harsh treatment of over 300 Palestinian youths being held in Israeli prisons was distributed by AP only on its international wire. In other words, it went to the U.K., Europe, Asia, South America—all over the world. The only place it didn't go was the United States. I read it on an Israeli newspaper web site. When I asked AP spokesman Jack Stokes why this report was considered newsworthy in Norway but not in New York, Stokes said that not all stories are sent out on all newswires; AP editors use their news judgment in making these decisions.

- A potentially explosive piece by investigative journalist and author Stephen Green exposing the fact that some of the nation's top officials have been repeatedly investigated for spying for Israel fizzled. No newspapers picked it up, no wire services sent it out, no television stations reported it.

- A letter to the national headquarters of the Presbyterian Church threatening to torch Presbyterian churches across the country—while worshipers were inside—unless church leaders changed their position opposing Israeli human rights violations was barely reported. There was nothing on CBS, nothing on CNN, nothing on PBS, nothing on NPR. Not a single major newspaper notified readers of this threat.

There are multitudes of such stories. In 1904 Joseph Pulitzer warned:

Our republic and its press will rise or fall together. An able, disinterested, public spirited press with trained intelligence to know the right and courage to do it can preserve that public virtue without which popular government is a sham and a mockery. A cynical, mercenary, demagogic press will produce in time a people as base as itself.

Over 100 years before Pulitzer's words, our forefathers similarly considered an informed population such a fundamental necessity for our democracy that they established freedom of the press in the very first sentence of the Bill of Rights.

Yet today, time after time in meeting with editors and publishers responsible for informing Americans fully and accurately on Israel-Palestine—one of the world's most destabilizing, tragic and longstanding conflicts—we have found people too partisan, too ambitious, too neglectful, too fearful, or too jaded to fulfill their profoundly important responsibilities.

It is critical that we repair our faltering press.

The Israeli-Palestinian conflict is central to grave events in the world—and in our nation—today. The United States is currently fighting a war against Middle East "terror" that contains neither temporal nor geographic limits. Our population is being whipped up to fear and oppose an entire religion and untold millions of people whose ethnicity make them "enemies." Our security is threatened, our children are in peril, and our national morality is up for grabs.

It is urgent that Americans become informed. It is urgent that we share our information with others, that we require honesty and accuracy from our media, and that we affirm the principles that make the world safe for all people.

We cannot wait for others to do this.

Update by the author, Alison Weir

Continuing Non-Coverage and Under-Coverage

Los Angeles, CA—Since I wrote this article, our organization has continued to find disturbing patterns in media coverage of Israel-Palestine. We conducted a study of Associated Press coverage of Israel-Palestine for 2004 (to match the time period of previous studies), again examining prominent coverage—i.e., headlines and lead paragraphs, which basically tell what the news report is about. Once more, the results were startling.

We discovered that AP had prominent reports on 131 percent of Israeli deaths (through multiple follow-up reports) and on 66 percent of Palestinian deaths. In other words, it covered Israeli deaths at twice the rate it reported Palestinian ones.

For children, the disparity was even greater. In a year in which eight Israeli children had tragically been killed by Palestinians and 179 Palestinian children had tragically been killed by Israelis, we found that AP had reported on 113 percent of the Israeli deaths and failed to report on at least 85 percent of the Palestinian ones—a differential of 7.5 to 1. When we looked at unique reports alone, taking out follow-up reports, we found that the differential remained immense, with AP reporting Israeli children's deaths at a rate 6.5 times greater than they reported Palestinian ones.

In our study we also found that pertinent subject areas had gone virtually unreported by AP, despite a multitude of stories on Israel-Palestine during this period (over 700 on deaths alone), and noted three of them:

- Torture in Israeli prisons is listed as a concern in the first paragraph of Amnesty International's report on Israel covering the year 2004, and, as I noted in my piece, the massive number of prisoners and their abusive treatment have been of continuing concern.

Yet, apart from four stories on a prisoner hunger strike, we could find only two stories that described Israeli prison conditions for Palestinians. Only one AP headline from the area mentioned torture—and this one was about Lebanese, not Palestinian, prisoners.

- During 2004 numerous Israelis refused to serve in the Israeli armed forces in the Occupied Territories. By year's end there were 1,392 such "refusers," and 37 had gone to prison. This movement was a topic of increasing discussion in Israel and the subject of numerous news reports. Yet AP had only one story on this.

- Palestinian resistance efforts have included numerous nonviolent marches and other activities, many joined by international participants, Israeli citizens, and faith-based groups. This nonviolence movement has been an important topic in the Palestinian territories, with growing numbers of people taking part—in 2004 the Palestinian News Network reported on 79 major demonstrations that were exclusively nonviolent. Yet, we did not find any reports in which AP had described a Palestinian demonstration or other activity as nonviolent or utilizing nonviolence.

Missing Footage

We have continued to look into the handling of video footage of Israeli soldiers shooting children. AP continued to refuse to answer questions on the erasing incident, even during "Sunshine Week," when its president was touring the country proclaiming the "public's right to know" and stating "secrecy is for losers." As our information spread on the internet, however, AP eventually issued a statement. It criticized my reporting, yet, when examined closely, didn't actually deny that they had once possessed footage of this incident, while also stating that they do not now have it.

Because of deadline and space considerations, I did not include in my *Link* article details indicating that CNN saw film footage of the shooting of Bashar Zabara, possibly its own or AP's. The evening of the killing I was sitting in a hotel in El-Bireh watching a CNN report on a suicide bombing in Israel; there was no mention of the killing of the 12-year-old Nablus boy. I phoned CNN, telling them that I was in the West Bank and had a news tip. When I described the incident, the person on the other end of the phone said, "I know. I saw the footage."

The person then said that s/he agreed with me that they should be showing it, saying that s/he had been the one who had convinced them to run the footage of Muhammed Al-Durrah. (Muhammed Al-Durrah is the young boy shot by Israeli soldiers while his father tried to shelter him—the only footage of a Palestinian child's killing to get significant, though brief, play in U.S. media.) In the course of our conversation, it became clear that it was unlikely that CNN would mention anything about this latest incident of Israeli soldiers killing a Palestinian child. As I watched the repeated updates on the suicide bombing, this turned out to be correct.

I'm still trying to investigate what this means. Whose footage did this person see? Who made the decision not to broadcast it? Why? Most important, how often does this occur?

As we all know, such images can be extremely powerful. Vietnam-era broadcasts of a running girl screaming in pain helped end public support of that war. Are similar images of Palestinian victims—with similar potential to end U.S. support of Israel—being withheld from the American public? This seems extremely possible. Palestinian cameramen are often in the thick of the action, at considerable personal risk. Many have been shot and injured, a number have been killed. Given the number of civilians and children that Israeli forces have killed in the past five years, it is quite likely that these cameramen have filmed numerous such events.

Where is their footage?

Part IV: Religion

Theodor Herzl, the father of political Zionism, was personally indifferent to religion. When Britain offered him Uganda to locate his Jewish state, over 60 percent of the delegates to the Fifth Zionist Congress in 1903 voted to accept it. The rejectionists, however, said no; they wanted Palestine, the land of the Bible. Herzl eventually sided with them.

Today, an estimated 80 percent of Israeli Jews consider themselves secularists; for them biblical history has cultural resonance. That leaves a significant minority, as in Herzl's day, who see the land of Palestine as their biblical patrimony, the land given them by God, the land they have a divine right to settle, even if other people have lived on it for centuries.

Sharing this belief is a significant number of evangelical Christians, who believe that the return of the Jews to the Promised Land is a sign of Christ's Second Coming. Lord Balfour, who wrote the famous Balfour Declaration in 1917, subscribed to such a belief, as do many of today's televangelists, such as Jerry Falwell and Pat Robertson. (When the secularist Ariel Sharon had his stroke, Robertson pronounced it a punishment from God for having withdrawn Jews from their divine patrimony in Gaza.)

Competing with Jewish claims to historic Palestine are Muslim organizations such as Hamas, the Palestinian military/social/political group whose name is an acronym for the Islamic Resistance Movement. With its landslide victory in the 2006 parliamentary elections came a new scrutiny of its covenant which states, "The land of Palestine is an Islamic trust left to the generations of Muslims until the day of resurrection. It is forbidden to anyone to yield or concede part or all of it."

The Link has featured numerous articles on the relevance of religion to the Palestine-Israel conflict. Here we select three that examine the impact of Jewish fundamentalists on the Christian community in Palestine (Halsell), the ethical question posed by the Bible's God-mandated genocide (Prior), and the emergence of neo-normative Islam (Haddad).

In the Land of Christ, Christianity Is Dying

By Grace Halsell

Journalist and lecturer Grace Halsell covered the Korean and Vietnam wars and served as a speech writer for President Lyndon Johnson. In 1982, Macmillan published her book Journey to Jerusalem, *which recounts her Holy Land experiences living with Jewish, Christian, and Muslim families. In 1985, Grace, an evangelical Christian, attended the first Christian Zionist Congress in Basel, Switzerland. To research her January–March 1995* Link *article she participated in several Holy Land tours sponsored by the Rev. Jerry Falwell. From 1982 until her death in 2000, Ms. Halsell served on AMEU's board of directors.*

In 1948, between 60 and 70 percent of the Palestinian Christians were driven from their ancestral homes with the creation of a Jewish state. Since the 1967 illegal Israeli occupation of their lands, an additional 20,000 Christians have felt a necessity to leave their homeland. Formerly the population of Jerusalem, in Christian tradition the "mother of all churches," was half Christian. Now Christians in the Holy City are so few that "with a couple of jumbo jets you could move them all out," said Jonathan Kuttab, a Jerusalem Christian, U.S.-educated attorney.

Under the British Mandate, Palestine officially was a Christian country, with Bethlehem having a population that was 90 percent Christian. Now the town that gave birth to Christ—and Christianity—has only about 10 percent Christians. The creation of a Jewish state on Palestinian soil meant "thousands of our people were uprooted," Bethlehem deputy mayor Hanna J. Nasser told me. "The war of 1948 forced more than 700,000 Palestinians—50,000 of them Christians—

to emigrate." Since 1948, the emigration of Palestinian Christians is over twice the rate for the overall Palestinian population. Why are so many Christians leaving? Are they "encouraged" to emigrate, and if so, by whom? Would getting rid of them remove a potentially "dangerous element" that might arouse sympathy from fellow Christians in the West? I learned there were at least four important reasons Christians were leaving:

First, the Christians have contacts in the outside world. Beginning in the mid-19th century, teachers sent to Christian missionary schools in Jerusalem, Bethlehem, and Nazareth provided overseas addresses—those of their own homes and churches—to those indigenous Christians who wished to emigrate. Christian forebears of Bethlehem mayor Elias Freij first traveled to Chile almost 100 years ago. Other Christian Bethlehemites as well as Christian Beit Jalans began immigrating to South America, while Christians from Jerusalem, Jaffa, and Ramallah started a trek to the United States. Family members followed those who had gone earlier. Today more Christians from the West Bank town of Ramallah live in the United States than live in Ramallah. "Christian emigration, rather than an individual undertaking, has been a family pattern," noted Bethlehem University's Dr. Adnan Musallam. Thus a visitor to San Diego, Chicago, Detroit, San Francisco, Sydney, as well as Santiago and Bogota can find whole Palestinian communities residing in those cities.

Christian Palestinians spoke of a second reason for emigration: housing, or lack of it. I did not meet a Palestinian who had not experienced, personally or by one of his family members, the loss of a home. Once, on a drive around West Jerusalem, a Christian Palestinian, Ibrahim Mattar, showed me his family home—seized in the 1948 war. His story repeats, tens of thousands of times. Then there was the 1967 seizure of Arab lands, including the West Bank.

Israelis using military law have for the past 28 years demolished Palestinian homes with impunity. Fawzi Kiswani, a hotel kitchen steward and father of nine children, watched as bulldozers and Israeli police arrived at his home in southeast Jerusalem. Two hours later, his house was a pile of stones. Kiswani was born where he lived; he had never moved. And the same was true for Cirres Nestas, whom I first met in 1979. In that year, I stayed awhile in the family home near Bethlehem. How long, I asked Nestas, had he and his forebears been Christian? "Oh," he replied, "about 2,000 years." In 1985 I returned for a visit. The house where I had stayed had been bulldozed. I saw nothing more than rubble. On a nearby site, I found Nestas rebuilding. What, I asked, happened to his home? "The Israelis said I did not have a permit to live over there, so they demolished that house."

Still, Nestas feels more fortunate than his Christian neighbors, whose land and homes were seized for a gigantic for-Jews-only settlement called Gilo. I drove through this settlement, accompanied by Jerusalem's Latin Patriarch liaison officer, Joseph Donnelly.

"All that land you see, for miles and miles, with its housing complexes—it's all confiscated land. The Israelis made this part of a string of settlements that wind their way around every dimension of Jerusalem. This was Beit Jala; it was mostly Christian. But the Palestinians who owned this land, they will never get their land back, they will never regain their property. Here the Israelis have built the biggest shopping mall in the Middle East, the largest in the Jewish state. It is called the Canyon—it is adjacent to Teddy Stadium, all built on lands confiscated from Palestinian families—to house tens of thousands of Jews coming here from Russia and Eastern Europe. None had roots in Palestine. And as you see, the units just go on and on—for miles." Donnelly added that when he showed American visitors around such billion-dollar settlements, "they are always surprised that they—the U.S. taxpayers—are paying for these illegal, vast housing units, all built on land taken by force from Palestinians."

Christians spoke of a third reason for emigration: they can't find jobs. Palestinian Christians generally live in urban areas. And about half of the West Bank Christians work in public services, which include such areas as education, health, and tourism. "It means they are employees, and being an employee becomes precarious when no one under occupation has control over the economic situation—and everyone must abide by laws imposed by Israeli authorities," said Bethlehem University's Dr. Bernard Sabella, who has written extensively on Christian emigration. Since 1967, he pointed out, the

Israelis have imposed over 1,300 military rules which restrict movement and turn ordinary tasks into obstacle courses. The laws restrict what Palestinians produce, while making them a captive market for Israeli goods. Fifty percent of Palestinian men and 85 percent of the women are unemployed. The average annual Palestinian income is only $1,000. "Those with secure jobs do not think of leaving," said Dr. Sabella.

Palestinians, who have the highest number of college graduates per capita of any Arabs, put a high premium on education, and this is a fourth reason for their emigration: they want a future for their children. "Since 1948, parents began saying: 'An educated mind is the one asset the Zionists can't take from us,'" said Dr. Hind Salman, whose Christian parents sent her to Cairo University, where she earned a degree in economics. She has taught economics at Bethlehem University since soon after its founding in 1973—and is one of 200 women with doctorate degrees from that university. Today, she noted, the university's graduates have a record unemployment rate reaching 50 percent. Studies show that Palestinians with a first university degree are those most likely to emigrate. Overall, the Palestinian Christian community, with its emphasis on education and its work experience, fits well the definition by migration experts of a "migrant community:" "A community with a high educational achievement and a relatively good standard of living but with no real prospects for economic security or advancement will most probably become a migrant community."

The Difference Between a Tour and a Pilgrimage to the Holy Land

Back in the 1980s, I became intrigued by Christian Zionists—those who put a cult of Israel above the teachings of Christ. To learn more about Christian Zionists, I began research on the TV evangelist Jerry Falwell. For some years, I made a habit of tuning into Falwell's *Old Times Gospel Hour* on TV. I learned Falwell talked more about Israel than about Christ. He liked to boast, "The Jewish people in America and Israel and all over the world have no dearer friend than

Jerry Falwell." Falwell found many opportunities to tell Americans that the fate of the nation stood or fell according to the attitude they took toward Israel. If Americans did not show an unflinching willingness to provide Israel with arms and dollars, Falwell said, America would lose all.

In 1983, I was one of 630 Christians who flew out of New York on a Holy Land tour sponsored by Falwell. In Tel Aviv, after being put in groups of about 50, we began traveling by bus. Throughout the tour, we had Israeli Jewish guides. Not once did we have a Christian guide. Not once was a service scheduled in a Christian church, nor the opportunity given to meet a Christian Palestinian. On the day we approached Nazareth, where Jesus grew up and had his ministry, our guide said, "There is Nazareth." He added we would not stop. "No time," he said. Minutes later, he changed his mind, announcing: "We will stop in Nazareth. To use the toilet facilities." Thus, the only site the Christians saw in Nazareth was the toilets.

In 1985, I signed to go on another Falwell-sponsored tour, and again I got a colored brochure, printed in Israel, with no mention of Christ or the Christian sites. While we were in Jerusalem, Falwell gave a banquet honoring Defense Minister Moshe Arens. Seated not far from the two men, I heard Falwell say, in an aside to Arens, "By the way, I want to thank you for that jet plane you gave me." Earlier on, in a visit to Lynchburg, Virginia, Falwell's home base, I had seen the jet, and been told by Lynchburg residents: "The Israelis gave the jet to Falwell—as payment for what he's done for them."

When I went on the Falwell-sponsored trips, I presumed it was only right-wing Christian supporters of Israel who put a cult of the land of Israel above the teachings of Christ. But once, at Washington, D.C., Foundry Methodist Church, which Hillary Rodham Clinton attends, I saw a brochure of a Holy Land tour to be led by assistant minister William Shropshire. As with Falwell's brochure, Shropshire's was printed in Israel. I learned his group would have only Israeli guides—and they had no plans to meet Christians.

Christians, said Canon Ateek of St. George's Cathedral, "should not be shepherded about by Israeli guides. . . . I am disturbed that Israelis who do not believe in Christ are interpreting—to the visitors—

the Christian sites. I think there is a message that goes with the Christian sites, to those stones; these stones can be living stones, also. The message is what happened here and what God in Christ has done. And yet we hear what some of the Israeli guides say, and it is regrettable."

Canon Ateek also said he fears that Israelis plan further commercialization of the holy sites: "We don't want this 'touristy' aspect, we don't want the Holy Land to become a religious theme park, a kind of museum, a kind of Disneyland—which is happening. I am deeply concerned about Israel's wanting and gaining almost total control over our lives—politically, and as Christians."

Christian human rights attorney Raja Shehadeh also voiced concern over the Israeli control of holy Christian sites and the resulting commercialization. He gave an example of how one might pay Israelis to be baptized: "The Israelis have taken a small tributary of the Jordan, they call it the 'Yardenit Baptismal Site.' It's open every day for business, except Yom Kippur. Christians from Israeli-arranged tour groups line up. They pay shekels to an Israeli to rent a white garment and towel, step into the water, and get immersed. They also pay $3— to an Israeli—for a certificate verifying they have been baptized. I didn't go in the water, but I got one of the $3 certificates—as an example of the commercialization."

From the moment they arrive until they depart the Holy Land, American Christian tourists generally see only Israelis. On my arrival in the Holy Land, I met a woman from Salt Lake who had been touring there for two weeks and was leaving that same day. Had she, I asked, met any Christians? Her face registered confusion, as if I had asked: Had she met anyone from Mars? She explained she had been with a tour, and had heard lectures "from Israelis who wore skullcaps. And we had Israeli guides" to the Christian shrines. Then she volunteered she had gone to Egypt for three days. "And in Cairo, I met a Christian." She had chatted with him, found him "a pleasant person." But as for Christians in the Land of Christ—they had all been invisible.

Most all U.S. Christians are like the woman from Salt Lake City. They book Holy Land tours exclusively with Jewish agencies and use only Israeli guides. "There are 4,000 licensed Israeli guides—and only 40 Christian guides," said Latin Patriarch liaison officer Joseph Donnelly. "A West Bank Palestinian Christian guide has not been given a license since Israel militarily seized the land in 1967." The few Christian guides still operating "are carefully monitored" by the Israelis.

"There are 56 million American Catholics and only 8,000 came last year—and most came with Jewish agencies." Donnelly said he favors having a Catholic pilgrimage office.

"Our role would not be to compete with commerce or anyone's right to have a commercial endeavor, but to expose more American Christians and Catholics to the resources available here in the non-Jewish community. We would let those desiring to visit the Holy Land know about experienced pilgrimage leaders, experienced pilgrimage agencies that would enable the people coming here to visit Christian hospices, Christian restaurants, as well as visiting Muslim and Jewish communities. Right now, there's only these package deals offered by Unity Tours and Educational Opportunities. Their package deals are completely exclusive of any encounter with the living church, the living communities that have businesses but that are largely ignored by all the tourists coming here. And certainly a good way to support the community is to patronize its businesses."

There are hundreds of Jewish agencies that book Christian tourists to the Holy Land. But one need not go as a tourist. As we approach the year 2000, one might like to go to the Land of Christ as a pilgrim. Here is a suggestion of how to do so.

Volunteers in Mission (of the Southeastern jurisdiction, United Methodist Church): Bonnie Gehweiler, who serves on Americans for Middle East Understanding's board, spearheads this group. "I was one of 20 Christian volunteers going to Bethany to live among Palestinians in 1992," she said. "And I was also in a group of 20 Christian volunteers going to Beit Sahour in 1993. Our trips are for 13 days. We do work projects for one week and then travel to Christian sites the second week. During our stay in Beit Sahour, we stayed in a small Palestinian hotel, but we took all meals with local Christians—and it was one of the most wonderful experiences I have had in all my life. We got to know the people, and this was most meaningful for all of us."

Last month in Beit Sahour I met several of the Christians who had been "family" for Bonnie Gehweiler and her group. "We were so pleased they wanted to stay awhile among us. They gave us great support—and much help," Beit Sahour's Jamal Salameh said, adding, "we hope to host many such groups. We are thinking 'grassroots,' people-to-people. We think the experience we had with the groups that came here, and the way we were able to interact with the visitors— that we were better than tour guides. We talked about Christianity and being a Christian in this country. We gave an explanation of our lives by talking about our Christian heritage and introducing them to some of the problems we are facing."

"We would also like to accompany pilgrims to other Palestinian towns," said Beit Sahour's Dr. Nassar.

"We have beautiful sights, interesting things. There is Hebron. What tourist goes to Hebron? Yet it is a very interesting place, very attractive; it is a city of commerce. Twenty-five to 40 percent of the national product comes from Hebron. Take Nablus, for example. It is a wonderful city, you have the Old City, you have a very old Turkish bath. There are Samaritans there, so one can go and visit them, talk to them and see how they are living and thinking, it is an experience. You only hear about the Good Samaritan in the Bible, but who are they? There are only 500 left in the world. We want to give the Christians who come here not a chance to meet politicians but some real persons, we need to give something more than that which they can read in any newspaper."

Readers wishing to go as pilgrims to the Holy Land can contact Americans for Middle East Understanding for a list of travel agents: 212-870-2053; ameu@aol.com.

Confronting the Bible's Ethnic Cleansing in Palestine

By Michael Prior

Until his death in 2004, Michael Prior was professor of biblical studies at the University of Surrey in England, and visiting professor at Bethlehem University. In his December 2000 issue of The Link*, he wrestles with the question that has confronted believers and nonbelievers alike: How can an all-just and all-loving God command genocide?*

It is mid-October 2000; to date, at least 98 Palestinians and seven Jews have been killed, and over 3,000, mostly Palestinians, injured in the Holy Land's most recent unholiness. That's the math of it.

It is, however, the morality of it that has engaged me over the past quarter of a century.

I would have been spared some pain had I not undertaken significant portions of my postgraduate biblical studies in the land of the Bible. And although the focus of my engagement was "the biblical past," I could not avoid the modern social context of the region. As a result, my studying the Bible in the Land of the Bible provoked perspectives that scarcely would have arisen elsewhere.

For me, as a boy and young man, politics began and ended in Ireland, an Ireland obsessed with England. Much later I recognized that the history I absorbed so readily in school was one fabricated by the nationalist historiographers of a newly independent Ireland, who had refracted the totality of its history through the lens of 19th-century European nationalisms. Although my Catholic culture also cherished Saint Patrick and the saints and scholars after him, the real heroes of Ireland's history were those who challenged British colonialism in Ireland. I had no interest in the politics of any other region—except that I knew that Communism, wherever, was wrong. Anyhow, the priesthood beckoned.

Prior to the June 5–10, 1967, war, I had no particular interest in the State of Israel, other than an admiration for the Jews for having constructed a nation-state and restored a national language. In addition to stimulating my first curiosity in the Israeli-Arab conflict, Israel's conquest of the West Bank, the Golan Heights, the Gaza Strip, and Sinai brought me "face to face," via TV, with wider, international political realities. The startling, speedy, and comprehensive victory of diminutive Israel over its rapacious Arab predators produced surges of delight in me. And I had no reason to question the mellifluous mendacity of Abba Eban at the United Nations, delivered with that urbanity and self-assurance characteristic of Western diplomats, however fraudulent, claiming that Israel was an innocent victim of Egyptian aggression.

Later that summer in London, I was intrigued by billboards in Golders Green, with quotations from the Hebrew prophets, assuring readers that those who trusted in biblical prophecy could not be surprised by Israel's victory. Up to then, my understanding was that biblical prophecy related to the period of the prophets, and was not about predicting the future. The prophets were "forth-tellers" for God, rather than foretellers of future events. I was intrigued that others thought differently.

I was to learn later, in the 1980s and 1990s, that the 1967 war inaugurated a new phase in the Zionist conquest of Mandated Palestine, one which brought theological assertions and biblical interpretations to the very heart of the ideology that propelled the Israeli conquest and set the pattern for Jewish settlement. After two more years of theology, ordination, and three years of postgraduate biblical studies, I made my first visit to Israel-Palestine at Easter 1972, with a party of postgraduate students from the Pontifical Biblical Institute in Rome.

Seeing and Believing

The visit offered the first challenge to my favorable predisposition toward Israel. I was disturbed by the ubiquitous signs of the oppression of the Arabs, whom later I learned to call Palestinians. I was witnessing some kind of "institutionalized oppression"—I cannot recall whether "apartheid" was part of my vocabulary at the time. The experience must have been profound since, when the Yom Kippur War broke out in October 1973, my support for Israel did not match my enthusiasm of 1967. I had no particular interest in the area for the remainder of the 1970s, but I recall watching on TV the visit of Egypt's President Sadat to the Israeli Knesset in November 1977, an initiative which would culminate in a formal peace agreement in Camp David in 1979. Things changed for me in the 1980s.

In 1981 I went with a party from my university to visit Bir Zeit University in the Israeli-occupied West Bank. Because the campus was closed by the military just before our arrival, carefully planned programs had to yield to Palestinian "ad-hocery." Bir Zeit put a bus at our disposal, and equal numbers of its and our students constituted a university on wheels.

I was profoundly shocked when I began to see from the inside the reality of land expropriation and the ongoing Jewish settlement of the West Bank. I began to question the prevailing view that the Israeli occupation was for security reasons, but even with such obvious evidence I could not bring myself to abandon it.

I spent my 1983–84 sabbatical year at Jerusalem's École Biblique researching the Pauline Epistles. Again, the day-to-day life in Jerusalem sharpened my sensitivities. I was beginning to suspect that the Israeli occupation was not after all for security reasons, but was an expansion toward the achievement of "Greater Israel," which, I was to learn later, was the goal of even mainstream Zionism.

I can date to that period also voicing my first displeasure at my perception that the land traditions of the Bible appeared to mandate the genocide of the indigenes of "Canaan." At the end of his public lecture in Tantur, I suggested to Marc Ellis, a young Jewish theologian who was developing a Jewish Theology of Liberation with strong dependence on the Hebrew prophets, that it would be no more difficult to construct a Theology of Oppression on the basis of other biblical traditions, especially those dealing with Israelite origins that demanded the destruction of other peoples.

Following my sabbatical in 1984, I returned to London where, later that year, a colleague told me of the plea of Abuna Elias Chacour of Ibillin to pilgrims from the West to meet the Christian communities, "the Living Stones" of the land, and not be satisfied with the "dead stones" of archaeological sites. Soon a group of interested people in London established the ecumenical trust Living Stones, which promotes links between Christians in Britain and the Holy Land, and appointed me chairman. In 1985 I co-led a study tour to Israel and the Occupied Territories, and led a group of priests on a "Retreat through Pilgrimage" in 1987, and made other visits in 1990 and 1991.

It took some time for my experiences to acquire an ideological framework. Gradually I read more of the modern history of the region. In addition to bringing a university group in 1992, I spent August in the École Biblique, and while there interviewed prominent Palestinians, including Latin Patriarch of Jerusalem Michel Sabbah; Greek Orthodox Archbishop Timotheos; Anglican Bishop Samir Kafity; Canon Naim Ateek; and the vice president of Bir Zeit University, Dr. Gabi Baramki.

I made three visits in 1993, one at Easter to prepare the Cumberland Lodge Conference on Christians in the Holy Land, one for study in August, and the third to bring a group of students. Although my academic concentration in that period was on the scene of Jesus in the synagogue in Nazareth (Luke 4.16–30), my growing unease about the link between biblical spirituality and oppression stimulated me to examine the land traditions of the Bible, and so I began to read the narrative systematically with that theme in mind.

Yahweh and Ethnic Cleansing

What struck me most about the biblical narrative was that the divine promise of land was integrally linked with the mandate to exterminate the indigenous peoples, and I had to wrestle with my perception that those traditions were inherently oppressive and morally reprehensible. Even the Exodus narrative was problematic. While it portrays Yahweh as having compassion for the misery of his people and as willing to deliver them from the Egyptians and bring them to a land flowing with milk and honey (Exodus 3.7–8), that was only part of the picture. Although the reading of Exodus 3, both in the Christian liturgy and in the classical texts of liberation theologies, halts abruptly in the middle of verse 8 at the description of the land as one "flowing with milk and honey," the biblical text itself continues, "to the country of the Canaanites, the Hittites, the Amorites, the Perizzites, the Hivites, and the Jebusites." Manifestly, the promised land, flowing with milk and honey, had no lack of indigenous peoples, and, according to the narrative, would soon flow with blood:

> When my angel goes in front of you, and brings you to the Amorites, the Hittites, the Perizzites, the Canaanites, the Hivites, and the Jebusites, and I blot them out, you shall not bow down to their gods, or worship them, or follow their practices, but you shall utterly demolish them and break their pillars in pieces. (Exodus 23.23–24)

Matters got worse in the narrative of the book of Deuteronomy. After the King of Heshbon refused passage to the Israelites, Yahweh gave him over to them, who then captured and utterly destroyed all the cities, killing all the men, women, and children (Deuteronomy 2.33–34). The fate of the King of Bashan was no better (3.3). Yahweh's role was central:

> When Yahweh your God brings you into the land that you are about to enter and occupy, and he clears away many nations before you—the Hittites, the Girgashites, the Amorites, the Canaanites, the Perizzites, the Hivites . . . and when Yahweh your God gives them over to you . . . you must utterly destroy them. . . . Show them no mercy. . . . For you are a people holy to Yahweh your God; Yahweh your God has chosen you out of all the peoples on earth to be his people, his treasured possession. (Deuteronomy 7.1–11; see also 9.1–5; 11.8–9, 23, 31–32)

And again, from the mouth of Moses:

> But as for the towns of these peoples that Yahweh your God is giving you as an inheritance, you must not let anything that breathes remain alive. You shall annihilate them—the Hittites and the Amorites, the Canaanites and the Perizzites, the Hivites and the Jebusites—just as Yahweh your God has commanded, so that they may not teach you to do all the abhorrent things that they do for their gods, and you thus sin against Yahweh your God. (Deuteronomy 20.16–18)

It was some shock to realize that the narrative presents "ethnic cleansing" not only as legitimate, but as required by the deity. The book ends with Moses's sight of the promised land before he dies (34.1–3). Although Moses was unequalled in his deeds, he left a worthy successor, Joshua, who, after Moses had lain his hands on him, was full of the spirit of wisdom (34.4–12). So much for the preparation for entry into the Promised Land.

The first part of the Book of Joshua (chapters 2–12) describes the conquest of a few key cities, and their fate in accordance with the laws of the Holy War. Even when the Gibeonites were to be spared, the Israelite elders complained at the lapse in fidelity to the mandate to destroy all the inhabitants of the land (9.21–27). Joshua took Makkedah, utterly destroying every person in it (10.28). A similar fate befell other cities (10.29–39): everything that breathed was destroyed, as Yahweh commanded (10.40–43). Joshua utterly destroyed the inhabitants of the cities of the north as well (11.1–23). Yahweh gave to Israel all the land that he swore to their ancestors he would give them (21.43–45). The legendary achievements of Yahweh through the agencies of Moses, Aaron, and Joshua are kept before the Israelites even in their prayers: "You brought a vine out of Egypt; you drove out the nations and planted it" (Psalm 80.8; see also Psalms 78.54–55; 105.44).

By modern standards of international law and human rights, what these biblical narratives mandate are "war crimes" and "crimes against humanity." While readers might seek refuge in the claim that the problem lies with the predispositions of the modern reader rather than with the text itself, one could not escape so easily. One must acknowledge that much of the Torah, and the book of Deuteronomy in particular, contains menacing ideologies and racist, xenophobic, and militaristic tendencies. The implications of the existence of dubious moral dispositions, presented as mandated by the divinity, within a book which is canonized as Sacred Scripture, invited the most serious investigation. Was there a way of reading the traditions which could rescue the Bible from being a blunt instrument of oppression, and acquit God of the charge of being the Great Ethnic-Cleanser?

In that August of 1994, the École library had just received a Festschrift consisting of studies in Deuteronomy. In addition to articles covering the customary source, historical-critical, and literary discussions, it contained one by F. E. Deist with the intriguing title, "The Dangers of Deuteronomy," which discussed the role of that book in support of apartheid.[1] It dealt with the text from the perspective of its reception history, especially within the ideology of an emerging Afrikaner nationalism. During that month I also read A. G. Lamadrid's discussion of the role of the Bible and Christian theology in the Iberian conquest of Latin America.[2] The problem, then, went beyond academic reflection on the interpretation of ancient documents.

Somebody must have addressed the moral question before, I presumed. Back in Jerusalem in August 1995, I realized that this was not the case. Even though Gerhard von Rad lamented in 1943 that no thorough investigation of "the land" had been made, no serious study of the topic was undertaken for another 30 years. Even W. D. Davies acknowledged later that he had written his seminal work *The Gospel and the Land* at the request of friends in Jerusalem who, just before the war in 1967, had urged his support for the cause of Israel. Moreover, he confessed that he wrote *The Territorial Dimensions of Judaism* in 1982 under the direct impact of that war, and his 1991 update because of the mounting need to understand the theme in the light of events in the Middle East, culminating in the Gulf War and its aftermath. I was intrigued by the frankness with which Davies publicized his hermeneutical key: "Here I have concentrated on what in my judgment must be the beginning for an understanding of this conflict: the sympathetic attempt to comprehend the Jewish tradition."[3]

While Davies considers "the land" from virtually every other conceivable perspective, little attention is given to broadly moral and human rights issues. In particular, he excludes from his concern, "What happens when the understanding of the Promised Land in Judaism conflicts with the claims of the traditions and occupancy of its other peoples?" He excused himself by saying that to engage that issue would demand another volume, without indicating his intention of embarking upon such an enterprise. I wondered whether Davies would have been equally sanguine had white, Anglo-Saxon Protestants, or even white Catholics of European provenance been among the displaced people who paid the price for the prize of Zionism. Reflecting a somewhat elastic moral sense, Davies, although perturbed by the aftermath of the 1967 conquest, took the establishment of the State of Israel in stride. Showing no concern for the foundational injustice done to the Palestinians in 1948, Davies wrote as if there were later a moral equivalence between the dispossessed Palestinians and the dispossessing Zionists. The rights of the rapist and the victim were finely balanced.

Walter Brueggemann's *The Land* brought me no further. While he saw land as perhaps "the central theme" of biblical faith, he bypassed the treatment to be meted out to the indigenous inhabitants, affirming, "What is asked is not courage to destroy enemies, but courage to keep Torah," avoiding the fact that "keeping Torah" in this context demanded accepting its xenophobic and destructive militarism. By 1994, however, Brueggemann was less sanguine, noting that while the scholastic community had provided "rich and suggestive studies on the 'land theme' in the Bible . . . they characteristically stop before they get to the hard part, contemporary issues of land in the Holy Land."[4]

It was beginning to dawn on me that much biblical investigation—especially that concentration on the past which is typical of the historical-critical method—was quite indifferent to moral considerations. Indeed, it was becoming clear that the discipline of biblical studies over the last hundred years reflected the Eurocentric perspectives of virtually all Western historiography and had contributed significantly to the oppression of native peoples. The benevolent interpretation of biblical traditions that advocate atrocities and war crimes had given solace to those bent on the exploitation of new lands at the expense of native peoples. While the behavior of communities and nation-states is complex, and is never the result of one element of motivation, there is abundant evidence that the Bible has been, and still is for some, the idea that redeems the conquest of the earth. This was particularly true in the case of the Arabs of Palestine, in whose country I had reached these conclusions as I studied the Bible.

By the autumn of 1995 I was well into a book on the subject, and in November I went to discuss with Sheffield Academic Press a draft manuscript on "The Bible and Zionism." The editor, apprehensive at my concentration on Zionism, persuaded me to use three case studies. The task ahead, then, would require further immersion in the histories of Latin America, South Africa, and Israel, as well as a more detailed study of the biblical narrative and its interpretation in the hands of the biblical academy.

Having had my moral being sensitized by the biblical mandate to commit genocide, I was amazed that scholars had a high esteem for the book of Deuteronomy. Indeed, commentators conventionally assess it to be a theological book par excellence, and the focal point of the religious history of the Old Testament. In the November 14, 1995, Lattey Lecture at Cambridge University, Professor Norbert Lohfink argued that it provides a model of a utopian society in which there would be no poor.[5] In my role as the formal proposer of a vote of thanks—I was the chairperson of the Catholic Biblical Association of Great Britain—I invited him to consider whether, in the light of that book's insistence on a mandate to commit genocide, the utopian society would be possible only after the invading Israelites had wiped out the indigenous inhabitants. The protocol of the Lattey Lecture left the last word with me, and subsequently I was given a second word, being invited to deliver the 1997 Lattey Lecture. I chose the title, "A Land Flowing with Milk, Honey, and People."[6]

O Little Bantustan of Bethlehem

The final revision of my study on the relation between the Bible and colonialism was undertaken in 1996–97 while I was visiting professor at Bethlehem University and scholar-in-residence in Tantur Ecumenical Institute, Jerusalem. My context was a persistent reminder of the degradation and oppression which colonizing enterprises inflict on their indigenes. I also became more aware of the collusion of Western scholarship in the enterprise.

Working against a background of bullet fire, and in the shadow of tanks, added a certain intensity to my research. Several bullets landed on the flat roof of Tantur on September 25–26, 1996. Two Palestinians, one a graduate of the university, were killed in Bethlehem, and many Palestinians and Israeli soldiers were killed in the disturbances elsewhere in the West Bank. However, with no bullets flying in Jerusalem on the 26th, I was able to deliver my advertised public lecture in the Swedish Christian Study Center, entitled "Does the God of the Bible Sanction Ethnic Cleansing?" By mid-December I was able to send the manusccript of "The Bible and Colonialism" to Sheffield Academic Press.

I preached at the 1996 Christmas Midnight Mass at Bethlehem University, presided over by Msgr. Montezemolo, the Holy See's Apostolic Delegate and a key player in the signing of the Fundamental Agreement between the Holy See and the State of Israel on December 30, 1993. I reflected with the congregation that, notwithstanding the Christmas rhetoric about God's Glory in the Highest Heaven and Peace on Earth, the reality of Bethlehem brought one back to reality rather quickly. I assured them that passing by the checkpoint between Bethlehem and Jerusalem twice a day made me boil with anger at the humiliation which the colonizing enterprise of Zionism had inflicted on the people of the region. I suggested that the Christmas narratives portray the ordinary people as the heroes and the rulers as the antiheroes, as if assuring believers that the mighty will be cast down, and that God is working for the oppressed. I would meet His Excellency again soon.

On December 30, I listened to Msgr. Montezemolo lecture in Notre Dame on the third anniversary of the Fundamental Agreement between the Holy See and Israel. The audience was composed exclusively of expatriate Christians and Israeli Jews, with not a Palestinian in sight.

Well into the question time, I violated the somewhat sycophantic atmosphere: "I had expected that the Agreement would have given the Holy See some leverage in putting pressure on Israel vis-à-vis the Palestinians, if only on the matter of freedom to worship in Jerusalem—Palestinians have been forbidden entry into even East Jerusalem, whether on Friday or Sunday, since March 1993."

His Excellency replied rhetorically, "Do you not think that the Holy See is doing all it can?" At the reception afterwards, a certain Ambassador Gilboa, one of the Israeli architects of the Agreement, berated me in a most aggressive fashion for my question. Rather than assuming the posture of a culprit, I took the attack to him on the matter of the Jews having "kicked out" the Palestinians in 1948. "No, they were not kicked out," he, who was a soldier at the time, insisted. "In fact, helicopters dropped leaflets on the Arab towns, beseeching the inhabitants to stay put, etc."

I told him I did not believe him, and cited even the Israeli revisionist historiographer Benny Morris, whom he dismissed as a compulsive attention-seeker. It was obvious all around the room that a not insignificant altercation was taking place. In the hope of discouraging him from trying to stifle the truth in the future, I assured him that he should have remained a soldier, because he had the manners of a "corner-boy," and not what I expected from a diplomat. I went home righteous.

Academic life rolled on. My February 28, 1997, lecture titled "The Bible and Zionism" seemed to perplex several of the students of Bethlehem Bible College. Most of the questions reflected a literalist understanding of the Bible, and I struggled to convey the impression that there were forms of discourse other than history.

Having visited the Christian Peacemaker Team in Hebron as a gesture of solidarity on March 6, I returned home for the Tantur public lecture on "The Future of Religious Zionism" by Jewish philosopher and professor David Hartman. It was an eventful occasion. Hartman gave a dazzling exegesis on the theme of covenant, from the Bible through the rabbis, to Zionism. My journal takes the matter up from the second half of his talk, devoted to questions:

> I made the fourth intervention, to the effect that in being brought through the stages of understanding of the covenant, from the Bible to Rabbinic Judaism, I was enchanted, and much appreciative. However, I was shocked to hear Zionism described as "the high point of covenantal spirituality." Zionism, as I saw it, both in its rhetoric and in its practice, was not an ideology of sharing, but one of displacing. I was shocked, therefore, that what others might see as an example of 19th-century colonial plunder was being clothed in the garment of spirituality.

Somewhat shaken, Professor Hartman thanked me for my question, and set about putting the historical record straight. The real problem was that the Arabs had not welcomed Jews back to their homeland. Moreover, the displacement of the Arabs was never intended, but was forced on the Zionist leadership by the attack of the Arab armies in 1948. Nevertheless, great developments in history sometimes require initial destruction: consider how the United States had defeated totalitarianism, although this was preceded by the displacement of the Indians.

On the following day, in the discussion after my final session of teaching on "Jesus the Liberator" in Tantur, one of the continuing-education students brought the discussion back to the previous day's deliberations. He was very embarrassed by my attack on "that holy man."

There was a particularly lively exchange, with several others getting into the discussion. A second student said that he was delighted with my question yesterday and was sure that it represented the disquiet of many of the group. A third responded enthusiastically to my liberation ethic, saying that it disturbed him, but he had to cope with the disturbance. An American priest came to me afterwards, saying how much he appreciated my courage in speaking yesterday and on a previous occasion, etc. His enthusiasm was not shared by everyone. After the class, an advertising notice appeared on the board from the overseer of the Scholar's Colloquium. It read, "Dr. Michael Prior presents a largish paper, 'Zionism: from the Secular to the Sacred,' which is a chapter from a book he is in the process of writing." The next paragraph read:

> Zionism is a subject on which there are hot opinions—not least from the author himself. Some have suggested to me that this disunity is a reason why we should not discuss such matters at all. I believe the opposite: the quality of hot opinions is best tested in a scholarly discussion, where they must be supported by evidence and good argument. One can even learn something. Welcome!

Swedish New Testament scholar Bengt Holmberg chaired the colloquium.

The first scholar to respond to my paper, a U.S. Catholic veteran of the Jewish-Christian dialogue, did so in a decidedly aggressive manner, accusing me of disloyalty to the church, etc. The second was long in praise.

The third intimated that there was nothing new in the paper, and rambled on about the Zionists' intentions to bring benefits to the indigenous population, etc. Losing patience, I asked him to produce evidence for his claims, adding that not only was there no such evidence, but the evidence there was showed that the Zionist ideologues were virtually at one in their determination to rid the land of Arabs.

A fourth scholar, a Dutch Protestant veteran of the Jewish-Christian dialogue, chastised me for my audacity in addressing the question at all, insisting that I should be silent, because I was an outsider and a Christian.

I rose to the challenge. Was I understanding him to say that, having seen the distress of the Palestinian people for myself, I should now not comment on it? Was he asking me to deny my experience, or merely to mute my critique? I assured the colloquium that as a biblical scholar, and an ongoing witness to what transpired in the region, I considered it an obligation to protest what was going on. Once again, the admiring remarks were made later, in private.

The proofs of *The Bible and Colonialism* arrived on Good Friday. I got my first taste of tear gas in the vicinity of Rachel's Tomb on my way to Easter Sunday Mass at St. Catherine's in Bethlehem. On April 3, I delivered the Tantur public lecture, "The Moral Problem of the Bible's Land Traditions," followed by questions, both appreciative and hostile. Uniquely for the series, the lecture was not advertised in *The Jerusalem Post*. In dealing with a trilogy of hostile questions, I availed of the opportunity to say that I considered Zionism to be one of the most pernicious ideologies of the 20th century, particularly evil because of its essential link with religious values.

Stars from the west studded the sky over Bethlehem for the celebrations of Tantur's 25th birthday (May 25–28, 1997). Under the light of the plainly visible Hale-Bopp comet, a frail Teddy Kollek was introduced at the opening ceremony as though he were the founder of the institute. A choir from the United States sang, one song in Hebrew. Palestinian faces, not least that of Afif Safieh, the Palestinian Delegate to the United Kingdom and the Holy See, looked decidedly out of joint throughout the opening festivities. But the Palestinians were not altogether forgotten, being thanked profusely for their work in the kitchen and around the grounds.

Moreover, for the lecture on "Christians of the Holy Land" given on May 27, prominent Palestinians were invited to speak from the floor. Although the lecture was billed to be presented by a distinguished expatriate scholar "with local presenters," in fact the Palestinian savants had been invited only to the audience floor. Having excused himself from dealing with the political context, the lecturer delivered an urbane, accomplished historical perspective.

The token Palestinians were invited to speak from the floor, first Naim Ateek, then Mitri Raheb, and then Kevork Hintlian. After two rabbis had their say, also from the floor, I was allowed to speak, wishing to make two points: that my experience with the Palestinians had impressed upon me their unity, rather than their diversity, and second, that the Jewish-Christian dialogue had been hijacked by a Zionist agenda. After one more sentence had escaped from my mouth, the chairman stopped me short. I had broken the Solemn Silence. This was the third time that year I had been prevented from speaking in public. I paused, producing a most uncomfortable silence, thanked him, and sat down.

Saturday, May 31, 1997, being the 28th anniversary of my ordination I determined to do something different. Since it was also the Feast of the Visitation, I decided that I would go to Ein Karem, the traditional site of Mary's visit to her cousin Elizabeth. But on the way, I would call at Jabal Abu Ghneim, the hill opposite Tantur, which, despite U.N. condemnation, was being prepared for an Israeli settlement. The teeth of the high-tech machinery had cut into the rock, having chewed up thousands of trees. Joseph Conrad's phrase, "the relentless progress of our race," kept coming at me.

On the way to Ein Karem, I visited Mount Herzl to see the grave of the founder of Zionism. Knowing that I would also visit the grave of Yitzhak Rabin, I was struck by the irony of the situation. Theodor Herzl was sure that Jews could survive only in their own nation-state. Nevertheless, he died a natural death in Europe, and was re-interred in the new state in 1949, while Prime Minister Rabin, born in Palestine, was gunned down by a Jewish religious zealot in what was intended to be the sole haven for Jews.

Back in England

I returned to London in July 1997. By December, *The Bible and Colonialism* and *Western Scholarship and the History of Palestine* were hot off the press. In *The Bible and Colonialism* I promised that I would discuss elsewhere the more theological aspects of Zionism, and, while still in Jerusalem in 1997, I had laid out my plans for writing the book I had really wanted to write some years earlier.

I submitted a draft manuscript to a distinguished publisher in November 1997, and even though the anonymous reader found it to be "a brilliant book which must be published," the press declined. I was informed orally that the press had "a very strong Jewish list" and could not offend its Jewish contributors and readers. While an American publishing company judged it to be "a prodigious achievement of historical and theological investigation" and "a very important work," it deemed that it would not really suit its publishing program. Routledge "bit the bullet," publishing it under the title *Zionism and the State of Israel: A Moral Inquiry.*[7]

On the basis of his having read *The Bible and Colonialism,* Professor Heikki Räisänen of the University of Helsinki invited me to address the most prestigious of the international biblical conferences, the Society of Biblical Literature International Conference (Helsinki-Lahti, July 16–22, 1999) on "The Bible and Zionism." The session at which I was invited to speak dealt with "Reception History and Moral Criticism of the Bible," and I was preceded by Professors Robert Jewett (U.S.) and David Clines (U.K.) on aspects of Paul and Job, respectively.

When my hour came, I invited biblical scholarship not to maintain an academic detachment from significant engagement in contemporary issues. I noted that "the view that the Bible provides the title-deed for the establishment of the State of Israel and for its policies since 1948 is so pervasive even within mainstream Christian theology and university biblical studies, that the very attempt to raise the issue is sure to elicit opposition. The disfavor usually took the form of personal abuse, and the intimidation of publishers."

In the light of what happened next I might have added that one is seldom honored by having the substantive issues addressed in the usual way.

After I had delivered my 25-minute lecture, the official respondent, who had my paper a month in advance, said he would bypass the usual niceties ("A very fine paper," etc.) and quickly got down to his objections, which were so standard as not to deserve my refutation. Instead I suggested that the chairman open up the discussion.

Some five Israelis in turn took up the challenge. "Jews have always longed for the land." "They never intended displacing anyone." "The land was empty—almost." "You were wrong historically: Herzl never intended dislocating the Arabs."

I interrupted, quoting Herzl's June 12, 1895, diary entry—in the original German for good measure—about his endeavor to expel the poor population, etc.

I was berated for having raised a "political matter" in an academic conference: "See what can happen when one abandons the historical critical method!" Another Israeli professor began by saying, "I am very pleased to have been here this morning," but added, "because I understand better now how anti-Semitism can present itself as anti-Zionism, all under the guise of academic scholarship." A cabal, including at least one Israeli and a well-known scholar from Germany, clapped. The chairman had to restore order.

In the course of my "defense" I reiterated that it was the displacement of another people that raised the moral problematic for me. I had witnessed the effects of the oppression rather more than even most of the audience. Having been given the last word, I professed that until Israelis acknowledge their having displaced another people and make some reparation and accommodation, there would be no future for the state.

In the course of the following day several who had attended expressed their appreciation, albeit in private. A Finnish scholar congratulated me on having raised a vital issue, adding, "The way you were received added sharpness to your argument." A distinguished biblical scholar from Germany, who was very distressed by my having raised the question, later pleaded that his people were responsible for killing six million Jews.

The Importance of the Issue

I have learned that, distinctively in the case of Zionist colonization, a determined effort was made to rid the terrain altogether of the native population, since their presence in any number would frustrate the grand design of establishing a Jewish state. The necessity of removing the Arabs was recognized from the beginning of the Zionist enterprise—

and advocated by all major Zionist ideologues from Theodor Herzl to Ehud Barak—and was meticulously planned and executed in 1948 and 1967. In their determination to present an unblemished record of the Zionist achievement, the fabricators of propagandist Zionist history are among the most accomplished practitioners of the strange craft of source-doctoring, rewriting not only their history, but the documents upon which such a history was based. The propagandist intent was to hide things said and done, and to bequeath to posterity only a sanitized version of the past.

In any case, the argument for the compelling need of Jews to settle in a Jewish state does not constitute a right to displace an indigenous population. And even if it had never been intended from the start, which it most certainly was, the moral problematic arises most acutely precisely from the fact that Zionism has wreaked havoc on the indigenous population, and not a little inconvenience on several surrounding states. Nor can the *Shoah* (Holocaust) be appealed to credibly to justify the destruction of an innocent third party. It is a dubious moral principle to regard the barbaric treatment of Jews by the Third Reich as constituting a right to establish a Jewish state at the expense of an innocent third party. Surely the victims of Auschwitz would not have approved.

My study of the Bible in the Land of the Bible brought me face to face with the turbulence of Israel-Palestine and raised questions not only about the link between biblical interpretation and colonial exploitation but about the nature of the biblical narrative itself. An academic interest became a consuming moral imperative.

Why should the State of Israel, any more than any other state, be such a challenge to morality? The first reason, I suggest, derives from the general moral question attendant upon the forcible displacement of an indigenous people from its homeland. The second springs from the unique place that the land has in the Sacred Scriptures of both Jews and Christians, and the significance attached to it as the location of the state for Jews. In addition, there is the positive assessment of the State of Israel on the part of the majority of religious Jews of various categories, as well as in certain Christian ecclesial and theological circles.

As a biblical scholar, I have been shocked to discover that the only plausible validation for the displacement of the Palestinians derived from a naïve interpretation of the Bible, and that in many church and academic parties—and not only the "fundamentalist" wing—biblical literalism swept away any concerns deriving from considerations of morality. I contend that fidelity to the literary genre of the biblical traditions and respect for the evidence provided mainly by archaeological investigation demands a rejection of such simplistic readings of the biblical narratives of land, and of the prophetic oracles of restoration.

And to these academic perspectives, one must add one of faith, namely, that God is fundamentally moral; and, for those espousing the Christian vision, that He loves all His people, irrespective of race, etc.

Rather than relate the establishment of the State of Israel to the Shoah, I have been led gradually to situate Zionism within the category of xenophobic imperialism so characteristic of the major European powers towards the end of the 19th century. I consider the espousal of it by a majority of Jews worldwide to mark the nadir of Jewish morality. Because I trust in a God before whom tyranny ultimately dissolves, and because one learns something from history, I have no doubt that a future generation of diaspora and Israeli Jews will repudiate its presumptions and repent for the injustices perpetrated on the Palestinians by their fathers and grandfathers.

While I regret the descent of Judaism into the embrace of Zionism, there is little I can do about it. However, the degree to which a thoroughly Zionized Judaism infects the so-called Jewish-Christian dialogue—which I prefer to designate "a monologue in two voices"—is a matter of grave concern. I am perturbed that concurrence with a Zionist reading of Jewish history—that Jews everywhere, and at all times, wanted to reestablish a nation-state in Palestine (with no concern for the indigenous population), etc.—is virtually a component of the credo of the dialogue. In that fabricated scenario, the planned, and systematically executed dislocation of the Palestinian population, far from incurring the wrath of post-colonial liberalism, becomes an object of honor, and even religious significance. While most Jews worldwide—there are notable exceptions—allow themselves to be deluded by such perspectives, I see no reason Christians should.

God the Ethnic Cleanser?

Often I am asked: How do you as a Catholic priest and biblical scholar explain to an ordinary believer the Yahweh-sanctioned ethnic cleansing mandated in some of the narrative of the Old Testament? Is not this also the Word of God? Such questions have forced themselves on me in a particular way as a result of my contact with the Holy Land. Let me indicate some of my perspectives. But first, let us look at the stakes.

Recently a full-page advertisement in the September 10, 2000, *New York Times,* signed by over 150 Jewish scholars and leaders, stated:

> Christians can respect the claim of the Jewish people upon the land of Israel. The most important event for Jews since the Holocaust has been the reestablishment of a Jewish state in the Promised Land. As members of a biblically-based religion, Christians appreciate that Israel was promised—and given—to Jews as the physical center of the covenant between them and God. Many Christians support the State of Israel for reasons far more profound than mere politics. As Jews, we applaud this support.

Here we see clothed in the garment of piety the Zionist enterprise, which was determined to create a state for Jews at the expense of the indigenous Arab people—a product of the nationalistic and imperialistic spirit of 19th-century Europe.

Whatever pangs of conscience one might have about the expulsion of a million Palestinian Arabs and the destruction of their villages to ensure they would not return, the Bible can salve it. Zionism, a program originally despised by both wings of Judaism, Orthodox and Reform, as being antireligious (by the Orthodox) and contrary to the universal mission of Judaism (by Reform Jewry), is now at the core of the Jewish credo. And credulous Christians allow themselves to be sucked into the vortex. Only when Zionism is being evaluated are normal rules of morality suspended; only here is ethnic cleansing applauded by the religious spirit.

Many theologians on seeing how the revered sacred text has been used as an instrument of oppression seek refuge in the view that it is the misuse of the Bible, rather than the text itself, that is the problem. The blame is shifted from the nonproblematic biblical text to the perverse predispositions of the interpreter.

This "solution" evades the problem. It must be acknowledged that several traditions within the Bible lend themselves to oppressive interpretations and applications, precisely because of their inherently oppressive nature.

Towards a Moral Reading of the Bible

My approach is set forth in a chapter of *The Bible and Colonialism: A Moral Critique*.[8] I begin by stressing how important it is to acknowledge the existence of texts of unsurpassed violence within Sacred Scripture, and to recognize them to be an affront to moral sensitivities. The problem is not only theoretical. In addition to being morally reprehensible texts, some have fuelled terrible injustices through colonialist enterprises.

The Holy War traditions of the Old Testament pose an especially difficult moral problem. In addition to portraying God as one who cherishes the slaughter of his created ones, they acquit the killer of moral responsibility for his destruction, presenting it as a religious obligation.

Every effort must be made to rescue the Bible from being a blunt instrument in the oppression of one people by another. If a naïve interpretation leads to such unacceptable conclusions, what kind of exegesis can rescue it?

Some exegetes note that Christians read the Old Testament in the light of the life and paschal mystery of Christ. In such a perspective, the writings of the Old Testament contain certain "imperfect and provisional" elements, which the divine pedagogy could not eliminate right away. The Bible, then, reflects a considerable moral development, which finds its completion in the New Testament. I do not find this proposal satisfactory.

The attempts of the fathers of the church to eliminate the scandal caused by particular texts of the Bible do little for me. The allegorical presentation of Joshua leading the people into the land of Canaan as a type of Christ who leads Christians into the true promised land does not impress.

The Catholic Church deals with the embarrassment of having divinely mandated ethnic cleansing in the biblical narrative either by excluding it altogether from public use or by excising the most offensive verses. The disjuncture between this censoring of the Word of God and the insistence on the divine provenance of the whole of the Scriptures has not been satisfactorily resolved.

There is another method that is more amenable to modern sensibilities, one which takes seriously the literary forms of the materials, the circumstances of their composition, and relevant nonliterary evidence. According to this view, the fundamental tenet of the Protestant Reformation that the Bible can be understood in a straightforward way must be abandoned. Narratives purporting to describe the past are not necessarily accurate records of it. One must respect the distinctive literary forms within the biblical narrative—legend, fabricated myths of the past, prophecy and apocalyptic, etc.

The relevant biblical narratives of the past are not simple history, but reflect the religious and political ideologies of their much later authors. It is now part of the scholarly consensus that the patriarchal narratives of Genesis do not record events of an alleged patriarchal period, but are retrojections into a past about which the writers knew little, reflecting the author's intentions at the later period of composition. It is naïve, then, to cleave to the view that God made the promise of progeny and land to Abraham after the fashion indicated in Genesis 15.

The Exodus narrative poses particular difficulties for any reader who is neither naïve nor amoral. It is the entrance (Eisodus) into the land of milk and honey which keeps the hope of the wandering Israelites alive. It is high time that readers read the narrative with sensitivity to the innocent third party about to be exterminated, that is, "with the eyes of the Canaanites."

Moreover, there is virtual unanimity among scholars that the model of tribal conquest as narrated in Joshua 1–12 is unsustainable. Leaving aside the witness of the Bible, we have no evidence that there was a Hebrew conquest. Evidence from archaeology, extra-biblical literature, etc., points in an altogether different direction from that propounded by Joshua 1–12. It suggests a sequence of periods marked by a gradual and peaceful coalescence of disparate peoples into a group of highland dwellers whose achievement of a new sense of unity culminated only with the entry of the Assyrian administration. The Iron I Age settlements on the central hills of Palestine, from which the later kingdom of Israel developed, reflect continuity with Canaanite culture, and repudiate any ethnic distinction between "Canaanites" and "Israelites." Israel's origins, then, were within Canaan, not outside it. There was neither invasion from outside nor revolution within.

A historiography of Israelite origins based solely or primarily on the biblical narratives is an artificial construct influenced by certain religious motivations obtaining at a time long postdating any verifiable evidence of events. Accordingly, contrary to the opinion of the 150-plus Jewish scholars and rabbis who signed *The New York Times* ad, the biblical narrative is not sufficient to transform barbarism into piety.

Conclusion

Western theological scholarship, while strong in its critique of repressive regimes elsewhere, gives a wide berth to Zionism. Indeed, a moral critique of its impact on the Palestinians is ruled out.

I try to break the silence in *The Bible and Colonialism* and *Zionism and the State of Israel*. The former explores the moral question of the impact which colonialist enterprises, fueled by the biblical paradigm, have had on the indigenous populations in general, while the latter deals with the impact of Zionism on the Palestinians. They are explorations into terrain virtually devoid of inquirers, which attempt to map out some of the contours of that terrain. They subject the land traditions of the Bible to an evaluation which derives from general ethical principles and criteria of human decency, such as are enshrined in conventions of human rights and international law.

Such an enterprise is necessary. When people are dispossessed, dispersed, and humiliated, not only with alleged divine support, but at the alleged express command of God, one's moral self recoils in horror. Any association of God with the destruction of people must be subjected to an ethical analysis. The obvious contradiction between what some claim to be God's will and ordinary civilized, decent behavior poses the question as to whether God is a chauvinistic, nationalistic, and militaristic xenophobe. It also poses the problem of biblical prophecy finding its fulfillment in what even unbelievers would regard as a form of ethnic cleansing.

I consider that biblical studies and theology should deal with the real conditions of people's lives and not satisfy themselves with comfortable survival in an academic or ecclesial ghetto. I am concerned about the use of the Bible as a legitimization for colonialism and its consequences. My academic work addresses aspects of biblical hermeneutics and informs a wider public on issues that have implications for human well-being, as well as for allegiance to God.

While such a venture might be regarded as an instructive academic contribution by any competent scholar, to assume responsibility for doing so is for me, who has witnessed the dispossession, dispersion, and humiliation of the Palestinians, of the order of a moral imperative. It is high time that biblical scholars, church people, and Western intellectuals read the biblical narratives of the promise of land "with the eyes of the Canaanites."[9]

The Islamic Alternative

By Yvonne Y. Haddad

Yvonne Haddad is professor of history of Islam and Christian-Muslim relations at Georgetown University. While her article for The Link *was written in 1982, her analysis of Islam as an emerging factor in global politics has proven to be remarkably perceptive. Dr. Haddad has written or edited more than a dozen books on Islam.*

To the careful observer of Muslim countries it is quite evident that a phenomenon hardly visible in the 1960s and the early half of the '70s appears to be gaining momentum and mass approval. A growing consensus among an increasing number of intellectuals as well as the common people suggests that "the time has come to try Islam."

This study will attempt to portray the Islamic perception of the world based on the Muslim understanding of reality, precipitating the current attitudes that dominate intellectual centers as well as governments in various countries. It is based on eight years of research of Islamic literature, particularly that coming from the Arab world, and on numerous conversations with those who find their primary identity in this Islamic nationalism. The study attempts to show that the search for Islamic answers is not restricted to a small fringe group, but rather has become the general deliberate search of elites as well as of the masses for Islamic answers to political, economic, social, and cultural questions.

The critical need for such answers has been mandated by what is perceived as the unsuitability of the Western models for Muslim countries, evidenced by the failure of these models in those Muslim countries that have adopted or experimented with them, and by what is perceived as the failure of the model even in the West itself.

The Colonial Challenge: A Question of Militancy

It is currently popular in some circles of the Western press to refer to the rise in Islamic consciousness and identity as "Militant Islam." For those Muslims engaged in the process of Islamization, Militant Islam appears to be their response to "Militant Secularism," "Militant Christianity," and "Militant Judaism."

The Muslim encounter with "the West" in the 19th and 20th centuries was most intimately experienced through European conquests of Muslim lands which facilitated Western political, economic, social, and cultural domination of the daily lives of the Muslims. By the end of World War I, only four Muslim nations—Afghanistan, Turkey, Saudi Arabia, and Yemen—had not experienced direct or indirect European rule.

European expansion, which began in the 17th century through the search for markets and natural resources, was by the 19th century enhanced through an ideological support system based on the teachings of social Darwinism: "natural selection" and the "survival of the fittest." This gave European man "scientific" proof that he was the acme of human evolution and that his civilization was the final state in human achievement and progress.

Colonialism was justified on "humanitarian" grounds. Its purpose was to share the enlightenment and its achievements with those of inferior development. The colonial conquests were thus cloaked in the image of the European man's "manifest destiny" which would lead the rest of humanity to become a replica of European man and to enjoy the benefits of the institutions he devised.

Meanwhile, many religious circles viewed Christianity in a similar way as the highest form of religion, affirming that all other religions were of human origin, leading people astray from the worship of the true God as He made Himself manifest in Jesus Christ in order to save the world. Armed with Bibles, printing presses, and a sense of service and mission, thousands of missionaries went into the world to Christianize it—many of them convinced that all humanity would be brought into the Christian fold within this century.

The Economic Front

Muslims, as well as other people in the developing world, experienced "militant Christianity" as a multipronged attack on their total existence. While Western businessmen scrambled throughout Asia and Africa to gain access to natural resources, the "natives" were informed that this was in their best interest, since they were allowing these resources to go to waste.

European merchants, on the other hand, supported by the political and military power of their respective nations, gained access to local markets. This led to severe economic dislocation throughout the third world. Not only did the colonial powers dictate what crops the various nations were to raise, but, through the competition of European-made products, they also eliminated local crafts. Formerly self-sufficient countries became economically dependent on Western powers.

Meanwhile European banks and financial institutions found a ready lending market for their accumulated capital. Rulers in various Muslim countries were encouraged and in some cases cajoled by unscrupulous men to borrow money for a variety of vanity and prestige projects (such as the opera house in Cairo) to help provide their nations with the benefits of Western civilization. High interest rates made the debts impossible to pay, since they were invested in projects that provided no return yield. Several governments defaulted in payments, providing further colonial pretext for assumption of power. It was evident in colonial circles that only European know-how could provide proper management of the financial resources of these countries, including the collection of taxes and the imposition of other sanctions in order to pay off the debt.

The Political Front

Europeans considered Muslim political institutions antiquarian and obsolete. Throughout the 19th century various Western powers exerted pressure on local governments to liberalize their institutions. This included at times political, economic, and military pressures to adopt changes in their policies as well as to incorporate Western "democratic" principles into their governments.

Western arrogance was finally sanctioned by the Versailles Treaty (1919), which implied that Arab nations were unfit to govern themselves. International agreements had promised the independence and autonomy of the Arabs in return for their rebellion against the Muslim Turks, their fellow religionists. Despite these promises, the European powers devised the mandate system which carved up the Ottoman Empire into several states to be ruled directly by Britain and France. This was justified as a "civilizing" mission. In effect, Arab countries were assured that they would become beneficiaries of the European enlightenment, which would help bring them into the 20th century by developing their political, economic, and social institutions after Western models. This was to prepare them to assume responsibility for themselves once they had learned how to emulate the Europeans.

The mandate system ascribed to them a new national identity. No longer Ottoman subjects or Muslims, they would now be defined by geographic boundaries manufactured in Europe; now they were Syrians, Jordanians, Palestinians, etc. The situation was further aggravated by the British policy to plant a "Jewish entity" in Palestine, the heart of the Arab world. Emigration and colonization rights were given to Jews all over the world to form a model "European" nation that would continue to carry the light of European civilization in the area and provide guidance in "modern" and "Western" ways.

The Social and Cultural Front

As European occupation policies were based on the assumed Arab and Muslim underdevelopment in the political sphere, they also affirmed the backwardness of the prevalent Islamic social and cultural institutions. Islamic law, the *shari'a,* developed over the centuries to coordinate with the injunctions of the Koran, was deemed incompatible with the modern world. The seemingly harsh Islamic justice and penal systems failed to reflect the humanitarian and reformative influences of the European concepts. Islamic family law and regulations affecting the role and status of women were ridiculed as obscurantist. Repeatedly the "native" elites were told they were backward because they had not given women equal rights. Polygamy, condemned as repressive to women, merely reflected the lower nature of Muslim men governed by lust and an insatiable sexual desire. Veiling was attacked as a form of slavery. In other words, it was made quite clear that if the Muslim Arabs wanted to take their place among the nations, they had better adopt Western ways, liberate their women, and reform their laws.

Reformism was further inculcated through the establishment of public education to prepare civil servants for the colonies. Students learned about the benefits of the Western system and were encouraged to promote them. European textbooks were adopted. Years later, the author heard an Arab, educated in Palestine, describe his first visit to London. "There was nothing strange about the place. I recognized it immediately. To my surprise I found out that I still remembered the names of all the subway stations!" With bitterness he added, "I was never taught the names of the cities and towns in Palestine."

The Religious Front

Since its initial spread, Islam has come into contact with Christianity. This coexistence, at times confrontation, led to a particular articulation of certain Islamic theological teachings honed over several generations of debate and apologetics. Although the Crusades did not bring about much formal theological discussion between the two religions, they did spawn an active Catholic mission among the Eastern-rite Christians living in Muslim lands in order to bring them under papal jurisdiction. This however did not impact on the Muslim community in any significant way.

It was not until the 19th century that Muslims found it necessary to reinterpret their religion in response to the Christian challenge—this time in the form of the evangelical Protestant. Many of the missionaries from Europe and the United States sought fervently to convert Muslims to Christianity by undermining the religion of Islam, its teachings, and its prophet. Several missionary texts refer to Islam as the religion of the "anti-Christ" or "Satan." The Prophet Muhammad was pictured as either unwittingly or through calumny the deceiver or the deceived one, the agent of Satan, fabricating the Koran to lead people astray. While this literature was mainly for the missionaries, it soon found its way into the public domain. To these missionaries, the validation of Christianity was evident through its power, its superior civilization, and its humanitarian doctrines that liberate men from bondage to anything save Christ. Islam was portrayed as an inferior religion because of its supposed notion of predestination, which was leading to indolence and an affirmation of the bliss awaiting the believers in the hereafter. In this way, Islam itself was presented as the central cause for the retardation of the Muslims.

From the beginning the "civilizational" challenge as experienced by Muslims was supported and advanced by military and political power, by various economic interests, and by a Christian theology that judged all values and ideals developed outside of Christianity as ungodly, or at best immoral and deficient. Thus the total encounter was seen as a struggle between a higher and a lower set of values, between the forces of light and darkness, of purity and corruption, of modernity and antiquated, obsolete systems.

The Islamic Response

The Western challenge elicited a variety of responses as Muslims attempted to maintain their dignity while charting a vision of the future that would guarantee authenticity and self-worth. At the outset their initial efforts focused on immediate crises. Every reform undertaken by the Ottoman Empire, for example, followed a military defeat. This led to an obsession with modernizing the armed forces in order to withstand aggression and guarantee freedom within one's borders. Thus the first efforts of Westernization centered not only on acquiring Western technology but on learning Western tactical skills as well. The concern for a modern army capable of defending the borders even led to the adoption of Western-style uniforms and, in the case of Muhammad Ali's Egypt in the 19th century, to the building of factories to manufacture uniforms for the army. The first government-sponsored schools where Western technology was taught prepared the officer corps for the armed forces. In a similar fashion, the first school for women in Egypt trained midwives who were to serve the families of the military.

This obsession with defense is still very much in evidence, as various countries continue to feel impotent against foreign "Western" incursions now experienced as the Israeli military machine. Losses in battle and perpetual defeats are an incentive for change. Recent changes are, for example, the development of coed military training in high schools as well as the formation of units of female paratroopers and parachutists in several Arab countries.

The Response Under Foreign Occupation

The Islamic response to Western domination took many forms, discussed within this study under three categories: (a) acculturationist, (b) normative, and (c) neo-normative. The term *acculturationist* refers to those Muslims who have accepted the Western definition of reality and have struggled to reform and redefine Islam to fit the models and norms thus appropriated. These include secularists, nationalists, Communists, and the romantics who in different ways have sought to replicate Western civilization in their respective countries. While some of them are convinced that only radical methods such as the separation of religion and state can provide the vitality necessary to rebuild their nations according to Western models, others strive to fuse various Western ideas into the prevalent structures, seeking Islamic precedents to justify their incorporation and validate their "Islamic" source.

The term *normativists* is used for those Muslim traditionalists who have never wavered in their rejection of the West as alien and its norms as ungodly.

Neo-normativists refers to the subsequent Islamic response to the struggle between the acculturationists and the normativists. It is used in discussion of various Muslims who in attempting to modernize Islam refuse to relativize it, trivialize it, or "patch it up." They are the ideological engineers who are striving to develop an Islamic identity that is totally Muslim and totally relevant to the modern world. The term *neo-normative* is assigned to them because, although they may disagree with each other on details, they are consistent in affirming that Islam is the norm by which all reality is measured and by which everyone is judged.

It has become fashionable in Western circles to refer to the Islamization process evident in various parts of the world as "fundamentalism," or Muslim "fanaticism." The term neo-normative is utilized in this essay to avoid the tendency of Western readers to dismiss "fanaticism" and "fundamentalism" as passing fads that need to be ignored because of their transient nature. Neo-normativists are not a small group of malcontents who, given the proper incentive, can be reincorporated in the general body of society. The quest for an Islamic identity is not restricted to the fringe, but is a deliberate effort on the part of thousands of leaders in all aspects of life in various Muslim countries to find an Islamic answer to the problems of their societies.

Neo-normative Muslims seek similar goals to those of the Moral Majority. In fact, their views on the family, the role of women, the type of society they strive to fashion are almost identical. Neo-normative Muslims insist on providing a modern view of the world; their teachings are aimed at redeeming society. Unlike traditional Islamic teachings of the normativists, their literature focuses on man, his duties and responsibilities in the world to himself, to God, and to the society. Neo-normativists have developed an anthropological dimension to Islamic theology, making Islam a comprehensive ideology seeking the fulfillment of a utopia here on earth. This vision is not new; it is not based on unfulfilled dreams. Rather it is an attempt to replicate the perfect society as it existed on earth in 622–632 A.D. in Medina under the rule of the Prophet Muhammad, in which all aspects of life were supervised and regulated under the aegis of the revelation of God transmitted in the Koran through the angel Gabriel to the Prophet Muhammad. This replication is not intended to be one of form or structure, i.e., a return to the seventh century, but rather it focuses on purpose (obedience to God) and method (guidance through the Koran).

The student of Arab history will find that all three forms of response developed quite early under Western political and military domination. However, they appear to have had a checkered history of success at different times. The prevalence of any one of these as a comprehensive ideology helping to analyze existent forces and attempting to plan, supervise, and implement future goals has varied with the fortunes of these countries. When not in ascendancy, they have assumed the role of the opposition.

It should come as no surprise that two kinds of acculturationists (nationalists and secularists) flourished under European colonial rule. It is evident that they were encouraged and supported by the colonial powers who found in them ready students. In the political field, parliamentary rule was established, with various segments of the population given the right to vote. Furthermore, new constitutions modeled after European precedents were written for the various countries. In the social sphere, there were several attempts to grant women full rights, not only to go to school and have access to public places, but in some places even to vote. These rights also extended into family life, previously the exclusive domain of the *shari'a*. Thus new interpretations were developed to restrict polygamy, easy repudiation, and other rights that the *shari'a* granted to males.

The economy, under the direct supervision of the colonial powers, became more intimately tied to that of the Europeans, with the various countries providing the natural resources for the European factories as well as the markets for their manufactured products. In most countries resident foreign nationals also acquired control of the utilities as well as of trade by dominating all import and export activities. The local land-owning class provided the rest of the capitalists who managed the local economies.

As for the Islamic religion and its values, the secularists and other acculturationists argued that Islam had always advocated Western ideals. The fusion of a religious and a temporal authority in the person of the caliph was a historical deviation. The prophetic function was unique, never to be repeated. Islam, they insisted, is in a position of retardation because it has assumed too much control of the daily lives of Muslims. Even the Prophet Muhammad had said that Muslims are better judges than he of the affairs of their daily lives; hence the secularists sought to dismiss many of the customs based on the example of the prophet's life. Islam must be relegated to the personal sphere and should have no impact on the political, economic, social, and cultural areas of life.

The normativists affirmed the classical arguments condemning the secularists as innovators. What they protested was the trivialization of religion. While they watched, Islam was being undermined and eliminated from having an impact in the affairs of the state. Not only had the divine laws revealed in the Koran for the governing of human affairs been undermined, but also special courts had been established to implement colonial justice in matters pertaining to relations between the indigenous people and the resident foreigners. Western legislation had also given license for the consumption of liquor and the sanctioning of prostitution.

Neo-normative Islam affirmed through its various advocates (the most notable of whom was Hassan al-Banna, founder of the Muslim Brotherhood) that Islam to be Islam must impinge on public policy and must be intimately concerned with all aspects of life. Islam then is perceived not only as a religion that supervises man's relationship to God, but also as intrinsically involved in creating a Muslim society regulating all aspects of man's relationship to man.

Islamic Response in the Post-Colonial Period

While World War I precipitated direct European intervention in several Arab countries, World War II brought European domination to an end. The new independent states came into being almost simultaneously with the State of Israel in 1948. Although the Western press has incessantly created an image of a tiny Israel being attacked by formidable armies from several Arab nations, a careful study will show that the army of Jordan continued to be under British leadership, while the British sat astride the Suez Canal in Egypt and were able to intercept armament shipments destined for Arab countries. Furthermore, the national government of Syria was trying to remove "the mercenaries" that supported French hegemony.

The defeat of 1948 and 1949 was seen to be the consequence of Arab lack of preparation and Israeli acquisition of a fresh arms supply from Czechoslovakia (despite the armistice stipulation against such acquisition by either party). It signaled the end of the democratic experiment in Arab Muslim countries. The parliamentary systems were tested by this war and found inadequate. Imitation of the West had not brought parity with the West.

It had become evident for some time that although the Arab countries had constitutions and elected parliaments, these institutions were not effective. Some Western observers have blamed the failure of the parliamentary systems on the alien nature of consultative democracy to the Arab mind. Clearly their failure was also hastened by the attitude of the colonial rulers towards such institutions. Whenever foreign governments or their representatives disliked what the democratically elected deputies decided, they tried to countermand their wishes by a variety of means, such as seeking their dismissal or applying relentless direct pressure, blackmail, or bribery. When Arab governments attempted to use European law to assure freedom and the implementation of the will of the people, it was these same colonial rulers who ridiculed them and treated them as upstarts.

Furthermore, the establishment of the State of Israel was proof of the inadequacy of the parliamentary nationalist experiment for those who were pained by the humiliation of defeat. In no time, coup d'etats in various Arab countries—e.g., Egypt, Syria, Iraq—removed the Westernized nationalist elites from office. Power evolved from a new breed of leadership, military officers originally recruited from the middle and lower middle classes. Their military training, it was hoped, would provide new direction to redeem the honor of the nation. They formed the most Westernized and modernized institution in these countries. Upon assumption of power they sought to speed the modernization process through the adoption of a socialist and/or Marxist model. Socialism became the dominant ideology of several Arab countries in the 1950s and '60s. It was believed that a new Arab man could be produced through intensified effort, development, and planning. It was during this period that education became truly public and available to the masses.

Under the colonial regimes very few schools were established to specifically provide cadres for the civil bureaucracy. (This set the precedent for the following generations who assumed that education entitled them to a government job.) Despite all claims to their "civilizing" mission, the colonial powers prepared only a small, select, Western-oriented group. Rarely was more than one small high school established in select urban centers. The availability of education to the masses in the postcolonial period has produced a new, educated elite, predominantly of lower class and peasant background, seeking upward mobility through education. The majority of these new graduates have had no direct experience of the Westernizing "brainwashing" undertaken under the colonial rule with the help of mission schools. For most of these students, socialism has provided an alternative ideology that leads to modernity, ascendancy, and acceptance in the international community.

The socialist and Marxist experiment has been dominated by a different group of acculturationists who find Marxism appealing because it is believed to have proven effective in transforming Russia from an agrarian economy into an industrial giant. This success can be replicated, it is hoped, if one acquires the correct ideology. Furthermore, socialism provides a speedy means of modernization and Westernization without Christianization.

It was with great enthusiasm that Egypt under Nasser embarked on the socialist experiment. Nasser's popularity was bolstered by the image of success and potency which he acquired after the 1956 Suez War when he nationalized the Suez Canal, withstood American political and economic pressure, and finally brought to completion the departure of British forces from Egypt.

Nasser was able to institute socialist laws because he effectively eliminated the neo-normative opposition that insisted that Islam must govern all life. By 1965, several leaders of the Muslim Brotherhood, including Sayyid Qutb, the most popular neo-normativist ideologue, were executed. Hundreds of members were imprisoned, while still others sought refuge outside Egypt. A number of them became the intellectual leadership of Saudi Arabia that sought to eliminate Nasser and his "anti-Islamic" socialist thought.

Encouraged by the United States, King Faisal of Saudi Arabia with the Shah of Iran sought to establish the Islamic pact, bringing together various Muslim nations which aimed at containing Nasser and the spread of socialism. Saudi Arabia supported the royal regime in Yemen, and Nasser supported the republican system by sending Egyptian troops to aid the Yemeni revolutionaries. (Nasser was later to speak about this as his Vietnam, since it sapped the Egyptian economy and impeded the progress in industrialization that Nasser fervently supported.)

The Arab-Israeli war of 1967 brought into serious question the hegemony of socialist ideology. The Arabs stood humiliated, and once again parts of Syria, Jordan, and Egypt were under foreign occupation. Socialism was seen by the masses to have failed. Marxist ideologues argued that the failure was not due to the ineffectiveness of socialism, but to Nasser's compromising attempt to cover socialism with Islamic garb in order to appeal to the masses. What went wrong, they said, was the compromise on ideology.

The Arab-Israeli war in 1967 initiated a frantic search for a new ideology. Neo-normative Islam once again began to appeal to the masses. Its appeal rested on the insistence of its advocates that true Islam had never been tried. While secularists (supporters of the European as well as the socialist models) bemoaned the fact that the defeat of 1967 was due to the inability of the leaders to eradicate the vestiges of religion from public life, the neo-normativists reasoned that the defeat was God's punishment inflicted on the Muslims because they had sought salvation in alien ideologies, preferring them to God's guidance in the Koran. They argued quite eloquently with supporting evidence from scriptural passages that had the Muslims taken God at His word, they would have been victorious. Their defeat was due to the fact that God had abandoned them to their enemies because they had abandoned Islam and the revelation of God.

The struggle for an Islamic alternative was supported by political considerations in various countries. With Sadat's ascendancy to power, an Islamization process was initiated in Egypt. This was an attempt to use Islamic coalitions to rid Sadat of the Nasserites and the socialists. Besides assuming the title of the Believer Muhammad Anwar al-Sadat, founder of the Believing Nation, he encouraged various Muslim groups to participate in public life, describing the program as the Rectification, instituted on the principles of Belief and Knowledge.

The religious trappings of the Sadat regime were enhanced by the 1973 victory in the Arab-Israeli war. The Islamic slogans utilized in the war, it was believed, vindicated the teachings of Islam that God will give the victory if Muslims will take Him at His word and stay faithful. Neo-normative Islam was also bolstered by the image of the rising political and economic power of the Arab world initiated by the oil boycott and evident in the increased wealth of members of the OPEC nations.

The Israeli Connection

The rise of Islamic consciousness in the Muslim world is also directly related to Israeli policies in the area. The formation of the State of Israel in 1948 had a dire effect on many of the intelligentsia of the Arab world. Secularists and Westernizers felt betrayed by Europe and America, the "defenders of justice and freedom." American policies in the area made it clear that while support was given to democratic principles and the right of self-determination to various peoples throughout the world, the same was denied to the Palestinians. Not only were they not to have the right of a homeland, but they were to be displaced, expelled from the land of their birth to make room for European Jews.

It was felt that the Christians and Muslims of Palestine were chosen to atone for the sins of European Christians who at various times through pogroms, inquisitions, and gas chambers had sought to annihilate European Jews.

While Westernized Arabs struggled to form nation-states based on equal citizenship for all ethnic and religious groups, they watched with disbelief as Israel, supported by American money and military might, instituted a state based on religious affiliation, with citizenship open to all born of a Jewish mother. Israeli policies aimed at the ingathering of Jews from all over the world while insisting that there was no room for the indigenous people. Those who had a Christian or a Muslim mother were condemned to refugee existence, unfit for a Jewish state based on religious discrimination.

From its inception, Zionism, whether religious or political in ideology, has been based on a religious understanding. It affirms the right of Jews to return to Palestine because of a promise that scriptures say God made 4000 years ago to the Hebrews. Despite the notion that many Israelis are atheists, and that some Zionist ideologists believe that Zionism is a form of nationalism, many Muslims believe that the essential core of the right that Zionism affirms is cloaked with religious legitimacy based on a religious claim.

Muslims in the last few years with great fascination have watched United States policy makers condemn the "fanaticism" of Islamic "fundamentalism" while ignoring the militancy of the Gush Emunim and the Jewish Defense League. Muslims from all walks of life have asked, "Why fanatical and obscurantist for Muslims to have religion impinge on public policy even if that government is Muslim, while it is progressive and enlightened if practiced in Israel?"

Sayyid Qutb, who spent 1949–51 in the United States, gave what a growing number of Muslims perceive as an eloquent and convincing answer when he said that the West, which he characterized as the coalition of the capitalist, Communist, and Zionist forces in the world, seeks the destruction of Islam because it fears the power of Islam, the only mobilizing force that can bring about the ascendancy for which the Muslims hope.

Qutb believed that at heart all Western wars against Muslim countries are the product of what he termed the Zionist-Crusader mentality, or what can be explained as the Judeo-Christian stance. Despite Western teachings that wars inspired by religion are obsolete, he wrote, they and their surrogates, the Israelis, attack and acquire land, claiming geographical or economic goals, seeking the destruction of Islam.

Qutb saw the establishment of Israel as a continuation of the anti-Islamic Crusader mentality. He and his supporters have recalled the words of Field Marshal Edmund Allenby who, on entering

Jerusalem in 1919, reportedly said, "Today the Crusades have come to an end." Thus for neo-normativists the State of Israel is an extension of Christian hatred of Islam. The West itself actually sanctions the fusion of religion and state in Israel, and Muslims must take heed to recognize that secularism, nationalism, socialism, or any other "ism" that seeks to separate religion and state is part of the Western conspiracy against Islam.

It should be noted here that Iranian students involved in their country's Islamic revolution cited Israel as a model. They were seeking to establish an Islamic modern state just as Israel had built a Jewish one. It became clear that American condemnation of Muslim "fanaticism" and "fundamentalism" was not out of distrust for a religious state per se, evident through the West's support of Israel, but out of an innate dislike and distrust of Islam. This realization provided the incentive for wide-reaching support of the Islamic revolution as a perceived way of striking fear into the heart of the American giant who had for so long intimidated them.

Israel and its policies have influenced the rise of neo-normative Islam in other ways. One of these is the "Islamization" of the Palestinian issue. The Organization of the Islamic Conference, born in the aftermath of the 1969 fire in the mosque in Jerusalem, is composed of 43 states that consider Jerusalem threatened by Israeli occupation. This feeling is strengthened by repeated threats from various Israeli sectors, including the chief rabbi of the Israeli armed forces, that the mosque should be destroyed to make room for the rebuilding of the temple.

Although different members of the Organization of the Islamic Conference vary in their respective policies, the point that binds them together is the fear that the third holy place of Islam is under occupation. Reinforced by President Reagan's statement of November 19, 1981, that "he preferred for Jerusalem to remain undivided under Israeli sovereignty," more than 850 million Muslims consider Jerusalem threatened by the continuing Israeli occupation. This was inflamed more recently when an American Jew shot and killed several Muslims at prayer in the mosque.

The American Connection

Unqualified American support of Israel is an added dimension for the radicalization of neo-normative Islam. It is obvious to Arabs that America has assigned a special low status to its Arab friends. Many question America's continued diplomatic, military, and economic support of Israel despite the fact that it acts against America's stated interests. After listening to a ringing defense by an American senator of Israel's destruction of a nuclear plant in Iraq, an Arab asked whether the senator thought he was running for the Knesset rather than the Congress of the United States.

Others have wondered at America's continued support of Israel despite its acts detrimental to American interests. Why is America supporting Israel when Israel sells arms to such countries as Communist-supported Ethiopia (with Cuba and Russia), and to Iran and Argentina? Others have questioned the American response to the deliberate sinking of the American ship *Liberty* in 1967 by the Israeli air force in which 34 American lives were lost.

Some Arabs point to the disdain with which Arab allies of the United States are treated. They mention King Hussein of Jordan who was not received at the White House by President Carter because he refused to sign the Camp David agreement. On June 13, 1982, then Secretary of State Alexander Haig, on ABC's *This Week with David Brinkley,* referred to King Fahd of Saudi Arabia as our "collaborator." Despite Saudi efforts to stabilize oil prices and supplies to help the American economy against their own national interest, Fahd is perceived not as a friend, but as merely a collaborator.

The influence of the United States in the Middle East became more dominant after World War II, through American intent and design rather than by default. The strategic importance of the Arabian Gulf area was heightened by increased American dependence on oil. With typical insensitivity to Arab feelings, United States foreign policy responded to the "vacuum" created in the Arabian Peninsula with the departure of the British. To those who lived there, the image of a "vacuum" was offensive; not only did it affirm their insignificance, it suggested their nonexistence.

To prevent Russia from filling the "vacuum," American foreign policy sought to contain Soviet influence through alliances and pacts, including the Baghdad Pact. All countries were urged to choose the forces of democracy, enlightenment, and freedom under the leadership of the United States. There was no middle position for those disinterested in the big power struggle. If they did not align themselves with the United States, they would be considered under the influence of Communism. Those who made the right choice would be rewarded with the benefits of aid and military training.

The pressure on third-world countries to choose one of the two systems gave rise to the "nonaligned movement," a position that neo-normative Muslims had advocated vehemently after the establishment of the State of Israel. Muslims, they had argued, will not benefit from either East or West, because both camps treat them with disdain and harbor nothing but enmity for Islam. Neither capitalism nor Communism helped the Palestinians and the Arabs in their confrontation with Israel. This "conspiracy" became more convincing to the masses with every Arab-Israeli clash, where each loss illustrated the inadequacy of the defensive weapons the Arabs were allowed to purchase.

The Nixon policy of detente between East and West left pro-Western Arab nations in a state of limbo. In 1972, for example, Jordan, which had long been under pressure from the United States not to recognize the Republic of China, found itself on the occasion of President Nixon's state visit to China supporting an apparently obsolete American policy. The United States either forgot to inform its ally of the impending recognition so it could take the necessary measures to save face, or it did not trust Jordan to have the maturity to handle a Communist country.

Detente which followed the Moscow Summit of 1972 changed the image of the world. Russian-American cooperation went into such spectacular shows as the Apollo-Soyuz space docking in 1975. American allies in the Arab world felt they could have the same friendly exchanges with Russia that the United States enjoyed.

For neo-normative Muslims, detente became more than "superpower equality:" it showed that Russia and the United States had decided to share the monopoly of power rather than compete for it. This left third-world countries unable to barter away their allegiance. In fact, some of them began to suspect that detente was concluded at their expense. Detente also "proved" to many Arabs that the superpowers had decided to parcel out areas of interest. In the 1973 war, it is believed that the "victory" of recapturing land lost in 1967 was taken from the Syrian and Egyptian forces when the United States supplied the Israeli armed forces and the Russians made declarations of support but did not deliver. The "collusion" between East and West was seen in the events that led to both Angola's and Ethiopia's coming under Communist influence, with the United States watching from the sidelines.

Neo-normative Muslims kept asking: How does friendship with the East or West benefit us? We need an alternative. Islam was proposed as the alternative, a total system that encompasses all aspects of life— social, political, and economic. Thus it is out of the experience of Israel and unlimited American support for its expansionist policies that the Islamic alternative began to make sense for a growing number of Arab Muslims. The Islamic alternative proceeds from an Islamic worldview that insists on the rejection of "followership" of either East or West and instead emphasizes self-worth, dignity, and authenticity.

Neo-Normative Islam: Basic Teachings

While all neo-normative Muslims continue to believe that the economic, political, social, and cultural aspects of life must be judged by God's truth, they do not agree on the specifics of the Islamic order, system or government that they seek. In recent years, a great deal of literature has been published advocating various positions as the Islamic one. However, concepts of Islamic justice, banking, economics, etc., appear to vary. There are those who have been called the Islamic Right and those who call themselves the Islamic Left, as well as those with an abundance of Islamic centrist positions. While they all utilize

Koranic verses and precedents from the life of the Prophet to justify their ideas, they do not seem to agree on any specific definition of that position. Some ideologues see room for a variety of Islamic systems or interpretations, and others restrict it to one, their own.

Despite the lack of consensus about the details of the Islamic system, there is agreement that the time for Islam has come. It is time to assume confidence in its teachings, to take it at its word and cease from all attempts to mimic the West. This does not mean a retreat to medieval times. Rather it is the summons to all Muslims to chart the future, utilizing modern technology and scientific knowledge while upholding the ethical teachings of Islam. The redemption of society is the final goal. The ardent supporters of neo-normative Islam come from the ranks of the best educated, modernized Muslim professionals, technicians, and scientists. While striving to master Western technology to modernize and develop their society, they are anxious to avoid what is perceived as Western pitfalls that have led to the collapse of Western society.

Although the quest for an Islamic alternative continues to be the primary goal of some committed groups in the various Muslim countries, it is difficult at present to assess the scope of its appeal or the number of adherents it has. This is due mainly to the absence of political parties and organizations in most Arab countries.

The popularity of the movement has been evident since the early 1970s, particularly among students in the science, engineering, law, and medical departments of various Arab universities, where it became fashionable for male students to grow beards and for female students to don Islamic garb (covering their hair and wearing long sleeves and ankle-length skirts). This phenomenon has been suppressed in Egypt (where, after Sadat's death, members of an estimated 30 different groups were arrested) and in Syria, where the government reportedly forced young men to shave their beards and used female paratroopers "to unveil" women in the streets of Damascus. In each of these states, as well as on the West Bank and Gaza, the Islamic alternative acts as a rallying point, a demonstration of opposition to the existent political order.

Meanwhile Saudi Arabia, Morocco, and Libya, though manifesting different forms of government, have what are considered to be states based on Islamic principles. Others, such as Tunisia (since 1972), utilized Islamic justification to explain government policies as authentic, while the Sudan has co-opted the Islamic ideologues by including them in the government to help shape and mold the expected Islamic future. It is also reported that there is a great deal of popular support for the Islamic Liberation Front in Kuwait and other states in the Gulf area.

The rise in Islamic consciousness and the growing consensus on an Islamic worldview as an alternative to that of capitalism and Marxism has not eradicated the acculturationists. In fact, some of them continue to rule in places like Syria, Iraq, and South Yemen. However, they find it increasingly necessary to provide an Islamic interpretation for their activities and the ideologies they advocate.

The nationalists, socialists, and secularists appear to be fighting a rearguard battle at present; unless Islam fails, and in a devastating manner, there will be ample room for it to revitalize itself. It is a sign of the times that a prominent secularist of the 1950s, Khaled Muhammad Khaled, whose book *From Here We Start* was translated into English, has written a new book defending the position that religion and government cannot be separated in Islam. He now believes that Islam must supervise and control the government in order to insure an ethical order.

The discussion thus far has centered on the growing general consensus for the imperative of finding an authentic ideology, one that is a total system equal in every way to those of capitalism and Marxism. The Islamic alternative frees Muslims from the necessity of being satellite dependencies of either the Eastern or Western orbit. It provides meaning, status, authenticity, and a sense of adequacy and assurance. Muslims no longer will have to strive to find out what is current in the West in order to be "with it." They themselves can determine what they want to do and think.

A significant number of Muslims, usually dismissed as radicals, insist that Islam is not *an* alternative, it is *the* alternative. They perceive the world as divided between the righteous: those who take the Koran seriously and try to live an Islamic life, and those who reject God's revelation and live under the influence of man-made systems and

sanctions. They continue to maintain that their definition of Islam
has an exclusive claim to veracity. Not only capitalists, Communists,
secularists, positivists, etc., but also all Muslims who do not agree
with them are outside the pale of Islam and need to be summoned
back to the truth. It is from their ranks that the assassins of Sadat
have emerged.

The Islamic Alternative: Future Prospects

United States foreign policy has been known to support the growth
of Islamic identity as a buffer against Communism in such places as
Iran under the Shah and Egypt under Sadat, in addition to the Saudi
form of Islam and the Mujahideen in Afghanistan fighting against
the Russian presence in their country. These policies have not necessarily
won friends among Muslims for the United States. In fact, neo-
normative Muslims see the American role as one that encourages the
traditional, ritualistic, and personalistic aspects of Islam, while
condemning activistic, political Islam. This kind of apolitical religion,
neo-normative Muslims believe, is a palliative to make Muslims accept
their condition of subservience to American policies as well as
oppressive rulers. Several have found it necessary to alert other Muslims
to American hypocrisy. They ask: "Why is America protesting the
Russian occupation of Afghanistan while sanctioning through vocal
and material support the Israeli occupation of Jerusalem?"

Others have pointed to the United States policy of support for
the Polish movement under the Catholic Church in Poland while
condemning the Muslim revolution against the Shah's oppression.
They ask: "Why is it good when the religious group supporting the
revolution is Christian, and evil when it is Muslim? Is it because
America hates Islam? Is it true that there is a separation between church
and state in the West, or is this something created for Muslims to
separate them from their only source of dignity and power?"

For many Muslims the potentials of Islam have not been realized.
Its promise is yet to come. The joy they experienced at the fall of the
Shah, the great oppressor, has been temporarily tainted by what some
are calling the "misdirection" of the Khomeini experiment. The

problems in Iran, however, do not detract from Islam or the Islamic system. The Iranian people proved what the Koran had promised: if a people are committed to God and united against oppression in the world, God will give them the victory over the greatest enemy. This can be replicated in other parts of the Muslim world, if people can be mobilized to heed this summons from God.

It is unfortunate that the United States, whose ideals of justice, freedom, and equality many Muslims have made their own, has been identified with the forces of oppression and exploitation. America's unconditional support of Israeli expansionism and the rejection of the rights of the Palestinian people has placed the United States for many in the role of enemy of the Arab people. At present, for an Arab leader to be cast as a friend of the United States, much less a "collaborator," may bring about his downfall. This is due not to a rejection of the ideals of America, but to the experience of the double standard in American policy. The death of an Israeli soldier is a loss of human life; the death of thousands of Christians and Muslims is "mopping up."

At present a growing number of Muslims believe that they have three alternatives to choose from in formulating their political institutions aimed at gaining parity with the West and the respect of the world. American support of Israel, which appears determined to bomb all their technological achievements out of existence and restore them to underdevelopment, may rule out the capitalist option. The Russian appeal has always been a reaction to defeat, a potential source of support and a source of arms. At present, Islam offers the best option—and, in the views of many, the only option. Experiments with national states and socialist governments have not been able to deliver on promises and goals. While the Lebanese civil war heralded the death of Arab nationalism as an option for the young, the liquidation of the present Palestinian movement in 1982 may seal its fate forever.

There is no consensus on what the Islamic alternative is or is supposed to be. On the one hand, there is Saudi Islam, supported by oil money, trying to contain the Islamic movement through the Muslim World League. For many neo-normative Muslims that is unacceptable. It is referred to as American Islam because of its American connection. They believe that the wealth is being used to maintain pro-American policies that are not necessarily in the interest of the Arabs.

The Organization of Islamic Conference offers another alternative, but it has proved ineffectual because many of these nations do not have a truly Islamic system, but rather pay lip service to Islam in order to keep themselves in power.

What neo-normative Muslims hope for is a truly democratic system that is not subservient to either East or West; a system working for the propagation of Islam, and the elevation of Muslims, to bring about a just order in the world, one nation under God, with liberty and justice for all.

Part 5: Warfare

In a private letter to his son in 1937, David Ben-Gurion, Israel's first prime minister, said, "We will expel the Arabs and take their place." And in his diary, dated December 19, 1947, he wrote: "In each attack, a decisive blow should be struck, resulting in the destruction of homes and the expulsion of the population."

The Zionists knew that it would take superior force to evict the Palestinians, and superior force to prevent them from retaking their land.

This has led to a bloody escalation of conflicts that have embroiled the entire Middle East.

Here we offer snapshots of three of them, from 1948 (Rantisi), 1967 (Ennes), and 2003 (AMEU).

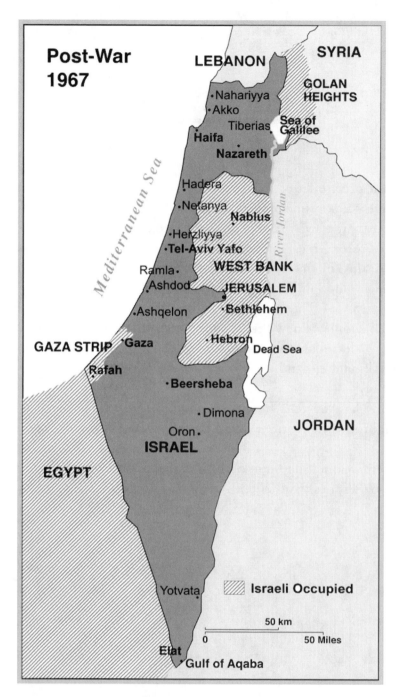

Extent of the Israeli Occupation after the 1967 War

The Lydda Death March

By Audeh G. Rantisi

Audeh G. Rantisi's birth certificate shows that he was born in "Lydda, Government of Palestine," on November 21, 1936. On July 13, 1948, he and his family became part of the more than 700,000 refugees who were forced to flee their homes. Rantisi, who would become a priest in the Arab Evangelical Episcopal Church, tells what happened that fateful July morning.

At 7:15, Monday morning, July 13, 1948, three Israeli soldiers came to our home in Lydda. I remember going to the door with my mother. I was 11 at the time. I heard the soldiers say in English: "Leave your house open and go outside."

We did as we were ordered. My father, George, 49; my mother, Fayqa, 38; my three younger brothers, Elias, 8, Philip, 6, and Mahfouz, 1; my two sisters, Adla, 14, and Sonia, 3; and my two grandparents—we all went outside and left our home unlocked.

At first my father thought the Israelis were doing what the British had done during the six-month strike in 1936, when they had everyone leave their homes and gather at the threshing-floor center in the city. Back then the British were checking for weapons, and they let the people return to their homes later in the day. We are Christian Palestinians, so my father thought we should wait in the compound of St. George's Church. Hundreds of people were heading in the same direction.

We never made it. At a turn in the road just before the church, Israeli soldiers directed us down a road that ended at a narrow gate that led into the mountains. By this time the number of people had grown, and panic began to set in. Word had spread about the mosque. The Israelis had herded over 136 men into the Dahmash mosque, the smaller of Lydda's two mosques, and machine-gunned them. Not one person survived.

When we saw Tawfeeq abu-S'oud, the headmaster of one of our schools, he told us how the soldiers had come to his home and told him that he and his family had to leave in three minutes or they'd all be killed. And what made our fear so rational, if that's the word, was the fact that the soldiers were not forcing us out onto one of the main roads, where it would have been easier to walk, but out onto rough, hilly terrain, littered with rocks and boulders and clumps of bleached thorn, a place where they could kill us and leave our bodies for the wildlife.

By now the heat had reached 100 degrees. The scene was chaotic. Women in black *abbahs* and heavily embroidered Palestinian dresses hysterically clutched their infants as they stumbled forward to avoid the expected spray of machine-gun fire. I remember holding the hand of my paternal grandfather, Audeh Rantisi, whose name I, as the eldest son, was given, as is our custom. In his other hand my grandfather held our only remaining possessions: a small tin of sugar and some milk for my aunt's two-year-old son Easa, who was sick with typhoid.

About a mile outside the city we came to a private vegetable farm, its entrance framed by a large gate. Atop the gate sat soldiers with machine guns, firing over our heads and shouting at us to hurry through the gate.

I did not know it at the time, but our death march had begun.

Behind us, forever, was our home, our family business, our clothing, and our food, along with those possessions we were never able to replace. When the editor of *The Link* asked me for photos of our home or my childhood in Lydda, I had to say we had to leave all that behind. The one thing I do remember my father taking with him was the key to the front door of our home.

Our house was located in the new section of Lydda in the district of Haqouret Al-Qura. My father and his father, Audeh, built it with their own hands sometime in the 1920s. Prior to the new home, our family had lived in the old section of Lydda. There we can trace our family history back at least 1,600 years. My father, like his father and his father before him, were soap makers. We made soap from olive oil. It was our family business.

In front of me, as we were prodded through the gate to the vegetable farm, an old cart on metal-rimmed wheels wobbled over uneven ground. Alongside the cart, a mother, clutching her baby, was being pressed by the crowd. Suddenly, in the jostling, the child slipped from its mother's arms and fell to the ground. I saw the cart's rickety wheel run over the baby's neck. The shrieks of the mother as she picked up her dead baby still ring in my ears.

Inside the gate, the soldiers had placed a blanket on the ground and were ordering everyone to throw all of their valuables onto the blanket. This included money, jewelry, wristwatches, pens, even wedding rings. Amin Hanhan and his wife had only been married six weeks. When the soldiers demanded a container with money that he was carrying, he refused. One of the soldiers lifted his rifle and shot him. He fell to the ground, his young bride beside him, screaming. It was the first time I had ever seen one human being kill another. I was so shocked and so afraid. It happened so fast, and so casually. I remember feeling I wanted to throw up.

Then the soldiers wanted to search my grandfather. He refused because he was afraid they would take the milk and sugar he had brought for Easa. When they pressed him, he held up his cane and shook it in their faces. They let him go.

Now the only thing that kept us going were the horrors we had witnessed. We stumbled on through the blinding sun, over stones and sharp undergrowth, placing one blistered foot in front of the other, the thirst within us growing.

Before we left the vegetable garden we picked some eggplants. The soldiers were telling us "Go to Abdullah," that is, to the area of Palestine under Jordanian control. If we had to walk, it meant a march of some 25 to 30 miles. Eggplants might be the only thing we'd find to sustain us.

By the evening of the first day we stopped on a mountain top near the village of Jimzu. Once the sun went down, we had to cope with the severe cold, and we had nothing to keep us warm. Some of us gathered twigs and made a small fire. But the Israeli planes must have spotted the light and headed low towards us. Afraid they might shoot at us, others in the group made us put out the fire, forcing us to use the precious little water we had left.

That night I cried myself to sleep.

Day Two

In the early hours of the next day, soldiers on horseback came riding at us shooting their guns. The soldiers were yelling for us to get moving. Everyone started running. It was a stampede.

At the time we were on a mountain, halfway down into a valley. In the confusion I lost sight of my family. I went down the mountain and stood in the valley, asking about my family. There was a donkey behind me. Suddenly a bullet missed my waist and hit the donkey, immediately killing it. I began to run in fear for my life.

A short while later I saw my sister, Adla. She too was lost. We began to ask people and to look for the rest of our family.

Then we came across my uncle, Suliman, with his family. He told us our parents were behind us and would be coming along soon.

They never did.

As the sun went down, we stopped for the night somewhere in the mountains in a particularly rocky place that offered us some protection from the cold. I remember eating for the first time that day. A camel that was about to die was slaughtered, and the meat was divided among all of us. Each got a very small bite.

With the darkness came an awful loneliness and anxiety. In my head I heard my father telling us what the soldiers had recently done in the village of Deir Yassin, how they rounded up the men, women, and children and killed them all in cold blood. I thought of the men in the Dahmash mosque. I thought of Amin, the young man shot in front of me. I thought of the bullet that almost killed me. Had the soldiers killed my family?

I had to know if they were still alive.

So, around 8 p.m., I got up and, without saying a word to my uncle, slowly began to retrace my steps down into the valley, in the pitch darkness, stumbling among the thousands of people on the ground. About 45 minutes went by when, in the distance, I heard my father's voice. I started shouting at him. Sounds carry long distances at night in such places, and I could hear my parents asking, "Are you safe?" and "Where is your sister?" I shouted back that we were both well. We kept shouting until we found each other. I will always remember that moment when he and my mother hugged me.

My father wanted to move that night to be with my sister and uncle. So he hired three donkeys for my mother and grandparents to ride.

I have been asked how he managed to hire donkeys in the dark out in the middle of nowhere. And where did he get the money, if he had to give it to the soldiers? As for the money, he never handed it over. I wonder had the soldiers found it would they have killed him, as they did Amin Hanhan. The donkeys belonged to local villagers along the way, who came out to see if they could help and also to see if they could make money. My mother and grandparents along with the youngest of the children rode the donkeys. The owners of the donkeys stayed with their animals until we reached the rocky area where my uncle and his family were. Then the owners took the animals back.

Reunited with my family, I went to sleep feeling that now I could face anything.

Day Three

This was the day most would die.

The heat felt worse than ever, and the lack of water began to take its toll. Many of us—4,000 by my estimate—staggered and fell by the wayside, either dead or dying in the scorching heat.

Scores of pregnant women miscarried, their babies left for jackals to eat.

I can still see one infant beside the road, sucking the breast of its dead mother.

The wife of my father's cousin, Yacoub, became so thirsty she could go on no longer. She slumped to the ground and died. Not being able to carry her, we wrapped her in cloth and, after saying a prayer, left her body beside a tree.

Eventually, as we neared the village of Budros, northeast of Lydda, we found a deserted cistern. But we had no way to get the water up. So some of the men tied a rope around my father's cousin, Ibrahim Rantisi, lowered him down, then pulled him out. Then we literally sucked the water from his clothing. The few drops helped, but the thirst still tormented me as we trudged along in the shadeless heat. Some people were so thirsty and desperate that they drank their own urine.

One of the people I saw on the death march was George Habash. George, then 23, was a medical student and, like me, came from a Christian family in Lydda. I've often thought of how this experience must have affected his life. As many know, he became a physician, graduating from the American University of Beirut. Brilliant as well as eloquent, in 1952 he co-founded the Arab Nationalist Movement which, in 1967, merged with the Syrian-based Palestine Liberation Front to form the Popular Front for the Liberation of Palestine. To this day George's organization is the only PLO splinter group that continues to reject the Oslo accords, claiming that they only sanction more Zionist expropriation of Palestinian land and expulsion of Palestinians from their homes.

By the end of the third day we had been forced to march for miles up rocky hills, then down into deep valleys, then up again, gradually going higher and higher. At long last, we reached a main road, where we were met by trucks that had come from Ramallah and other places the Israelis had not occupied. The truck drivers came to search for their family members and to help the people who had been evicted. A man who came to transport his relatives gave us a lift on his truck. There were over 50 persons packed like sardines on that truck. But it got us to Ramallah.

Our death march was over. Our life as refugees had begun.

Day Four to the Present

The 13 members of my family arrived in Ramallah carrying nothing but the clothes we wore. I lived in a refugee tent camp for the next three and one-half years. For the first three of those years I had no formal schooling.

We were not alone. Of the 1.3 million Arabs who lived in Palestine in 1948, between 700,000 and 900,000 of us lost our homes, some forcibly driven out, as we were, others fleeing to escape the terrorism of the invaders.

The winter of 1948 was one of the severest on record. For the first time I saw snow on the ground. I looked out of the tent window one morning and found the whole ground completely white. It did not take long to discover the seriousness of such weather. Water began to bubble up from underneath our tents. In one tent there were my parents, brothers, sisters, grandparents, aunt, and her child and uncle.

My father died in 1979. He spent most of his 31 years in exile doing odd jobs. He always held on to the large metal key to our home in Lydda.

My mother passed away in 1987. She remained in Ramallah, traveling once with my father in 1975 to Toronto to see her sons Elias, Philip, and Mahfouz. During her last years she lived with me and my wife.

My grandfather, Audeh, died in Ramallah. Every day he would go to the Orthodox Church for evening prayers. One day, in 1952, while waiting outside for the church to open, he died.

My three brothers, as I noted, ended up in Canada. Elias works for a medical company. Mahfouz studied in Nova Scotia and is an architect. Philip is a carpenter who worked for the Ministry of Education in Kuwait, where he was responsible for all courses in carpentry; he moved to Canada after suffering a back accident, requiring the insertion of a steel plate in his spine.

My sister Adla lives in Bir Zeit, here in Palestine's West Bank. She has nine children, four of whom live in the United States.

My other sister, Sonia, lives in Ramallah. She has seven children, three of whom live in the United States.

My father's cousin, Ibrahim, the one they lowered into the well, has since died. He lived for a while in Ramallah, then moved to Amman. He had a daughter and two sons, both of whom are goldsmiths in Jordan.

My cousin Easa, who had typhoid, still lives in Ramallah. He worked for a while as an X-ray technician, then worked for a Lutheran bookshop in Jerusalem. Presently he is unemployed. He has a daughter and a son, who studied in Germany.

Yacoub, my father's cousin, whose wife died on the march, died himself a long time ago.

I went on to study at the Bible College of Wales in Swansea, South Wales, and then attended Aurora College in Illinois. I served as a missionary in Khartoum, eventually being ordained a priest in the Arab Evangelical Episcopal Church. In 1965, I founded the Evangelical Home for Boys in Ramallah to care for Palestinian orphans. What motivates me, I believe, is the desire to give these youngsters the childhood I never had.

Also, in 1965, I married Patricia Greening, whom I had first met in Swansea. The daughter of an Anglican clergyman in England, Patricia had gone on to work in Peru as a missionary nurse. We had kept in touch by letters, and in 1963, she visited Ramallah. Soon after, I asked her to marry me, and we were wed in Shrewsbury, England. After a honeymoon in North Wales, we took a ship for the Gulf of Aqaba. There we were driven to Amman, and crossed the Jordan River to our home in Ramallah. Pat and I have been blessed with three daughters, Susan, Hilary, and Rosemary.

In 1967, I again came under Israeli military rule, when Israel occupied Ramallah and all of the West Bank. In 1976 I was elected deputy mayor of Ramallah. In 1991, I wrote a book about my death march experience, *Blessed Are the Peacemakers: A Palestinian Christian in the Occupied West Bank,* co-authored with Dr. Ralph Beebe, Professor of History at George Fox College, Newberg, Oregon. The first edition of the book faced a strong wave of criticism from the Zionist lobby in the United States. Zondervan Books eventually bowed to the pressure and decided not to reprint the book.

Soon after Israel's 1967 occupation of the West Bank, a group of us who had been driven out of Lydda took a bus trip back to see our former homes. I knew that two Jewish families were living in my father's home. As the bus drew up in front of the house, I saw a young boy playing in the yard. I got off the bus and went over to him.

"How long have you lived in this house?" I asked.

"I was born here," he replied.

"Me too," I said.

The USS *Liberty* Affair
By James M. Ennes, Jr.

Jim Ennes was the lieutenant on watch at the time of Israel's attack on the USS Liberty. *In 1980 Random House published his account of the attack,* Assault on the Liberty. *His* Link *issue was written four years after his book appeared.*

Seventeen years ago, in one of the worst peacetime naval disasters in American history, Israeli air and naval forces attacked the U.S. Navy intelligence ship *Liberty* on the high seas.

Even before the story appeared in the American press, U.S. government public affairs officers went to work promoting a version of the story that was satisfactory to Israel, while representatives of the American-Israel Public Affairs Committee descended on the press and Congress to help keep the story under control. Almost immediately, Jacob Javits in the Senate and Roman Pucinski in the House of Representatives took to the floor of Congress to lament the "tragic mistake" that had directed "friendly fire" toward an American ship.

The campaign was so effective that most American newspapers and all commercial television networks dropped the story almost overnight, before most of the facts were known. No American newsman probed for the inside story of the USS *Liberty* affair. No member of Congress called publicly for the facts. No crewmen were interviewed on the evening news. Even today, few people anywhere have ever heard of the USS *Liberty*.

One who tried to reverse the trend was *Liberty*'s engineer officer, Lieutenant George Golden. A Jew and former enlisted man, Golden was disturbed about the government's seeming unconcern for the truth.

So he sought out Associated Press reporter Colin Frost in a Maltese bar while the Navy Court of Inquiry into the incident was still in session and told him why he thought the attack was deliberate.

The resulting story appeared in newspapers around the world,[1] but it failed to excite the press as Golden had hoped. Instead, it brought further pressure for crewmen to keep quiet.

Yet, despite the paucity of news and the fact that the Israeli government promptly apologized and called the attack an accident, insiders knew that "America's closest ally in the Middle East" had done its best to sink a ship that it knew to be American. One unsatisfied official was Secretary of State Dean Rusk, who complained bitterly and officially to the Israeli government. But the complaining voices were never heard by the American public, and the official protests were classified top secret to avoid embarrassing the attacking nation. Publicly the Lyndon Johnson administration considered the attack on the USS *Liberty* an understandable error in the heat of war.

As officer-of-the-deck aboard the *Liberty* that day, I had a ringside seat. I personally observed the close-range reconnaissance that preceded the attack. I saw the Israeli reconnaissance pilots wave to our crewmen. I talked to my shipmate, Chief Petty Officer Melvin Smith, moments after he intercepted Israeli radio messages in which Israeli pilots informed their headquarters that we were an American ship. I spent a year in military hospitals recovering from injuries received in the attack that followed. And for the next 12 years I probed government files and interviewed everyone who would agree to talk about what happened to our ship and why our government looked the other way.

Worldwide Fleet of Spy Ships

In 1967, *Liberty* was the newest and most elaborate of nearly a dozen intelligence-collection ships operated by the American Navy. Newsmen like to call them "spy ships." Akin to the Soviet intelligence trawlers that haunt the Western world, the American counterparts were fewer, but larger and better manned. At least six were at sea at any one time, and whenever tension developed anywhere in the world, the closest ship would be sent to the area.[2]

Thus 13 days before the outbreak of the Arab-Israeli Six Day War in 1967, middle-of-the-night orders from Washington moved the *Liberty* from her usual patrol area on the west coast of Africa to a new position near the scene of the expected fighting in order to report on the war's progress.

Unfortunately the decision-makers in Washington failed to consider that the Israeli government rarely tolerates "observers," particularly during wartime. This time, Israeli officials were even more sensitive because, among other things, they planned to capture the Golan Heights from Syria despite heavy White House opposition. If the Golan grab was to succeed, it had to be done quickly and in secret before the Americans could interfere.

When war broke out between Israel and the Arab states on June 5, 1967, General David Elazar assembled his troops near Lake Tiberias in preparation for an assault on the Syrian (Golan) Heights, set to begin at 11:30 on June 8.

One obstacle remained. Israeli leaders had learned, probably through observers in Spain, that the USS *Liberty* had stopped overnight at the U.S. Naval Base in Rota en route to the Gaza Strip. If the ship arrived on schedule, *Liberty* would be within easy radio range of the invasion site hours before the invasion of Syria was to start.

On *Liberty*'s third deck almost a 100 men with earphones, computers, and sensitive radio-frequency scanning equipment were already recording every radio signal from either side, while linguists and other specialists analyzed the results.

Everything of conceivable value was relayed instantly to Washington, where larger teams of specialists and even more sophisticated computers resifted and reanalyzed the results of *Liberty*'s work. *Liberty* was still far out at sea, but soon she would be in perfect position to report every detail of the war—including the fact that Israel was proceeding with an invasion against the strongest possible protests of the United States.

And if that weren't enough to frustrate the Israeli generals, Secretary of State Dean Rusk learned of the invasion plan more than a day beforehand, possibly from the *Liberty*'s work while the ship was still far at sea. Rusk immediately cabled Israeli leaders demanding that they de-escalate the war and, particularly, that they cancel the plan to invade Syria.[3]

Although Israeli leaders ignored the Secretary of State, they did not ignore the approach of the USS *Liberty.*

Early in the afternoon of June 7, a Central Intelligence Agency observer in the office of the United States Defense Attache in the American Embassy at Tel Aviv reported to CIA seniors in McLean, Virginia, that Israeli leaders had decided to sink the USS *Liberty* if the ship came near the war zone.[4]

Liberty Ordered to Move

American military leaders took the warning very seriously and immediately issued an order for the *Liberty* to move at least 100 miles from the embattled areas.[5]

The military communications fiasco that followed was described by a House Armed Services Investigating Subcommittee as "one of the most incredible failures of communications in the history of the Department of Defense."[6] As far as the USS *Liberty* was concerned, the entire worldwide military communication system, indeed the entire United States military command and control apparatus, failed.

Because an American naval vessel was being threatened, officers in the Joint Chiefs of Staff War Room at the Pentagon did not rely exclusively upon the then-antiquated military communication system. Too much was at risk.

Military communications in 1967 depended upon a worldwide series of manual relay stations. Every message was received as a ribbon of punched paper tape, typically from 5 to 20 feet long. Young operators, often with minimal training, were expected to "read" the punched tape, make duplicate copies when necessary, and insert the tape into the proper machine for transmission to the next relay point. The problem was that the system, designed for World War II, could not handle communications in the 1960s. In times of crisis, backlogged message tapes often covered the floor up to the operator's knees.

So, instead of trusting the message system, a Major Breedlove in the Pentagon's Joint Reconnaissance Center placed a trans-Atlantic telephone call to U.S. Navy headquarters in London relaying the order from the Joint Chiefs of Staff to move the USS *Liberty* far away from the Israeli-Egyptian coast.

But because the order came by telephone, and because it was not telephoned personally by a senior officer, the London headquarters chose to await a confirming message before taking action. The confirming message, unfortunately, went astray in the communications morass.[7] It was sent not to London but to the Philippine Islands. Twice! Follow-up messages were lost repeatedly. Still other messages were delayed by "more important" messages—particularly by a lengthy transcript of a press conference given by Defense Secretary Robert McNamara.[8]

Every military command in the world promptly received about 50 pages of transcript from the press conference, since it was given a speed-of-handling precedence rating suitable for event contact reports. *Liberty*'s urgent movement orders, however, were given a relatively low urgency rating, which caused them to be handled after most other naval messages. As a result, messages that could have saved the ship were delayed, mishandled, and not received.

Careful Examination by Israeli Aircraft

Before midnight on June 7, as *Liberty* passed about 50 miles from Port Said, the first Israeli reconnaissance aircraft began to observe our ship. And from the start they did not act like friendly or even neutral visitors. Instead, they trained their missile guidance radar on our ship as though preparing to fire deadly guided missiles.[9]

Liberty's trained technicians recognized the radar immediately as Israeli and attempted to report the incident to Washington. Unfortunately, a supervisor determined that the operators must be mistaken. "Israel would never aim guided missiles at an American ship," the supervisor insisted, and he thus refused to sign the report. He had much to learn.

When daylight came, we saw a procession of Israeli reconnaissance aircraft flying over us at an incredibly low level, while our intercept operators eavesdropped on the radio conversations between pilots and their headquarters. By this time I had relieved the watch on the bridge in order to assume the forenoon watch as officer-of-the-deck.

"No sweat, Lieutenant," Chief Petty Officer Melvin Smith, our leading enlisted cryptologist, whispered to me. "We can hear the pilots reporting by radio that we are American."

"It's good they're looking us over so closely," Captain McGonagle, the ship's commanding officer, said. "This way there can be no mistakes." (In the Israeli War Room, a green peg marked the location of the USS *Liberty*. The green color signified a neutral vessel. Alongside the peg were the words, "Liberty, an electromagnetic, audio surveillance ship of the U.S. Navy."[10])

In eight hours of daylight we were visited eight times by Israeli aircraft that circled our ship 13 times, sometimes as close as 200 feet directly overhead.[11] Visibility was unlimited. Off-duty officers in swimsuits waved to the pilots and could see the pilots waving back.

My shipmates relaxed. It looked like the war was over.

At 2:00 p.m., as I was preparing to go below after nearly seven hours on the bridge, radar operators detected three jet aircraft and three motor torpedo boats approaching from the east. Expecting another reconnaissance flight, I stood stupidly watching the aircraft approach, when suddenly a pattern of orange flashes danced the length of our ship accompanied by a deafening roar. Men on the ship's forecastle were thrown high into the air, while men around me fell to the deck. My left leg shattered from the impact of fragments from an Israeli rocket.

We were under intense fire, first by Israeli supersonic Mirage jets that momentarily knocked out our four puny 50-caliber machine guns and disabled all radio antennas, then by slower Israeli Mystere jets that plastered the stack, gun mounts, open bridge, and superstructure with an inferno of napalm. Flames were everywhere.

When *Liberty*'s radiomen tried to call for help, they found that all the ship's usual radio frequencies were blocked by a loud buzz-saw sound generated by sophisticated jamming equipment, apparently operated from the jets.[12] As they tried to find an unjammed frequency, a napalm bomb exploded outside their compartment, overheating the room and causing paint to smolder within. The space filled with smoke, but the ship's safety depended upon these men, and they would not leave their post. Instead, they lay flat on the deck, below most of the smoke, choking in the foul air, calling into their microphones as they continued to search for an unjammed radio frequency. In less than 10 minutes Chief Radioman Wayne Smith and his men found a clear channel and got a message through to U.S. Navy forces operating near Cyprus about 300 miles away.

On the bridge of the Sixth Fleet carrier *Saratoga,* Captain Joseph Tully received *Liberty*'s call for help and promptly turned his ship into the wind. A tough, no-nonsense skipper, Tully didn't wait for someone to tell him what to do. He started launching aircraft even as he relayed our message to his seniors. But just before his aircraft were out of sight, they were gruffly recalled by orders from Washington.

By this time a radio receiver on the carrier's bridge had been tuned to *Liberty*'s distress calls. Even today, *Saratoga*'s officers recall their frustration as they heard frantic calls for help from fellow Americans and knew that the aircraft that could have saved them were now flying under order back toward the carriers.

We may never know the reason, but we do know that the aircraft which might have arrived in time to save American lives were recalled. A radioman who relayed the order reports that it was given personally by Defense Secretary McNamara. Even a fly-over was forbidden while officials in Washington mulled over the fate of the USS *Liberty.*

Meanwhile, after 25 to 30 minutes of intense air attack by a dozen or more aircraft unobstructed by Sixth Fleet air power, three Israeli torpedo boats arrived to finish the job. Our ship was an easy target.

The boats approached at high speed and fired five torpedoes. Luckily, the first shots went wild. One torpedo passed safely astern, where it missed by a bare 25 yards. Another passed so close ahead of the ship that it vanished under the point of the bow, "sounding like a motorboat" to Petty Officer Rick Aimetti, who stood, astonished, on the forecastle. Two torpedoes passed safely, unseen. And one torpedo made a direct hit on the ship's cryptologic spaces, where it killed 25 men and temporarily trapped at least 50 more in the flooded compartment.

When *Liberty* miraculously remained afloat despite severe flooding from a 40-foot torpedo hole, the torpedo men circled the ship at close range, machine-gunning anyone who came on deck. Finally, at 3:15 p.m., it appeared that the USS *Liberty* was going to sink. Orders came from the bridge to prepare to abandon ship, and *Liberty* crewmen responded by launching three rubber rafts—the only boats not damaged in the attack. Almost immediately the torpedo men machine-gunned the empty rafts, plucked one out of the water, and set a course for their base at Ashdod.

Liberty was alone, in flames, dead in the water, and sinking. She had no usable lifeboats. Her radios were dead. From a crew of 294, 34 men were dead or dying, and 171 more were wounded.

Almost two hours after receiving our call for help, U.S. Navy commanders were given White House permission to come to the *Liberty*'s defense. For a second time that day, rescue aircraft streaked toward the *Liberty*. Immediately, as though aware the game was ending, the Israeli government summoned the U.S. Naval Attaché to report that Israeli forces had "erroneously attacked a maybe U.S. ship" and to offer "abject apologies."

At 4:32 p.m., the torpedo boats returned to ask: "Do you need help?" The reply from the bridge was profane. The attack, after more than two and one-half hours, was over.

Inquiry Leads to Inaccurate Report

The cover-up began. *Liberty* sailors were told daily that they could say nothing about the attack to anyone, not even to members of their own families. A Court of Inquiry was to be held, the men were told, and nothing could be said until the court had completed its work.

But the hearings were limited, and some of the most important witnesses were not asked to testify. Lookouts who might have described pre-attack reconnaissance were not questioned by the court. My sworn statement as officer-of-the-deck was read to the court, but was not accepted as evidence or entered into the official record. Vital deck logs were rewritten, and most references to reconnaissance were deleted. Evidence that failed to support the Israeli version was often changed, lost, or ignored by the official body assigned by the Navy to "inquire into all aspects" of the attack.

Despite the inadequacy of the Court of Inquiry, the final report did contain damning testimony and evidence—much of which conflicted directly with the "Findings of Fact" reported by the same court. Unfortunately, the entire 707-page report was classified top secret, and only a 28-page, watered-down excerpt was released to the public.

Instead of describing repeated reconnaissance flights as low as 200 feet overhead, the U.S. government disregarded the crew's sworn testimony and reported publicly that the attack was an understandable case of mistaken identity which was preceded by only three distant and casual reconnaissance flights. The government ignored the ship's logs and sworn testimony that the American flag stood clearly displayed in a 12-knot wind and reported instead that the flag probably hung limp and indiscernible on a windless day.

Instead of describing a prolonged and carefully coordinated attack in which the ship was under heavy fire for 75 minutes and called desperately for help for another 75 minutes, the U.S. government reported publicly that the air attack lasted only 6 minutes and that all firing ended when the torpedo boats drew close enough to see the American flag. The American government repeated Israel's claim that the ship was mistaken for the Egyptian freighter *El Quseir,* but failed to note that *El Quseir,* a rusted-out, 40-year-old horse carrier then awaiting the salvage yard of Alexandria, was a most unlikely candidate for a *Liberty* look-alike.

Meanwhile, the American government complained bitterly but privately to Israel that *Liberty* was indeed identified before the attack. Secretary of State Rusk officially informed the Israeli government that the attack was "quite literally incomprehensible (and) must be condemned as an act of military recklessness reflecting wanton disregard for human life."[13] But such candor was only for diplomatic channels. Publicly, the Johnson administration portrayed the attack as brief, spontaneous, casual, and mistaken—a story they knew to be untrue.[14]

American-Israeli Debate Continues

The *Liberty* crew had been told early in the cover-up that they would be free to talk to the press once the Court of Inquiry report was declassified and released. But this was not to be. When the press blanket was "lifted," the men were told that the Court of Inquiry had reported everything that could be said about the affair. The crew, therefore, could say only what had already been reported by the court and only in the same words the court had used.

Omitted from the government's published version of the Court of Inquiry report were the facts that the radios were jammed, that napalm was used, that the life rafts were shot up in the water, that American forces failed to arrive during a two-and-one-half-hour ordeal, and anything indicating that the attack was planned and deliberate. No one was allowed to describe the close-range reconnaissance that preceded the attack. Particularly forbidden was any description of the American flag or the steady breeze that displayed the flag clearly for the Israeli pilots to see.

It was clear from the beginning that such a complex, carefully orchestrated, thoroughly reconnoitered military operation could not have been an accident. Over the past 17 years, the Israeli government has churned out a fascinating series of "rebuttals" and "official versions," each different and each readily disproven. Meanwhile, several former U.S. government officials and scores of *Liberty* survivors have stepped forward to support the previously untold story. And government files continue to reveal telling evidence that the United States government knows that the attack was deliberate, that the story was covered up and is still being covered up.[15]

Book Receives Favorable Response

Even before I was discharged from the hospital I started interviewing other survivors. Research for my eventual book, *Assault on the Liberty,* spanned more than 12 years. For much of that time I was a Navy lieutenant commander, stationed in Germany and

Washington, D.C. Throughout that period I was in constant contact with other survivors and with officers who had watched the affair unfold from Washington. But documentation was hard to come by because the government steadfastly denied access to most records that could provide written evidence to support the recollections of survivors.

All this changed when the Freedom of Information Act was passed in 1974. For the first time, Americans could demand access to government information with a reasonable chance of success. Important files could no longer be legally withheld. To be sure, there were delays and foot-dragging. At one point I filed suit in Federal court just to get the Department of State to answer one of my requests under the act.[16] For two years they had simply ignored my requests. But eventually I gathered proof for most of the story of the attack on the USS *Liberty.*

Although columnist Jack Anderson and others had speculated in print that the attack must have been deliberate,[17] until now no one had ever presented proof. No one had ever shown, step by step, how the attack was conducted, how the American rescue was mismanaged, how the American government had covered up the truth, and why the Israeli excuse for the attack was plainly untrue.

Finally, in January 1980, my findings were published by one of the world's most respected publishers, Random House, in New York.

The reviews exceeded my fondest hopes. The widely read *Hartford Courant* called *Assault on the Liberty* "a balance between *The Cruel Sea* and *Mister Roberts*—the most important book you'll read this year." The U.S. Naval Institute at Annapolis called *Assault* "probably the most important naval book of 1980." *Military Review,* the professional journal of the U.S. Army, hailed the book as "a meticulous account, unemotional and detailed," while the *Naval War College Review* called it "an instructive reading exercise."

People magazine did a two-page spread, while leading newspapers found the book "convincing," "provocative," "haunting," "absorbing," "indelible," "lively," "stirring," "revealing," "exciting," and "fascinating."

The Washington Post ran two book reviews, two news stories, and an editorial on the subject, and gave the book its highest rating, "Choice." Two retired chiefs of naval operations praised the book publicly, as did several leading members of Congress and four Pulitzer-winning authors.[18] Even the independent Jewish press wrote that *Assault on the Liberty* exemplifies "the best traditions of quiet investigative journalism."[19]

Interest soared. I did a two-hour interview with Larry King on his national radio network and about seven hours on Washington, D.C., stations alone. Eventually there were over 150 radio and television interviews, including 12 hours in a series of talk-show appearances on KGO, a powerful San Francisco radio station that is heard in 11 states. The *Radio Reader* at Michigan State University selected my book to read in its entirety on a coast-to-coast radio network—a minimum of 9 hours of air time on each of 44 stations. Most stations broadcast the reading twice.

One would expect that such priceless publicity would sell books. Indeed, four booksellers told me that *Assault on the Liberty* was their best-selling title, accounting for over 1,000 sales for each dealer. But these stories were not typical.

Campaign to Discredit Begins

An early disappointment was *Newsweek.* The news magazine had covered the story objectively in 1967, and its "Periscope" column set about doing a story on the book. The story was written, edited, and ready to run when, according to Random House Publicity Manager Cheryl Merser, it was pulled moments before press time—supposedly for "hotter news." It never ran.

Columnist Jack Anderson had written twice about the *Liberty,* once stating flatly that the attack "was planned in advance." Anderson also writes for Random House. But the book I arranged to send him was received in stony silence. When I called his office, I found a hostile staff that did not want to talk about the USS *Liberty.*

The first indication of the likely source of the problem was a report from a newspaper reporter in Washington, D.C., who called to warn of trouble. The Israeli government, he said, was working hard behind the scenes, particularly in New York and Washington, to discredit my story. I soon learned that he was correct.

The Israeli Foreign Office in Jerusalem, I discovered, had prepared and distributed a four-page criticism of my book. "Ennes," said the Israeli government, "is illogical and unrealistic. His conclusions fly in the face of logic and the military facts." The paper made no attempt to refute my evidence and produced no evidence of its own; instead, Israeli officials simply discounted my story out of hand, ignored the evidence and testimony of eyewitnesses, and repeated their original claims of mistaken identity. Unfortunately, that was enough to provide ammunition for other spokesmen for Israel.

Soon the American-Israel Public Affairs Committee published a six-page attack drawn heavily from the Israeli document. Similar language was published by Israeli counsels general in Chicago, San Francisco, and Atlanta. Identical phrases and paragraphs surfaced in "fact sheets" and "background papers" prepared by other pro-Israeli organizations. In one striking case, my name appeared in a published list of "Who's Who in Arab Propaganda" distributed by the American-Israel Public Affairs Committee. (Former U.S. representative Paul Findley explores the depth of AIPAC's influence on Congress and the media in his forthcoming book, *They Dared to Speak Out.*)

Before long, language from the Israeli propaganda mill began to appear in letters to editors and media managers whenever my book was mentioned publicly. Most radio talk-show callers were friendly, but the unfriendly ones invariably used arguments taken from the Israeli literature. In California, 20 members of an Oakland B'nai B'rith chapter signed a letter to radio station KQED asking to cancel a scheduled reading of my book. In another case, a statement drawn from the Israeli document was read on radio station KUOW in Seattle by an Anti-Defamation League chairman, and the same statement reappeared word for word 3,000 miles away in a letter to the editor of *The Jacksonville Times-Union* in Florida. A Jewish reader who objected to this organized campaign mailed an Anti-Defamation League circular to an editor of *The San Diego Union* after the *Union* supported my book editorially.[20] In the circular, ADL members were instructed never to be first to mention the USS *Liberty,* but to respond quickly with a canned protest if the subject were mentioned publicly.

Book Orders Disappear

Meanwhile, I began to receive reports that orders for the book were not being filled. Booksellers who failed to receive a book order usually assumed that it was out of print and so informed their customers. The book has never been out of print; Random House has reprinted it three times. Nevertheless, many orders vanished without a trace somewhere in the distribution pipeline.

Would-be readers from several states wrote to tell me that, when they bypassed local retailers to place orders directly with my publisher, an order clerk told them that the book was out of print, or that Random House had suspended distribution to avoid a lawsuit. In one case a determined New York City reader argued at length with a Random House clerk who insisted that Random House had never published a book called *Assault on the Liberty.*

Random House traced a large order at my request and discovered that all West Coast orders from Ingram Book Company, a major wholesale book dealer, had simply "vanished." All orders for *Assault on the Liberty* had ostensibly been "lost." Following several important reviews and talk shows, the manager of the popular Washington, D.C., Pentagon branch of Brentano's bookstore told me that my book had been unavailable for months—even though Random House had an abundance of books at that time.

Waldenbooks, a large national chain, dropped *Assault on the Liberty* prematurely from stock despite steady demand.[21] The naval base in San Diego returned a large supply of books to the publisher after a chaplain at the base filed a complaint.

Even the advertising department of the venerable *Washington Post* may have yielded to the pressure of hundreds of complaining letters and telephone calls in response to the *Post's* two book reviews and two news stories. According to *Post* military editor George Wilson, "It seemed that every phone in the building had someone calling to complain about our mention of the book." A few days later, when Seattle bookseller Karen Smith called the *Post* to place an ad offering to sell *Assault on the Liberty* by mail, the ad clerk warned: "I don't know if we can accept an ad for that book. There have been a lot of complaints that we should not have reviewed such a controversial book."

The ad did not run. Several weeks later, after repeated apologies for unexplained delays and missed publication dates, *Post* advertising manager Robert Rawls returned the bookseller's check with apologies for the "foul-up." (Although the advertising department may have folded under pressure, the *Post*'s editors did not. They eventually published yet another review and a feature story about the *Liberty* crew.)

On radio station WIND in Chicago, interest in the subject was so intense that a talk show scheduled for one hour was extended to three hours while studio phone lines buzzed with callers. Then came the complaints. When I waited near my telephone for a scheduled follow-up interview two weeks later, the phone never rang.

When I complained to WIND's program director, Tom LaPorte, he apologized grandly. It was a "terrible oversight." It was something that had never happened before at WIND, he assured me, and it would never happen again. He promised to investigate the "inexcusable error" and to call back within the hour to reschedule the interview. He did not call. When I called him, he refused to accept my calls. He did not answer my letters and he declined to discuss the matter with a Chicago citizen who did manage to reach him by telephone. Apparently the truth about the "oversight" was too embarrassing to discuss.

Television Coverage Cancelled

The campaign to suppress the *Liberty* story was probably most effective with the national commercial television networks. A producer for ABC's popular *Good Morning America* invited me to an interview set for March 10, 1980. She said she would invite the Israeli embassy to send a representative to appear with me. Then she phoned the embassy and dropped me cold. Weeks later, when asked about guest appearances, the ABC computer reported, "Ennes, James—cancelled." ABC still will not discuss the reasons for the cancellation.

ABC's late-night news show *Nightline* scheduled a *Liberty* story three times, but cancelled the segment each time. Most notable was in June 1982, when *Nightline* interviewed four *Liberty* crewmen for three hours in the *Nightline* studios and prepared a complete show on the history and circumstances of the loss of the ship. The program was fully edited and ready to run when, shortly before air time, *Nightline* producer Pat Cullen called me at home to say the *Liberty* story was to be pushed aside temporarily for news of the Israeli invasion of Lebanon. "Don't worry," she told me, "the *Liberty* story is too big to ignore."

Anchor Ted Koppel confirmed that intention a few days later in a letter to a San Francisco viewer. "I cannot just now say when we will be able to air this program," Koppel wrote, "but it is still our intention to do so."

Yet when producers tried to resurrect the aborted story, they found that the valuable, fully edited studio tape and more than 15 reels of supporting raw film had mysteriously disappeared from the *Nightline* film library.

At the request of Ira Rosen, producer of the popular *60 Minutes* television series, I spent a week preparing a detailed *Liberty* synopsis, complete with copies of key documents and a long list of suggested guests. Apparently Mike Wallace and Rosen wanted to do the story, but anything as controversial as the USS *Liberty* story needed approval from CBS management. And there the plan died. "Nothing short of direct testimony from a defecting Israeli official will justify doing this story," producer Rosen told me reluctantly.

When NBC news producer Robert Toombs in New York City asked his office for permission to interview a group of *Liberty* survivors for the evening news, he was told, "NBC is not interested in the USS *Liberty.*" Toombs seemed surprised. The survivors were not. We have seen it all before.

Now a Hollywood company is hard at work writing a screenplay and doing other preproduction work for a full-length motion picture based on *Assault on the Liberty*. Theater distribution has already been offered in both the United States and Europe, and some leading Hollywood personalities have offered their support, even though skeptics and naysayers predominate.

Incredibly, a common response from friends as well as foes is, "Israel will never allow this movie." If that is true, the film's backers have decided, then the United States is in deep trouble. They are determined to complete the film.[22]

Liberty Crew and Friends Step Forward

Soon I began to hear from other survivors, most of whom told me they found the book almost therapeutic. The book, they said, relieved a weight from their shoulders; for the first time they felt free to discuss the attack with friends.

One of the first to call was retired master chief petty officer Stan White, the senior enlisted man aboard the *Liberty*. Stan had helped with some of my research. Now he wanted to help tell the story. Starting with my list of about 40 survivors, he almost single-handedly tracked down more than 150 former crewmen and their families.

A few of the men just wanted to forget the *Liberty*. Many were bitter. Most felt that they had been ravaged by an ally and then betrayed by their own government. Many were frustrated and angry that the "official" story told by both governments was so different from what they had experienced. And nearly every man wanted to help tell the *Liberty* story to a wider audience.

Stan set to work immediately on planning for a reunion of the *Liberty* crew.

A Visit to Washington

A big boost came late in 1980 when I was invited to discuss the attack with Senator Adlai Stevenson of Illinois. Senator Stevenson quizzed me privately for two hours about the attack, the evidence, and my sources of information. Then he invited me back on another day to be grilled by members of his staff and that of Senator Barry Goldwater of Arizona.

While everyone seemed to agree that my story was sound, Senator Goldwater's staff argued (incredibly, I thought) that the matter should not be pursued because "nothing can be gained" by probing this ugly matter.

Senator Stevenson did not agree. He argued that "to tell the American people the truth" was reason enough, and his staff stood behind him. He went to work trying to get the support of Senator Goldwater and others.

Soon Senator Stevenson published in the *Congressional Record* (S13136, September 22, 1980) the full text of a review from *The Washington Post* written by Commander Lloyd Bucher, former USS *Pueblo* skipper, and he urged every member of Congress to read the book. Then he gave UPI reporter William J. Small a remarkable interview that was broadcast by radio and widely printed in newspapers on September 28.

In that interview, Senator Stevenson said: "I intend to use the [Intelligence] Subcommittee as a means of looking into this matter further. . . . One possibility would include providing [crewmen] with an opportunity to tell their story to the American people. Those sailors have one story to tell, and that story leaves no doubt but that this was a premeditated, carefully reconnoitered attack against our ship."

The story quoted three government officials who were not interested in examining the matter. "That's the explanation Israel brought forward, and that's what we have to go with," said State Department spokesman Jack Toohey, neatly dismissing the value of the logs, files, and testimony of survivors. "To Israel it would only be an irritant with little purpose," said Ted Cubbison on the State Department's Israel desk, apparently untroubled by the charges and unwilling to examine the evidence. "The findings of the Court of Inquiry have not been revised," said a Navy spokeswoman, as if that settled the matter. Then the story closed with these astounding remarks by Senator Stevenson:

[Congressmen are] intimidated by a lobby which at the moment takes its orders from an extremist minority within Israel. It's about time we indicated that Mr. Begin is wrong when he says they can go on defying the United States. If you acquiesce even in an attack against your own ship, and the killing of your own countrymen, you lose all credibility, in the world as well as in Israel. You lose your self-respect, ultimately, and you may lose the peace of the world.

Unfortunately, Senator Stevenson did not prevail. He had not run for reelection and his term in Congress was about to expire. Other senators were simply unwilling to risk their futures by openly challenging the Israeli government. Just before he left Congress, Senator Stevenson wrote to me that most members of Congress are "timid" about the USS *Liberty* and that Barry Goldwater, though initially interested, had chosen to take the path [of caution] advised by his staff.

UPI reporter William Small's story, however, did have one apparent result. After years of procrastination and refusal to pay the $14 million demanded by the United States for loss of the ship itself (actually worth more than $40 million) the Israeli government suddenly offered $6 million to settle the score. President Carter accepted, and his decision was announced by the Department of State on December 18 with a press release entitled, "The Book Is Now Closed on the USS Liberty Affair."

Adlai Stevenson remarked that the book would not truly be closed until the government acknowledged the truth, but that rhetorical book-closing was more than enough to satisfy several hundred congressmen.

USS *Liberty* Reunion

Meanwhile, Stan White continued to work toward a *Liberty* reunion. On June 4, 5, and 6, 1982, more than 100 former crewmen of the USS *Liberty* met a block from the White House at the Hotel

Washington for their first gathering in 15 years. It was a joyful, tearful, emotional occasion.

All the men had been ordered (illegally, we now believe) never to say anything about the *Liberty* to anyone. For the first time, they felt free to discuss the attack, and most found that speaking out relieved a heavy burden.

Virgil Brownfield described what it was like to see his best friend die. "People don't die like they do on TV, you know. They sort of die . . . like chickens. And everyone is falling—the navigator and the executive officer, and the officer of the deck—and you wonder if you should just stand up and get it over with."

"At one point I got madder than hell. I just wanted to kill somebody," said Chuck Jones. "But I got over that, because there were just too many things to do. In my own mind it wasn't a mistake, but I don't hate those guys."

"We're not blaming the Israeli people," said Ron Grantski. "The Israelis had some people in charge who should be held responsible."

"We should have stood up a little bit, instead of accepting their apology just like that," added Gene Kirk.

Joe Meadors asked, "How many Russian intelligence trawlers have been wiped out? You know if one of those were sunk, they'd go to war over that."

Crewmen had sent the ambassador from Israel a polite invitation to attend the reunion or to send a representative to ask questions. We were hoping he would come, as we felt it would be impossible for him to defend his government's actions after hearing firsthand from men who had survived the attack. Instead, the journalist Wolf Blitzer, then working for *The Jerusalem Post,* phoned, promising to attend. But he didn't show up either. Apparently a public meeting with men who knew the truth about the *Liberty* attack was more than the government of Israel wanted to risk.

The gathering did have other results. A reporter called former secretary of state Dean Rusk to ask his opinion. "Sure the attack could have been deliberate," he said. "They had sightings beforehand of the ship. I don't buy the Israeli explanation. We were never able to get to the heart of what happened."[23]

Perhaps the most outspoken of all was retired chairman of the Joint Chiefs of Staff Admiral Thomas H. Moorer, who did not hesitate to tell the crew and assembled reporters that the attack "could not possibly have been a case of mistaken identity. I have never been willing to accept the Israeli explanation." Later he added, "Even a rag-tag Navy could not make a mistake like that."

Soon after the reunion, a heavily censored report by the super-secret National Security Agency revealed the true feelings of another government servant. Scribbled in a margin next to the still-officially-censored Israeli excuse was a note by the agency's deputy director, Dr. Louis Tordella. Never intended for public exposure, the note read: "A nice whitewash."

Even retired admiral Isaac C. Kidd, who headed the official Navy inquiry into the attack, agreed by telephone to a request by *Liberty* survivor Don Blalock that he reexamine the evidence and rethink the conclusions of his 1967 court. If he ever did reread the file, he kept his findings to himself.

Veterans Organizations Lend Support

Liberty crewmen are now supported by almost every major veterans organization except the American Legion. Strangely, the American Legion was first to cry out publicly about the *Liberty.* In 1967 the Legion passed a national resolution calling for a proper investigation (and rejecting the official Navy investigation), but according to Legion staff member Dr. Frank Maria, who proposed the original resolution, the American Legion failed to follow through because they came under heavy pressure from pro-Israel organizations.

The Disabled American Vets, the Retired Officers Association, the Veterans of Foreign Wars, and most others have laid wreaths on the *Liberty* graves at Arlington, but the American Legion, still stung by the charges, has been conspicuously absent.

Liberty veterans were supported when they complained to the Veterans Administration that the gravestone marking the final resting place of six men at Arlington National Cemetery was evasive and improper. The stone was changed to read "Killed—USS Liberty" instead of "died in the Eastern Mediterranean."

The Veterans of Foreign Wars, in a letter from National Commander James Currieo, called officially upon the Reagan administration to join the VFW in sending a representative to "render long overdue honors" in a ceremony at the *Liberty* grave site. Not surprisingly, the White House ignored the request. But the Jewish War Veterans did not. Jewish War Veterans published a scathing attack by National Executive Director Harris Stone on the VFW for having "dredged up an ancient and discredited story,"[24] and then ignored a carefully documented request for rebuttal space from the USS *Liberty* Veterans Association.

But the VFW was not intimidated. VFW members attending the 1983 national convention passed Resolution Number 685 calling upon the United States to establish "a fitting memorial . . . honoring those men lost on the USS *Liberty.*"

The Israeli Government Persists

Largely through the efforts of *Liberty* crewmen working together, the story has now been told on the front pages of *The New York Times, The Baltimore Sun,* and *The Los Angeles Times,* and in major stories in many other pages including *The Washington Post.* It has been covered repeatedly in national wire service stories and on national radio networks. According to columnists Evans and Novak, President Reagan even mentioned the *Liberty* attack to his staff as an example of Israeli treachery.[25]

Meanwhile, the Israeli government periodically releases another "official version" of the incident. The latest, prepared by the History Department of the Israeli Defense Forces, was released in 1982 on the eve of the *Liberty* reunion. Like those before it, the report ignores hard evidence, laws of physics, and testimony of crewmen. Instead it dwells on the incredible claims that the ship flew no flag and was tracked by radar from patrol boats that were in fact far beyond radar range.

As this is written, another salvo is about to be fired. According to a correspondent in Jerusalem, two leading Israeli writers will publish a 7,000-word essay on the USS *Liberty* in the summer issue of *Atlantic Monthly.* The authors reportedly believe that their article "refutes all that has ever been written about the Israeli attack."

To do that, the article will have to resolve all inconsistencies found in the official Israeli excuses. Why do *Liberty* crewmen recall waving to reconnaissance pilots when Israel claims there was no reconnaissance? And why do *Liberty* crewmen remember seeing the torpedomen deliberately destroy life rafts at 3:15 when Israel claims that the last shot was fired before 2:40? It will have to explain away CIA reports that Moshe Dayan directed the attack[26] and that the decision to attack the *Liberty* was made a day in advance.[27] It should make interesting reading.

Update by the author, James Ennes

USS *Leper* AGTR5

Seattle, Washington—Nearly 40 years after Israeli forces attacked and almost sank USS *Liberty*, the ship has become a pariah. Indeed, some survivors have come to calling their ship USS *Leper*. The name fits. Probably no ship in the history of the United States has become so universally despised by the very people who should be its strongest supporters.

Despite the fact that dozens of senior U.S. military and government officials agree that the attack was deliberate and was a war crime (see www.ussliberty.org/supporters.htm), few have ever been willing to support the crew while still holding government office. Their often courageous support usually comes only after they have retired. Officially, the United States government has silently acquiesced to the false claims that the attack was investigated and that no evidence was found that it was deliberate. However, according to Richard Helms, former director of Central Intelligence, the CIA conducted a still classified investigation "that concluded the Israelis

knew exactly what they were doing when they attacked USS *Liberty*."
To this day there has not been a single congressional investigation.

In June 2005, with the help of an experienced prosecuting
attorney, survivors prepared and filed with the Secretary of the Army
a carefully detailed and thoroughly documented 300-page "Report of
War Crimes Committed Against USS *Liberty*." The report includes
sworn affidavits from surviving eyewitnesses, a sworn statement by
the legal counsel to the Navy Court of Inquiry attesting that the court
proceeding was fraudulent, a sworn statement by the counsel to the
court's convening authority (who also served as the Navy's senior legal
officer) attesting that the legal process was deeply flawed, and evidence
that a serious crime was committed. All this is supported by
appropriate legal citations which require the government's action.

That report (www.ussliberty.org/report/report.pdf) was delivered
by Federal Express to the Secretary of the Army. Additional copies
were hand-delivered by a former Chief Judge Advocate General of
the Navy along with his own supporting letter.

Meanwhile, about a dozen retired flag and general officers (brought
together by the late Admiral Thomas Moorer and the late General
Ray Davis and now led by Rear Admirals Merlin Staring and Mark
Hill) work diligently along with surviving crewmen to seek some
measure of justice for the crime against our ship.

These efforts have so far been ignored, despite an absolute
requirement in U.S. law and international treaties that allegations of
war crimes be promptly investigated by the United States.

On April 20, 2006, Rear Admirals Staring and Hill appealed once
again to the Secretary of the Army to respond appropriately to our
report. They write, in part:

> . . . . [these matters] have never been addressed or investigated
> at all. The fact that the state of Israel may have admitted to
> the attack upon the LIBERTY after the fact, claiming it to
> have resulted from a mistaken identification of the ship—or
> that it ultimately paid some damage claims—is in no way
> responsive, or even relevant, to the Report of War Crimes—

War Crimes which, quite simply, have never been investigated. Those War Crimes have been properly reported now, and they should now be investigated, at long last, with appropriate corrective action to follow in accordance with the system implemented by the DoD Directives cited above.

The full letter and supporting correspondence can be found online at http://freewebs.com/gidusko/crimes/.

Meanwhile, USS *Liberty* sinks even lower in official esteem. A new amphibious ship, now in planning stages, was to have been named USS *Liberty* LCS-2. That name appears widely in planning documents. But in April the Navy announced that the new ship is to be named USS *Independence*. No one in Washington will explain why the "USS *Liberty*" name became inappropriate.

Timeline for War

By Jane Adas, John Mahoney, and Robert Norberg

Jane Adas lectures at Rutgers University and is vice president of AMEU. John Mahoney has been AMEU's executive director since 1978. Bob Norberg is a journalist by profession and serves as AMEU's president.

March 1992: The Pentagon. Paul Wolfowitz, undersecretary of defense for policy for President Bush, drafts an update of America's overall military strategy called the "Defense Planning Guidance." In it he argues that the U.S. might be faced with taking preemptive military action to prevent the use or development of WMD. The official ultimately responsible for the document is Bush's defense secretary Dick Cheney. The draft is actually written by Wolfowitz's protégé and top assistant Lewis Libby.

September 1, 1992: New York. Ramzi Yousef, the nephew of Khalid Shaikh Mohammed, arrives at JFK Airport. Born of a Palestinian mother, his goal is to punish the United States for its support of Israel, knowing that the U.S. government every year sends military and financial aid worth billions of dollars to Israel. Ramzi says that he and his uncle, an engineer who had studied higher mathematics and jet propulsion in the U.S., have been planning to bring down the towers of the World Trade Center, the ultimate symbol of America's worldwide financial muscle.

February 26, 1993: New York. Ramzi Yousef, with others, sets off explosives at the World Trade Center. Later in the day he flies out of JFK for Karachi, disappointed that both towers were still standing, and determined to bring them down at another time.

February 27, 1993: New York. A group calling itself the "Liberation Army" sends a letter to *The New York Times* saying the World Trade Center bombing was in retaliation for American support of Israel, and warning that if America did not change its Middle East policy, more terrorist missions would be carried out, some by suicide bombers.

April 15, 1993: Kuwait. Kuwaiti police say they have prevented an assassination attempt on former president George H. W. Bush, his wife, two sons, and daughter-in-law Laura. Most in the CIA promptly point the finger at Saddam Hussein; others, including investigative journalist Seymour Hersh, doubt the Iraqi president had any involvement in the plot.

January 7, 1995: Manila. Ramzi Yousef and a colleague, Abdul Hakim Murad, accidentally set off an explosion in their apartment. Murad is captured and, under torture, tells the Philippine police of a plan to board an American commercial aircraft, hijack it, control the cockpit, and dive the plane into the CIA headquarters. The chief of intelligence command for the Philippine National Police tells the Associated Press that its office shared the information immediately with FBI agents in Manila, along with the message they found on Yousef's laptop explaining why they were doing it: "If the U.S. government keeps supporting Israel . . . then we will continue to carry out operations inside and outside the United States."

April 18, 1996: Lebanon. Israel attacks a U.N. refugee camp at Qana, killing women and children. Israel says it was a mistake. The U.N. and Amnesty International say it was intentional. Shortly afterwards, Osama bin Laden moves to the mountains of Afghanistan, where he uses the Qana massacre to recruit fighters in a war against the U.S. and Israel.

July 9, 1996: Washington, D.C. Douglas Feith, the Washington, D.C., partner of an Israeli firm soliciting American business for Israel's right-wing settler movement, joins with other pro-settlement supporters Richard Perle, David Wurmser, and Wurmser's wife, Meryav, to develop a foreign-policy position paper for Israeli prime minister Benjamin Netanyahu. Titled "A Clean Break: A New Strategy for Securing the Realm," it calls for Israel to overthrow

Saddam Hussein and put a pro-Israel regime in his place. Netanyahu rejects it.

July 25, 1996: Al Khobar, Saudi Arabia. A truck bomb rams a high-rise complex housing U.S. airmen. Nineteen are killed. The bombing is blamed on Hezbollah and its Iranian sponsors, although the U.S. commission investigating the 9/11 attacks will later conclude that Osama bin Laden may have had an involvement—but not Saddam Hussein.

August 23, 1996: Afghanistan. Bin Laden, with his new mastermind for worldwide operations, Khalid Shaikh Mohammed, issues a call to action: "My Muslim Brothers of the world . . . your brothers in Palestine and in the land of the two Holy Places [Saudi Arabia] are calling upon your help and asking you to take part in fighting against the enemy—your enemy and their enemy—the Americans and the Israelis. . . . The horrifying pictures of the massacre of Qana in Lebanon are still fresh in our memory. . . . They [Americans] are not exonerated from responsibility, because they chose this [their] government and voted for it despite their knowledge of its crimes in Palestine, Lebanon, Iraq, and in other places."

January 26, 1998: Washington, D.C. Richard Perle, Paul Wolfowitz, Donald Rumsfeld, Richard Armitage, and 14 others send a letter to President Clinton urging regime change in Iraq and a more aggressive Middle East policy. The letter is sponsored by the Project for the New American Century (PNAC), founded by William Kristol, editor of *The Weekly Standard.*

July 31, 1998: New York. David Wurmser meets with Israel's permanent representative to the U.N., Dore Gold, in an effort to get Israel to put pressure on the American Congress to approve a $10 million grant to Ahmad Chalabi 's Iraqi National Congress, an exile group based in London with a guerilla army based in northern Iraq, whose purpose is the overthrow of Saddam Hussein.

August 7, 1998: Tanzania and Kenya. Suspected Al Qaeda cells bomb U.S. embassies in both countries, killing 258, including 12 Americans.

August 20, 1998: Afghanistan and Sudan. President Clinton orders missile attack against Al Qaeda camps in Afghanistan and a pharmaceutical plant in Sudan said to produce nerve gas and to be linked to bin Laden. Bin Laden survives and doubts are raised about the pharmaceutical plant, which Sudanese say produced infant formula. Shortly after, bin Laden tells ABC News that, if the liberation of the Al-Aqsa Mosque in Jerusalem and the Ka'aba in Saudi Arabia is a crime, he indeed is a criminal.

February-March 1999: Afghanistan. Osama bin Laden summons Khalid Shaikh Mohammed to tell him that his proposal to use aircraft as terror weapons against the U.S. has the full support of Al Qaeda.

September 28, 2000: Jerusalem. Israeli prime minister Ariel Sharon, flanked by 1,000 armed police, visits site of the Al-Aqsa Mosque. Bin Laden reacts by asking that the planned attacks against the U.S. be moved up.

October 12, 2000: Yemen. The USS *Cole* is attacked; 17 sailors are killed and 39 wounded. Bin Laden, the suspected mastermind, praises the suicide attackers, then reads a poem he wrote in honor of Palestinian children killed in their struggle against Israel's occupation of their land.

January 1, 2001: Washington, D.C. David Wurmser recommends to President-elect Bush that America and Israel join forces to "strike fatally, not merely disarm, the centers of radicalism in the region—the regimes of Damascus, Baghdad, Tripoli, Tehran, and Gaza," and he suggests that "crises can be opportunities" to implement this plan.

January 30, 2001: The White House. President Bush holds his first high-level National Security Council meeting. Two topics are on the agenda: Israel and Iraq. He says he plans to "tilt it [U.S. policy] back toward Israel" and—in what turns out to be the prime focus of the meeting—he says he wants to remove Saddam Hussein. Condoleezza Rice explains: "Iraq might be the key to reshaping the entire region."

February 5, 2001: The White House. Rice chairs a principals' committee meeting to review Iraq policy. All agree that the sanctions were hurting only the Iraqi people, not Saddam. Powell proposes stricter U.N. sanctions on Saddam's military programs.

April 2001: The White House. Cabinet deputies meet to review terrorism policy. Richard Clarke warns that the network of terrorist organizations called Al Qaeda, led by Osama bin Laden, presents an immediate and serious threat to the U.S., and that the U.S. had to target bin Laden and his leadership by reinitiating flights of the Predator drone. Wolfowitz replies that Iraq is just as much a terrorist threat. Clarke says he is unaware of any Iraqi-sponsored terrorism directed at the U.S. Deputy CIA director John McLaughlin backs up Clarke. Wolfowitz tells Clarke he gives bin Laden too much credit and that he had to have a state sponsor. Clarke replies that bin Laden has made plain his terrorist aims and, as with Hitler in *Mein Kampf,* you have to believe these people will actually do what they say. Wolfowitz responds that he resents comparing the Holocaust to "this little terrorist in Afghanistan." Clarke replies: "I wasn't comparing the Holocaust to anything. I was saying that like Hitler, bin Laden has told us in advance what he plans to do, and we would make a big mistake to ignore it."

June 21, 2001: Afghanistan. Bin Laden aide Ayman al-Zawahiri announces over the Middle East Broadcasting Company that "the coming weeks will hold important surprises that will target American and Israeli interests in the world."

August 6, 2001: Crawford, Texas. President Bush receives a President's Daily Brief entitled "Bin Laden Determined to Strike in U.S." It warns that the FBI has intelligence indicating that terrorists might be preparing for an airline hijacking in the U.S. and might be targeting a building in lower Manhattan. No action is taken.

September 4, 2001: The White House. Counterterrorism czar Richard Clarke meets with the president to walk him through a proposed National Security Presidential Directive, whose goal is to eliminate bin Laden and Al Qaeda leaders. Clarke had asked for the meeting, calling it "urgent," back in January, but is only now allowed to see him. He tells Bush that the use of minimum-wage rent-a-cops to screen passengers and carry-on luggage at airports has got to stop. The president agrees.

September 11, 2001: New York; Washington, D.C.; Pennsylvania. Nineteen Middle Eastern hijackers, 15 from Saudi Arabia, commandeer four commercial airplanes, crashing two into the World Trade Towers in Manhattan, one into the Pentagon in Washington, and one in a field in Pennsylvania. Nearly 3,000 are killed. Rumsfeld directs Pentagon lawyer to talk to Wolfowitz about Iraq's connection to the attacks.

September 12, 2001: Germany. Seven members of Rumsfeld's brain trust meet at an airport in Frankfurt and board an Air Force refueling plane sent to ferry them back to Washington. Group includes Douglas Feith, now undersecretary of defense for policy. On the flight back they sketch out a plan for the defense secretary according to which the U.S. would first topple the Taliban government of Afghanistan, then go after other terror states, including Iraq. Feith appoints David Wurmser to put together a secret intelligence unit in his Pentagon office that will bypass the normal channels and report directly to him; called the Policy Counterterrorism Evaluation Group, its purpose is to find loose ties between Saddam Hussein and Al Qaeda in order to counter the CIA, whose analysts had found no credible links between the two. Later in the day, counterterrorism coordinator Richard Clarke attends White House meetings of the inner circle of Bush's war cabinet and is stunned to learn that Rumsfeld and Wolfowitz were going to take advantage of the national tragedy to promote their agenda about Iraq. Rumsfeld specifically asks if the attacks did not present an "opportunity" to launch war against Iraq.

September 15, 2001: Camp David. Bush gathers closest advisers. Much discussion is on Afghanistan, but Wolfowitz advocates attacking Iraq, maybe even before Afghanistan. He says there's a 10 to 50 percent chance Iraq was involved in 9/11. Bush sends note to Wolfowitz saying he doesn't want to hear more on Iraq that day. Cheney, Powell, Wolfowitz, and Rice vote against hitting Iraq first; Rumsfeld abstains. Powell, who is appalled at the idea of hitting Iraq, finds Rumsfeld's abstention interesting. Richard Perle, who is also present, says Wolfowitz planted the seed.

September 16, 2001: Washington, D.C. Richard Perle and other neoconservatives send letter to Bush urging him to focus immediately on a war with Iraq, whether or not a connection with 9/11 can be shown.

September 17, 2001: The White House. Bush signs a top-secret order that lays out his plan for going to war in Afghanistan and directs the Pentagon to begin planning military options for an invasion of Iraq.

September 19, 2001: The Pentagon. Perle convenes a two-day meeting of the Defense Policy Board, a group that advises the Pentagon. He introduces two guest speakers: Professor Bernard Lewis of Princeton, a longtime friend of Cheney and Wolfowitz, who says U.S. must respond to 9/11 with a show of strength, and must support such democratic reformers in the Middle East as Ahmad Chalabi. The second speaker, in fact, is Ahmad Chalabi, who tells the group that Iraq does possess WMD, although as yet there is no evidence linking Iraq to 9/11.

October 7, 2001: Afghanistan. U.S. and U.K. planes bomb Taliban bases; the war against Al Qaeda begins.

November 13, 2001: Afghanistan. The capital, Kabul, falls. Most of the Taliban leaders flee.

November 21, 2001: The White House. At the end of a National Security Council meeting, President Bush secretly directs Rumsfeld to prepare for war on Iraq.

November 27, 2001: Florida. Rumsfeld flies to see General Franks at CENTCOM headquarters in Tampa and tells him to update the Top Secret Operation Plan on attacking and invading Iraq.

December 4, 2001: The Pentagon. Franks presents a slightly revised plan on invading Iraq. Estimated force level is reduced from 500,000 to 400,000. Rumsfeld thinks fewer forces will be needed in light of the Afghanistan success. Franks agrees.

December 12, 2001: The Pentagon. Franks returns with updated plan. Rumsfeld tells him he has to look at a plan that he could do "as early as April or May."

December 20, 2001: New York. *New York Times* reporter Judith Miller has front-page interview with Iraqi defector Adnan Ishan Saeed al-Haidere, who says he has recently been working in Baghdad in secret facilities for biological, chemical, and nuclear weapons. Miller secures the interview through Ahmed Chalabi's Iraqi National Congress, which has close contacts with Donald Rumsfeld, Richard Perle, and Douglas Feith. Miller will later say that it is Chalabi who provided most of the front-page exclusives on WMD to *The New York Times.*

December 28, 2001: The White House. Franks tells Bush that, with support from other Muslim countries, Iraq could be invaded with an initial 105,000 U.S. forces, but 230,000 eventually would be needed.

January 2002: The White House. Bush's top speechwriter, Michael Gerson, gives instructions to David Frum, a Canadian, to write a speech making the best case for war in Iraq.

January 29, 2002: Washington, D.C. Bush gives State of the Union address; he calls North Korea, Iran, and Iraq an axis of evil and pledges not to wait while dangers gather.

February 1, 2002: The Pentagon. Franks tells Rumsfeld a unilateral U.S.-only invasion of Iraq could be readied in 45 days with an initial force of 105,000; ultimately, 300,000 would be needed to stabilize Iraq after it fell.

February 7, 2002: White House Situation Room. Rumsfeld introduces notion of "shock and awe," i.e., building up such a carrier force and bombing onslaught that it might, by itself, trigger regime change.

February 12, 2002: Washington, D.C. Powell tells the Senate Budget Committee there are no plans to go to war with Iran or North Korea, but U.S. is looking into ways of bringing about regime change in Iraq.

February 16, 2002: White House. The National Security Council ratifies Policy Directive on Iraq, committing the U.S. to examining ways of bringing about a CIA-backed coup and providing military support for Chalabi's Iraqi National Congress.

February 20, 2002: Iraq. CIA survey team secretly enters northern Iraq to prepare for deployment of CIA paramilitary teams.

February 28, 2002: Pentagon. Franks brings Rumsfeld a list of nearly 4,000 possible bombing targets in Iraq. Rumsfeld tells him to prioritize the list.

March 6, 2002: The White House. In preparation for his upcoming visit to the Middle East, Cheney is briefed by Franks, who tells him what the U.S. will need in its invasion of Iraq from other Arab and Muslim countries. When he does go to the Middle East, the vice president is surprised to learn that Israel's occupation of the

West Bank and Gaza is seen by Arab leaders as a greater threat to the region than Saddam Hussein.

March 9, 2002: Washington, D.C. CIA tells the White House that reports that Niger was supplying Iraq with uranium were investigated by Ambassador Joseph Wilson and were found not to be credible.

March 14, 2002: The White House. The Joint Chiefs of Staff report that an invasion of Iraq "would place severe strains on personnel and cause deep shortages of certain critical weapons."

April 20, 2002: Camp David. Bush tell Franks he wants the invasion of Iraq done "right and quickly."

April 24, 2002: Doha, Qatar. Franks tells his major commanders to do whatever it takes to prepare for an invasion, no matter the costs.

May 11, 2002: Camp David. Franks presents a five-front war plan to Bush.

June 19, 2002: The White House. Franks tells Bush he could do the invasion within 30 days with a little over 100,000 ground assault troops.

Late August 2002: The Pentagon. Office of Special Plans is set up at the Pentagon to plan for the war and its aftermath. Picked to head the OSP is longtime protégé of Richard Perle, Abram Shulsky. As part of its mission, the OSP forges close ties to a parallel intelligence unit within Ariel Sharon's office in Israel, whose job is to provide key Bush administration people with cooked intelligence on Saddam's Iraq. One Pentagon official, Air Force Lt. Col. Karen Kwiatkowski, later relates how she had escorted six or seven Israeli generals to Feith's OSP office. The generals surged ahead of her, waved aside the required sign-in book, and entered the OSP office; seeing Feith's office door closed, the generals demanded to know from his secretary who Feith was talking to.

September 7, 2002: The White House. Bush tells reporters that an International Atomic Energy Agency report estimates that the Iraqis are six months away from developing a nuclear weapon. The new report, however, turns out to be an old IAEA document from 1996 that described a weapons program that the inspectors had long ago destroyed.

September 12, 2002: New York. Bush addresses U.N. General Assembly, saying the U.S. will work with the U.N. Security Council for the necessary resolutions to go to war with Iraq.

September 16, 2002: New York. U.N. Secretary General Kofi Annan says he has received a letter from Iraqi authorities allowing inspectors access "without conditions." Bush administration is livid because it did not say "unfettered access," meaning "anytime, anyplace."

September 19, 2002: Washington, D.C. Rumsfeld, speaking before the Senate Armed Services Committee, says current U.N. inspection team is weak. At the White House, Bush says if U.N. Security Council won't deal with Iraq, "the U.S. and some of our friends will." Bush also meets with 11 House members, telling them the biggest threat is that Saddam, with his WMD, "can blow up Israel, and that would trigger an international incident."

October 1, 2002: Langley, Virginia. CIA prepares secret National Intelligence Estimate on the case for war with Iraq. NIE claims Saddam has chemical and biological weapons, including mobile labs, and that it is building nuclear weapons. Bush wants condensed version for the public in the form of a White Paper. The White Paper, however, distorts the facts to make the strongest possible case for war. (For specific examples of distortion, see *Vanity Fair,* May 2004, "The Path to War," Eugenia Peretz, David Rose, and David Wise, pp. 230–294.)

November 8, 2002: New York. U.N. Security Council passes Resolution 1441, which gives Iraq a "final opportunity" to come clean on its WMD, adding that the council would meet again, following the inspectors' report, to "consider the situation." The French, who oppose war with Iraq, say off the record that they understand the resolution is enough to give America and Britain legal cover for going it alone, if they felt Iraq hadn't complied to their satisfaction.

December 7, 2002: Baghdad. Iraqi government delivers a 12,000-page document in Arabic to UNMOVIC. It is intended to account for the state of its weapons programs. The U.S. takes possession of it, has it translated, submits it to the Security Council with large portions deleted, then dismisses it as a "material breach" of Resolution 1441.

January 13, 2003: The White House. The French call for a meeting that is held in Rice's office. Attending are Chirac's top adviser,

Maurice Gourdault-Montagne, and the French ambassador to the U.S., Jean-David Levitte. Both explain their country's reasons for opposing the war, then Levitte says that if the U.S. was determined to go to war, it should not seek a second U.N. resolution, that 1441 arguably gave the White House enough cover, and that France would keep quiet if the U.S. went ahead. White House dismisses the offer because it has promised Tony Blair it would seek a second resolution. The French are angry. On the same day, Bush tells Powell in the Oval Office, "I'm really going to do this." Powell asks if he understands the Pottery Barn principle: if he breaks Iraq, he'll own it. Bush says he understands.

January 20, 2003: New York. French foreign minister Dominique de Villepin announces that France will not support military intervention in Iraq. The White House is irate.

January 21, 2003: The White House. Franks delivers final war plan to Bush. He estimates fewer than 1,000 U.S. killed. No public pictures of returning coffins and no body count of Iraqis killed will be permitted, as both practices created bad PR during the Vietnam War.

January 25, 2003: White House. Lewis Libby makes presentation on Saddam's WMD and ties him to bin Laden. Much of the material comes from Feith's Office of Special Plans. Richard Armitage, the second in authority at the State Department, sees it as drawing the worst conclusions from fragmentary threads; Wolfowitz finds it convincing. Bush aides Karen Hughes and Karl Rove think Powell should make the U.N. presentation. Powell agrees to do it.

January 27, 2003: New York. Hans Blix delivers his first inspections report to U.N. He acknowledges that no WMD have been found but notes that Iraq has failed to account for undetermined quantities of the nerve agent VX and anthrax, and for 6,500 chemical bombs.

January 28, 2003: Washington, D.C. Bush gives State of the Union address in which he claims: "The British Government has learned that Saddam Hussein recently sought significant quantities of uranium from Africa."

January 29, 2003: The State Department. Powell gives his chief of staff, Larry Wilkerson, a 48-page dossier that the White House wants Powell to use in his U.N. speech making the case for war with Iraq. The dossier is prepared in Cheney's office by a team led by Cheney's chief of staff, Lewis Libby, and his deputy assistant for national security affairs, John Hannah.

January 30, 2003: Langley, Virginia. Wilkerson, with several staff members and CIA analysts, sets up shop at CIA headquarters to prepare Powell's speech. Meanwhile, the White House supplies 45 more pages on Iraq's links to terrorism and human rights violations.

January 31, 2003: Langley, Virginia. Wilkerson throws out the White House dossier, suspecting much of it originated with the Iraqi National Congress and its chief, Ahmad Chalabi, whose information in the past often proved suspect or fabricated. Powell is convinced that much of the material had been funneled to Cheney by the separate OSP unit set up by Rumsfeld. "We were so appalled at what had arrived from the White House," says one staff member.

February 5, 2003: New York. At 2 a.m. on the day of his U.N. speech, Powell receives a call from the CIA's George Tenet, who says he wants another look at the speech. Tenet is afraid Powell has cut too much about Saddam's supposed links to terrorism, especially the 9/11 attack. For days the White House and Cheney have pressed Powell to include a widely discredited Czech intelligence report that Mohamed Atta, the 9/11 ringleader, had met in Prague with an Iraqi intelligence officer. Powell had thrown out the Prague material as suspect and unverified. But Powell does keep much of what the White House wants, including mobile biological weapons labs, ties to Al Qaeda, and anthrax stockpiles. One of the sources for the mobile labs is an Iraqi major known to the CIA to be a liar. That morning at the U.N., Powell insists that Tenet sit behind him as a signal that he is relying on the CIA to make the case for war.

February 8, 2003: The White House. President Bush, in his weekly radio address, says: "Saddam Hussein has longstanding, direct and continuing ties to terrorist networks. Senior members of Iraqi intelligence and Al Qaeda have met at least eight times since the early 1990s. Iraq has sent bomb-making and document-forgery experts to work with Al Qaeda. Iraq has also provided Al Qaeda with chemical and biological weapons training. And an Al Qaeda operative was sent to Iraq several times in the late 1990s for help in acquiring poisons and gases. We also know that Iraq is harboring a terrorist network headed by a senior Al Qaeda terrorist planner. This network runs a poison and explosive training camp in northeast Iraq, and many of its leaders are known to be in Baghdad."

February 14, 2003: New York. Hans Blix goes before the U.N. Security Council. He contradicts Powell, saying the trucks Powell had described as being used for chemical decontamination could just as easily have been used for routine activity, and he contradicts Powell's statement that the Iraqis knew in advance when the inspectors would be arriving. And he adds that Iraq is finally taking steps toward real cooperation with the inspectors, allowing them to enter Iraqi presidential palaces, among other previously prohibited sites. Disarmament through inspections is still possible, he concludes.

February 15, 2003: Worldwide. Tens of millions participate in an unprecedented, antiwar demonstration. The biggest crowds are in the countries that support the war: Britain, Italy, and Spain.

February 24, 2003: New York. Claiming Iraq has failed to take the final opportunity afforded it in Resolution 1441, the U.S., Britain, and Spain propose the second resolution Tony Blair has been seeking.

February 27, 2003: The White House. Holocaust survivor and author Elie Wiesel visits Bush and tells him Iraq is a terrorist state that should be invaded as a matter of morality, otherwise Saddam will unleash a weapon of mass destruction on Israel. Bush later remarks, "If Elie Wiesel feels that way, I am not alone."

March 1, 2003: Turkey. The Turkish government rejects U.S. request to move troops through its country.

March 3, 2003: The White House. Pope John Paul II's envoy, Cardinal Pio Laghi, visits Bush and tells him war with Iraq would be unjust and illegal because it would cause so many civilian casualties, create a wider gap between the Christian and Muslim worlds, and overall would not make things better. Bush replies it would absolutely make things better.

March 7, 2003: France. The French announce they will veto a second resolution to authorize the automatic use of force. The U.S. begins lobbying the six undecided members of the Security Council:

Pakistan, Chile, Mexico, Cameroon, Guinea, and Angola, having first wiretapped their offices. Chile and Mexico say they will not support a second resolution.

March 10, 2003: France. French president Chirac goes on TV and announces, "My position is that, regardless of the circumstances, France will vote 'no.'" U.S. and Britain blame France for the diplomatic breakdown, and use it as the reason for not seeking the second resolution.

March 14, 2003: The White House. As a concession to Blair, Bush announces agreement on a road map for resolving the Palestinian-Israeli conflict.

March 16, 2003: The Azores. Bush, Blair, and Spanish prime minister Aznar meet. Bush says they need to start the war soon because antiwar sentiment will only get worse if they delay. He says he is going to give Saddam a 48-hour ultimatum to leave Iraq.

March 17, 2003: The White House. Bush reneges on his commitment to seek U.N. approval, claiming 1441 provides ample authorization. In a TV announcement he gives Saddam the 48-hour ultimatum. Prior to the announcement he calls Australian prime minister Howard and Israeli prime minister Sharon to tell them of his decision. Meanwhile, Cheney tells congressional leaders of the decision, noting that Israel will not be part of the coalition, "but we are working closely with them on their reaction."

March 18: 2003: London. Blair wins a Commons vote for war, barely carrying his own party.

March 19, 2003: The White House. Bush gives Franks order to execute Operation Iraqi Freedom. Around 4 p.m., CIA information is received that Saddam and his two sons are or will be in a bunker in Baghdad. Cheney advises Bush to strike at the target, effectively beginning the war. Bush agrees. At 7:30 p.m., Rice phones Israeli finance minister Benjamin Netanyahu, telling him the war had begun; he says he knows. Rice then summons Saudi ambassador Prince Bandar to come to the White House. Around 8:30 p.m. she tells him that, within a half-hour, all hell will break loose. At 10:10 p.m., Bush informs the nation the war has started.

April 7, 2003: Washington. Rumsfeld appoints Gen. Jay Garner to direct Pentagon's new Office of Reconstruction and Humanitarian Assistance for Iraq. Garner, a JINSA (Jewish Institute for National Security Affairs) advisor, says the first person he will invite to work with him is former Israeli defense minister Benjamin Ben-Eliezer.

May 2, 2003: The USS *Lincoln*. President Bush tells nation, "In the battle of Iraq, the United States and our allies have prevailed."

May 6, 2003: Washington. L. Paul Bremer III is appointed administrator of Iraq, replacing Jay Garner.

June 5, 2003: Washington, D.C. *The Washington Post* reports that VP Cheney and his aide Lewis Libby paid multiple visits to the CIA in the months leading up to the Iraq war. Later, former CIA counterterrorism chief Vince Cannistraro will tell a congressional hearing that prior to the war, the White House exerted unprecedented pressure on the CIA and other intelligence agencies to come up with evidence linking Iraq to bin Laden and Al Qaeda.

June 8, 2003: Washington, D.C. David Kay, former chief weapons inspector for the U.N., is asked to take over the search for WMD in Iraq.

July 6, 2003: New York. Former U.S. ambassador Joseph Wilson IV writes column in *The New York Times* saying he was sent on a fact-finding mission to Niger by the CIA and that, well before the president's State of the Union Address, he reported his finding that no uranium had been shipped to Iraq.

August 27, 2003: Washington, D.C. Newly available documents reveal that Halliburton, the company VP Cheney formerly headed, wins contracts for more than $1.7 billion out of Operation Iraqi Freedom and stands to receive hundreds of millions more under a no-bid contract awarded by the U.S. Army Corps of Engineers.

September 17, 2003: The White House. President Bush tells a reporter, "No, we've had no evidence that Saddam Hussein was involved with September 11."

October 2, 2003: Washington, D.C. Kay delivers interim report to Congress saying, "We have not yet found stocks of weapons."

December 13, 2003: Iraq. Saddam Hussein is captured.

January 23, 2004: David Kay resigns.

January 28, 2004: Washington. Regarding the existence of WMD in Iraq, Kay tells Senate Armed Services Committee, "We were almost all wrong." His testimony forces White House to name a presidential commission to investigate the prewar intelligence on Iraq.

February 5, 2004: Washington, D.C. Tenet admits in a speech at Georgetown University that as far back as May 2002 the Defense Information Agency had issued a "fabrication notification" to steer clear of the Iraqi major who had attested to the mobile biological labs mentioned in Powell's U.N. speech. Somehow the CIA never saw it.

February 24, 2004: Washington, D.C. CIA director Tenet tells the Senate Select Committee that, despite our invasion of Afghanistan and occupation of Iraq, the worldwide threat from bin Laden and Al Qaeda has grown, not diminished.

March 11, 2004: Madrid. Train bombs kill 200 people. Search leads to a widening web of organizations that may have few ties to Al Qaeda but share its goals.

March 14, 2004: Madrid. Conservative prime minister José Aznar is defeated by Socialist challenger José Luís Rodríguez Zapatero, who ran on a pledge to withdraw Spanish troops from Iraq unless they were placed under U.N. sanction. The new prime minister calls the Iraq war an error, saying: "It divided more than it united, there were no reasons for it, time has shown that the arguments for it lacked credibility, and the occupation has been poorly managed."

April 18, 2004: Madrid. Spain withdraws all its troops from the Coalition of the Willing.

April 19, 2004: Nicaragua. President Maduro says Nicaragua will withdraw its forces from Iraq.

April 28, 2004: CBS's 60 *Minutes II* shows U.S. troops mistreating Iraqi detainees at the Abu Ghraib prison in violation of the Fourth Geneva Convention.

April 29, 2004: Santo Domingo. The Dominican Republic withdraws its troops from Iraq, citing security concerns. Wolfowitz tells a congressional hearing that Iraq is still a combat zone, "and until it becomes peacekeeping, a lot of countries are probably going to stay on the sidelines."

May 20, 2004: Baghdad. Iraqi police and U.S. military raid home of Iraqi National Council finance minister Ahmad Chalabi as part of an investigation into suspected fraud. CIA also charges him with informing Iran that the U.S. had cracked its secret codes and was eavesdropping on its intelligence messages. The Pentagon stops monthly payments of $340,000 to Chalabi's Iraqi National Congress.

May 26, 2004: New York. *The New York Times* acknowledges that its reporters, among them Judith Miller, used questionable sources in affirming the existence of WMD in Iraq, and that Ahmad Chalabi, the INC leader, was feeding bad information to journalists and the White House, information the White House eagerly received.

May 29, 2004: Baghdad. Iyad Alawi, a longtime CIA operative, is chosen interim prime minister of Iraq.

June 4, 2004: Langley, Virginia. CIA Director George Tenet resigns.

June 16, 2004: Washington, D.C. The 9/11 Commission investigating the September 11 attacks reports that there did not appear to be a collaborative relationship between Al Qaeda and Saddam Hussein.

June 22, 2004: Washington, D.C. Wolfowitz tells a House Armed Services Committee that the Pentagon had underestimated Iraq's postwar insurgency and that the U.S. may have to keep a significant number of troops in Iraq for years to come.

July 5, 2004: Former U.S. Army general Janis Karpinski, who had been in charge of the Abu Ghraib prison when Iraqi detainees were abused and humiliated, tells BBC radio that she knew of at least one Israeli involved in the prisoner interrogation.

July 9, 2004: Washington, D.C. The Senate Select Committee on Intelligence concludes in its report that the most pivotal assessments used to justify the war against Iraq were unfounded and unreasonable. Senator Jay Rockefeller, vice chairman of the committee, concludes: "We in Congress would not have authorized that war—we would NOT have authorized that war—with 75 votes if we knew what we know now." The second part of the report on whether the White House and Pentagon tried to influence intelligence agencies is postponed until after the November election.

July 12, 2004: The Philippines. President Arroyo announces that her country will withdraw from the Coalition of the Willing in order to save the life of a Filipino hostage held by Iraqi insurgents.

August 1, 2004: Number of U.S. killed in the Iraq war reaches 910. The media is barred from showing their returning coffins. Number of Iraqi civilians killed is not available from official U.S. sources; independent sources estimate the number to be between 11,305 and 13,315. (For updates on Iraqis killed and wounded, see www.iraqbodycount.org.)

Update by the editors

December 12, 2005: Washington, D.C. In a major policy speech, President Bush says that "Israel's long-term survival depends upon the spread of democracy in the Middle East."

March 16, 2006: Washington, D.C. General John Abizaid, Commander of U.S. Central Command, tells the Senate Armed Services Committee that "Iraq remains a long way from civil war."

April 23, 2006: Former highest-ranking CIA officer in Europe, Tyler Drumheller, tells *60 Minutes* that he had warned the White House that the sole human source for information on Saddam's mobile biological weapons labs, an Iraqi emigré called Curveball, was mentally unstable and a known liar. In the same interview, the CIA officer says the White House ignored credible intelligence from a highly placed Iraqi, identified as Iraq's foreign minister, Naji Sabri, who said there were no WMDs and no active weapons program in Iraq prior to the U.S. invasion.

May 1, 2006: *Sunday Times of London* publishes the Downing Street memo, the transcribed minutes of a July 23, 2002, meeting of British prime minister Tony Blair with his senior advisors. In it, Sir Richard Dearlove, head of British Secret Intelligence Service, says that Bush wants to remove Saddam through military action and justify it on the basis of terrorism and WMD. "But," Dearlove concludes, "the intelligence and facts were being fixed around the policy," and "there was little discussion in Washington of the aftermath of military action."

July 28, 2006: Iraq. A federal audit finds that the U.S. State Department agency in charge of $1.4 billion in reconstruction money used an accounting shell game to hide ballooning cost overruns and schedule delays from Congress. Bechtel is cited as one contractor whose project to build a hospital in Basra had a hidden overrun of nearly 100 percent and an unreported schedule delay of 273 days.

August 3, 2006: Washington, D.C. General Abizaid tells the Senate Armed Services Committee that the sectarian violence is as bad as he's seen it in Baghdad and that "it is possible that Iraq could move toward civil war."

September 14, 2006: U.S. military killed in the Iraq war reaches 2,677; U.S. military wounded is estimated at 19,910. Number of Iraqi civilians killed is estimated between 41,931 and 46,613.

September 23, 2006: Washington, D.C. Report surfaces that 16 intelligence agencies inside the U.S. government conclude in a National Intelligence Estimate that the Iraq war has made the overall threat of terrorism worse, not better, since 9/11.

Projected Palestinian State under the "Road Map" 2006

Epilogue

By Robert Norberg

Apologizing for the brevity of a book in excess of 400 pages may strike the reader as odd, but apologize we must. The Editors were constrained by considerations of expense, not to mention portability, to select only a few dozen of the 197 *Links* published since AMEU's founding in 1967. When we circulated early drafts of *Burning Issues,* some readers familiar with AMEU's complete archive called our attention to the absence in this anthology of their favorite issues and authors. Indeed, this anthology would be incomplete without the mention of the following writers and their contributions:

The Rev. Humphrey Walz was pastor of a Presbyterian church in New York City during World War II. His work on behalf of refugees from Nazism, Communism and Palestine was widely recognized, and he was granted the British Government's George VI medal for "service in the cause of freedom." From 1948 until his death in 2003—more than 55 years—Walz never lost faith that Americans, once they understood the plight of the Palestinians, would bring justice to bear. He co-founded AMEU in 1967, edited *The Link* for its first two years, and drew on his personal bank account on more than one occasion to keep AMEU from having to close its doors.

Walz's approach to the controversial United Nations Resolution equating Zionism and racism was typical of his expository writing. "Zionism? Racism? What Do You Mean?" appeared in print in little over a month after the controversial 1975 resolution was approved by the General Assembly. (The resolution was revoked 16 years later after intense U.S. lobbying during the presidency of George H. W. Bush. Although marketed as encouraging Middle East peace, ostensibly to reward Israel for participating in the 1991 Madrid Peace Conference, Bush was anxious to restore his political standing with Jewish leaders angered by his threat to veto $10 billion in loan guarantees to pressure Israel to stop expanding settlements.) In an easy read that nonetheless is fully sourced, Walz covers alternative definitions of the key terms, *Zionism* and *racism*; leads the reader through political Zionism's origins; laces the narrative with quotes from Zionist luminaries from Herzl to Meir; and describes Israel's strange-bedfellow alliance with millenialist Christians. A resident of Janesville, WI, since 1988, Rev. Walz died there in 2003 at the age of 92.[1]

James Abourezk, born in South Dakota and of Lebanese descent, was the first Arab-American to serve in the U.S. Senate (1973–79). Abourezk, who chose not to run for a second term, would no doubt agree with *Wikipedia*, the online encyclopedia, which termed him a "maverick who questioned the political status quo." Abourezk's enduring legacy is the American-Arab Anti-Discrimination Committee (ADC), which he founded in 1980 to intercede for Arab-Americans in incidents of discrimination and civil rights violations. One of the most referenced *Link* issues is "A Brief History of the Middle East Conflict," written by Sen. Abourezk in 1974 and revised for the AMEU web site in 2002. Sen. Abourezk is chairman of the board of ADC and practices law in Sioux Falls, SD.[2]

Francis Boyle's *Link* is critical to understanding that the one constant underlying Israel's peace negotiations from 1992 forward has been the Bantustan arrangement—a fragmented Palestine entity, with virtually no control over its borders. Arafat couldn't be hustled into that at Camp David, and Israel—to a continuing drumbeat of media praise for courage in "giving up" land and settlements— embarked on the Wall and a unilateral disengagement that will enshrine the Bantustan plan. Dr. Boyle, a scholar in the areas of international law and human rights, is currently a professor of law at the University of Illinois, Urbana-Champaign.[3]

Norman Finkelstein. In March 2006, before a large crowd at Columbia University, Professor Norman Finkelstein delivered a talk in which he accused Israel of state terrorism, criticized Columbia's president for not supporting his faculty's proposal calling for the university to divest from firms dealing with the Israeli military, and alleged that Harvard Law professor Alan Dershowitz had plagiarized large portions of his 2006 book *A Case for Israel* from Joan Peters's 1984 title *From Time Immemorial.* Familiar subjects to readers of *The Link.*

Finkelstein first appeared in our January-March 1985 issue in which he challenged the Peters contention that there were no Palestinians in Palestine prior to the Zionist colonization. He next appeared in our December 1992 issue, where he traced the roots of political Zionism back to the ethnic nationalism of German Romanticism. Both above issues were based on his thesis on Zionism written for his doctoral degree from Princeton University. In our December 1999 *Link,* Norman compared Israel's treatment of the Palestinians to America's treatment of native Americans, particularly the Cherokee nation. And in our "Reflections on September 11, 2001" issue, he wrote that the easy explanation to the 9/11 tragedy is to blame it on these "crazed-lunatic-fanatic-fundamentalist-Middle-Eastern-Arabs-Islamic-whatever." The tougher answer, he went on, "is to recognize the humanity in these people, to acknowledge their suffering and degradation—and toughest of all—to take a hard look at ourselves and the responsibility we bear for their torment."

Dr. Finkelstein now teaches at DePaul University in Chicago. Prior to that he had taught for 10 years at City University of New York's Hunter College. In 2001, he was forced out by an administration that, he believes, was under pressure to drop him. What sustains him, he says, are the words of his mother, a survivor of the Maijdanek concentration camp and two slave-labor camps; she told him to make sure that Jews don't do to others what was done to them. Faced with the sufferings of African-Americans, Vietnamese and Palestinians, she said, "We are all holocaust victims."[4]

Muhammad Hallaj. Americans with only a passing interest in the Middle East hold opinions largely shaped by well-promoted myths and propaganda regarding Israel's creation, accepting as fact the fictional *Exodus* account of Jews whose only desire was to flee persecution and live in peace if only the Palestinians would accept them. Dr. Hallaj, more than any other single writer for *The Link* has meticulously researched the Zionist archives to demonstrate that whatever might have to be said otherwise to the Arabs and the world at large, the Zionist project was colonialist and expansionist in nature and would require force of arms and violence to persuade Palestinians to leave or to acquiesce as a largely voiceless minority.

In four major *Link* articles from 1982 to 1988, Dr. Hallaj wrote on Israel's cultural suppression of the Palestinians, the Israeli thesis that "Jordan is Palestine," on the falsification of Palestinian history epitomized by Joan Peters's *From Time Immemorial*, and on Zionist violence against Palestinians.

After a 25-year career as a professor, college administrator, researcher and author, Dr. Hallaj is now retired and living in Fairfax, VA.[5]

Ilan Pappe. The "new" Israeli historians largely accept the Palestinian narrative of how they were targeted by Zionists for dispossession, that the victory of Israel over Arab forces in 1948 was a foregone conclusion, and that hundreds of Arab villages were ethnically cleansed and deliberately destroyed to make return impossible. Since his 1998 *Link* issue, Dr. Pappe has spoken widely outside Israel, called for economic and academic boycotts of Israel, recommended that an international force be deployed to protect Palestinians living under occupation, and advocated a "multinational democratic state" in lieu of the two-state solution.[6]

Cheryl Rubenberg. The power of the "Israeli Lobby," widely acknowledged but seldom explored in the mainstream media, was thrust into public debate in 2006 when two distinguished academicians—John J. Mearsheimer, University of Chicago, and Stephen M. Walt, Harvard University—contended that the U.S. subordinated its own national interests, including security, with

Middle East policies responsive almost entirely to the Israeli Lobby and domestic politics. The media, led by *The New York Times*, *The Washington Post*, and *U.S. News and World Report*, eventually were drawn into addressing the issue and, as the authors had anticipated, the charge of anti-semitism, or aiding and abetting anti-semitism, was laid at their feet by some commentators.

While many *Link* authors over the years have decried the lobby's stranglehold on Middle East policy, only one—Cheryl Rubenberg—has devoted a full *Link* to the subject. She joins such rare voices as James Forrestal, William Fulbright, Paul Findley, and most recently professors Mearsheimer and Walt, who have sought to make the critical distinction between American and Israeli national interests. In 1982, when Israel brutally punished all of Lebanon for the PLO presence in its midst— causing more than 20,000 deaths, presiding over the Sabra and Shatila massacres, and driving 700,000 from their homes—even staunchly pro-Israel senator Alan Cranston issued a stinging public rebuke in a letter to then Prime Minister Begin. Years later, in the summer of 2006, as the world community outside of the U.S. and Israel, recoiled at the death and destruction visited on all Lebanese for the actions of Hezbollah, there was not a single Cranston-like response, only a rush to sign on to an AIPAC-authored resolution of total support for Israel.

Dr. Rubenberg taught political science for 20 years at Florida International University. She recently published *Palestinians in Search of a Just Peace* (Lynne Rienner, 2003) and is currently editor of *The Encyclopedia of the Israeli-Palestinian Conflict* (forthcoming 2007, Lynne Rienner).[7]

Jack Shaheen. While AMEU claims only serendipity, not cause and effect, a number of writers whose early efforts were published in *The Link* later expanded their articles to full-length books—and subsequently gained a measure of renown in their chosen fields of expertise. Jack Shaheen's 1980 *Link* "The Arab Stereotype on Television" became the basis for his book *The TV Arab* and today Shaheen is recognized as the foremost authority on Arab stereotyping. While Shaheen might have been content to merely document transgressions (as he has done most recently in his book *Reel Bad Arabs*, which looks at slurs, stereotypes and anti-Arab propaganda in more than 900 films), he has distinguished himself by pressing executives in the media and entertainment industries to effect change, using a style of congenial but persistent persuasion that has come to be his trademark. CBS News and Warner Brothers have solicited his input, and *Nightline*, *The Today Show*, and *Good Morning America* have interviewed him.

Before leaving academia in 1998, Dr. Shaheen taught journalism at Southern Illinois University, Edwardsville. He now resides in Hilton Head, SC, where he remains active as an author and media consultant.[8]

* * *

The name of AMEU's principal publication, *The Link*, was chosen to highlight what its founders specified as a principal objective of the organization: to call attention to the programs, activities, and educational materials of other groups with similar interests and objectives. The early format of *The Link* was designed to that end—a number of brief items calling attention to books, rallies, speeches, relief efforts, peace initiatives, cultural events and other activities centered on the Middle East.

In closing, we refer our readers to Appendix II, which lists more than 40 organizations currently in operation to inform, educate, and advocate, and to provide relief, human rights protections and legal representation.

In particular, the Editors call attention to the Israeli organizations that take the same risks—both in physical danger and social ostracism—that faced American activists of the 1950s and 60s who chose confrontation over comfort in solidarity with Blacks oppressed by segregation, discrimination and unanswerable violence. Five thousand Israelis came into the streets to protest their government's July 2006 indiscriminate attacks in Lebanon, while officials of America's legislative and executive branches marched in lockstep with Israel. Israeli mothers are sentinels at Israeli checkpoints and intervene against gratuitous insult and humiliation. Israeli soldiers decline to play a further role in occupation. Rabbis rise to the defense of suppressed Palestinians. Protesters anticipate gas and batons in standing in solidarity with Palestinians whose homes face demolition. While many Israelis, including Amira Hass and Gideon Levy of *Haaretz* newspaper, aggressively question the rationale and Draconian tactics of occupation, few Americans are aware that Israeli discourse has a range that the American mainstream media has yet to embrace.

Appendix I: *The Link* Catalogue

AMEU carries the entire archive of past Link *issues on its web site (www.ameu.org). Since the inaugural* Link *in 1968, 197 issues have been published through July 2006. The archive will continue to be expanded with the addition of each new* Link *as it is published. From time to time AMEU has covered special subjects in its Public Affairs Series. Papers from this series that are available on the web site are listed as a concluding part of the Catalogue.*

1968, Volume 1
Issue 1: How The Link Was Born and Can Grow, Humphrey Walz
This, the first issue of *The Link*, sets forth its goals and programs.
Issue 2: U.N. Struggles for Mideast Peace, Humphrey Walz, ed.
U.S. Secretary of State Dean Rusk demands prompt action on U.N. Resolution of November 22, 1967 calling for withdrawal of Israeli troops from recently occupied territories, and justice for the refugees.

1969, Volume 2
Issue 1: Black Bids New Administration Face Facts, Humphrey Walz, ed.
Features excerpts from speech by past president of the World Bank, Eugene R. Black.
Issue 2: Mosque to Add Minaret to NYC Skyline, Humphrey Walz, ed.
Announcement of new mosque in Manhattan.
Issue 3: Church Statement Stresses Mideast Needs, Humphrey Walz, ed.
Summary of "Policy Statement on the Middle East" submitted to the General Board of the National Council of Churches at its meeting in New York City.
Issue 4: End UNRWA Deficit for Refugee Aid, Humphrey Walz, ed.
Analysis of report by UNRWA Commissioner-General Laurence Michelmore.
Issue 5: Churches Plan for Refugees and Peace, Humphrey Walz, ed.
Report on World Council of Churches upcoming consultation between Christians and followers of other faiths next March in Beirut.

1970, Volume 3
Issue 1: Responses to Palestine Information Proposal, Humphrey Walz, ed.
Report on World Council of Churches determination to raise over $1million for Palestinians. Lectures by Simha Flapan, Elmer Berger, John Davis and Ruth Knowles.
Issue 2: *Sequel* Offered Free to Refugee Agencies, Humphrey Walz, ed.
A review of upcoming conferences, U.N. reports, recent books, and church editorials.
Issue 3: Mayhew Reports on Arab-Israeli Facts, Christopher Mayhew
Text of lecture by British Member of Parliament Christopher Mayhew given during his U.S. tour.

Issue 4: Council of Churches Acts on Middle East Crisis, Humphrey Walz
Includes statements by Metropolitan Philip Saliba and Raymond Wilson of the American Friends.
Issue 5: Is the Modern State, Israel, A Fulfillment of Prophecy?, Bradley Watkins
Frequently we confront the contention that the land belongs to the Jews "because God promised it to them." The author sets forth his refutation of this claim.

1971, Volume 4
Issue 1: At Stake in UNRWA's 1971 Budget, Humphrey Walz, ed.
UNWRA's financial squeeze.
Issue 2: Arab-Israeli Encounter in Jaffa, Humphrey Walz, ed.
Palestinian refugee visits his family home in Jaffa that is now occupied by a Jewish family from Beirut.
Issue 3: Why Visit the Middle East?, Humphrey Walz, ed.
Suggested pilgrimage to the Holy Land.
Issue 4: Invitation to the Holy Land, Humphrey Walz, ed.
A sequel to issue 3.
Issue 5: Peace and the Holy City, Humphrey Walz
Religious factors affecting problems and hopes of Jerusalem.
Issue 6: Computer Age Answers to M. E. Problems, Humphrey Walz, ed.
A look at ways computer-age techniques can speed the solving of problems even as complex as those in the Holy Land.

1972, Volume 5
Issue 1: Religion Used to Promote Hatred in Israel, Humphrey Walz, ed.
Summary of article by B. Shefi: "Israel: The Jewish Religion Abused."
Issue 2: A Look at Gaza, Humphrey Walz, ed.
Includes reports on Gaza from American Near East Refugee Aid (ANERA) and United Nations Relief and Works Agency (UNWRA).
Issue 3: Foreign Policy Report: Nixon Gives Massive Aid But Reaps No Political Harvest, Andrew Glass
Examines U.S. policy towards the Middle East: how it is determined and what forces influence it.
Issue 4: Some Thoughts on Jerusalem, Joseph Ryan
Archbishop Ryan speaks on: The gravity of the present situation, the expansion of Zionism, the Vatican's position.
Issue 5: Toward a More Open Middle East Debate, Humphrey Walz, ed.
Includes profiles of various sources of information on the Palestinian-Israeli conflict.

1973, Volume 6
Issue 1: The Arab Market: Opportunities for U.S. Business, Humphrey Walz, ed.
Examines present supply and demand for energy fuels; the challenge and opportunity for Arab economic development; and what this means for U.S. businesses.

Issue 2: <u>A Prophet Speaks in Israel</u>, Norton Mezvinski
Profile of Dr. Israel Shahak, founder of the Israeli League for Human and Civil Rights.

Issue 3: <u>US Middle East Involvement</u>, John Richardson
A survey of U.S. voluntary organizations involved in relief and rehabilitation for Palestinian refugees and other needy individuals in the Middle East.

Issue 4: <u>American Jewry and the Zionist Jewish State Concept</u>, Norton Mezvinski
Author traces American Jewry's support for the Zionist Jewish State since 1948.

Issue 5: <u>Christians in the Arab East</u>, Humphrey Walz
In 1973, it was estimated that there were some 9 million Christians in the "Arab East." Author Humphrey Walz noted: "To many Christians in the West . . . it's downright startling that [there is] so much as a single co-religionist left in the lands that cradled their faith and exported it to the world . . . "

1974, Volume 7

Issue 1: <u>Arab Oil and the Zionist Connection</u>, Jack Forsyth
Analyzes how and why the Rogers Plan for peace in the Middle East failed, and why the Mobil Oil Company ad in *The New York Times* titled "The U.S. Stake in Middle East Peace" backfired.

Issue 2: <u>History of the Middle East Conflict</u>, Sen. James Abourezk
One of the most frequent requests that AMEU receives is for a "brief history of the Middle East Conflict." This article by Senator James Abourezk answers this need.

Issue 3: <u>Holy Father Speaks on Palestine</u>, Pope Paul VI
The official text of Pope Paul's apostolic exhortation "concerning the increased needs of the Church in the Holy Land."

Issue 4: <u>The Palestinians Speak. Listen!</u>, Frank Epp and John Goddard
Interviews with 28 Palestinians.

Issue 5: <u>The Arab-Israeli Arms Race</u>, Fuad Jabber
Author traces the arms race between Israel and its neighbors and warns that, if diplomacy proves sterile, the race will presage an increase in both the tempo and the scale of armed violence.

1975, Volume 8

Issue 1: <u>Crisis in Lebanon</u>, Jack Forsyth
Author documents Israel's increasing military intervention inside Lebanon and concludes that Lebanon has quietly turned the corner towards full involvement in the Arab-Israeli conflict. Issue contains a chronology of the victims of Israeli attacks on Lebanon from 1968-1975.

Issue 2: <u>The West Bank and Gaza</u>, John Richardson
John Richardson, President of American Near East Refugee Aid (ANERA), focuses on the Palestinian territories occupied by Israel since 1967.

Issue 3: <u>Saudi Arabia</u>, Ray Cleveland
In the wake of the recent murder of King Faisal, Prof. Ray Cleveland, author of "The

Middle East and South Asia," looks at the foreign policy of the kingdom under King Khalid.

Issue 4: Syria, Marcella Kerr, ed.

Includes: history of Syria; social data; Syrian economy; government; foreign policy; Syrian Jews; education; and the women's movement in Syria.

Issue 5: Zionism? Racism? What Do You Mean?, Humphrey Walz

Title article by L. Humphrey Walz. Other articles and their authors include: "The U.N., Zionism and Racism," by Donald Will; "The Racist Nature of Zionism and of the Zionistic State of Israel," by Prof. Israel Shahak; "A Letter from an American Rabbi to an Arab Ambassador," by Rabbi Elmer Berger; and a review of Jakob J. Petuchowski's book, *Zion Reconsidered*, by Rabbi Berger.

1976, Volume 9

Issue 1: Islamic/Christian Dialogue, Patricia Morris, ed.

Summary of an international conference held in Tripoli in February 1976.

Issue 2: America's Stake in the Middle East, John Davis

A speech by AMEU director and former Commissioner General of UNRWA given at a Washington Islamic Center Symposium on February 5, 1976.

Issue 3: Egypt, Allan Klaum

A look at Egypt, its past, present and future.

Issue 4: New Leader for Troubled Lebanon, Minor Yanis

On September 23, 1976, Lebanon's sixth president was sworn in. This issue looks at Elias Sarkis and the decimated country he now heads.

Issue 5: Unity Out of Diversity: United Arab Emirates, John Sutton

A profile of the seven states that comprise the United Arab Emirates.

1977, Volume 10

Issue 1: Carter Administration. & the Middle East, Norton Mezvinski

A professor of history at Central Connecticut State College offers a scenario for changes in U.S. policy towards the Middle East that are anticipated in the incoming Carter Administration.

Issue 2: Literary Look at the Middle East, Djelloul Marbrook

A comprehensive look at the most current and relevant books and periodicals on the Middle East plus a brief look at films that are available.

Issue 3: Prophecy and Modern Israel, Calvin Keene

A critique of the Biblical arguments offered by Christians who believe that the reestablishment of Israel today is part of God's apocalyptic plan.

Issue 4: Concern Grows in U.S. Over Israeli Policies, Allan Brownfeld

Author describes the split in U.S. Administration over the proper handling of Israel's flouting of the U.S. on the settlements question.

Issue 5: War Plan Ready If Peace Effort Fails, Jim Hoagland

Author writes that Israel "is actively preparing to fight a war of annihilation against the Egyptian and Syrian armies if the Carter Administration's new Middle East peace effort fails."

1978, Volume 11
Issue 1: <u>The Palestinians</u>, John Sutton, ed.
Includes: "A People Scattered, Bewildered and Divided," by James Markham; "Looking at Reality," by Anthony Lewis; "Palestinians Cling to a Vision of a Homeland," by John Darnton, and "The P.L.O. Is Palestinians' Only Voice."
Issue 2: <u>The New Israeli Law: Will It Doom the Christian Mission in the Holy Land?</u>
Humphrey Walz
Presbyterian leader and AMEU director L. Humphrey Walz examines the new Israeli "Anti-Missionary Law" passed by the Israeli Parliament on December 27, 1977. It makes it an offense—punishable by five years in prison or a 50,000-pound fine—to offer material inducement to an Israeli to change his religion. (For those who convert under such circumstances, the penalty is three years imprisonment or a 30,000-pound fine.)
Issue 3: <u>The Yemen Arab Republic</u>, Alan Klaum
Alan Klaum, an international consultant on the Middle East and Asia, looks at the history, culture, and politics of Yemen, and the problems it faces.
Issue 4: <u>The Arab World: A New Economic Order</u>, Youssef Ibrahim
This survey of the business environment in the Middle East is by Youssef Ibrahim, a business reporter for The New York Times, who has been covering the region since 1973.
Issue 5: <u>The Sorrow of Lebanon</u>, Youssef Ibrahim
Issue focuses on the uprooted people of Lebanon and a list of donor organizations that are helping them.

1979, Volume 12
Issue 1: <u>Palestinian Nationhood</u>, John Mahoney
Issue includes interview with U.S. Ambassador to the U.N. Andrew Young on the need for a new Palestinian policy; an address by John Reddaway, director of the Council for the Advancement of Arab-British Understanding on "International Recognition of Palestinian Nationhood," and an article from The Arab Report, "Trauma and Triumph of a Nation in Exile."
Issue 2: <u>The Child in the Arab Family</u>, Audrey Shabbas
Audrey Shabbas looks at roles in the Arab family: choosing a child's name; early child care and development; educational patterns; styles of dress; simple toys; nursery rhymes and riddles; Arab songs; children's games and stories. There is a special section on "Iraq: Pacesetter in Children's Services."
Issue 3: <u>Jordan Steps Forward</u>, Alan Klaum
Article examines the: history of Jordan; the West Bank's annexation; Jordan's Constitution; political parties; military; educational system; role of women; economic climate; and tourism.

Issue 4: The Muslim Experience in the US, Yvonne Haddad
Muslim contact with America occurred quite early. It was revealed at the quincentennial celebration of Columbus's birth in 1955 that the explorer's private library contained a copy of the work of the Arab geographer, al-Idrisi. This book, which describes the East coast discovery of the "new continent" by eight Muslim explorers, is said to have inspired Columbus's own expedition. Arab involvement in the discovery of America also rested with Columbus's interpreter, Louis Torres, a Spaniard of Arab descent who had converted to Christianity after the reconquista. This issue goes on to discuss Islamic Centers in the United States, Islam and American blacks, Islamic practice in America, and Islam's future in America.

Issue 5: The West Bank and Gaza: The Emerging Political Consensus, Ann Lesch
Draws upon the research of Dr. Ann Lesch, who was the Associate Middle East representative in Jerusalem for the American Friends Service Committee from 1974 to 1977.

1980, Volume 13

Issue 1: The Presidential Candidates: How They View the Middle East, Allan Kellum
A look at the men who would be president and what they say about the Middle East.

Issue 2: The Arab Stereotype on Television, Jack Shaheen
Article is based on author's research for an upcoming book intended to make television producers and executives more aware of the media's responsibility to reflect a wide range of positive roles for all people.

Issue 3: American Jews and the Middle East: Fears, Frustration and Hope, Allan Solomonow
Allan Solomonow was the first Program Director for the Jewish Peace Fellowship, a national inter-religious effort to bring together resources and programs to stimulate a national dialogue on peaceful alternatives for resolving the Arab-Israeli conflict, all of which he describes in this issue.

Issue 4: Kuwait, Alan Klaum
Examines Kuwait's history, culture, economy, and political role in the Middle East landscape.

Issue 5: National Council of Churches Adopts New Statement on the Middle East, Allison Rock and Jay Vogelaar
When the 266-member governing board of a national organization, representing 32 Christian denominations with more than 40 million members, reaches unanimous agreement on a policy statement pertaining to the Middle East, that statement at once becomes noteworthy, as this issue points out.

1981, Volume 14

Issue 1: Europe and the Arabs: A Developing Relationship, John Richardson
Traces the historical contacts between Europe and the Middle East and looks at how

Europe's independent dialogue with the Arab countries evolved and what effect it might have on U.S. foreign policy.

Issue 2: <u>A Human Rights Odyssey: In Search of Academic Freedom</u>, Michael Griffin
When the Israel Teachers' Union announced that it was organizing a November 1980 International Teachers Conference to Combat Racism, Anti-Semitism and Violations of Human Rights to be held in Tel Aviv, Michael Griffin applied to AMEU for a travel grant. We gave it to him. We also asked him to visit academic institutions on the West Bank to see how they were faring. Then we invited him to report his findings in this issue of *The Link*.

Issue 3: <u>The Palestinians in America</u>, Elias Tuma
An estimated 4.4 million Palestinians now live in the diaspora that followed the 1947-48 and 1967 Middle East wars. Approximately 100,000 of these Palestinians are American citizens today. This issue look at how they view the situation in the Middle East.

Issue 4: <u>Arms Buildup in the Middle East</u>, Greg Orfalea
The United States in 1980 sold $15.3 billion worth of military equipment abroad, of which 53 percent or $8.1 billion went to the Middle East. Should we be concerned? The distinguished diplomat George Kennan gave his answer recently when he compared us to lemmings racing to the sea. Col. Yoram Hamuzrahi, Chief Officer of the Israeli Defense Forces, gave his answer when he told a group of visiting Americans, "We will not concede an inch to the Arabs, even if it means atomic flames in New York." Greg Orfalea, editor of the National Association of Arab Americans' political action report, explains why we should be concerned.

Issue 5: <u>The Disabled in the Arab World</u>, Audrey Shabbas
The United Nations resolution to designate this year as the International Year for Disabled Persons was first put forth in 1976 by the Libyan Arab Republic out of concern for the world's estimated 450 million physically and mentally disabled persons, most of whom live in developing countries. Audrey Shabbas looks at the situation of the disabled in the Arab World.

1982, Volume 15

Issue 1: <u>Palestine: The Suppression of an Idea</u>, Muhammad Hallaj
In this issue, two questions which go to the core of Dr. Hallaj's life are examined: how an indigenous Palestinian culture is faring today under Israeli occupation, and why Zionism is bent on erasing it.

Issue 2: <u>Tourism in the Holy Land</u>, Larry Ekin
Tourism is the world's biggest industry. For many world capitals it represents over 40 percent of their total revenues. Far less appreciated, however, are the political and ethical dimensions of the industry. That is particularly true of tourism in the Holy Land.

Issue 3: <u>Yasser Arafat: The Man and His People</u>, Grace Halsell
Despite his worldwide recognition as Chairman of the Palestine Liberation Organization, little is known of Yasser Arafat's early life, his education, his politics,

his religion, his living habits, etc. To fill in some of these blanks, Grace Halsell went twice to Beirut, once in December 1981, and again in April 1982. Halsell is the author of 11 books, including *A Biography of Charles Evers, Bessie Yellowhair, Soul Sister,* and *Journey to Jerusalem.*

Issue 4: The Islamic Alternative, Yvonne Haddad

Article is based on author's eight years of research of Islamic literature, particularly that coming from the Arab world, and on numerous conversations with those who take their primary identity in Islamic nationalism.

Issue 5: US-Israeli Relations: A Reassessment, Allan Kellum

Reassessment is one of those catchall words that implies anything from substantial change to a slight variation on an old theme. In the lexicon of U.S.-Middle East diplomacy, notes Allan Kellum, publisher of *The Mideast Observer,* it has a lineage all its own.

1983, Volume 16

Issue 1: Military Peacekeeping in the Middle East, William Mulligan

Individual commanders of U.N. peacekeeping forces have written of their experiences in the Middle East. A compilation of their experiences has yet to appear in English, and practically all of the individual accounts are now out of print. William Mulligan, who has spent most of his 35 years in the Middle East in the area of Government Relations for the Arabian American Oil Company, was able to contact some of the major participants. Their reflections add relevancy to a history from which the United States and the multinational force now in Lebanon can learn a great deal.

Issue 2: The Land of Palestine, L. Dean Brown

President Reagan's recent call for a Palestinian "homeland" on the West Bank elicited from Moshe Arens, Israel's Defense Minister, the response that "a Palestinian homeland and state exists — Jordan." In this issue, former U.S. Ambassador to Jordan, L. Dean Brown, responds.

Issue 3: Prisoners of Israel, Edward Dillon

For the past 15 years, Father Edward Dillon has worked with prisoners in the Philadelphia area. In this issue, Fr. Dillon reports on the plight of prisoners inside Israeli-run prisons in south Lebanon and the Occupied Territories.

Issue 4: Christian Zionism, O. Kelly Ingram

Christian Zionism seeks the return of Jews to Palestine as a necessary prelude to the Second Coming of Christ and expects the wholesale conversion of Israel to belief in Jesus as the true Messiah. It is part of a movement begun in 17th-century England which Jewish historian Cecil Roth calls "philo-semitism."

Issue 5: US Aid to Israel, Samir Abed-Rabbo and Mohamad El-Khawas

In 1982, the U.S. General Accounting Office (GOA) began a study of U.S. aid to Israel. In March 1983, the completed study was submitted to Secretary of State George Shultz. Three months later a highly censored version was released to the public. Shortly thereafter, a copy of all but six pages of the GOA report was leaked to the press. This issue analyses that uncensored report.

1984, Volume 17

Issue 1: The Middle East Lobbies, Cheryl Rubenberg
The American Israel Public Affairs Committee (AIPAC) is the most powerful pro-Israel lobby in the United States. Its Arab-American counterpart is the National Association of Arab-Americans. In addition to these registered lobbyist groups, there are, at last count, 33 pro-Israel Political Action Committees and two pro-Arab ones. How these and other pro-Arab and pro-Israel groups operate, how they influence our national elections and foreign policy decisions, and what their objectives are for 1984, are some of the questions examined here by Dr. Cheryl Rubenberg, Assistant Professor in the Department of Political Science at Florida International University.

Issue 2: The USS *Liberty* Affair, James Ennes, Jr.
Survivors of Israel's 1967 attack on the USS *Liberty*, an unarmed intelligence ship sailing in international waters, wonder to this day why rescue planes from the Sixth Fleet were called back by Washington, why Congress has never investigated the incident, and why they were forbidden to discuss the attack – even with their own families. Thirty-four American servicemen were killed and 171 wounded – but it remains a miracle that there is even one survivor left to tell what happened that day.

Issue 3: Shrine Under Siege, Grace Halsell
According to author Grace Halsell, efforts to rebuild the Jewish Temple on the site of the earliest remaining Islamic monument in the world are championed by a significant number of Christian Zionists in this country and by a well-organized group of Jewish Zionists in Israel, many of whom hold dual U.S.-Israeli citizenship. This issue tells who they are, how they are financed, what their motives are and how they have already attempted to realize their aims.

Issue 4: Israel's Drive for Water, Leslie Schmida
In October 1953, [then President] Eisenhower's Science Advisory Committee responded to Israeli Prime Minister David Ben-Gurion's call for the settlement in Israel of an additional two million European Jews by warning that "this unrealistic approach can only lead to further economic and financial difficulties, and will probably result in additional pressure to expand Israel's frontiers into the rich lands of the Tigris and Euphrates Valley, and northward into the settled lands of Syria." Writes author Leslie Schmida in this 1984 issue: "Israel's appropriation, time after time, of Arab property and water resources in abrogation of all commonly accepted international standards seems well on the way to realizing this dismal prospect."

Issue 5: The Lasting Gift of Christmas, Hassan Haddad
For historian Hassan Haddad this issue is not only a return to his childhood memories of Christmas in northern Lebanon as the son of a Protestant minister, it is also a return of 1,400 years to the Qu'ran and its beautiful retelling of the Annunciation and virgin birth, of 2,000 years to the Gospel stories of Matthew and Luke, of centuries earlier to the Sumerians and Egyptians, the Nabateans and Zoroastrians, and beyond the Middle East, to Asia and the birth of Buddha. Along the way, Professor Haddad, who teaches at St. Xavier College in Chicago, is not uncritical of

the ways Christmas has been exploited by one group or another. Still, he finds in the Christmas story, a universal longing.

1985, Volume 18

Issue 1: From Time Immemorial: The Resurrection of a Myth, Muhammad Hallaj
Last year an American writer, Joan Peters, produced a book that claimed that Palestinians never did constitute an indigenous majority in those areas of Palestine which became Israel in 1948. Ms. Peters recently promoted her book, cross country, on radio, television and in newspaper interviews. Dr. Muhammad Hallaj's purpose in this issue is to locate the Peters book in the context of 20th century Zionist writings on the Arab-Israeli conflict. What does the Peters book add to previous Zionist claims? Hallaj's conclusion may surprise Ms. Peters, who tells us it took her seven years to reach her new findings.

Issue 2: The Middle East on the US Campus, Naseer Aruri
The first Middle East study center in the U.S. was founded in 1946 at the Johns Hopkins School of Advanced International Studies in Washington, D.C. Since then, at least 17 major Middle East centers have been established, including centers at Princeton, Harvard and Columbia, with more than 115 colleges and universities now offering Middle East area courses. With growth, however — as Naseer Aruri points out — has come a disturbing awareness.

Issue 3: The Palestine-Israel Conflict in the US Courtroom, Rex Wingerter
The attachment between the United States and Israel has been described most often as a "special relationship." As Rex Wingerter points out in this issue, that attachment has found expression in the United States courtroom.

Issue 4: US-Israeli-Central American Connection, Benjamin Beit-Hallahmi
According to the author, a professor of psychology at Haifa University who wrote a book on Israel's relations with the third world, "Only once, in 1981, has the United States admitted to a direct and explicit request to Israel to help a Central American country; that request came from Secretary of State Alexander Haig and the country in question was Guatemala. Otherwise, U.S. officials admit to 'a convergence of interests.'"

Issue 5: Humphrey Goes to the Middle East, John Law
Humphrey, a well-meaning but aggressively obtuse and monumentally uninformed fellow, drops by John Law's office from time to time to pick his brains on the Middle East.

1986, Volume 19

Issue 1: The Israeli-South African-US Alliance, Jane Hunter
In March 1985, Denis Goldberg, a Jewish South African sentenced in 1964 to life imprisonment for "conspiring to overthrow the apartheid regime," was released through the intercession of his daughter, an Israeli, and top Israeli officials, including Israel's president. Arriving in Israel, Goldberg said that he saw "many similarities in the oppression of blacks in South Africa and of Palestinians," and he called for a total

economic boycott of South Africa, singling out Israel as a major ally of the apartheid regime. Pledging not to stay in a country that is a major supporter of South African apartheid, Dennis Goldberg moved to London. Just how big a supporter Israel is, is the subject of this issue.

Issue 2: The Making of a Non-Person, Jan Abu Shakrah

This issue is about a people without passports—four million people, dispossessed of their land, intimidated, tortured, massacred, facing an uncertain future. Sociologist Jan Abu Shakrah traces the dehumanization of the Palestinian and dissects with clinical precision the matter of their statelessness.

Issue 3: The Vatican, US Catholics, and the Middle East, George Irani

Why has the Vatican never officially recognized the state of Israel? Why did Pope John Paul II agree to meet with P.L.O. Chairman Yasser Arafat? Why do 81 percent of U.S. Catholics support an independent Palestinian state in the West Bank and Gaza? George Irani, author of "The Papacy and the Middle East: The Role of the Holy See in the Arab-Israeli Conflict," explains.

Issue 4: Misguided Alliance, Cheryl Rubenberg

Writes author Cheryl A. Rubenberg: "The once open debate of the 1940s on whether the U.S. should support a state for the Jews in the Arab heartland has evolved into a political orthodoxy of the 1980s that considers the U.S.-Israel ties the most important–and unquestionable–cornerstone of American Middle East policy. How did the transformation occur?" This issue explores the question in depth.

Issue 5: The Demographic War for Palestine, Janet Abu-Lughod

What is the current and projected ratio of Jews leaving Israel to those migrating to Israel? What is the current and projected ratio of Palestinians born in historic Palestine to those who either die, emigrate, or are forcibly expelled? What role does the United States play in this demographic chess match? And, finally, what does all this mean for the political future of Arabs and Jews in the Middle East? The conclusion reached by Professor Abu-Lughod may surprise many for whom demography is the classical stratagem for checkmating the opponent. Suppose, however, the latest data suggests not checkmate but stalemate, what then? This issue looks at all these questions.

1987, Volume 20

Issue 1: Archaeology, Politics in Palestine, Leslie Hoppe

In the Holy Land, where praying at a particular shrine can be construed as a political act and where disputes over ownership and control of land are supercharged with religious and nationalistic overtones, archaeologists are beset with problems that challenge the skill of the most tactful diplomat. Leslie Hoppe, author of "What Are They Saying About Biblical Archaeology?, explains.

Issue 2: England, the US in Palestine, W. F. Abboushi

The recent Tower Commission Report, in analyzing causes of the Iran-Contra debacle, cited the failure by U.S. officials to realize that Israel's foreign policy goals at times stand in direct opposition to those of the United States. As this issue points out, it's a lesson we could have learned from the British.

Issue 3: Public Opinion and the M.E. Conflict, Fouad Moughrabi
Looks at U.S. public opinion in the aftermath of Israel's 1982 invasion of Lebanon and the Jonathan Pollard espionage case. Some of the findings are unexpected.
Issue 4: The Shadow Government, Jane Hunter
Tom Dine, executive director of the American Israel Public Affairs Committee, said earlier this year that Secretary of State George Shultz privately had told him of a desire "to build institutional arrangements so that...if there is a [future] secretary of state who is not positive about Israel, he will not be able to overcome the bureaucratic relationship between Israel and the U.S. that we have established." This issue suggests that institutional arrangement is already well established.
Issue 5: The US Role in Israel's Arms Industry, Bishara Bahbah
A December 1986 article in *The New York Times* said that Israel has become one of the world's top ten arms exporters. Bishara Bahbah is author of "Israel and Latin America: The Military Connection." In this issue he looks at Israel's worldwide arms industry.

1988, Volume 21

Issue 1: The US Press and the Middle East, Mitchell Kaidy
Mitch Kaidy worked 20 years as a reporter and editor of three daily newspapers and one television channel. He was part of a team of reporters who won a Pulitzer Prize for the Rochester (NY) Democrat and Chronicle. As an Arab-American, Mitch is not always pleased with the way our media portrays Arabs in general and Palestinians in particular. Yet, as a newspaper man, he's not without a few suggestions.
Issue 2: Dateline: Palestine, George Weller
George Weller is a prize-winning war correspondent whose professional work in the Middle East spans 45 years. Here he recounts events he covered and leaders he interviewed for the Chicago Daily News.
Issue 3: Zionist Violence Against Palestinians, Mohammad Hallaj
Why are Palestinians revolting against the occupation? Israeli Prime Minister Yitzhak Shamir said it happened when a lone Palestinian from southern Lebanon, using a hang-glider, assaulted an Israeli army post and, single-handedly, killed several Israeli soldiers. He broke the barrier of fear, explained Shamir, adding that all Israel had to do to put down the uprising was to "reestablish the barrier of fear." To that end, he warned that any Palestinian challenging Israel's rule "will have his head smashed against the boulders and walls of these fortresses." His quote prompted this *Link* issue.
Issue 4: Israel and South Africa, Robert Ashmore
In this 1988 issue, Ashmore describes in depth the mutual affinity and cooperation between Israel and South Africa, including production of nuclear weapons, the training by Israel of South African white soldiers, and the transfer by Israel to South Africa of U.S. technology for Israel's Lavi aircraft. The latter issue was raised by Rep. George Crockett of the Congressional Black Caucus with Prime Minister Shamir on

March 16, 1988. Crockett described the Lavi deal with South Africa as an "unconscionable" use of U.S. aid. He went on to question the Israeli Prime Minister on "his government's brutal response to the Palestinian uprising" and asked when "the curfews, the closed military zones, the beatings, the house raids, the gunshots, the rubber bullets, the tear-gassing and mass deportations would end."

Issue 5: The Shi'i Muslims of the Arab World, Augustus Norton

For most Americans the emergence of Ayatollah Khomeini and the subsequent holding of U.S. hostages in Iran provided the first media exposure to Shi'i Muslims. This issue looks more closely at this religiously and politically important community.

1989, Volume 22

Issue 1: Cocaine and Cutouts: Israel's Unseen Diplomacy, Jane Hunter

When a government needs large sums of quick cash for questionable adventures, narcotrafficking offers a lucrative avenue. For this an ally is required, one who has the international networks of contacts and cutouts, i.e., a cover that can provide his or her government with public deniability, should the deal go sour. Israel, according to Jane Hunter, editor of *Israeli Foreign Affairs*, provides such service to various governments, including the United States.

Issue 2: US Aid to Israel, Mohamed Rabie

Reacting to the U.S. State Department's 1988 Human Rights Report charging Israel with "a substantial increase in human rights violations," both chairmen of the Congressional panels that appropriate foreign aid, Rep. David Obey of California and Sen. Patrick Leahy of Vermont, have advised Israel it could no longer count on the billions it receives each year if it continues to shoot at Palestinian demonstrators, deport them, detain them without trial, and blow up their houses. How many billions Israel gets each year is the subject of this issue.

Issue 3: An Interview with Ellen Nassab, Hisham Ahmed

Ellen Nassab gave this interview to Hisham Ahmed on Feb. 18, 1989. On June 9 she died of cancer. She was a wife, mother, nurse and, as this issue makes so poignantly clear, she was much, much more.

Issue 4: The International Crimes of Israeli Officials, John Quigley

This issue goes beyond Israel's human rights violations to the more significant question: Are Israeli officials—specifically Menachem Begin, Shimon Peres, Ariel Sharon, Yitzhak Shamir —guilty of war crimes against the Palestinian people?

Issue 5: Diary of an American in Occupied Palestine, by 'Mary'

A young American woman in occupied Palestine shares her diary entries from October 24, 1988 to June 17, 1989, during the height of the first intifada.

1990, Volume 23

Issue 1: American Victims of Israeli Abuses, Albert Mokhiber

An alarming number of Americans visiting Israel and Palestine have had to contact the U.S. consulate in Jerusalem because they have been harassed, illegally arrested, even tortured. When these Americans return home, they have filed affidavits describing their ordeals. Those affidavits form the basis of this feature article.

Issue 2: My Conversation with Humphrey, John Law

Last time Humphrey visited John Law in the pages of *The Link* was back in December 1985. That issue proved popular, particularly with teachers. True to his threat, the inquisitive Humphrey has shown up again on John Law's literary doorstep.

Issue 3: Protestants and Catholics Show New Support for Palestinians, Charles Kimball

In May of this year, Mayor Elias Freij of Bethlehem predicted that the military occupation of his land will continue as long as the U.S. Congress continues to finance Israel's expansionist policies which, in turn, will continue until the churches in the United States exert their moral influence more vigorously — a prospect he did not anticipate.

Issue 4: What Happened to Palestine?: The Revisionists Revisited, Michael Palumbo

Michael Palumbo is an American researcher who has spent much of his professional life poring over long-classified documents dealing with the immediate post-World War II period. Many of these documents from American, British and United Nations archives deal with the Israeli/Palestinian war of 1948. In this issue Dr. Palumbo invites us to look more critically at what the Israeli revisionists are saying in light of the new facts that they either did not have at their disposal or else opted not to use.

Issue 5: Arab Defamation in the Media, Casey Kasem

After Iraq invaded Kuwait in 1990, hate crimes and threats against Arab-Americans were reported across the United States. "America's DJ," Casey Kasem, writes about how anti-Arab stereotypes on television and in movies create a climate for such violence.

1991, Volume 24

Issue 1: The Post-War Middle East, Rami Khouri

Four weeks after Iraq's invasion of Kuwait, the MacNeil/Lehrer NewsHour featured an extensive interview with Rami Khouri, a highly regarded Jordanian journalist. The interview generated so many calls the NewsHour had to engage additional operators. Subsequently, the interview led to a book contract, an op-ed piece in *The New York Times*, and to this issue of *The Link*.

Issue 2: Beyond the Jewish-Christian Dialogue: Solidarity with the Palestinian People, Marc Ellis

Marc Ellis is a Jewish theologian who directs the Justice and Peace Program at the Catholic School of Theology in Maryknoll, N.Y. In his writings and lectures Marc regularly proposes that Christians and Jews break their long-standing "gentlemen's agreement" of not talking publicly about the one matter that has come to define their relationship: how each group views the Palestinian people.

Issue 3: A New Literary Look at the Middle East, John Mahoney

Books are reviewed which over the years have become our "bestsellers" in addition to recent books that are popular with teachers and those which are often requested by church groups.

Issue 4: <u>Visitation at Yad Vashem</u>, James Burtchaell

This September the U.S. Congress will consider Israel's request for an extra $10 billion for resettling hundreds of thousands of Russian Jews into Israel. Pro-Israel supporters will profess the humanitarian need of ingathering persecuted Jews. But who will speak for the persecuted Palestinians as they face the threat of yet another displacement? Father James Burtchaell does in this issue.

Issue 5: <u>The Comic Book Arab</u>, Jack Shaheen

Jack Shaheen, a Fulbright scholar, is Professor of Mass Communications at Southern Illinois University in Edwardsville. His 1980 *Link* issue, "The Arab Stereotype on Television," became the basis for his book *The TV Arab*. In this issue Professor Shaheen presents his research into Arab stereotyping in comic books, a preview of his forthcoming book, "The Comic Book Arab."

1992, Volume 25

Issue 1: <u>Facing the Charge of Anti-Semitism</u>, Paul Hopkins

In 1980, Paul Hopkins became the Presbyterian Church's Overseas Mission Secretary to the Middle East. His first visit to the West Bank and Gaza brought him face to face with hundreds of thousands of Palestinian refugees languishing under Israel's military rule. When he came home to report what he had seen, his criticism of Israel brought him face to face with something else he didn't expect: the charge of anti-Semitism. Paul's experience is not unique. Nor is that of the Presbyterian Church. Many Americans, Protestants and Catholics, have sought justice for the Palestinians, as have Americans of no religious affiliation. And many Jews, risking the charges of "self-hating Jew" have also said No to Israel's brutal occupation. This issue is dedicated to all those who have looked beyond the polls, beyond politics and, perhaps most difficult of all, beyond the fear of being smeared, to speak out on behalf of a people in pain.

Issue 2: <u>AMEU's 25th Anniversary Issue</u>, Various Authors

In this 25th anniversary issue, authors of previous *Links* revisit their subjects, including Muhammad Hallaj, Grace Halsell, Edward Dillon, Cheryl Rubenberg, James Ennes, John Law, Jane Hunter, George Irani, John Quigley, Mohamed Rabie and L. Humphrey Walz.

Issue 3: <u>Covert Operations: The Human Factor</u>, Jane Hunter

U.S.-Israeli covert operations have sealed the fate of millions of people worldwide. This issue looks at some of these operations that range from selling illegal arms to Third World dictators, to training these dictators' security forces, to cocaine trafficking, to multimillion dollar money laundering, to assassination squads.

Issue 4: <u>Beyond Armageddon</u>, Don Wagner

Some Evangelical Christians believe that the return of Jews to the Promised Land is the sign of the imminent Second Coming of Christ, when "true" Christians will be raptured into the upper air, and the rest of humankind will be slaughtered. 144,000 Jews will bow down before Christ and be saved, but the rest of Jewry will perish in this mother of all holocausts. This issue looks at who these Evangelicals are (some prominent TV personalities), why they are wooed by Israeli officials, and what their impact is on U.S. foreign policy in the Middle East. It also looks at a growing number of Evangelicals who are concerned about what happens to the indigenous Palestinians when hundreds of thousands of Jews colonize their land. The Commandment, Thou Shalt Not Steal, comes to mind.

Issue 5: A Reply to Henry Kissinger and Fouad Ajami, Norman Finkelstein
As a graduate student at Princeton University Norman Finkelstein challenged the accuracy of Joan Peters's "From Time Immemorial," which claimed that the Palestinians never did constitute an indigenous majority in those areas of Palestine that became Israel in 1948. [See *The Link*, Jan.-March 1985.] Since then, at considerable detriment to his own career, Dr. Finkelstein continues to challenge those myths that suggest that Palestinians deserve what they got and, moreover, are even blessed that they ended up with such benevolent occupiers.

1993, Volume 26
Issue 1: Islam and the US National Interest, Shaw Dallal
In its 1992 monograph entitled "Islam in America," the American Jewish Committee acknowledges attempts by "some Western commentators" to stimulate what has been termed "the threat which Islam poses to western civilization." What it fails to do, however, is to say who these commentators are, why they are turning Islam into a global villain, and how such a worldwide view affects U.S. national interests. For answers to these questions, AMEU turned to Professor Shaw Dallal of Utica College. He holds a degree in International Law from Cornell University, and is a frequent writer and lecturer on the Middle East.

Issue 2: An Open Letter to Mrs. Clinton, James Graff
Mrs. Clinton has voiced concern about the rights and well-being of children around the world. Now as First Lady she can accomplish even more on behalf of children. That's what prompted James Graff to write to her about Palestinian children. He writes to ask her help in ending a foreign government's practice of shooting, beating, terrorizing, and de-educating an entire generation of youngsters — a government, moreover, that is doing it with our tax money.

Issue 3: Censored, Colin Edwards
On April 14, 1993, 19 people filed a class action suit against the Anti-Defamation League of B'nai B'rith, et al. The plaintiffs, represented by former U.S. Congressman, Paul N. "Pete" McCloskey, are seeking damages for invasion of privacy. Colin Edwards is one of the class action plaintiffs. Here he writes about the law suit and about the wider issue of censorship of Middle East news in the United States.

Issue 4: Save the Musht, Rosina Hassoun
Rosina Hassoun delivered the first of four papers on "The State of Palestine," a panel sponsored by the American-Arab Anti-Discrimination Committee at its National

Convention, last April, in Alexandria, Virginia. The other three presenters talked about politics—everything from Israeli annexation of the Territories to Palestinian sovereignty over them. When the time came for questions, the 500-plus audience directed all their queries to the political analysts. Then something unexpected happened. The session ended and the three analysts gradually made their way out of the room. But not Rosina. She literally was surrounded by reporters and interviewers (one from the Arabic version of the BBC), as well as other participants just fascinated by what she had to say; they wanted to hear more.

Issue 5: <u>The Exiles</u>, Ann Lesch

Fifteen years ago, Ann Lesch, writing in the *Journal of Palestine Studies*, compiled a list of 1,151 Palestinians who had been deported by Israel between 1967 and 1978. Now, in this issue, Ms. Lesch updates her list to include the names of 547 Palestinians expelled from their homeland between the years 1980 and 1992. The issue also includes a 1988 letter by Umar Abd al-Jawad describing the midnight arrest and deportation of his father, al-Birah mayor Abd al-Jawad Salem, 14 years earlier.

1994, Volume 27

Issue 1: <u>Will '94 Be '49 All Over Again?</u>, Rabbi Elmer Berger

This was Dr. Berger's last major writing before his death. For 26 years he served as president of American Jewish Alternatives to Zionism (AJAZ), and for over 50 years he lectured and wrote on Judaism and Jewish nationalism as a rabbi of American Reform Judaism. In this issue Dr. Berger lists three "problems" that must be faced before any meaningful peace will come to Palestinians and Israelis: the biblical account of the Hebrew/Israelitist tribes; the Balfour Declaration; and the 1948-49 Armistice.

Issue 2: <u>Bosnia: A Genocide of Muslims</u>, Grace Halsell

She forded the Rio Grande with Mexican illegals, worked as a Navajo Indian in California, a black woman in Harlem and a speech writer for President Johnson. Now this veteran journalist — and AMEU board member — reports on the rape of some 50,000 Muslim women as part of the slaughter and expulsion of Muslims in Bosnia, Kosovo and Macedonia.

Issue 3: <u>The Post-Handshake Landscape</u>, Frank Collins

Have the Israelis left Gaza? Have they stopped expropriating Palestinian lands? A year after "the" handshake on the White House Lawn, journalist Frank Collins looks at how the situation has changed for Palestinians on the ground.

Issue 4: <u>Humphrey Gets the Inside Dope</u>, John Law

Another attempt to educate an American "Everyman" on the basics behind the ongoing struggle in the Middle East.

Issue 5: <u>Refusing to Curse the Darkness</u>, Geoffrey Aronson et al.

Former U.S. Attorney General Ramsey Clark once said that "The truest test of any individual's commitment to human rights in our society...lies in the commitment to human rights for Palestinians." This issue profiles eight Americans who embody that commitment.

1995, Volume 28

Issue 1: <u>In the Land of Christ, Christianity Is Dying</u>, Grace Halsell

In this *Link*, Halsell explains the reasons for the precipitous decline in the proportion of Christians—the "Living Stones"—in the land of their origin. She also comments on how Christian visitors to the Holy Land are systematically routed away from their co-religionists. As one of 630 Christians who flew to Israel in 1983 on a Holy Land tour sponsored by the Rev. Jerry Falwell, Halsell observed that during her tour by bus, not one Christian guide was provided, nor was time allocated to meet Christian Palestinians or attend a Christian service. She writes: "On the day we approached Nazareth, where Jesus grew up and had his ministry, our guide said, 'There is Nazareth.' He added we would not stop. 'No time,' he said. Minutes later, he changed his mind, announcing: 'We *will* stop in Nazareth. To use the toilet facilities.' Thus, the only site the Christians saw in all of Nazareth were the toilets."

Issue 2: <u>A Survivor for Whom Never Again *Means* Never Again</u> [An Interview with Israel Shahak], Mark Dow

Israel Shahak is a Nazi concentration camp survivor, a renowned chemist, and Israeli citizen. He has been called a prophet, a Renaissance man, and a self-hating Jew. However, he'd rather be known for his thoughts on democracy, fascism, ethnicity and human rights — which is what he focuses on in this issue.

Issue 3: <u>Jerusalem's Final Status</u>, Michael Dumper

Since its military take-over of East Jerusalem in 1967, Israel has confiscated over 18,000 acres of Palestinian land. On it the Jewish State has built 38,500 housing units, all of which are exclusively for Jews. Prior to 1967, when the Holy City was divided, West Jerusalem was 100 percent Jewish while East Jerusalem was 100 percent Arab. Today West Jerusalem is still 100 percent Jewish while East Jerusalem is 48 percent Arab. Israel's plan to judaicize the Holy City is working. Dr. Dumper concludes that there will be little to negotiate if Israel continues in this fashion.

Issue 4: <u>Teaching About the Middle East</u>, Elizabeth Barlow

Teachers, libraries and students comprise about 25 percent of our readership. *The Link* is also listed in various educational directories that offer teachers free and inexpensive curricular materials. And teachers do write to us. What we never could send them — because, as far as we know, none existed — was a concise up-to-date survey of the best resources available for teaching about the culture, history, and current events in the Middle East. Now we can, thanks to Elizabeth Barlow.

Issue 5: <u>Epiphany at Beit Jala</u>, Donald Neff

Donald Neff served as *Time* magazine's Jerusalem Bureau Chief from 1975-78. He had never worked in the Middle East before going to Israel in 1975. "My attitude toward the region [at that time] reflected pretty much the pro-Israel biases of the media and of Americans in general, unleavened by history or sophistication about Zionism," he writes in this issue. What he saw of the Israeli occupation began to change his attitude. His epiphany came at a two-story Palestinian middle school in Beit Jala in 1978.

1996, Volume 29

Issue 1: <u>Hebron's Theater of the Absurd</u>, Kathleen Kern

" . . . some broke ranks and attacked a line of Christian women peace activists who regularly placed themselves between the Jews and Palestinians, knocking two of them down and dragging them by their hair" was how *The New York Times* described a group of Jews led by Yigal Amir, the confessed assassin of Prime Minister Rabin, as he swaggered into Hebron. We thought that the U.S. media would have descended upon these women to get their eyewitness account, the assassination being, after all, a major story. One of the women, Kathleen Kern, was even back in the country for a few weeks. But when we tracked her down, she said we were the only publication to ask for her story.

Issue 2: <u>Meanwhile in Lebanon</u>, George Irani

The target was a school bus. Twenty-five children, returning from school, with flowers. It was Mother's Day 1994. Had the explosion occurred in Israel, it would have made news. As it was, it happened in South Lebanon. Part of South Lebanon still bleeds under Israel's military occupation, while 450,000 refugees in Lebanon, most of them clustered in 12 camps, struggle not to despair. As the world focuses on Gaza and the West Bank, Lebanon, its seems, has been forgotten.

Issue 3: <u>Palestinians and Their Days in Court: Unequal Before the Law</u>, Linda Brayer

Linda Brayer was born in South Africa to a Jewish family. Her parents were from Palestine and her grandfather was one of the founders of the first Jewish modern settlement, Petah Tikvah. She went to Israel on "aliya" in 1965. After obtaining her liberal arts degree (cum laude) from the Hebrew University, she continued on for her law degree and entered private practice in 1986. The following year the first intifada broke out. "My world was shattered," she writes. "I found myself facing the void of the lie of Zionism."

Issue 4: <u>Deir Yassin Remembered</u>, Dan McGowan

For McGowan, a professor of economics, it was a matter of parity: If his college was going to pull its investments out of South Africa because of its apartheid, why not pull them out of Israel for the same reason? The question led him to Deir Yassin.

Issue 5: <u>Slouching Toward Bethlehem 2000</u>, Betty and Martin Bailey

Ever been to the Holy Land? Ever think of going? Chances are you'll get on a tourist bus, get off at Manger Square, see the traditional site of Jesus' birth, buy a few souvenirs, be whisked back on the bus, and move on to the next holy place. In this issue, the authors suggest that, while you may see the site of Jesus' birth, you have not walked in the footsteps of Jesus.

1997, Volume 30

Issue 1: <u>The Children of Iraq: 1990-1997</u>, Kathy Kelly

More Iraqi children have died as a result of our sanctions on Iraq than the combined toll of two atomic bombs on Japan and the recent scourge of ethnic cleansing in the former Yugoslavia. Kathy Kelly, it should be noted, is a pacifist She's against all wars.

But her article is about these children. And the legitimate question for all peoples of good will, pacifist or not, American or not, is whether the preventable deaths of over 600,000 children under 5 years of age is an appropriate sanction to levy on any country, anywhere, any time.

Issue 2: AMEU's 30th Anniversary Issue, Various Authors

For the 30th anniversary issue of *The Link*, eight authors were invited to update readers on their earlier articles. Contributors are Lynda Brayer, Norman Finkelstein, James Graff, Grace Halsell, Rosina Hassoun, Kathleen Kern, Daniel McGowan, and Donald Wagner.

Issue 3: Remember the [USS] *Liberty*, John Borne

This issue includes a memorandum by Admiral Thomas H. Moorer, former chairman of the Joint Chiefs of Staff. "I have never believed that [Israel's] attack on the *USS Liberty* was a case of mistaken identity," Moorer writes. "[It was] a wanton sneak attack that left 34 American sailors dead and 171 seriously injured. . . . I have to conclude that it was Israel's intent to sink the *Liberty* and leave as few survivors as possible."

Issue 4: U. S. Aid to Israel: The Subject No One Mentions, Richard Curtiss

The United States has leverage over Israel—annual grants and loans in the billions of dollars—if it ever chooses to exercise it. In addition to the familiar figure of $3 billion or so that is handed over every year to Israel, the true cost to the American taxpayer is far more. From 1949 through October, 1997, benefits to Israel from U.S. aid totaled nearly $85 billion, including grants, loans, "non-foreign aid," and interest Israel accrued by receiving its foreign aid as a lump sum early in the fiscal year, rather than quarterly as is the case with all other foreign aid recipients. It cost American taxpayers $50 billion in interest costs to provide that aid. In that time period, Israelis received nearly $15,000 per citizen from the U.S. alone, and more than $20,000 when German assistance is included.

Issue 5: *People and the Land*: Coming to a PBS Station Near You?, Tom Hayes

Filming the Israeli occupation is to risk death or serious injury, but then just try and get the resulting documentary on U. S. television. Filmmaker Tom Hayes tells both parts of the story in *People and the Land*.

1998, Volume 31

Issue 1: Israeli Historians Ask: What Really Happened 50 Years Ago?, Ilan Pappe

This issue's feature article by Ilan Pappe, an historian at Haifa University, challenges Israel's official account of what happened 50 years ago in Palestine. Dr. Pappe is one of a growing number of Israeli historians whose analyses of newly released documents by the U. S., England and Israel have led them to conclude that what really happened back then is far closer to what Palestinians have been saying all along.

Issue 2: The Jews of Iraq, Naeim Giladi

In our previous *Link*, Israeli historian Ilan Pappe looked at the hundreds of thousands of indigenous Palestinians whose lives were uprooted to make room for foreigners who would come to populate confiscated land. Most were Ashkenazi Jews from

Eastern Europe. But over half a million other Jews came from Islamic lands. Zionist propagandists claim that Israel "rescued" these Jews from their anti-Jewish, Muslim neighbors. One of those "rescued" Jews—Naeim Giladi—knows otherwise.

Issue 3: Politics *Not* As Usual, Rod Driver

Rod Driver is running for the United States Congress from Rhode Island's second district. No stranger to politics—he was elected four times to Rhode Island's state legislature—Driver is now doing something no other candidate for federal office has ever done. He's telling his constituents how their tax dollars are being used to dispossess and torture Palestinians. And he's doing it by showing on television graphic film of Palestinian parents and their children being dragged kicking and screaming from their home as a bulldozer moves in to turn it all to rubble. (Channel 12 in Rhode Island prefaces Driver's TV ad with the disclaimer: "The following political advertisement contains scenes which may be disturbing to children. Viewer discretion is advised.") Why, at 65, spend thousands of your own dollars on behalf of Palestinians? That's what we asked Professor Driver to explain in this issue.

Issue 4: Israel's Bedouin: The End of Poetry, Ron Kelley

A cable TV programmer in Manhattan called AMEU's John Mahoney to ask if he would like to see a documentary on the Bedouin of Israel. It's rather extraordinary, he said. The day after viewing Ron Kelley's documentary, Mahoney phoned him at his home in Michigan and invited him to tell his story to our *Link* readers. He agreed in the hope that "the article can draw a little attention to the problem at hand." The problem at hand is the destruction of a people.

Issue 5: Dear NPR News, Ali Abunimah

Ali Abunimah, widely known today for his association with the Electronic Intifada web site, confronted National Public Radio in 1997-98 with a stream of e-mails about its Middle East coverage, using plain facts, humor and irony to call attention to historical inaccuracies, the use of Israeli euphemisms (i.e., "rubber bullets"), and failures to report on settlement growth, Palestinian deaths, home demolitions and collective punishments. Several of Abunimah's most compelling letters to NPR are reprinted in this issue.

1999, Volume 32

Issue 1: Sahmatah, Edward Mast

This is the story of one American playwright's willingness to question the world according to the U.S. media. And it is the story of a Palestinian-American's search for a past that had eluded him. Central to both stories is a village in the Upper Galilee, where horses and cows now graze. "Sahmatah" is a one-act play for two actors. It debuted in the Pacific Northwest and Western Canada in 1996. In 1998, it was produced in Arabic in the Masrah al-Midan theater in Haifa, and on the ruins of the village of Sahmatah in the Upper Galilee.

Issue 2: The Camp, Muna Hamzeh-Muhaisen

What is it like to be on the receiving end of the longest military occupation in modern history? Muna Hamzeh-Muhaisen lived in Dheisheh, a refugee camp on the outskirts of Bethlehem, for more than a decade, including the period of the first intifada. This is her account of the people who have lived in Dheisheh all of their lives.

Issue 3: Secret Evidence, John Sugg

This issue focuses on a country whose Supreme Court recently ruled that its government, for political reasons, can target particular groups within its non-citizen population for deportation. While deportation is being pursued, the aliens can be jailed indefinitely on the basis of evidence that neither they nor their lawyers are permitted to see. It focuses on a university professor forcibly taken in handcuffs from his home where for years he had lived peaceably with his wife and three young daughters. There are two authors for this issue of *The Link*. John Sugg is a reporter in Florida, where a Palestinian professor is spending his third year in jail for no known reason. Kit Gage of the National Coalition to Protect Political Freedom monitors other cases of prisoners of Middle Eastern origin languishing in our prisons for reasons known neither to them nor to their lawyers.

Issue 4: Iraq: Who's To Blame?, Geoff Simons

Many — most? — Americans believe that while the effects of economic sanctions on the Iraqi people are cruel, "we" are not to blame. Time and again it is said: "Saddam could end it today if he wanted to." When Geoff Simons agreed to write about the situation, we specifically asked him to address the question of culpability.

Issue 5: Native Americans and Palestinians, Norman Finkelstein and Zoughbi Zoughbi.

In 1998, a delegation of Palestinians visited the Lakota Indians on their Pine Ridge Reservation. Soon after, a delegation of Native Americans visited Palestine. What they found is the subject of this issue.

2000, Volume 33

Issue 1: Muslim Americans in Mainstream America, Nihad Awad

Between six and eight million Muslims live in the U.S. African-Americans represent 43%, Asian-Americans 26%, Arab-Americans 14%, Iranian-Americans 4%, Turkish-Americans 3%, European-Americans 3%, with 7% unspecified. Until recently, most lived in well defined Muslim communities. Today, however, Muslims are moving into the mainstream and, like minorities before them, many are facing discrimination, intolerance, even violence. To counter this bias, Nihad Awad helped to found CAIR, the Council on American-Islamic Relations.

Issue 2: The Syrian Community on the Golan Heights, Bashar Tarabieh

The author of this issue, Bashar Tarabieh, is a member of the Arab Academic Association for Development of the Golan. Bashar presently lives in Atlanta, Georgia. The story he tells in these pages is indeed the untold story of his people's oppression under foreign occupation. Much has been reported in the U.S. media of what the 17,000 Israeli colonizers on the Golan might lose should negotiations with Syria succeed. But what of the 140,000 Syrians expelled by Israel in 1967, or the

17,000 who remain there today? What about their 33 years of lost freedoms. This is their story.

Issue 3: <u>The Lydda Death March</u>, Audeh Rantisi and Charles Amash

On July 12 [1948] Ramle and Lydda were occupied by Zionist forces and a curfew was imposed. At 11:30 a.m., many Lydda inhabitants, shut up in their houses, took fright at the sudden outbreak of shooting outside…. Some rushed into the streets, only to be cut down by Israeli fire…In the confusion, many unarmed detainees in the detention areas in the center of town – in the mosque and church compounds – were shot and killed…. At 13:30 hours, July 12, before the shooting had completely died down, Operation Dani HQ issued the following order to Yiftah Brigade: "The inhabitants of Lydda must be expelled quickly without attention to age."—*Israeli historian Benny Morris, "The Middle East Journal," vol. 40, No. 1, Winter 1986, pp. 86-87*

Issue 4: <u>On the Jericho Road</u>, James M. Wall

In 1973, upon assuming the editorship of *Christian Century*, Jim Wall received an invitation from the American Jewish Committee to take an all-expenses paid trip to Israel. He began his journey a solid, pro-Israel supporter, a position his AJC host had hoped to reinforce. But, then—in a twist of fate not planned by his host—he met LeRoy Friesen, a Mennonite, who convinced him to spend a day with him in the Israeli-occupied, Palestinian West Bank. Now, 23 years later, the editor-politician-minister looks back upon an event that happened that day as a turning point in his understanding of Palestinians and their history.

Issue 5: <u>Confronting the Bible's Ethnic Cleansing in Palestine</u>, Michael Prior, C.M.

Is Yahweh the Great Ethnic-Cleanser? Did He not instruct the Israelites to rid their Promised Land of its indigenous people? Few biblical scholars want to wrestle with these questions. Rev. Michael Prior needs to wrestle with them. He's been to today's Holy Land and has seen today's variation on biblically sanctioned genocide. Dr. Prior is Professor of Biblical Studies in the University of Surrey, England, and visiting professor in Bethlehem University, Palestine. He is a biblical scholar and author of *Zionism and the State of Israel: A Moral Inquiry* and *The Bible and Colonialism: A Moral Critique.*

2001, Volume 34

Issue 1: <u>Israel's Anti-Civilian Weapons</u>, John F. Mahoney

Because they are the targets, Palestinian youngsters have become authorities of sorts on rubber-coated steel bullets. They collect them much like American kids collect baseball cards. And they've learned to discern what's coming at them.

Issue 2: <u>Today's Via Dolorosa</u>, Edward J. Dillon

In Ed Dillon's country parish in upstate New York, church members reenact the Stations of the Cross on the Friday before Holy Week. Tracing the Stations of the Cross has been a pious custom, especially for Latin Catholics, since the time of the Crusades. The *Link* asked Pastor Dillon to go to Jerusalem and to construct a modern parable while following the course of the original Via Dolorosa and reflecting on the figures who found themselves there 2,000 years ago. Who could be cast today as Jesus, Dillon asked himself. "For those who come to the Holy Land with eyes to see and ears to hear," he writes, "the answer is the Palestinian people."

Issue 3: Americans Tortured in Israeli Jails, Jerri Bird

Forty-five thousand United States citizens of Palestinian origin are living in or visiting the West Bank, according to U.S. officials. Some of these citizens are imprisoned by Israel, some without ever being charged. Some have their U.S. passports taken from them. All report that they were tortured. Jerri Bird profiles several cases in this issue, relying on the sworn affidavits of the tortured.

Issue 4: Inside H-2 [Hebron], Jane Adas

The most populated West Bank city after Jerusalem, Hebron today is a city cut in two. In 1997, following 30 years of Israeli occupation, 80 percent of Hebron came under Palestinian control—though Israel still controls the main access routes. This is H1. H2, the remaining 20 percent, remains under Israeli military control. It counts an estimated 30,000-35,000 Palestinians and approximately 400 Jewish settlers, protected by 1,200 Israeli soldiers.

Issue 5: Reflections on September 11, 2001, Various Authors

Post-9/11 commentaries by James M. Wall, *Christian Century* magazine; Dr. Ilan Pappe, Haifa University; Dr. Norman Finkelstein, DePaul University; Sen. James Abourezk; Muhammad Hallaj, political analyst; Rabbi Marc Ellis, Baylor University; and Ali Abunimah, media analyst.

2002, Volume 35

Issue 1: Law & Disorder in the Middle East, Francis A. Boyle

Francis Boyle served as legal adviser to the Palestinian delegation to the Middle East peace negotiations from 1991-1993 and worked closely with the head of that delegation, Dr. Haider Abdel Shafi. Part of his responsibilities was to review all preceding peace proposals put forward by Israel with respect to the Palestinians, going back to the Camp David Accords. This is his account.

Issue 2: A Style Sheet on the Palestinian-Israeli Conflict, compiled by J. Martin Bailey

J. Martin Bailey has compiled and defined 117 terms whose use, misuse and non-use by the media contribute mightily to what newspaper readers, radio listeners and TV watchers perceive as "the truth" about the Palestinian-Israeli conflict and the religious, cultural and ethnic ingredients of that conflict. The AMEU web site has made the lexicon into a permanent feature (see Resources) so that it can be expanded and amended as needed.

Issue 3: The Crusades, Then and Now, Robert Ashmore

Crusading is a concept that applies to successive campaigns against the East and even against foes in the West during medieval times, as well as to actions of the imperial powers in the 19th and 20th centuries. A clear understanding of crusading reveals that it characterizes much that is occurring today, from U.S.-headed economic sanctions on Iraq to Israel's expansionist settlement policy in Arab territory to Russia's devastating campaign in Chechnya.

Issue 4: <u>A Most UnGenerous Offer</u>, Jeff Halper
If you look at the blueprint of a prison, it looks like the prisoners own the place. They have 95 percent of the territory. The prisoners have the living areas. They have the cafeteria, the visiting area, the exercise yard. All the prison authorities have is 5 percent: the surrounding walls, the cell bars, a few points of control, the keys to the door. When you consider Israeli Prime Minister Barak's "generous offer" to the Palestinians at Camp David, keep that prison blueprint in mind.

Issue 5: <u>The Making of Iraq</u>, Geoff Simons
Geoff Simons has written four books on Iraq, his most recent being *Targeting Iraq: Sanctions and Bombing in US Policy*, published this year. Denis Halliday, former U.N. Assistant Secretary-General and head of the U.N. Humanitarian Program in Iraq, says of this work, "There is no doubt this is an important book." And *The Times of London* added: "Books either written or edited by Simons can be bought with confidence." If ever Americans had a need to know the history of Iraq—"from Sumer to Saddam," as the title of one of Geoff's books puts it—that time is at hand.

2003, Volume 36

Issue 1: <u>Veto</u>, by Phyllis Bennis
Thirty-four times over the past 30 years the United States has vetoed United Nations Security Council resolutions critical of Israel. Efforts by the vast majority of the world's nations to halt Israel's occupation of Arab lands, expropriation of Palestinian property, and violation of the human rights of a civilian population under military rule have been repeatedly thwarted by Washington's intervention. While U.S. dollars fuel Israel's colonization, U.S. vetoes shield Israel from international censure. The history behind these vetoes is the topic of this issue. Our author, Phyllis Bennis, has been a Middle East affairs analyst for over 20 years.

Issue 2: <u>Political Zionism</u>, by John F. Mahoney
AMEU Executive Director John Mahoney surveys political Zionism's origins under Theodor Herzl, traces its evolution from the early 1900s, describes its successful strategy of finding a world power patron, and documents its influence over U.S. foreign policy. The issue is dedicated to Alfred Lilienthal and Fayez Sayegh, whose seminal writings have had a sustained influence on the literature of the Palestine-Israeli conflict.

Issue 3: <u>In the Beginning, There Was Terrorism</u>, by Ronald Bleier
"Blowing up a bus, a train, a ship, a café, or a hotel; assassinating a diplomat or a peace negotiator; killing hostages, sending letter bombs; massacring defenseless villagers—this is terrorism, as we know it. In the modern Middle East it began with the Zionists who founded the Jewish state." Author Ronald Bleier's meticulous documentation includes Livia Rokach's *Israel's Sacred Terrorism*, which is based in large part on former Israeli Prime Minister Moshe Sharett's diary.

Issue 4: <u>Why Do They Hate US?</u>, by John Zogby
Practically all polls show that Americans are less esteemed by the world community today than ever before. Is it because, as many U.S. commentators suggest, non-Americans envy our power, or our way of life, or our technology? Or perhaps they revile our culture as they see it filtered through our movies and television? John Zogby, president of the international polling firm of Zogby International, looks at all these possibilities and concludes that none of them is right. So what is the answer? While Zogby's polling results may surprise many Americans, they will not come as a surprise to the rest of the world, and certainly not to the people of the Middle East.

Issue 5: <u>Rachel</u>, by Cindy Corrie
Rachel Corrie went to the Occupied Territories believing in (1) the right to freedom of the Palestinian people based on the relevant United Nations resolutions and international law; and (2) exclusive reliance on nonviolent methods of resistance. On March 16, 2003, Rachel was crushed to death by an Israeli bulldozer while trying to prevent the demolition of the home of a Palestinian pharmacist, his wife and three young children near the Egyptian border. She was 23 years old. Her mother wrote this issue of *The Link*.

2004, Volume 37
Issue 1: <u>Beyond Road Maps & Walls</u>, by Jeff Halper
Jeff Halper believes the time for a two-state solution has run out. If he's right, the question is, What do we do now? And, is a genuine Middle East peace possible? For if time is running out on the two-state option, that means time is running out on seriously considering the other options. In this issue, Dr. Halper looks at those options.

Issue 2: <u>Mordechai Vanunu</u>, by Mary Eoloff in collaboration with her husband, Nick
On April 21 of this year Dr. Mordechai Vanunu will have served out a prison sentence of 18 years for having publicly exposed Israel's nuclear weapons program. More than 11 of those years were spent in solitary confinement. Waiting for his release at the gate of Ashkelon prison will be a couple from St. Paul, Minnesota, Mary and Nick Eoloff. Nick is a retired lawyer and Mary taught Spanish before raising six children. Through adoption, Mordechai Vanunu has become the Eoloffs' seventh child.

Issue 3: <u>The CPT Report</u>, by Peggy Gish
Once the digital photos surfaced, the mainstream media suddenly became interested in a December 2003 report on prisoner abuse in Iraq prepared by the Christian Peacemaker Teams. Investigative journalist Seymour Hersh mentioned CPT in interviews he gave, and CNN interviewed a CPT member in Baghdad. Meanwhile, Peggy Gish, a member of CPT's Iraq delegation, was preparing this issue of *The Link*. CPT documented abuse not only in the Abu Ghraib prison but in prisons throughout U.S.-occupied Iraq.

Issue 4: <u>Timeline for War,</u> by Jane Adas, John Mahoney and Robert Norberg
A date-by-date account of how the war with Iraq came about. Beginning in 1992 and running through August, 2004, the chronology is drawn from books by Bob Woodward, James Bamford, James Mann, and Richard Clarke. A Reader's Guide on pages 8 & 9 provides background information on persons who figure prominently in the timeline. The Guide is based on two articles, "The Men from JINSA and CSP," by Jason Vest in *The Nation*, and "Serving Two Flags: Neocons, Israel and the Bush Administration," by Stephen Green in the *Washington Report on Middle East Affairs*.

Issue 5: <u>When Legend Becomes Fact,</u> by James M. Wall
James M. Wall, Senior Contributing Editor of *Christian Century* magazine, explains that Americans have been deprived of a valid and compelling alternative to the Israeli version of the basic elements of the Israeli-Palestinian conflict. Israel's mythic descriptions of why millions of Palestinians were condemned to expulsion and lives under occupation are accepted wholesale, while facts that confront the legend are ignored by the media. The book and movie *Exodus* are cases in point.

2005, Volume 38

Issue 1: <u>Iran,</u> by Geoff Simons
A comprehensive survey of Iran, beginning in antiquity. From World War II onward, there are many familiar American names and U.S.-influenced events embedded in this account: John Foster Dulles; the C.I.A. and Iranian Prime Minister Mossadegh; Kermit Roosevelt; the Rockefellers; Jimmy Carter and the Americans taken hostage during his presidency, President Ronald Reagan, Oliver North, and Iran-Contra.

Issue 2: <u>The Day FDR Met Saudi Arabia's Ibn Saud,</u> by Thomas W. Lippman
Former *Washington Post* Middle East Bureau Chief Thomas Lippman provides a fascinating, anecdote-laced account of the 1945 meeting of President Franklin D. Roosevelt with Saudi Arabia's legendary King Ibn Saud. Roosevelt's probing of Ibn Saud's views on Jewish settlement in Palestine elicited the King's response that Germany, being the perpetrator of the Holocaust, should be made to pay the price with appropriated land within Germany. Col. William Eddy, translator between the two principals, is relied upon for the substance of what was discussed, and the Eddy book, *F. D. R. Meets Ibn Saud*, can be accessed on the AMEU web site.

Issue 3: <u>The Coverage—and Non-Coverage—of Israel-Palestine,</u> by Alison Weir
The New York Times is called "the newspaper of record," in part because hundreds of other newspapers across the country and around the world subscribe to its New York Times News Service. So, if *The Times* skewers the news, it's skewered worldwide. Which is exactly what is happening with its coverage of Palestine/Israel, according to Alison Weir, executive director of If Americans Knew.

Issue 4: <u>The Israeli Factor,</u> by John Cooley
John Cooley, former correspondent for the *Christian Science Monitor* and *ABC News*, writes that President Bush, Prime Minister Blair and their real or nominal allies had the active or tacit cooperation of many in the media in the run-up to the "war of

choice" with Iraq. Cooley adds: "For this writer, after covering Arab and Muslim regions for nearly half a century, there is another issue. Our mainstream media, almost without exception, tip-toe around the role played by Israel in influencing the Bushites toward war in March 2003."

Issue 5: A Polish Boy in Palestine, by David Neunuebel

Frequently the path to discovering the plight of the Palestinians begins with acts of conscience with respect to racism, discrimination and civil rights in the U.S. And so it was with David Neunuebel, who recalls the perjoratives and ill treatment meted out to his mother solely for being Polish and poor, and the segregation visited upon blacks simply because of skin color. When Neuneubel returned from visiting Palestine for the first time, he felt compelled to tell other Americans about what he had learned. In addition to producing two film documentaries on life for the Palestinians under occupation, he also created an organization, Americans for a Just Peace in the Middle East.

2006, Volume 39

Issue 1: Middle East Studies Under Siege, by Joan W. Scott

In 2001, shortly after the terrorist attacks on the trade towers in New York, the American Association of University Professors set up a special committee to report on Academic Freedom in a Time of National Emergency. Joan W. Scott, professor of Social Science at the Institute for Advanced Study in Princeton, N.J., was a member of that committee and, at the time, chair of A.A.U.P.'s committee on academic freedom and tenure. The author describes the "well-organized lobby that, on campus and off, has been systematically attacking Middle East studies programs under various guises" in an effort to limit expression on the Israeli-Palestinian conflict to pro-occupation viewpoints.

Issue 2: Inside the Anti-Occupation Camp, by Michel Warschawski

In 1984, along with Palestinian and Israeli activists, Michel Warschawski co-founded the Alternative Information Center, which combines grassroots activism with research, analysis, dialogue and the dissemination of information on Palestine-Israel. He was arrested by Shin Bet in 1987 and refused, during 15 days of interrogation, to reveal the names of Palestinian counterparts and others active in opposing the occupation. The author is a Polish Frenchman and a rabbi's son who went to Israel to study the Talmud and ultimately chose to risk his personal security in the cause of peace with justice for Palestinians.

Issue 3: Why Divestment? And Why Now? by David Wildman

From 1976 to 1994, the author was involved in the South African anti-apartheid movement and in 2001 he became active with the U.S. Campaign to End the Israeli Occupation. He reports on the movement to use boycotts and divestment to pressure Israel to end its military occupation and its systematic denial of Palestinian human rights.

Issue 4: <u>For Charlie,</u> by Barbara Lubin
Barbara Lubin, a Jewish-American activist, begins her *Link* with these words: "Israel's recent invasion of Lebanon brought back painful memories to me of its 1982 invasion for more reasons than one. While Israel's actions in 2006 were similar to 1982—widespread bombing of civilians and civilian infrastructure, the destruction of entire neighborhoods, and the indiscriminate killing of women and children—my reactions then and now were very different. These opposite reactions tell the story of who I was and who I have become."

AMEU's Public Affairs Series

Since its establishment in 1967, AMEU has published 34 pamphlets in its Public Affairs Series. The following are available on the web site under Resources/AMEU Publications:

<u>Camp David and Palestine: A Preliminary Analysis,</u> by Dr. Fayez A. Sayegh.
Although Dr. Sayegh's thorough-going critique of Camp David was prepared in less than a month following the signing of the agreement by Israel and Egypt (17 September 1978), time has not diminished the accuracy of his "preliminary" analysis. Writes the author: "The Camp David accords envisage a final resolution of the Palestine problem which precludes the exercise of the inalienable national right of the Palestine people to self-determination and statehood in Palestine, the natural human right of dispersed Palestinians to return to their homes, and the elementary right of the Palestine people to choose and designate its national representatives. Both Israel and the United States had all along denied the Palestinian people those rights; it was the concurrence in that denial by Egyptian negotiators, headed by President Sadat, that constituted the astonishing feature of the Camp David Palestine formula." (www.ameu.org/uploads/campdavid_march10_03.pdf)

<u>The Role of International Law in Achieving Justice and Peace in Palestine-Israel,</u> by W. T. and Sally Mallison.
Writing in 1974 in the midst of a Middle East Peace Conference, W. T. and Sally Mallison observed: "It may be predicted with considerable assurance that if the present [conference] is to reach toward peace based upon justice, it will have to employ the principled criteria of international law. Another so-called 'practical settlement' based upon naked power bargaining and calculation will, at best, provide a short interlude between intense hostilities." (www.ameu.org/uploads/maillison_feb21_03.pdf)

<u>The USS *Liberty*</u>
A chronology of Israel's attack on a virtually defenseless intelligence-gathering ship in international waters off the coast of Gaza during the June 1967 Israeli-Arab war.

Thirty-four American crewmen were killed and 171 were injured. Rescue aircraft from U.S. carriers in the Mediterranean were called back on the orders of President Lyndon Johnson, survivors were placed under "gag orders" and Congress has never seen fit to investigate Israel's claim that it was a case of mistaken identity—a claim that eyewitness survivors unanimously repudiate. (www.ameu.org/uploads/ Liberty_Nov19_2002.pdf)

U.S. Middle East Policy and the Israeli Settlements, by Sen. George McGovern.
Speaking in 1991 during the presidency of the first George Bush, Sen. George McGovern said: "For the 22 years that I served in Congress, like most of my colleagues, I supported Israel, out of a combination of conviction and self-interest. We were constantly aware of the power of the lobby for that country. Sometimes, against our best instincts, we bowed to pressure. Now, thanks in large part to the leadership of the president [who was holding up $10 billion in loan guarantees for Israel to gain some leverage over Israeli policies], more members of Congress may be able to follow their consciences." (www.ameu.org/uploads/mcgovern_feb16_03.pdf)

"Why *Did* the United Nations Resolve that Zionism Is a Form of Racism?"
In 1991, under intense U.S. pressure, the United Nations General Assembly rescinded its 1975 "Zionism Is Racism" resolution. AMEU's paper explores the rationale that led to the Resolution's initial passage. (www.ameu.org/uploads/ zionismracism_feb14_2003.pdf)

Zionist Ideology and the Reality of Israel, by Nahum Goldmann, former President of the World Zionist Organization.
In reprinting the paper, AMEU noted that its Public Affairs Series "enables prominent authorities on various American-Middle Eastern issues to share views respected by, but not necessarily in total agreement with, [AMEU]." Goldman died in 1982 at age 87. (www.ameu.org/uploads/goldmann_feb23_03.pdf)

Appendix II: Peace Groups and Information Resources

Al-Haq - Al-Haq (also known as Law in the Service of Man) was established in 1979 by Palestinian lawyers intent on addressing the lack of human rights protection mechanisms in the Occupied Territories. Al-Haq was one of the first human rights organisations established in the Arab world. *The Link* v. 19, #2.

www.alhaq.org

Alternative Information Center - A joint Palestinian-Israeli organization, based in Jerusalem, that combines grassroots activism with critical research and dissemination of information on Palestine-Israel. *The Link* v. 39, #2.

www.alternativenews.org

American-Arab Anti-Discrimination Committee - Founded by former senator Jim Abourezk, ADC is the foremost organization confronting anti-Arab bias in the United States. *The Link* v. 7, #2; v. 18, #3; v. 23, #1.

www.adc.org

American Educational Trust - Publisher of the *Washington Report on Middle East Affairs*, the most comprehensive periodical on the Middle East available today. Referenced *Link*, by *Washington Report* co-founder Richard Curtiss, addresses U.S. aid to Israel. *The Link* v. 30, #4.

www.wrmea.com

American Friends Service Committee - AFSC has had a long history of involvement in Palestine, particularly in the area of education. *The Link* v. 22, #5.

www.afsc.org

Americans for a Just Peace in the Middle East - AJPME has produced several outstanding documentaries on life under military occupation. *The Link* v. 38, #5.

www.ajpme.org

The Association for Civil Rights in Israel - The Association was founded in 1972 as a non-political and independent body, with the goal of protecting human rights in Israel, the territories that are, in effect, subject to its control, and anywhere that a violation of human rights is a direct result of action taken by Israel's state authorities.

www.acri.org.il

Bat Shalom - A feminist peace organization of Israeli women, Bat Shalom works toward a just peace that includes recognition of a Palestinian state with Jerusalem as a shared capital. *The Link* v. 39, #2.

www.batshalom.org

Breaking the Silence - Some Israeli soldiers serving in Hebron initiated a photo exhibit in Tel Aviv to portray the military methods and mind-set that go into "protecting" Israel's security. They inspired colleagues positioned elsewhere in the occupation to express their support.

www.breakingthesilence.org.il

B'Tselem - Israeli Information Center for Human Rights in the Occupied Territory carefully documents torture, abuse and collective punishments. *The Link* v. 38, #5.

www.btselem.org

Catholic Near East Welfare Association - For many years the Association's administrator was Bishop John Nolan, a long-time member of AMEU's board of directors and president of The Pontifical Mission for Palestine. Publishes a monthly magazine, *One*. *The Link* v. 7, #3; v. 19, #3.

www.cnewa.org

Christian Century - James Wall, editor and publisher of *Christian Century* from 1971-1999, has written two *Link* issues and is an AMEU board member. Currently senior contributing editor of *Christian Century*, his commentaries on the Middle East appear regularly in the magazine. *The Link* v. 33, #4; v. 37, #5.

www.christiancentury.org

Christian Peacemaker Teams - A Christian nonviolent organization that attempts to protect innocent civilians caught in conflict situations. It has had a presence in Hebron since 1995. *The Link* v. 29, #1; v. 34, #4; v. 37, #3.

www.cpt.org

Council on American-Islamic Relations - CAIR is the major U.S. organization that monitors anti-Islamic bias. *The Link* v. 33, #1.

www.cair-net.org

Deir Yassin Remembered - Founded in 1987 to build a memorial to the Palestinians massacred in Deir Yassin in 1948. The referenced *Link,* "Deir Yassin Remembered," is included in this anthology. *The Link* v. 29, #4.

www.deiryassin.org

Dheishe Refugees - Children of the Dheisheh camp near Bethlehem tell about their lives in a refugee camp. *The Link* v. 32, #2.

www.dheisheh.acrossborders.org

Doctors Without Borders - Doctors Without Borders/Médecins Sans Frontières (MSF) is a medical humanitarian organization that delivers emergency aid to people affected by armed conflict, and disasters. It has long been active in the Occupied Territories. *The Link* v. 34, #4.

www.doctorswithoutborders.org

The Edward Said Conservatory of Music - Established in 1990 to fill the huge gap in music education in Palestinian society.

www.ncm.birzeit.edu

Electronic Intifada - Excellent web site for up-to-date Mideast commentary, often featuring Ali Abunimah, author of referenced *Link* issue titled "Dear NPR News." *The Link* v. 31, #5.

www.electronicintifada.net

Foundation for Middle East Peace - Publishes bimonthly Report on Israeli Settlement in the Occupied Territories, which provides up-to-date maps and statistics on the settlements. *The Link* v. 27, #5.

www.fmep.org

Gush Shalom - Israeli group calls for Israeli withdrawal from Occupied Territories and for Jerusalem to be shared capital of Israel and future Palestinian state.

www.gush-shalom.org

Ha'aretz - A widely circulated Israeli newspaper whose reports and commentaries by Gideon Levy and Amira Hass are sharply critical of the abuse of Palestinians under Israeli occupation, a viewpoint seldom seen in America's mainstream media.

www.haaretz.com

If Americans Knew - Organization founded by Alison Weir to monitor reporting on Israel-Palestine by the mainstream media. *The Link* v. 38, #3.

www.ifamericansknew.org

International Solidarity Movement - ISM is a Palestinian-led movement committed to resisting the Israeli occupation non-violently. Rachel Corrie was a 23-year-old American ISM volunteer when she was crushed to death by an Israeli military bulldozer in March, 2003. In April, Tom Hurndall, 21, also wearing the fluorescent orange vest of a noncombatant, was shot in the head by Israeli soldiers as he tried to help two young Palestinian girls to safety. He died of his injuries in the U.K. *The Link* v. 36, #5.

www.palsolidarity.org

Israeli Committee Against House Demolitions - Israeli Jeff Halper, ICAHD's founder, has recently been proposed for the Nobel Peace Prize. Originally established to oppose and resist demolition of Palestinian homes in the Occupied Territories, the organization expanded its resistance activities to land expropriation, settlement expansion, bypass road construction, policies of "closure" and "separation" and the wholesale uprooting of fruit and olive trees. Halper's two *Link* issues, referenced here, debunk the so-called "generous offer" at Camp David and describe the Bantustan arrangement Israel seeks to impose on the Palestinians. *The Link* v. 35, #4, v. 37, #1.

www.icahd.org

Jewish Voice for Peace - JVP, based in California, calls for an end to the occupation, a U.S. foreign policy based on promoting respect for international law, and a resolution of the Palestinian refugee problem consistent with international law. *The Link* v. 39, #2

www.jewishvoiceforpeace.org

Jews Against the Occupation - "Progressive, secular and religious Jews of all ages throughout the New York City area" come together in this organization to call for a restoration of human and civil rights for Palestinians under occupation, noting that "Israeli military fires bone-crushing rubber bullets and live ammunition at unarmed Palestinian civilians engaged in peaceful protest . . . [and demolishes] houses and crops ... while allowing Jewish settlers — many of them American — to illegally occupy the same land."

www.jatonyc.org

Land Defense Committee - Palestinian NGO has a presence in each district of the West Bank and uses volunteers from the legal and scientific professions to monitor settlements and attempt to prevent further Israeli confiscation of Palestinian land through the Israeli military court system. *The Link* v. 34, #4.

www.badil.org

Machsom Watch - Israeli women station themselves at Israeli checkpoints to help protect the civil and human rights of Palestinians and to report abuses to the widest possible audience. *The Link* v. 34, #4.

www.machsomwatch.org

Middle East Children's Alliance - Since 1988, oganization has delivered millions of dollars in humanitarian aid to children's clinics, hospitals, schools and women's organizations in the Occupied Territories and Iraq. *The Link* v. 39, #4.

www.mecaforpeace.org

Middle East Council of Churches - Group of 40 mainstream churches concerned with the Middle East. The Council notes that it "brings together a family of families—the Eastern Orthodox, the Oriental Orthodox, the Catholic and Protestant families." *The Link* v. 3, #4; v. 23, #3.

www.mec-churches.org

Middle East Crisis Committee - Publishes "The Struggle," a graphic, revealing report on human rights abuses. *The Link* v. 27, #5.

www.thestruggle.org

Middle East Studies Association - Association of college and university departments of Middle East studies. *The Link* v. 18, #2, v. 39, #1.

www.mesa.arizona.edu

Norman Finkelstein - Finkelstein, author of two *Link* issues, presents his work and commentary on this web site, including his critique of Alan Dershowitz. Referenced *Links* are titled "A Reply to Henry Kissinger and Fuad Ajami" and "Native Americans and Palestinians." *The Link* v. 25, #5; v. 32, #5.

www.normanfinkel-stein.com

Not In My Name - Not In My Name, a predominantly Jewish organization based in Chicago, advocates an end to the occupation and collective punishments, dismantlement of the "illegal" separation wall, a shared Jerusalem, and the right of return for displaced Palestinians.

www.nimn.org

Partners for Peace - Organization sponsors speaking tours and emphasizes nonviolent efforts to achieve peace. *The Link* v. 34, #3.

www.partnersforpeace.org

Rabbis for Human Rights - Founded in 1988 in response to serious abuses of human rights by the Israeli military authorities in suppression of the first Palestinian intifada. *The Link* v. 34, #4

www.rhr.israel.net

Rachel Corrie Foundation - The Foundation was established by her parents after Rachel, a pacifist and peace activist, was crushed and killed by an Israeli military bulldozer as she protested against the demolition of a home in Gaza. "Rachel," the *Link* written by her mother Cindy, appears in this anthology. *The Link* v. 36, #5.

www.rachelcorrie.org

Sabeel Center for Liberation Theology - Grassroots, ecumenical organization based in Palestine but with branches worldwide, including one in North America. Founded in 1990 by Naim Ateek, former canon of St. George's Cathedral in Jerusalem. *The Link* v. 34, #2; v. 39, #3.

www.sabeel.org

Search for Justice and Equality in Palestine/Israel - SEARCH focuses on informing journalists and opinion page readers. It publishes "Palestine/Israel File," a concise fact sheet on current Middle East events. *The Link* v. 27, #5.

www.searchforjustice.org

St. Ives Society - A legal advocacy group based in Jerusalem that represents Palestinians in Israeli civil and military courts. *The Link* v. 29, #3.

Ta'ayush - *Ta'ayush* means "coexistence" in Arabic. Jewish-Israeli and Palestinian-Israeli men and women interact under this philosophy as they undertake interventions together, helping Palestinian farmers harassed by Israeli settlers during olive harvests, and demonstrating solidarity with Palestinian Bedouins threatened with eviction by settlers and the Israeli military. *The Link* v. 39, #2.

www.taayush.org

Temporary International Presence in Hebron - TIPH was deployed for a three-month period following Israeli settler Baruch Goldstein's massacre of Palestinian worshippers on 25 February 1994. As part of the 1997 Hebron Accords, TIPH returned to Hebron with a new mandate. It is a civilian observer mission staffed by personnel from Denmark, Italy, Norway, Sweden, Switzerland and Turkey. *The Link* v. 34, #4.

www.tiph.org

U.S. Campaign to End the Israeli Occupation - A diverse coalition of U.S. based organizations that focuses on corporations and other institutions that sustain Israel's domination of the Palestinian people and denial of their human rights, including an end to the occupation, full equality for Palestinian citizens of Israel, and the right of return for Palestinian refugees. *The Link* v. 39, #3.

USS *Liberty* Survivors Association - Member newsletter reports on survivors' efforts to investigate the June, 1967 attack on their ship by Israeli war planes and gun boats. *The Link* v. 17, #2; v. 30, #3.

www.ussliberty.org

Voices in the Wilderness - A pacifist organization that was present in Iraq just prior to the first Gulf War, and then campaigned on humanitarian grounds for the end of sanctions that contributed to widespread malnutrition, disease and loss of life in Iraq. *The Link* v. 30, #1.

www.vitw.org

Wi'am - The Palestinian Conflict Resolution Center began operation in 1995. Known as *Wi'am*, which in Arabic means "cordial relationships," the Center helps to resolve disputes within the Palestinian community by complementing the traditional Arab form of mediation, called Sulha, with Western models of conflict resolution. *The Link* v. 32, #5.

www.planet.edu

Women in Black - Women in Black, an international peace network, was begun in Israel in 1988 by women who staged vigils to protest Israel's occupation of the West Bank and Gaza. *The Link* v. 39, #2; v. 24, #4.

www.womeninblack.net

Yesh Gvul - Israeli group supports soldiers, whether conscripts or reservists, who for reasons of conscience refuse assignments of a repressive or aggressive nature. *The Link* v. 39, #2.

www.yeshgvul.org

Appendix III: Members of the AMEU Board of Directors, 1967-2007

Jane Adas, Lecturer, Rutgers University

Hugh D. Auchincloss, Jr., Atwater, Bradley & Partners, Inc.

Elizabeth D. Barlow, Outreach Director, Center for Middle East and North African Studies, University of Michigan

John V. Chapple, Director of C.A.R.E., Gaza Strip Project

Bertram C. Cooper, Editor

Norman F. Dacey, Author

John H. Davis, First Commissioner General of U.N.W.R.A.

Edward Dillon, Chaplain and Professor, Marymount College

Harry G. Dorman, Jr., Middle East & Europe Department of the National Council of Churches

John Dorman, Director, American Research Center, Cairo

Paul Findley, Member, U.S. Congress

Henry G. Fischer, Curator in Egyptology, Metropolitan Museum of Art

Bonnie Gehweiler, Bethlehem 2000 Project

John Goelet, Businessman

Grace Halsell, Writer

Robert J. Hayes, Ergon Corporation

Ulric S. Haynes, Jr., U.S. Ambassador to Algeria

Robert M. Henry, Aramco

Helen C. Hilling, Professor of Public Administration, New York University

Richard Hobson, Jr., Olayan America Corporation

L. Emmett Holt, Board Chairman, American Middle East Rehabilitation

O. Kelly Ingram, Professor, Duke University

Anne R. Joyce, Editor, Middle East Policy

Robert V. Keeley, U.S. Ambassador to Greece, Zimbabwe and Mauritius

Robert Kerrigan, Attorney

Carl M. Kortepeter, Professor, Middle East History, New York

Kendall Landis, Middle East Supervisor, Citibank

Nell MacCracken, Consultant

Sister Blanche Marie, Professor, College of St. Elizabeth, N.J.

Robert E. Marsh, Consultant

Paul N. McCloskey, Member, U.S. Congress

David Nes, U.S. Foreign Service Officer

John G. Nolan, President, Pontifical Mission for Palestine

Robert L. Norberg, Aramco

Edward L. Peck, U.S. Ambassador

David C. Quinn, Assistant Attorney General, New York State

Lachlan Reed, President, Lachlan International

Joseph L. Ryan, S.J., Rector, Holy Cross College

Talcott W. Seelye, U.S. Ambassador to Syria

Donald L. Snook, Esso Middle East

Robert L. Stern, Secretary General, Catholic Near East Welfare Association

Jack B. Sunderland, President, Coroil, Inc.

John M. Sutton, Director, Near East Foundation; Executive Director of AMEU, 1969-1978

Elizabeth Thomas, Egyptologist

Henry P. Van Dusen, President, Union Theological Seminary

James M. Wall, Editor Emeritus, The Christian Century

L. Humphrey Walz, Associate Executive, Presbyterian Synod of the Northeast

Miriam Ward, R.S.M., Professor, Trinity College

Mark Wellman, Consultant

Charles T. White, Near East Foundation

Marshall M. Wiley, U.S. Ambassador to Oman

End Notes

Political Zionism by John Mahoney

[1] Joseph Weitz, "My Diary and Letters to the Children," Massada, 1965, III, p. 293, cited in Davar, Sept. 29, 1967.

[2] Samuel Landman, *Great Britain, the Jews and Palestine,* London, New Zionist Press, 1936, p. 4.

[3] Chaim Weizmann, *Excerpts from His Historic Statements, Writings and Addresses,* New York, Jewish Agency for Palestine, 1952, p. 48.

[4] Letter to Lord Curzon, Aug. 11, 1919, in *Palestine Papers 1917–1922: Seeds of Conflict,* Doreen Ingrams, ed., New York, George Braziller, 1973, p. 73.

[5] George Ball, *The Passionate Attachment: America's Involvement with Israel, 1947 to the Present,* New York, W. W. Norton, 1992, p. 316.

[6] Truman papers, Palestine-Jewish Immigration Files, Truman to Panby, Oct. 22, 1946.

[7] Harry S. Truman, *Memoirs,* Vol. II, Garden City, NY, Doubleday, 1956, p. 225, cited in A. Lilienthal, *The Zionist Connection: What Price Peace,* New York, Dodd, Mead & Co., 1978, p. 62.

[8] Clifford Wright, *Facts & Fables: The Arab-Israeli Conflict,* London and New York, Kegan Paul International, 1989, pp. 115–116.

[9] Paul Findley, *Deliberate Deceptions: Facing the Facts about the U.S.-Israeli Relationship,* Washington D.C., American Educational Trust, 1993, p. 7.

[10] Lilienthal, *The Zionist Connection,* p. 66.

[11] Ibid. The Truman administration's lobbying efforts and Eddie Jacobson's visit are based on chapter III, pp. 46–102.

[12] References to Fayez Sayegh are based on his speech before the Third Committee of the U.N. General Assembly that was reprinted in *Zionism: A Form of Racial Discrimination,* Office of the Permanent Observer of the Palestine Liberation Organization to the United Nations. The entire speech is available on AMEU's web site at www.ameu.org.

[13] Lilienthal, *The Zionist Connection,* pp. 91–92.

[14] Thomas Dine, from a transcript of his talk, "The Revolution in U.S.-Israeli Relations," delivered at AIPAC's annual conference in Washington, D.C., April 6, 1986.

[15] Dan Raviv and Yossi Melman, *Friends in Deed*, New York, Hyperion, 1944, p. 404.

[16] Ibid., p. 406.

[17] Elmer Berger, *A Partisan History of Judaism*, New York, Devon-Adair, 1951, p.136.

[18] Sayegh, *Zionism: A Form of Racial Discrimination,* p. 28.

[19] Dilip Hiro, *Sharing the Promised Land,* New York, Olive Branch Press, 1996, p. 50.

[20] Jason Vest, "The Men from JINSA and CSP," in the *Nation*, Oct. 2, 2002, p. 18. Other prominent JINSA members listed include Dick Cheney, James Woolsey, Jeane Kirkpatrick, and Michael Ledeen; CSP members include Elliott Abrams and Frank Gaffney. See also www.israeleconomy.org/strat1.htm.

In the Beginning by Ron Bleier

[1] For history of Zionist conquest and occupation, see Norman Finkelstein, *Image and Reality of the Israel-Palestine Conflict,* London and New York, Verso, 1995; for documentation of specific acts of Zionist terrorism, e.g., letter bombs, kidnapping, bombing cafes, theaters, markets, see Issa Nakhleh's *Encyclopedia of the Palestine Problem*, New York, Intercontinental Books, 1991, pp. 65–230.

[2] Stephen Green, *Taking Sides: America's Secret Relations with a Militant Israel,* New York, W. Morrow, 1984, pp. 38–40.

[3] Baylis Thomas, *How Israel Was Won: A Concise History of the Arab-Israeli Conflict (1900–1999),* Lanham, MD, Lexington Books, 1999, p. 93, note 39.

[4] Green, *Taking Sides*, p. 40.

[5] Written by Prof. Yehuda Lapidot on the Irgun web site: http://www.etzel.org/english/index.html.

[6] Thus, according to Irgun accounts, when the attack took place on July 22, the Haganah had officially withdrawn its approval.

[7] According to the Irgun, from the time of the first call at 12:10 pm, 22 minutes were allowed for the evacuation.

[8] R. Curtiss in the *Washington Report on Middle East Affairs*: www.wrmea.com/backissues/031885/850318011.html.

[9] Livia Rokach, *Israel's Sacred Terrorism*, Belmont, MA, Association of Arab-American University Graduates, 1980, pp. 5–6.

[10] Ibid., p. 11.

[11] Ibid., p. 13.

[12] Ibid.

[13] Ibid., p. 29.

[14] Rachel Corrie in e-mail to her family, cited in *Harper's* "This Happens Every Day," June 2003.

[15] Green, *Taking Sides,* pp. 94–123.

[16] "A Dangerous Liquidation," in *Yediot Achronot*, Nov. 25, 2001.

[17] Donald Neff, *Warriors at Suez: Eisenhower Takes America into the Middle East*, New York, Simon & Schuster, 1981, p. 33.

[18] Ehud Ya'ari, in Rokach, *Israel's Sacred Terrorism*, p. 62.

[19] Ibid., pp. 39–40.

[20] Ibid., p. 47.

[21] Ibid.

[22] Neff, *Warriors at Suez*, pp. 365–368, 371–376.

Deir Yassin Remembered by Daniel A. McGowan

[1] Menachem Begin, *The Revolt,* London, W. H. Allen, 1964, pp. 162–166.

[2] Ibid.

[3] *New York Times,* March 13, 1948, p. 7.

[4] Jacques De Reynier, *1948 in Jerusalem*, [translated from French to English by Sophie Elkin, Geneva, NY, October 1995], p. 73 in original.

[5] *Jerusalem Post* magazine, May 31, 1996, p. 23.

[6] James E. Young, *The Texture of Memory: Holocaust Memorials and Meaning*, New Haven, Yale University Press, 1993, pp. 243–247.

Censored by Colin D. Edwards

[1] See the *Jewish Encyclopedia*, the *Encyclopedia Judaica*, the *Encyclopedia Britannica*; Arnold Toynbee's *A Study of History;* H. G. Wells's *An Outline of History;* C. Roth's *The World History of the Jewish People (Vol. II);* Harry I. Shapiro's *The Jewish People;* H. H. Graetz's *History of The Jews;* W. Ripley's *The Races of Europe;* the writings of Dr. Hillel Nathan of Hebrew University-Hadassah Medical School and Dr. Norman Golb of the University of Chicago on the subject; the 10th Century "Khazar Correspondence" (between the Spanish Jew Hasdai ibn Shaprut and the Khazar Khan) and other Hebrew documents translated by Judah Halevi in 1140 and published by J. Buxtorf in 1660.

[2] Calvin Kephart, *Races of Mankind: Their Origin and Migration,* New York, Philosophical Library, 1960, pp. 157, 316, 516.

[3] Irving Calderon, a henchman of JDL leader Meir Kahane, is quoted by Robert I. Friedman in his book *The False Prophet*, New York, Lawrence Hill Books, 1990, p. 120, as saying that the JDL directed two JDL man-and-wife teams to go to London to assassinate Miss Khaled. One team, Avraham Herschkovitz and his wife Nancy, were arrested when they tried to board a BOAC flight in New York. The other team, already in London, fled to Israel when they heard of the arrest.

[4] See "FBI Analysis of Terrorist Incidents and Terrorist Related Activities in the U.S." These reports were issued annually from 1982 to 1986 but then ceased to be made public. JDL founder and leader Meir Kahane did some spying for the FBI, and several memos from the FBI's New York office and its Division Five (racial intelligence section) proposed using the JDL against militant black groups there, according to Friedman's *The False Prophet*, pp. 2–3, 94–95. See also *Heil Kahane* by Israeli journalist Yair Kotler, translated from the Hebrew by Edward Levin, New York, Adama Books, 1986.

[5] In 1971, Meir Kahane had ordered JDL bomb makers to serrate the outside of their pipe bombs to make them more lethal. This came about when Kahane saw that the results of JDL bombings of black institutions in New York were not up to his expectations. From Friedman, *The False Prophet*, p. 119.

[6] On his mother's side he was descended from the founder of the Lubavich wing of hasidism and had spent part of his time as a small boy in the "court" of his uncle, the chief rabbi, in Lubavich, west of Smolensk, and later became a student at a "Heder," a religious school, in Palestine.

[7] For a succinct summary of Zionist collaboration with the Nazis and also with the Italian fascists and Japanese militarists before and during World War II, read Lenni Brenner's *Zionism in the Age of the Dictators*, Westport, CT, Lawrence Hill; and Beckenham (U.K.), Croom Helm both in 1983.

[8] Whenever I visited Palestinian schools, including those for orphans of killed PLO guerrillas who were enrolled in the Ashbul (Young Lions) movement to provide them with some military training, I always asked what they thought about Jews. Invariably they would mention the names of Jews they had been taught about who were friends of the Arabs.

[9] With regard to the Middle East, one only has to read the excellent books by former correspondents in the region, such as Kenneth Love's *Suez: The Twice Fought War*, New York, McGraw-Hill, 1969, and Donald Neff's *Warriors at Suez*, New York, Simon & Schuster, 1981, and New York, Amana Books, 1988, *Warriors for Jerusalem*, New York, Simon & Schuster, 1984, and New York, Amana Books, 1988, and *Warriors against Israel*, New York, Amana Books, 1988, to recognize how much important material and how many valuable insights they had to offer that did not get into the columns of, respectively, *The New York Times* and *Time*. It is a national tragedy that they are not reporting from the Middle East today, and a national disgrace that their thinking on the situations there is not featured prominently in the mass media.

[10] University of Alberta Press and Ramparts Press, 1985.

[11] *San Francisco Weekly*, July 29, 1992.

[12] Ibid., August 19, 1992.

Confronting the Bible's Ethnic Cleansing by Michael Prior

[1] F. E. Deist, "The Dangers of Deuteronomy: A Page from the Reception History of the Book," in F. Garcia Martinez, A. Hilhorst, J.T.A.G.M. van Ruiten, and A. S. van der Woud (eds.), *Studies in Deuteronomy. In Honour of C. J. Labuschagne on the Occasion of his 65th Birthday,* Leiden/New York/Köln, Brill, 1994, pp. 13–29.

[2] A. G. Lamadrid, "Canaán y América. La Biblia y la Teologia medieval ante la Conquista de la Tierra," in "Escritos de Biblia y Oriente. Bibliotheca Salmanticensis," Estudios 38, Salamanca-Jerusalén, Universidad Pontificia, 1981, pp. 329–346.

[3] W. D. Davies, *The Gospel and the Land. Early Christianity and Jewish Territorial Doctrine,* Berkeley, University of California Press, 1974. See also his *Territorial Dimensions of Judaism*, Berkeley, University of California Press, 1972; and his *Territorial Dimensions of Judaism. With a Symposium and Further Reflections*, Minneapolis, MN, Fortress, 1991.

[4] Walter Brueggemann, *The Land. Place as Gift, and Challenge in Biblical Faith,* Philadelphia, Fortress, 1977. See also his "Forward" in W. Eugene March, *Israel and the Politics of Land. A Theological Case Study,* Louisville, KY, Westminster/John Knox Press, 1994.

[5] Norbert Lohfink, "The Laws of Deuteronomy: Project for a World without any Poor," in *Scripture Bulletin*, 1996, 26, pp. 2–19.

[6] Michael Prior, *A Land Flowing with Milk, Honey, and People,* Cambridge, Von Hügel Institute, 1997; and in *Scripture Bulletin,* 1998, 28, pp. 2–17.

[7] Michael Prior, *Zionism and the State of Israel: A Moral Inquiry*, London and New York, Routledge, 1999.

[8] Michael Prior, *The Bible and Colonialism. A Moral Critique*, Sheffield, U.K., Sheffield Academic Press, 1997.

[9] My study of the Bible in the Land of the Bible obviously aided me in seeing "with the eyes of the Canaanites." Others, surely, have had no less interesting experiences to tell, some of which I have collected in *They Came and They Saw: Western Christian Experiences of the Holy Land,* Michael Prior, ed., London, Melisende, 2000.

The USS *Liberty* Affair by James M. Ennes Jr.

[1] *New York Times*, June 18, 1967, p. 20. Although the story is attributed to a "senior officer" of the *Liberty*, Golden now admits freely to having been the source. At the time of the interview he was *Liberty's* acting commanding officer.

[2] For a detailed look at *Liberty's* mission and capabilities and her relationship with the National Security Agency, see James Bamford, *The Puzzle Palace*, Houghton Mifflin, 1982.

[3] From documents in the Mideast File of the Lyndon B. Johnson Library obtained in 1983 by author Stephen Green under the Freedom of Information Act.

[4] Stephen Green, *Taking Sides: America's Secret Relations with a Militant Israel*, New York, Wm. Morrow, 1984, pp. 238–239.

[5] JCS Top Secret message 080110Z, JUN 67, reproduced in Navy Court of Inquiry file and elsewhere.

[6] Review of Department of Defense Worldwide Communications, Report of the Armed Services Investigating Subcommittee of the Committee on Armed Services, House of Representatives, May 10, 1971.

[7] Proceedings of Navy Court of Inquiry, Exhibit 47.

[8] From documents in the Mideast File of the Lyndon B. Johnson Library obtained in 1983 by author Stephen Green under the Freedom of Information Act.

[9] From interview with cryptologic technician Charles Rowley, who was present.

[10] Sources: Israeli Defense Forces Preliminary Inquiry File 1/67 of *Liberty* hearing before Sgan-Aluf (Lt. Colonel) Y. Yerushalmi, July 21, 1967; also, Report on the Liberty Incident by History Department of the Israeli Defense Forces for senior officers of the U.S. Navy, June 1982.

[11] The Israeli government insists that there was no reconnaissance whatsoever and that my claims of 13 reconnaissance orbits "may be dismissed as exaggerated." However, a careful reading of survivors' testimony in the Navy Court of Inquiry file verifies that all 13 orbits did occur. A top-secret study by Department of State legal adviser Carl F. Salans dated September 21, 1967, cites testimony from crewmen of "overflights of the Liberty at 0515, 0850, 1030, 1056, 1126, 1145, 1220, and 1245." Dozens of crewmen are willing to testify publicly that they recall repeated overflights at masthead level.

[12] This report of radio jamming is ridiculed in the IDF History Department report as untrue and impossible. However, the original source of this report is the U.S. Navy Court of Inquiry, which concluded as a "Finding of Fact" that *Liberty* radios were jammed, apparently by equipment operated from the jets. The use of jamming is confirmed by *Liberty*'s chief radioman Wayne Smith and by radio logs of the affected radio circuits, which reflect loud and unusual circuit noise. See also Green, *Taking Sides*, p. 230.

[13] Navy Court of Inquiry file.

[14] President Johnson's press secretary, George Christian, told me in 1978 during my research for *Assault on the Liberty*, "There was considerable skepticism in the White House that the attack was accidental, even though tragic mistakes are rather common during wartime." Later, Christian said, he became convinced that "an accident of this magnitude was too much to swallow." Yet the Johnson White House nevertheless chose to look the other way. Donald Neff, in *Warriors for Jerusalem*, New

York, Linden Press, 1984, examines in detail the Israeli influences on the Johnson White House that caused that reaction.

[15] Probably the single most explosive revelation is Green's finding in *Taking Sides* that the United States knew a day in advance of the Israeli plan to attempt to sink the USS *Liberty*.

[16] James M. Ennes Jr. versus Department of State, Civil Action # 80-1126, in United States District Court for the District of Columbia.

[17] Syndicated column by Drew Pearson and Jack Anderson, June 30, 1967.

[18] Admiral Arleigh Burke, Admiral Thomas Moorer, Senator Adlai Stevenson, Senator Barry Goldwater, Congressman Paul Findley, Congressman Paul McCloskey, Seymour Hersch, George Weller, and Philip Geyelin.

[19] *St. Louis Jewish Light, Winnipeg Jewish Post, Jewish Western.*

[20] December 24, 1980. The editorial was then picked up for national distribution by a national newspaper editorial service and probably appeared in many other newspapers.

[21] The national bookseller restored the book to stock after I discussed the problem with Walden vice president Kay Sexton.

[22] For more information about the *Liberty* film, write to The Liberty Limited Partnership, PO Box 8008, San Marino, California 91108.

[23] *Los Angeles Times*, June 30, 1982, "Survivors Still Seek Answers," p. 1.

[24] *Jewish War Veteran* magazine, April-May-June 1983, p. 7.

[25] Rowland Evans and Robert Novak, syndicated column, "New Tactics of the Israeli Lobby," February 9, 1983, distributed by Field Enterprises.

[26] CIA Information Report, "Attack on USS Liberty Ordered by Dayan," based on the report of an informant obviously present in the Israeli War Room. The CIA has since discounted the report as "unevaluated," even though it is consistent with other reports and has not been discredited.

[27] This writer has received five separate reports, including one from a highly placed CIA official, that the United States learned in advance that Israel had decided to attack the *Liberty*. Stephen Green in *Taking Sides* is the first to produce a credible witness, in this case former congressman Robert Sikes of Florida, who is willing to stand behind that information publicly.

Epilogue by Robert Norberg

[1] "Zionism? Racism? What Do You Mean?," Dec. 1975, v. 8, #5.

[2] "A Brief History of the Middle East Conflict," Mar.-Apr. 1974, v. 7, #2.

[3] "Law and Disorder in the Middle East," Jan.-Mar. 2002, v. 35, #1.

[4] "From Time Immemorial: The Resurrection of a Myth," Jan.-Mar. 1985, v. 18, #1; "A Reply to Henry Kissinger and Fouad Ajami," Dec. 1992, v. 25, #5; "Native Americans and Palestinians," Dec. 1999, v. 32, #5; "Reflections on September 11, 2001," Nov.-Dec. 2001, v. 34, #5.

[5] "Palestine—The Suppression of an Idea," Jan.-Mar., 1982, v. 15, #1; "The Jordanization of the Palestine Question," May-June 1983, v. 16, #2; "From Time Immemorial: The Resurrection of a Myth," Jan.-Mar. 1985, v. 18, #1; "Zionist Violence Against Palestinians," Sept. 1988, v. 21, #3.

[6] "Israeli Historians Ask: What Really Happened 50 Years Ago?" Jan.-Mar. 1998, v. 31, #1.

[7] "The Middle East Lobbies," Jan.-Mar. 1984, v. 17, #1; Cranston letter, Dec. 1982, v.s15, #5.

[8] "The Arab Stereotype on Television," Apr.-May 1980, v. 13, #2; "The Comic Book Arab," Nov.-Dec. 1991, v. 24, #5.

Index

A